P.O. # DW04460851

Visual QuickStart Guide

DIRECTOR 5

For Windows

ANDRE PERSIDSKY

Peachpit Press

Visual QuickStart Guide
Director 5 for Windows
Andre Persidsky

Peachpit Press
2414 Sixth Street
Berkeley, CA 94710
510/548-4393
800/283-9444
510/548-5991 (fax)
Find us on the World Wide Web at: http://www.peachpit.com
Peachpit Press is a division of Addison Wesley Longman

Cover design: The Visual Group

ISBN 0-201-88643-X

9 8 7 6 5 4 3 2 1

Printed and bound in the United States

♻ Printed on recycled paper

Thank you.

Roslyn Bullas, ***Kate Reber***, and the rest of the staff at ***Peachpit Press***.

William Karneges at ***Pax Publishing***

Table of Contents

Chapter 5: Control Panel

Chapter 6: Paint Window

Chapter 9: Animation Techniques

Chapter 10: Digital Video

Chapter 11: Creating Text in Director

Introduction

Macromedia's Director is a powerful and extensive multimedia development tool. Use it to create animation, interactive movies, marketing presentations, technical simulations, and even full scale commercial productions such as entertainment titles for CD-ROM. The multimedia productions that you can synthesize with Director's powerful features are endless.

This book teaches the fundamentals of using **Director 5**, and covers the latest features and enhancements. It applies to **Windows 95**, **NT**, and **3.1** systems running Director. A version of this book is available for the Macintosh platform.

This book teaches all the steps involved in creating a **movie**—the term used to describe any multimedia piece created in Director. You will learn how to create cast members and assemble them in cast windows; how to animate cast members on the stage and build your movie frame-by-frame using the score window. You will learn how to control movie playback, set scene transitions, alter color palettes, use digital video, and add interactive controls to your movies using **Lingo**—Director's scripting language. Coverage on **Xtras** is also provided.

In the *Visual QuickStart Guide* format, this book provides step-by-step instructions, supported by numerous screen shots and tips. Where necessary, concise explanations are given. The emphasis is to get you up and running as quickly as possible through practical examples.

Chapter 2 provides an overview of the steps involved in creating a simple Director movie. Once you have mastered the basic techniques, the multimedia presentations you can create are limitless!

The Director screen and main windows

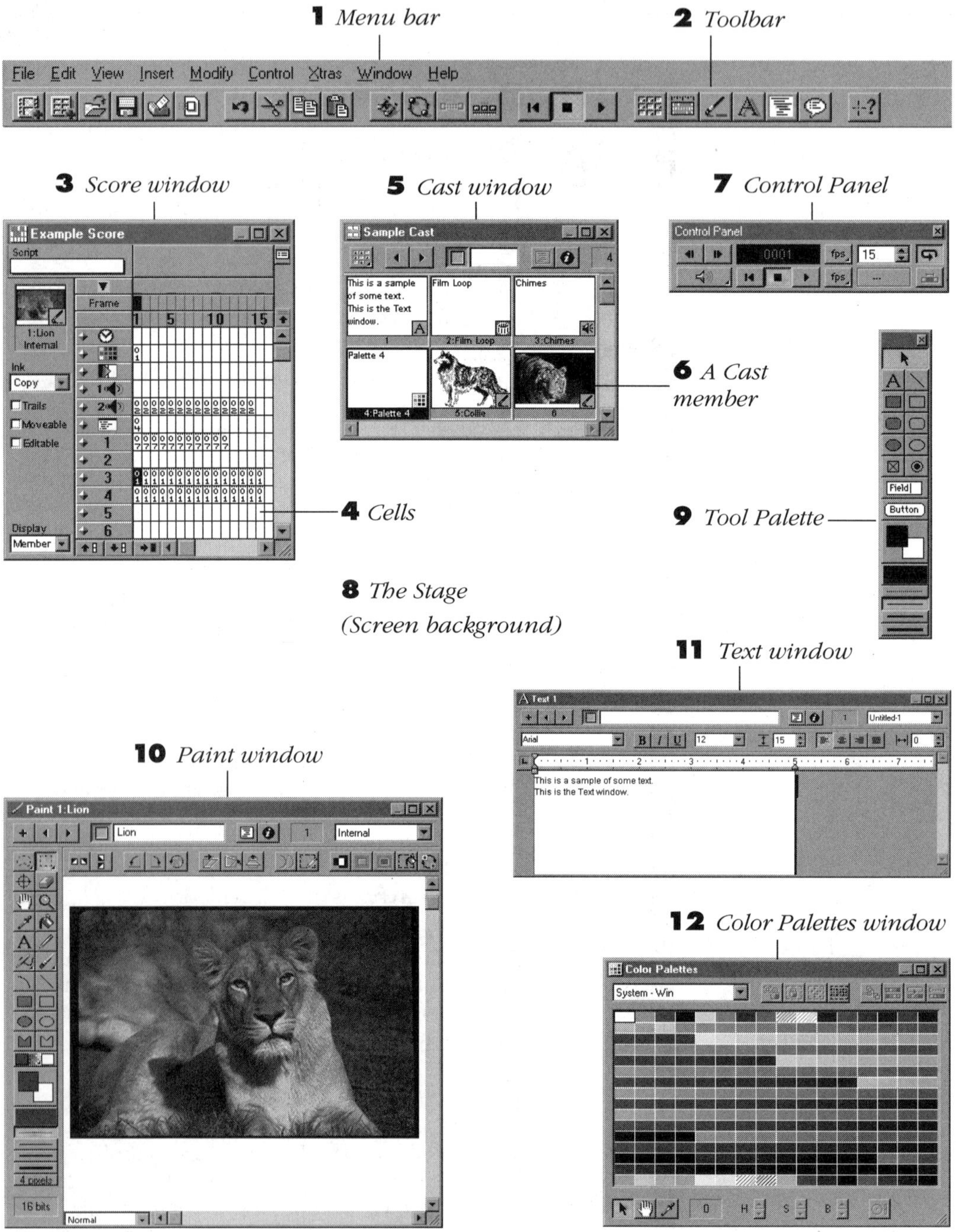

Key to the Director screen and windows

1 *Menu bar*

There are nine standard menu choices available in Director's menu bar—File, Edit, View, Insert, Modify, Control, Xtras, Window, and Help menus.

2 *Toolbar*

The Toolbar provides a convenient way to open frequently used windows such as the score, cast, and paint windows, and to select commonly used commands found under the File, Edit, Modify, and Control menus.

3 *Score window*

The score window is a frame-by-frame record of your Director movie. It is organized into frames and channels, which store all the components of your movie. These components include information such as the positions of each of your sprites during each frame, sound effects, color palette transitions, tempo changes, scene transitions—in short, all details pertaining to your movie.

4 *Cells*

The score is composed of cells, the storage units that hold all the information about your movie. Columns of cells are organized into frames, while rows of cells make up the score channels.

5 *Cast window*

Cast windows are the storage places for cast members in Director. A cast window is arranged into rows and columns of small windows, each of which can hold a unique cast member.

6 *A Cast member*

A cast member is a multimedia component such as a bitmapped image, or a sound effect, that you can incorporate into a Director movie. There are many different cast member types such as sounds, color palettes, text, buttons, bitmapped images, and shapes.

7 *Control Panel*

The control panel provides VCR-type control over the playback of your movie. You can rewind, play, fast forward, stop, and pause your movie from the control panel, as well as set the movie tempo.

8 *The Stage*

The stage is the background on which your movie plays.

9 *Tool Palette*

The Tool Palette allows you to create QuickDraw shapes, text, fields, and buttons on Director's stage.

10 *Paint window*

The paint window is Director's built-in paint program that allows you to edit and create bitmapped cast members. The paint window offers a menubar of effects such as rotate and distort that can be applied to your images.

11 *Text window*

The text window is used to create and edit text cast members.

12 *Color Palettes window*

The color palette displays the current set of colors used to draw your cast members on the stage.

About menus.

Director has nine standard menus in its menu bar—File, Edit, View, Insert, Modify, Control, Xtras, Window, and Help. Menu selections in the Edit and View menus change depending on which Director window is active. Selections in the Insert and Xtras menus change when you install additional Xtras into Director.

The File menu

The File menu selections such as Save, Open, Import, Preferences, and Create Projectors apply to your Director movie as a whole.

The Edit menu

The Edit menu provides standard editing commands such as cut and paste, which are applied in various windows in Director. The Edit commands vary according to which Director window is currently active. Below, the Edit commands apply to cells since the score window is the active window.

The Find command is located in the Edit menu, which allows you to search for specific cast members, handlers, and text.

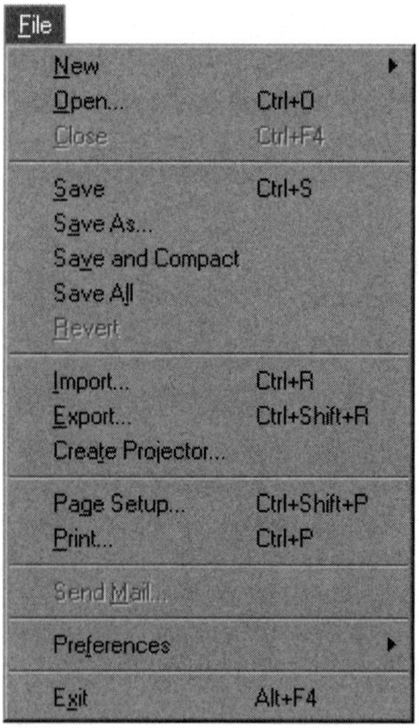

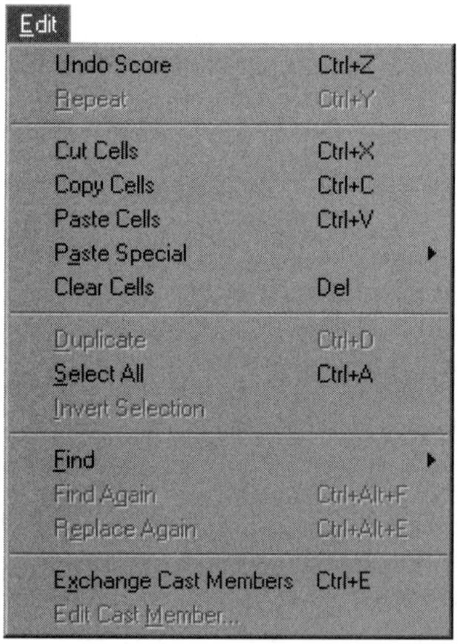

The View menu

The View menu commands generally deal with displaying or hiding certain visual guides and tools such as the stage grid, and the Onion Skin toolbar. Use the Panel command in the View menu to show or hide the paint window tool palette, or the text toolbar in the text window, giving you more room to work with in those windows. The Panel command changes depending on which window is active. Using the View menu, you can also display specific markers with the Marker command, and enlarge cast member artwork in the paint window with the Zoom command.

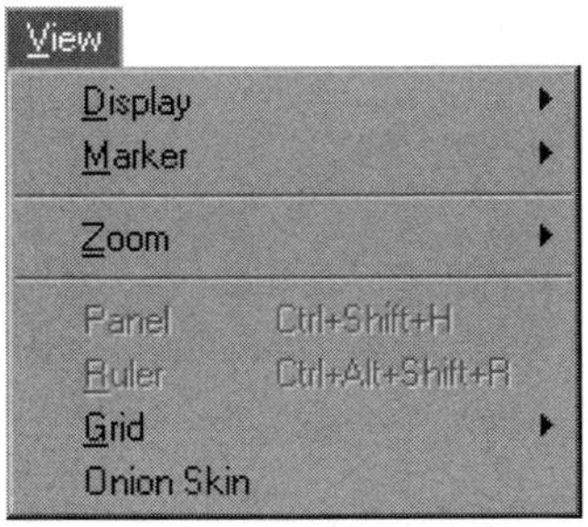

The Insert menu

The commands under the Insert menu allow you to insert and remove frames from the score, and insert media elements such as bitmaps and text into a cast window.

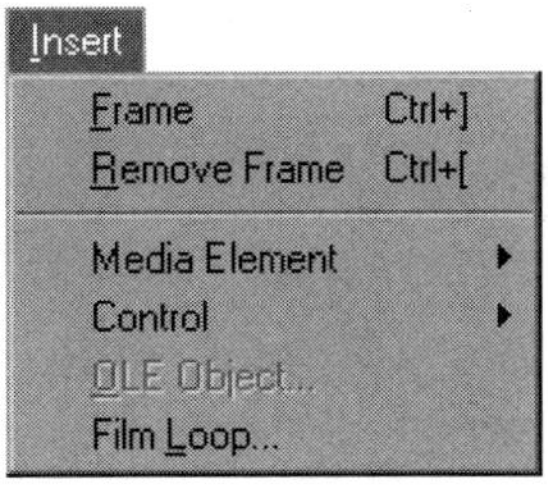

The Modify menu

The Modify menu commands allow you to modify the properties of casts, cast members, sprites, frames, and set parameters that affect your overall movie, such as stage size, and the default color palette. Commands which alter properties of cast members include Font, Transform Bitmap, and Convert Bitmap. Commands which change properties of sprites include Sprite, Align, and Tweak. The Modify menu commands also allow you to change the arrangement of sprites in the score. These include In Between, Arrange, Reverse Sequence, and Space to Time. You can also change the arrangement of cast members in a cast window using the Sort command.

The Control menu

The commands in the top half of the Control menu direct the playback of your movie. These include Play, Rewind, and Loop Playback. You can access these same commands using Director's control panel.

The commands in the bottom half of the Control menu deal with debugging Lingo scripts. These include Toggle Breakpoint, and Recompile All Scripts.

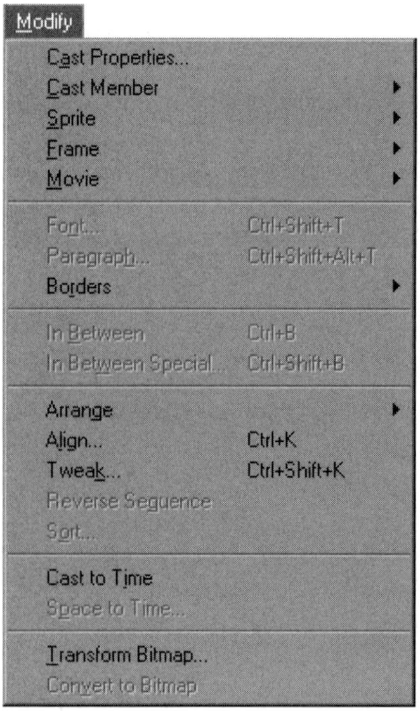

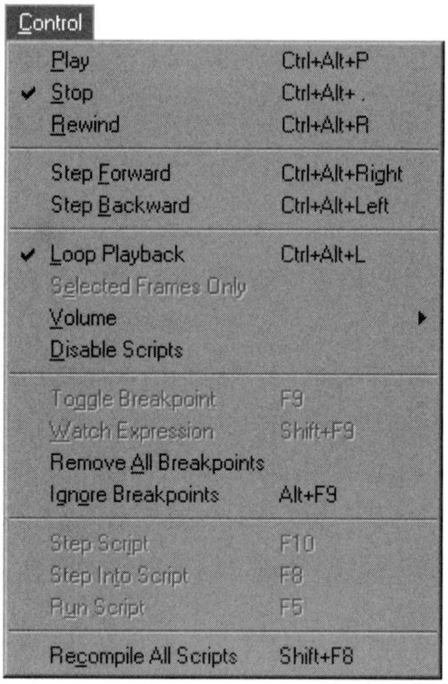

The Xtras menu

The commands in the Xtras menu generally deal with accessing Xtras (third party software modules), which expand the functionality of Director. The Filter Bitmap and Auto Filter commands allow you to apply Photoshop image filters to your bitmapped cast members. Any menu selections at the bottom portion of the Xtras menu are Tool Xtras, which become available when placed in the Xtras folder in the Director application folder. Tool Xtras enhance the authoring environment in Director.

The Update Movies command updates older version of Director movies, and the Auto Distort command is used to automatically generate a sequence of cast members.

The Window menu

Choosing a selection in the Window menu either opens or closes the corresponding window. Open windows have checkmarks beside their names.

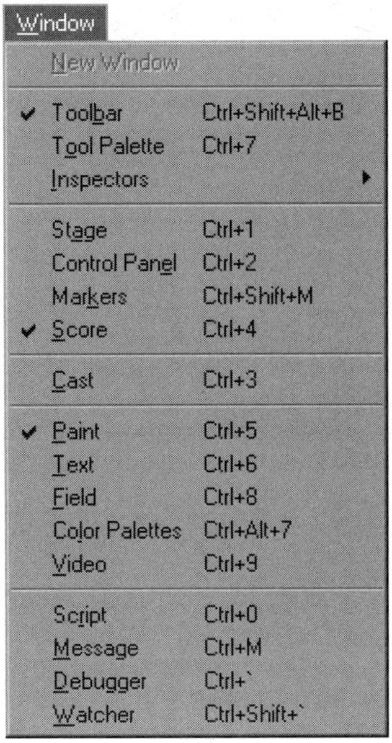

The Help menu

Use the Help menu commands to access online help in Director, and to electronically register Director with Macromedia.

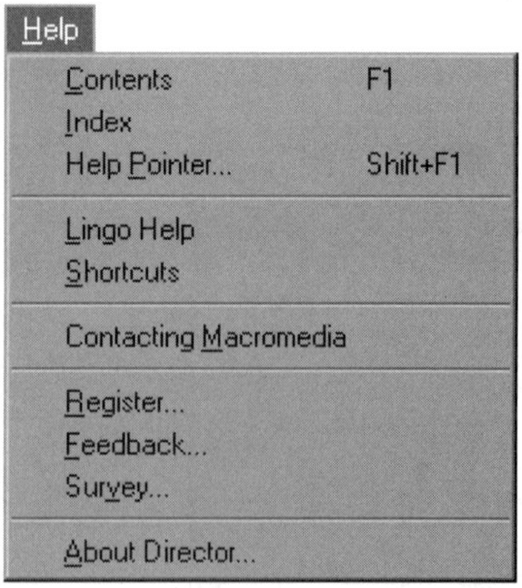

Hardware requirements to create movies

In order to create movies with Director for Windows, you need the following minimum hardware:

486/66 processor.

8 megabytes RAM, more is advised.

Double-speed CD-ROM drive (quad speed is preferable).

Hardware requirements to playback projector movies

To play a projector, you need at least a 386/33 processor with 4 megabytes of RAM. This is the bare minimum.

If you intend to play Director movies that are extensive productions—that feature 24-bit color, intensive animation, or digital video—you will realistically need at least a 486/33 with 8 megabytes of RAM.

Director's Toolbar

You can use the Toolbar **(Figure 1)** as a shortcut to select commonly used commands found under the File, Edit, Modify, and Control menus, and to open frequently used windows such as the score, cast, and paint windows.

Choose Toolbar from the Window menu **(Figure 2)** to either show or hide Director's Toolbar.

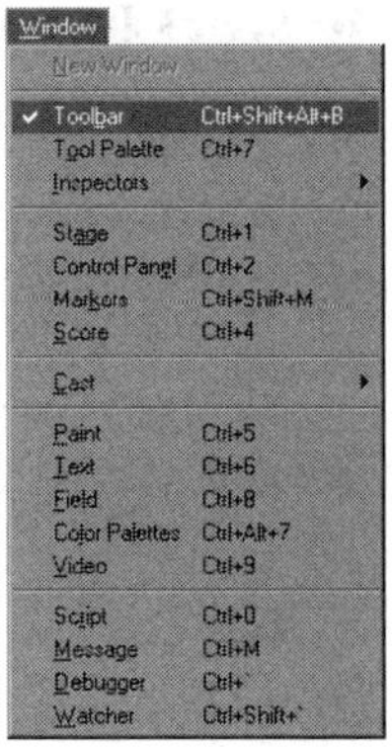

Figure 2. Choose **Toolbar** from the **Window** menu to either show or hide the Toolbar.

Figure 1. The Toolbar.

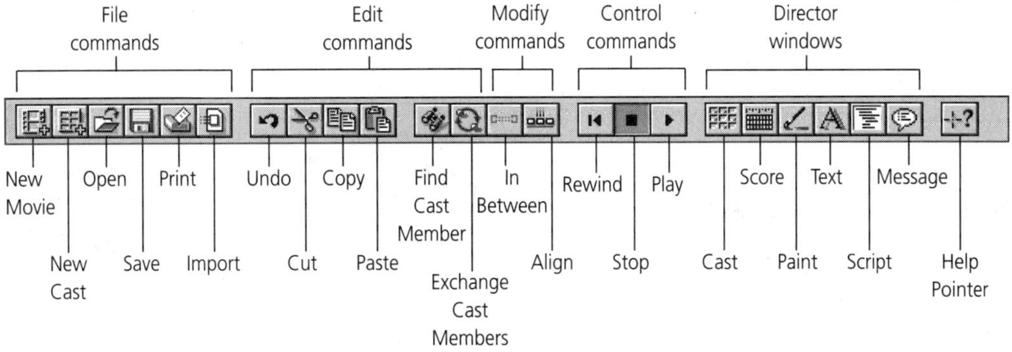

Shortcut menus

Click the right mouse button in any Director window or on a sprite to display a shortcut menu of commonly used commands that apply in that window or for that sprite.

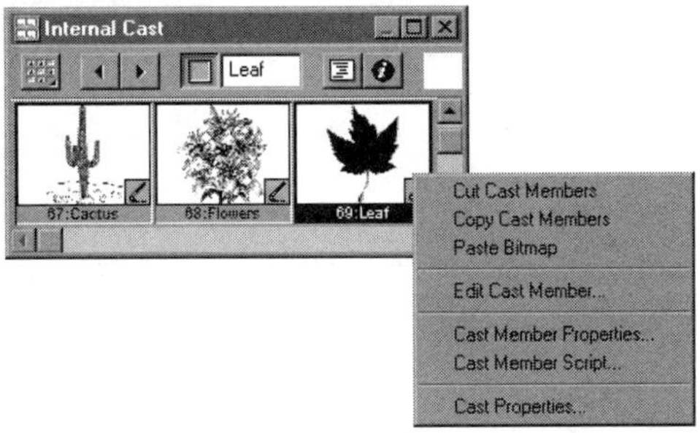

Keyboard shortcuts:

Most Director commands that you choose from the menus have a keyboard equivalent called a keyboard shortcut. To perform a keyboard shortcut, hold down one or more keys such as Control and Alt, and then press and release another key to execute the Director command.

(See Appendix B for a list of keyboard shortcuts)

To choose the Open command using a keyboard shortcut:

1. Hold down the Control key.
2. Press and release the "O" key.
3. Release the Control key.

To start Director:

Open the Director folder that was installed on your hard drive by double-clicking it. Then double-click the Director application icon **(Figure 3)**.

or

Double-click a Director movie icon **(Figure 4)**.

Figure 3. Double-click the Director application icon to start Director.

Figure 4. A Director movie icon.

✔ Tip

■ You can create a shortcut for Director that allows you to launch the program easily from the desktop. Single-click the Director application icon and choose Create Shortcut from the File menu. Now drag the shortcut icon onto the desktop for convenient access.

To create a new movie:

When you start Director, it is ready for you to begin creating a new movie. If at any point you wish to start over from scratch, choose New from the File menu and select Movie from the pop-up menu. **(Figure 5)**. You assign a name to a movie when you save it—by choosing Save from the File menu.

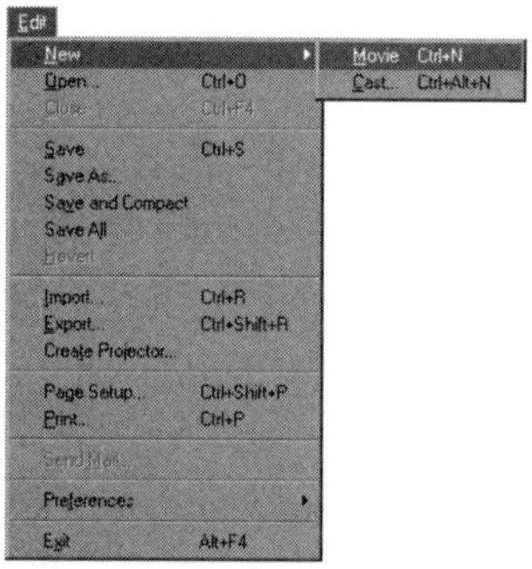

Figure 5. Choose **New** from the **File** menu and select **Movie** from the pop-up menu.

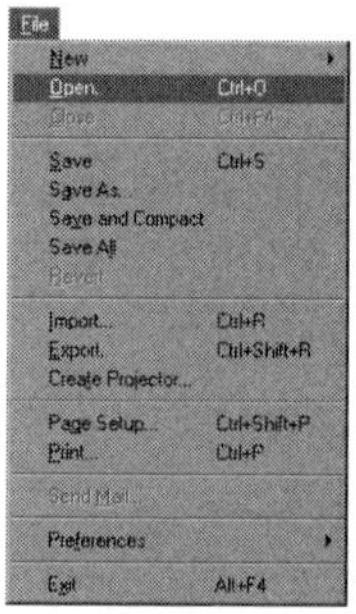

Figure 6. Choose **Open** from the **File** menu to open an existing movie.

To open an existing movie:

Choose Open from the File menu to open a Director movie or an external cast **(Figure 6)**. In the Open dialog box, select the movie's name and click the Open button, or double-click the movie's name **(Figure 7)**. The dialog box displays both cast files and the names of Director movies.

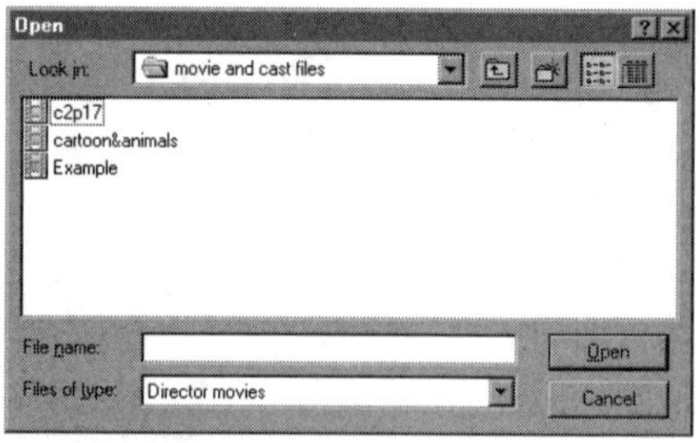

Figure 7. In the **Open** dialog box, select the movie's name from the file directory and click **Open**.

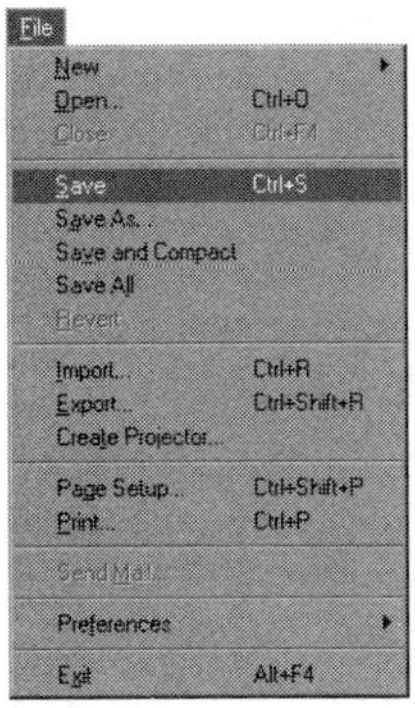

Figure 8. Choose **Save** from the **File** menu to save the current version of your movie.

To save a movie:

Choose Save from the File menu to save the current version of your movie to disk, writing over the movie's previous saved version **(Figure 8)**. You should save often to preserve your most recent work in case Director crashes, or your PC loses power.

When you save a movie for the first time, Director brings you to the Save As dialog box, where you can name your movie and choose the area of your hard disk the movie should be saved to.

To save and compact a movie:

Choose Save and Compact from the File menu to save an optimized version of your movie under its original file name **(Figure 9)**. This takes longer than the Save command since Director reorders the cast, reduces the movie to its minimum size, and eliminates any unused space that might have accumulated in the original file. Use this command to gain optimal playback performance on a CD-ROM.

If your multimedia production consists of a multiplicity of movie and external cast files, you can compact all of them at once for optimal playback by using the Update Movies command. *(See page 12)*

Figure 9. Choose **Save and Compact** from the **File** menu to save an optimized version of your current movie.

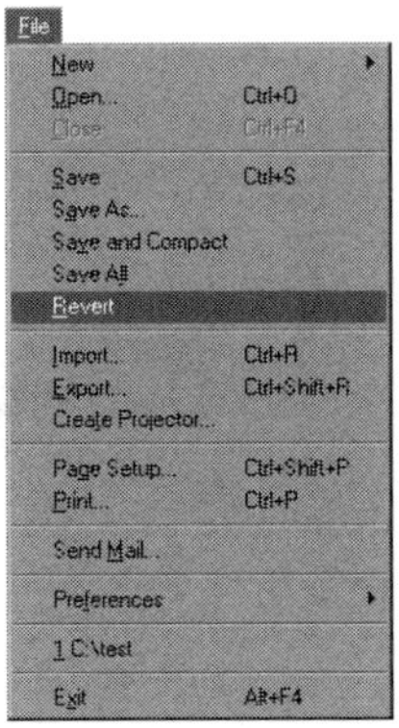

Figure 10. Choose **Revert** from the **File** menu to open the last saved version of your current movie.

Revert

Choose the Revert command from the File menu to open the last saved version of your current movie **(Figure 10)**. This is useful if you have made some undesirable changes to your movie, and wish to quickly go back to the previous saved version.

UPDATE MOVIES

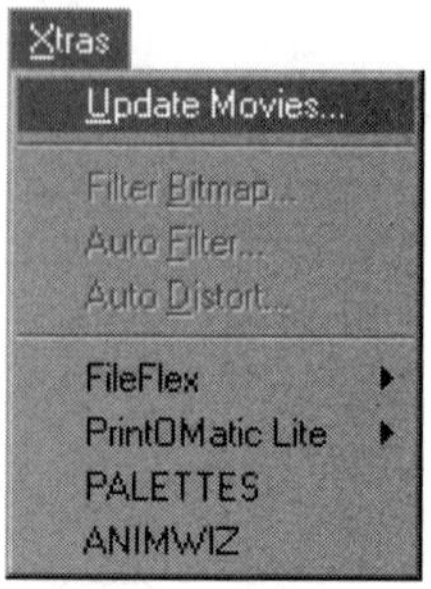

Figure 11. Choose **Update Movies** from the **Xtras** menu.

The Update Movies command under the Xtras menu is used for three different purposes:

- Convert Director 4.x movies to the Director 5 file format.
- Compact current Director movies for optimal playback (same as Save and Compact, except compacts multiple files at once).
- Protect movies from being opened or edited. *(See page 199 in the Create a Projector chapter)*

To update or compact Director movies:

Follow the steps below to either update Director 4.x movies, or to compact current Director movies. *(See page 199 in the Create a Projector chapter on Protecting movies)*

If you have a Director 4.x movie that uses a shared cast (a file called shared.dir), you must update that movie before you can use it with Director 5. The shared cast becomes a linked external cast named shared.cst. Make sure that you add the shared.dir file along with the Director 4.x movie file in step 5 below.

Director 4.x movies which don't have a shared cast can be opened in Director 5, but it is still a good idea to update them first since this converts them into the Director 5 file format, and compacts the file by removing any fragmented data.

1. Choose Update Movies from the Xtras menu **(Figure 11)**.

2. Click the Update and Compact radio button **(Figure 12)**.

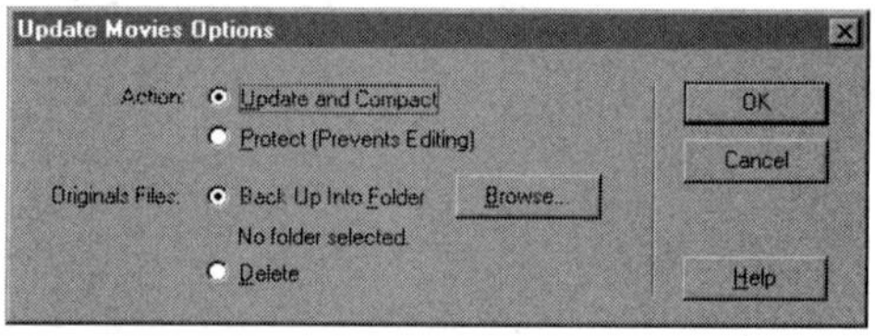

Figure 12. Click the **Update and Compact** radio button in the **Update Movies** dialog box.

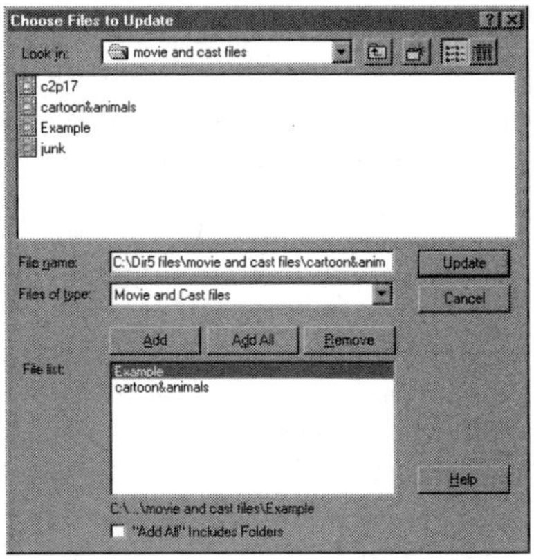

Figure 13. Add the files you wish to update or compact in the **Choose Files to Update** dialog box.

3. Click the Back Up into Folder radio button if you wish to place the original files into a specified folder. Click the Browse button to select the folder in which to place these original files.

or

3. Click the Delete button if you wish the new updated or compacted files to overwrite the originals. Make sure that you have backed up the original files since you cannot undo this conversion.
4. Click OK
5. In the Choose Files to Update dialog box, select a Director 4.x movie file you wish to update, or a Director 5 movie file or external cast you wish to compact. Click Add **(Figure 13)**. Repeat this step to add all the files you wish to update or compact to the list at the bottom of the dialog box. Click Add All to add all the files in the current folder to the list of files to update or compact.
6. Click Update.

THE HELP WINDOW

To open Director's Help window, choose Contents from the Help menu. The Help window's main screen or contents screen displays six help categories to choose from.

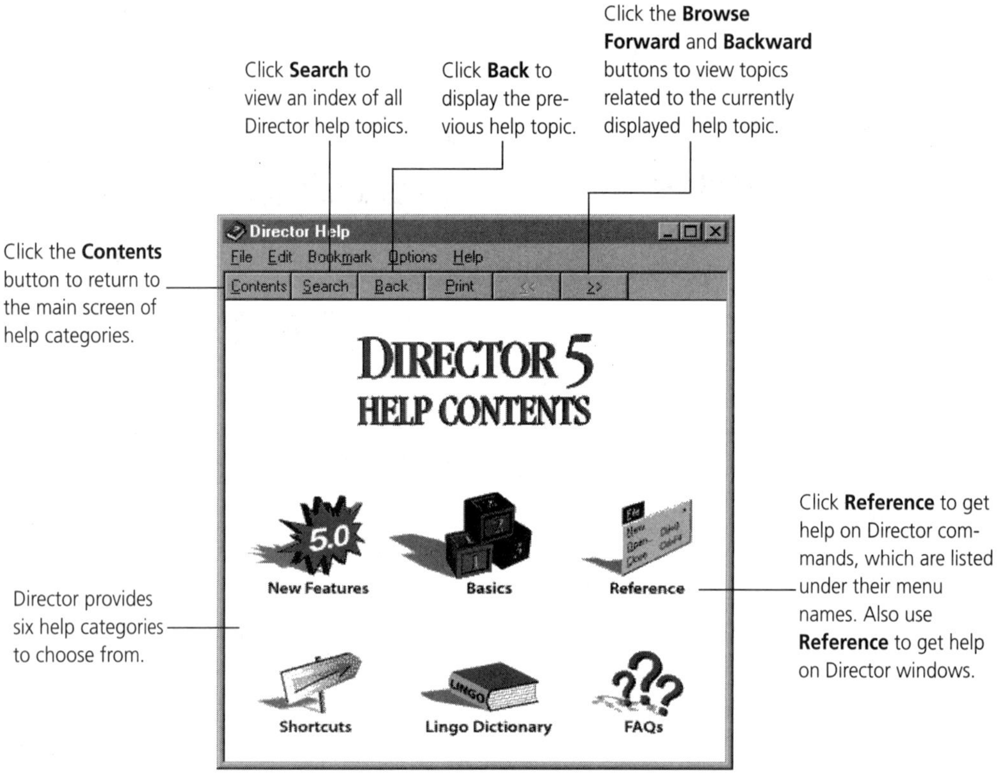

✔ Tip

- Choose Help Pointer from the Help menu, or click the Help Pointer button in the Toolbar to get context-sensitive help. The mouse pointer turns into a question mark, and when you choose a command or click in a window, an appropriate help screen is displayed.

GENERAL PREFERENCES

Use the General Preferences dialog box if you wish to change properties of Director's stage and user interface. Choose Preferences from the File menu and select General from the pop-up menu to open this dialog box. You don't need to change any of the default settings to start creating a Director movie.

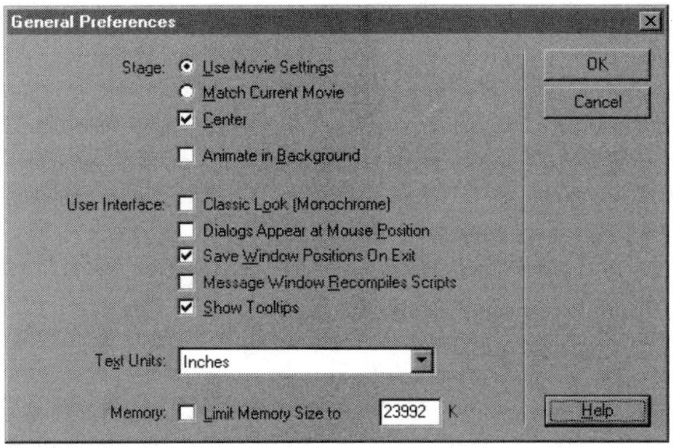

Stage Size

Use Movie's Settings

Select this option for the stage size to take on the dimensions of any new movie that is opened.

Match Current Movie

When set, any movie that is opened takes on the stage dimensions of the current movie.

Center

The stage is automatically centered on the screen (this comes in handy when the stage is smaller than the full screen dimensions).

Animate in Background

When checked, your movie can run in the background. This allows you to work in other applications while your movie plays on the stage behind the application windows.

Memory

Limit Memory Size to

When checked, Director is limited in the amount of memory it uses by the value entered in the box at the right.

User Interface

Classic Look (Monochrome)

When checked, Director displays the user interface in black and white. This improves performance since Director doesn't need to update any colors in the user interface when the current color palette is switched.

Dialogs Appear at Mouse Position

When checked, dialog boxes are displayed at the position of the mouse pointer. If this option is not selected, the dialog boxes will be centered on the monitor.

Save Window Positions On Exit

Saves the positions of all Director windows each time you quit.

Message Window Recompiles Scripts

This is checked by default. If not checked, your scripts should be manually recompiled using the Recompile All Scripts command under the Control menu before any Lingo is entered in the Message window.

Show Tooltips

When checked, definitions appear when the mouse pointer is positioned over tools. This is checked by default.

Text Units

Use the Text Units pop-up menu to select which units of measure are displayed on the text and field windows' ruler.

MOVIE PROPERTIES

Use the Movie Properties dialog box to set a number of properties that affect the current movie, such as the default palette and stage location. You don't need to change the default settings to start creating a Director movie. Choose Movie from the Modify menu and select Properties from the pop-up menu to open the Movie Properties dialog box.

Stage Location

Centered
The stage appears in the center of your monitor.

Upper Left
The stage is placed starting from the top left corner of the screen.

Other
Allows you to enter values into the Left and Top fields to indicate by how many pixels the stage should be offset from the top left corner of the screen.

Stage Size

You can change the size of the stage by choosing a monitor size from the pop-up menu, or by entering values into the Width and Height fields. This is useful when you wish to display movies on a smaller or larger monitor.

Stage Color

Sets the color of the stage. Click the color chip to select a new stage color from the pop-up color palette.

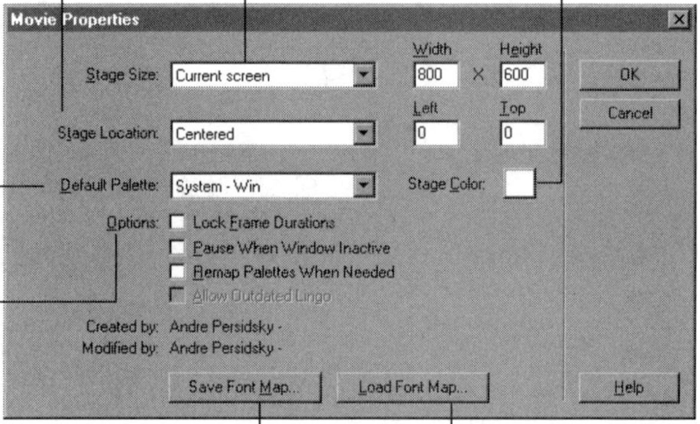

Default Palette

The Default Palette pop-up menu allows you to set the default color palette for your movie. This palette remains in effect until Director encounters a different palette setting in the palette channel.

Options

Lock Frame Durations
The current playback rate is locked so that your movie plays back at the same speed on all types of computers. The movie won't play faster, but may play slower if a computer is not fast enough to keep pace.

Pause When Window Inactive
When set, a movie in a window plays only when the main movie is playing.

Remap Palettes When Needed
If this box is checked, all cast members displayed on the stage that have a color palette different from the currently active palette are remapped to a common palette that Director creates. This is a useful feature to enable when you have many cast members that use many different palettes.

Allow Outdated Lingo
Allows you to include Lingo commands from Director 4 that have been eliminated in Director 5.

Save Font Map

Click to save current font map settings in a specified text file.

Load Font Map

Click to load font map settings.

HOW DIRECTOR WORKS 2

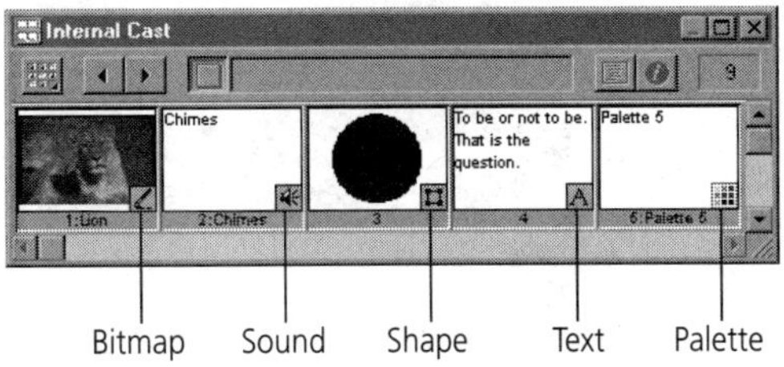

Figure 1. Cast members are stored in Director's **Cast** windows. Each cast member occupies a small numbered window, and its type is indicated by a small icon in the lower right corner.

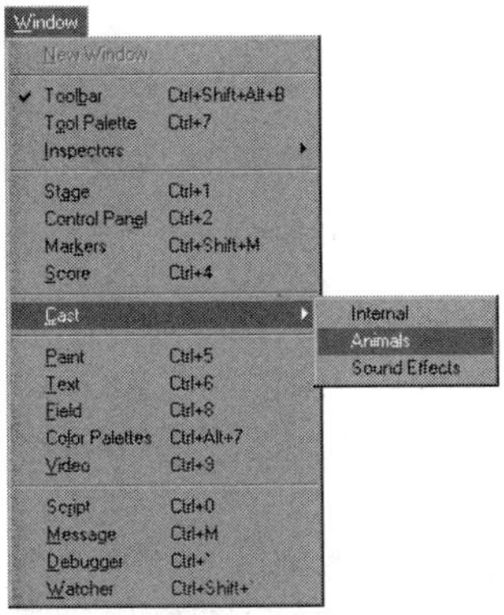

Figure 2. Choose **Cast** from the **Window** menu. If multiple casts are being used, select the cast you wish to view from the pop-up menu.

CREATING MOVIES

The steps involved in creating a Director movie mirror many of the ideas behind traditional Hollywood film production. You start by assembling a group of **Cast members**, which in Director are the multimedia elements that comprise your movies. Cast members can include graphics, sounds, text, buttons, digital videos, and color palettes, among others.

You create a movie by assigning cast members to various parts of the score. The **Score** is a detailed record that tells Director what your cast members should do on a frame-by-frame basis, very much like a script *(see page 20)*.

Your movie plays out on Director's **Stage**, which is the background upon which graphical cast members are animated.

Cast window

Your cast members are stored in a **Cast window**, which is a kind of multimedia database **(Figure 1)**. Cast members are numbered in the small windows they occupy, and their type is indicated by a small icon in the lower right corner. Director 5 allows you to organize your cast members into separate casts. Each cast is viewed in its own cast window. *(See the Cast Windows chapter on page 25 for more details)*

To open a cast window:

1. Choose Cast from the Window menu **(Figure 2)**. If multiple casts are present, choose the cast you wish to view from the pop-up menu.

Creating cast members

Director has its own set of in-house tools for producing cast members. These tools include the paint window, Tool Palette, text window, and field window. For high end production, you may prefer to create your cast members using an application such as Photoshop, which offers more advanced graphics tools. Director allows you to import externally generated cast members. *(See page 28)*

The **Paint window** in Director is actually quite extensive and can be used to create fairly elaborate bitmap cast members **(Figure 3)**. The paint window includes a variety of tools in its tool palette **(Figure 4)** such as the Air Brush, Shape, and Text tools. The paint window also offers a menu bar of special effect commands, such as Rotate and Warp, which can be applied to your bitmap cast members. *(See the Paint Window chapter on page 75 for more details)*

Figure 3. The paint window is used to create and edit bitmap cast members.

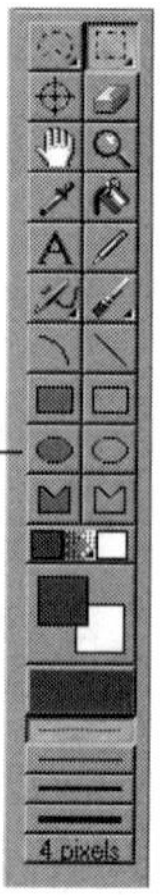

Figure 4. The paint window tool palette.

To create a cast member using the paint window:

1. Choose New from the File menu and select Movie from the pop-up menu **(Figure 5)**.
2. Choose Paint from the Window menu to open the paint window **(Figure 6)**.
3. Click the Filled Ellipse tool in the tool palette **(Figure 4)** (in this example we create a shaded ellipse).
4. Select a foreground color by clicking and holding the Foreground color chip **(Figure 3)**. Choose a color from the pop-up color palette that appears.
5. Drag in the paint window to size and draw your ellipse.
6. When you close the paint window, your drawing automatically becomes a bitmap cast member. It is placed into the first available slot in the current cast window.

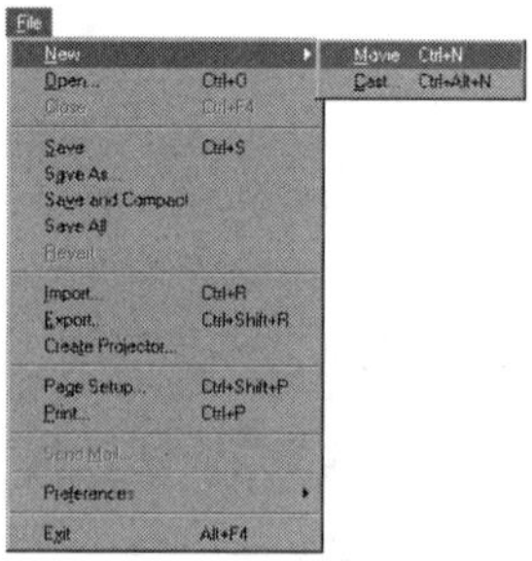

Figure 5. Choose **New** from the **File** menu and select **Movie** from the pop-up menu to open a new untitled movie.

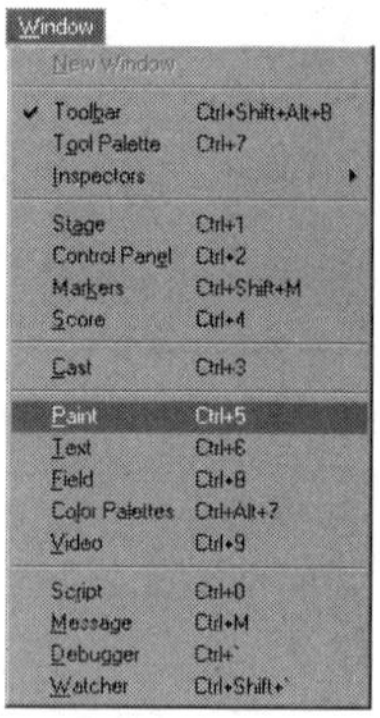

Figure 6. Choose **Paint** from the **Window** menu.

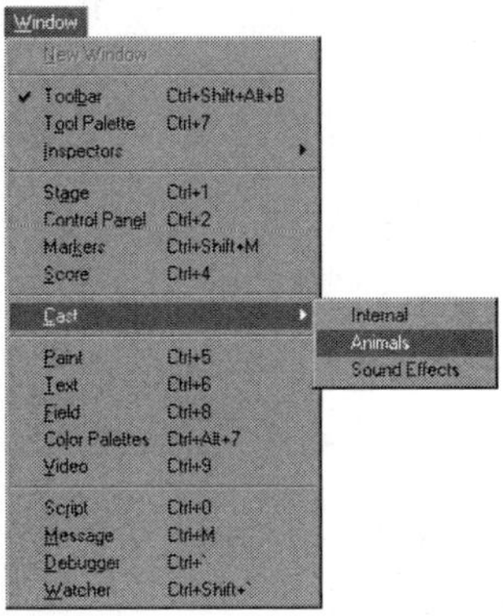

Figure 7. Choose **Cast** from the **Window** menu. If multiple casts are being used, select the cast you wish to view from the pop-up menu.

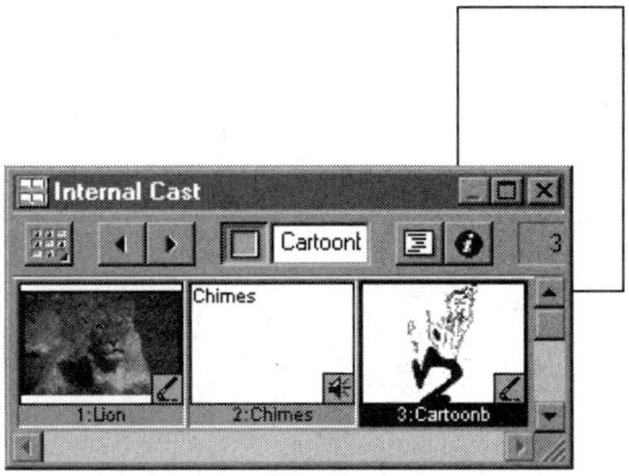

Figure 8. Dragging a cast member from a cast window onto the stage automatically places it in a single frame of the score. (The rectangular outline represents the cast member being dragged from the cast window to the stage.)

Optional

7. Choose Cast from the Window menu. The cast window appears and you should now see your ellipse in the first cast member position. Notice that the cast member type is a bitmap as indicated by the small icon.

✔ **Tip**

■ Double-click a bitmap cast member in a cast window to open it in the paint window.

To place a cast member onto the stage:

Once you have assembled your cast members in a cast window, you will want to start building your movie. You incorporate cast members into your movie by placing them into the score, or by dragging them onto the stage—the background upon which they are animated.

1. Choose Cast from the Window menu to open a cast window **(Figure 7)**.
2. Drag a cast member onto the stage, that is, onto any area of the screen not occupied by an open window **(Figure 8)**. This action places the cast member into your movie and automatically records it in a single frame of the score. If the cast member is a graphical type, its location on the stage is also recorded in the score.

Frames

A Director movie, like any movie, is broken down into a series of frames. A **Frame** is a snapshot of your movie that holds all the information about what's happening in a particular time segment. This information includes such things as the positions of each of your cast members, and what sound effects are being played at that instant.

Score window

Director's score window is a frame-by-frame record of your movie **(Figure 9)**. You use the score to orchestrate all the components of your movie on a frame-by-frame basis. Movie components include all cast member types like sounds and bitmaps, as well as events such as color palette and scene transitions. All these components are stored in the frames of the score, which are organized into vertical columns of cells, and numbered at the top. Each **Cell** stores an individual movie component that is part of a frame.

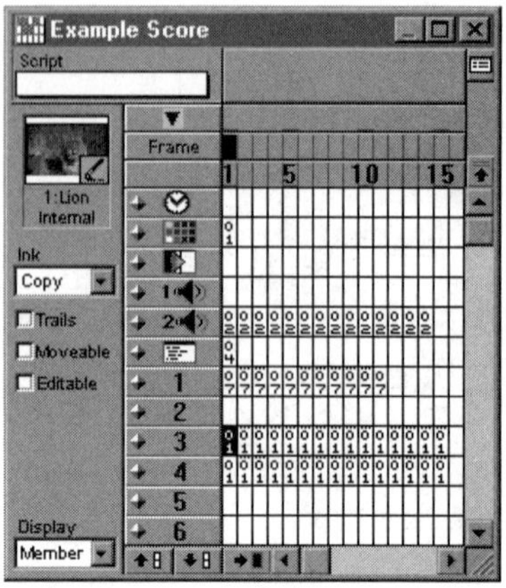

Figure 9. The score window is a frame-by-frame record of your Director movie.

The cells that make up a frame each belong to a particular score channel. **Score channels** are organized into rows of cells, and hold specific types of movie components **(Figure 10)**. For instance, when a graphical cast member appears in a certain frame, it's stored in a cell which belongs to one of the score's animation channels. Likewise, sound effects that play over a range of frames are stored in one of the two sound channels.

There are 54 score channels in all, five of which are called effects channels (tempo, palette, transition, sound 1 & 2), one script channel, and 48 animation channels, which keep track of the positions of individual cast members on the stage. *(See the Score, Stage, and Sprites chapter on page 43 for more details)*

The position of the **Playback head** in the score indicates which frame of the movie is currently displayed on the stage **(Figure 10)**. You can drag the playback head to display any single frame of your movie on the stage.

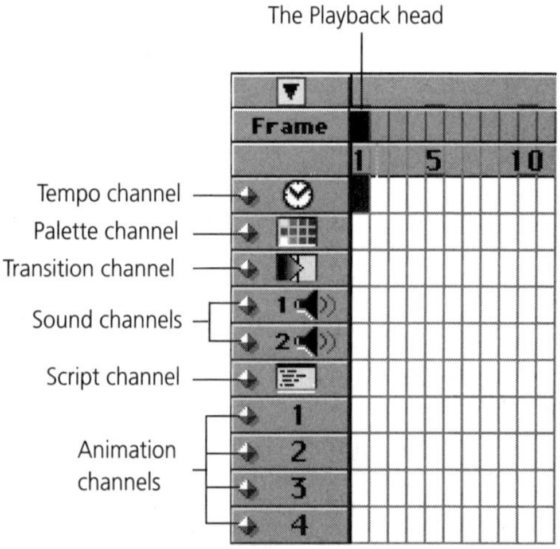

Figure 10. The score channels run vertically along the left side of the score window. Each channel forms a row of cells.

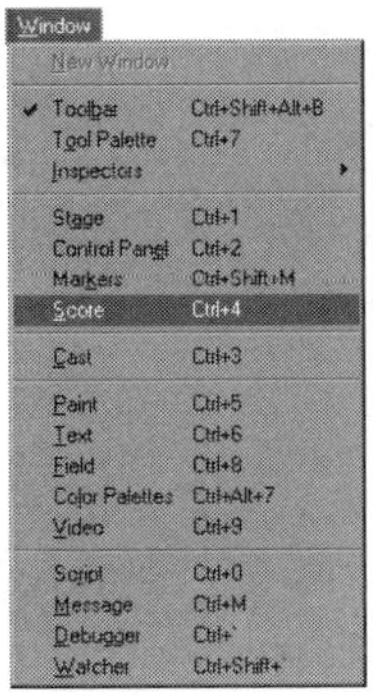

Figure 11. Choose **Score** from the **Window** menu.

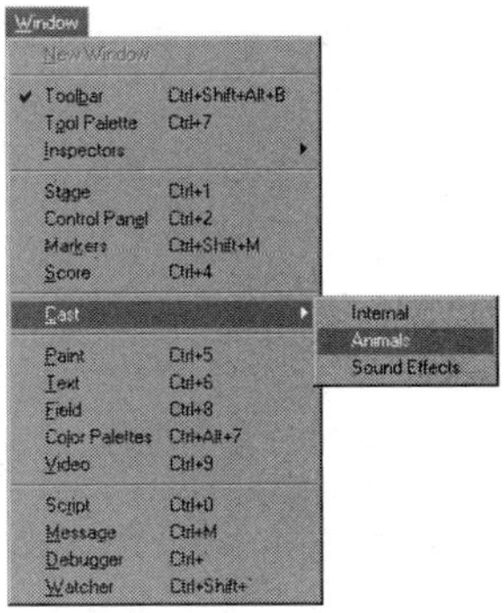

Figure 12. Choose **Cast** from the **Window** menu. If multiple casts are being used, select the cast you wish to view from the pop-up menu.

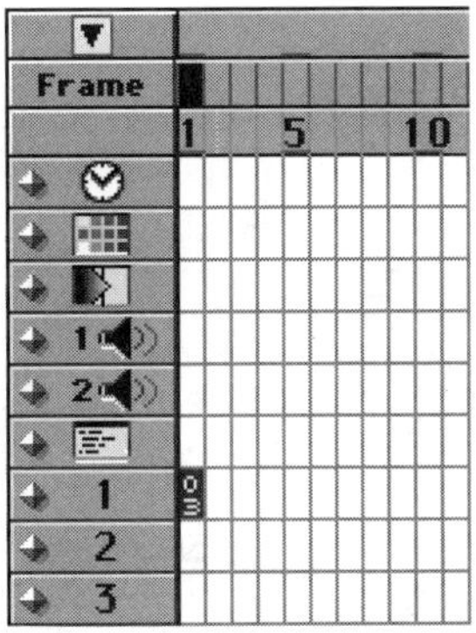

Figure 13. Drag a graphical cast member from a cast window into the first animation channel in the first frame of the score window.

Figure 14. Director can automatically generate a series of frames that lie between two key frames using the **In Between** command.

To place a cast member into the score:

You can enter a cast member into the score (and therefore into your movie) by dragging it from a cast window and placing it into a specific frame and channel. If the cast member is a graphical type (bitmap, shape, or PICT) it automatically appears centered on the stage in the frame you place it in.

1. Choose Score from the Window menu to open the score **(Figure 11)**.
2. Choose Cast from the Window menu to open a cast window **(Figure 12)**.
3. In this example, drag a graphical cast member from a cast window into the first animation channel in the first frame of the score **(Figure 13)**. The cast member is recorded into the score and appears centered on the stage.

Animation

An animation is created by positioning cast members on the stage, and then slightly changing the positions of each of these cast members in the successive frames of your movie. When the frames are played back at a high speed, animation is achieved. Director provides several techniques to expedite the process of animating your cast members. These include the In Between command and Real-time recording feature.

With the **In Between** command, you set up the **key frames**—the first and last frames in your animation—and Director automatically fills in all the intermediary frames, sparing you from having to manually create each frame (**Figure 14**). Director's **Real-time recording** feature lets you record the path of mouse movements and then substitute a cast member to follow this recorded path to produce animation. *(See the Animation Techniques chapter on page 145 for more details)*

Control panel

Director's control panel offers you VCR-type control over the playback of your movie. You can rewind, play, jump forward to any frame, and even change the tempo setting of your movie by using the control panel **(Figure 15)**.

Figure 15. Director's control panel offers VCR-type control over the playback of your movie.

A simple movie example:

The following steps create a simple movie animation. Before proceeding, follow the steps on page 18 to create the bitmap cast member of an ellipse that's used in this example:

1. Open the cast and score windows by choosing them from the Window menu.

2. Drag the ellipse from the cast window into frame 1, animation channel 1 in the score **(Figure 16)**. The ellipse appears in the center of the stage.

3. Drag the ellipse from the center of the stage to the left-hand-side.

4. Drag the ellipse again from the cast window but now place it into frame 15, animation channel 1 in the score **(Figure 17)**. The ellipse appears in the center of the stage.

5. Drag this ellipse from the center of the stage to the right-most-side.

6. In the score, drag to select all the cells in animation channel 1 that lie between frames 1 and 15, including frames 1 and 15 **(Figure 18)**.

7. Choose In Between from the Modify menu **(Figure 19)**. Director fills in all the empty frames between frames 1 and 15 with the ellipse cast member, but slightly shifting it to the right in each successive frame, creating an animation.

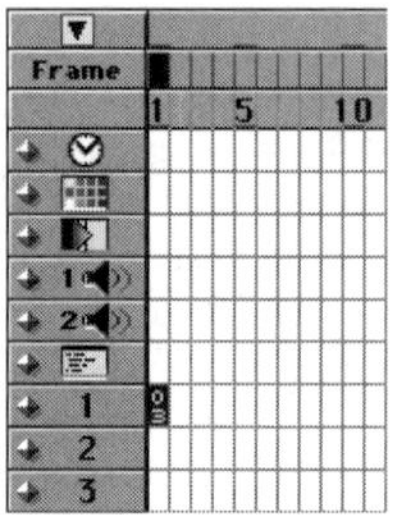

Figure 16. Drag the ellipse from the cast window into frame 1 in animation channel 1.

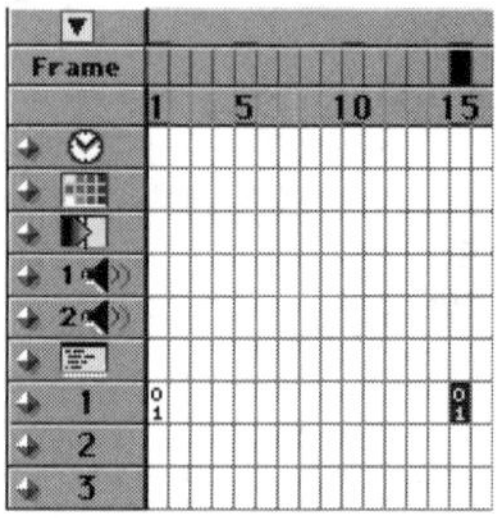

Figure 17. Drag the ellipse from the cast window into frame 15 in animation channel 1.

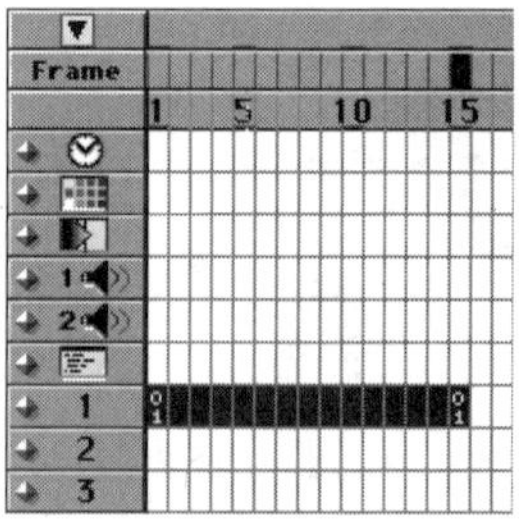

Figure 18. Select all the cells between frames 1 and 15 in animation channel 1.

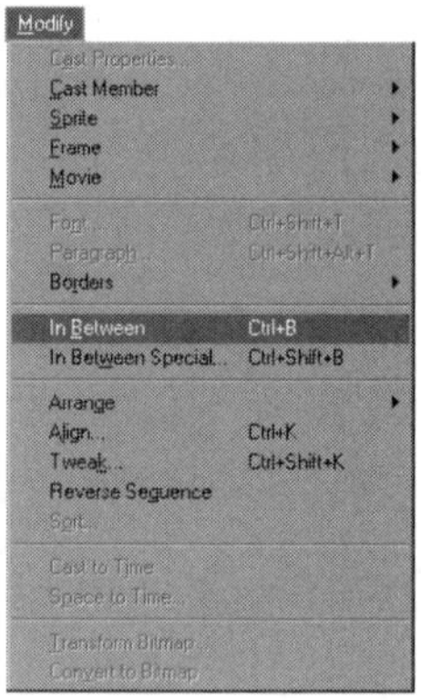

Figure 19. Choose **In Between** from the **Modify** menu.

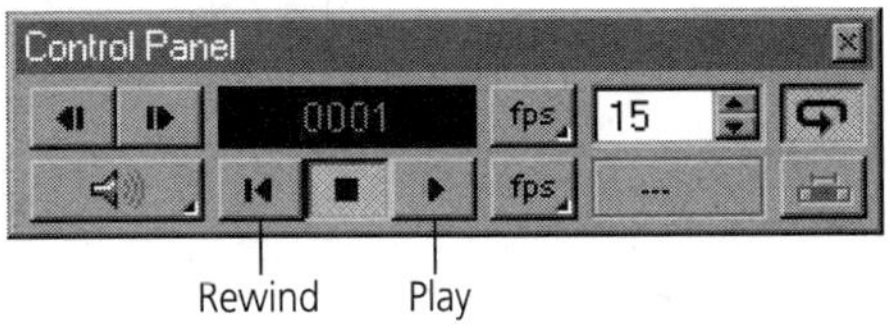

Figure 20. The control panel.

8. Choose Control Panel from the Window menu to open the control panel **(Figure 20)**.

9. Click the Rewind button to set the playback head to frame 1.

10. Click Play to watch your movie. The ellipse moves across the stage from left to right.

Lingo and interactivity

Director movies, unlike traditional animation or video, can incorporate interactive features, which allow your viewers to become active participants. They can change the course of your movie in many different ways, using mouse and keyboard input. Such interactivity is created by using Lingo—Director's scripting language.

Lingo scripts are instructions written in the script window **(Figure 21)** that tell Director how your movie should respond to user input, and to other changing conditions. For example, you can write a script that creates interactive buttons, which allow your viewers to navigate through the scenes of your movie at will. This is very common in an information kiosk set up. *(See the Interactivity through Lingo chapter on page 203 for an introduction to script writing)*

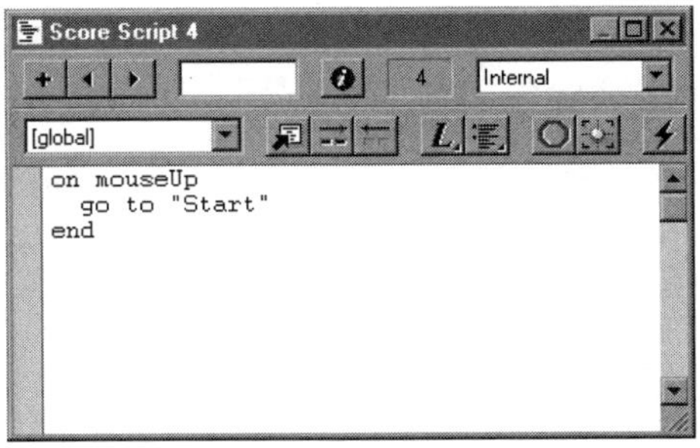

Figure 21. The script window.

CAST WINDOWS 3

Cast window.

Choose Cast from the Window menu to open a cast window, or press Control-3. If multiple casts are being used, select the cast you wish to view from the pop-up menu **(Figure 1)**.

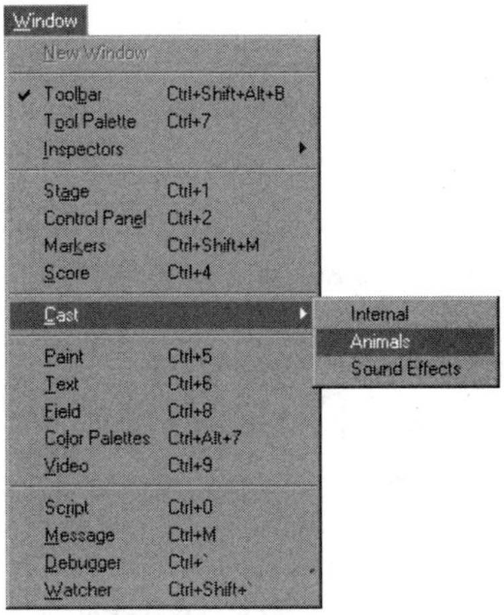

Figure 1. Choose **Cast** from the **Window** menu. If multiple casts are being used, select the cast you wish to view from the pop-up menu.

Figure 2. A cast window showing four cast members.

Director's **Cast windows** act as the viewing and storage areas for the cast members used in your movie (remember that cast members include pictures, sounds, strings of text, color palettes, digital videos, film loop animation, and interactive scripts, among others). When you're ready to incorporate a cast member into your movie, simply drag it from a cast window onto Director's stage or right into its score window. *(See the Score, Stage, and Sprites chapter on page 47 for more about incorporating cast members into Director's score)*

Director 5 allows you to create and work with multiple independent casts within a single movie. Each cast is displayed in its own window. Casts are either internal or external. (*See page 31 for more about internal and external casts*)

In order for a cast member to become available for your movie, it must first be placed in a cast window **(Figure 2)**. If the cast member has already been created and saved by some other program (for instance, a background created in Photoshop, or a sound effect mixed with Wave Lab), the cast member must first be imported into a cast window before it can be incorporated into your movie (*see page 28 for importing cast members*). However, if you're creating a cast member within Director itself (for instance, by using Director's paint window, or its Tool Palette), **the cast member is automatically added to the cast window**.

A cast window can contain up to 32,000 cast members available for use in your movie. Each cast member is represented by a thumbnail image, and identified by a number that's respective to the position it occupies.

Cast member types

Each cast member in a cast window has a small icon in its lower-right corner that identifies its type **(Figure 3)**.

Cast selector

Use the Cast Selector **(Figure 4)** to choose which cast is displayed in the current cast window, or to create a new cast. You can choose from all internal casts, and external casts that have been linked to the current movie. These casts are displayed in the pop-up menu. (*See page 31 for more about internal and external casts*)

Previous, Next arrows

Click the Previous or Next arrow to select the previous or next cast member (in relation to whatever cast member is currently selected) in the cast window **(Figure 4)**. The key combination Control-Left Arrow selects the previous cast member, and Control-Right Arrow moves to the next cast member.

Place button

The Place button is useful when you wish to move some cast members to a new position in a cast window, where the new position is beyond the visible range of the selected cast members. First click the cast member in the cast window you wish to move **(Figure 4)**. You may Shift-click to select more than one cast member at a time and move them together. Now scroll through the cast window to the position to which you wish to move the selected cast member(s). Drag the Place button to the new position in the cast window. Release the mouse button to move the selected cast member(s) **(Figure 5)**.

✓ Tip

- Hold the Alt key while dragging the Place button to copy selected cast members to their new position.

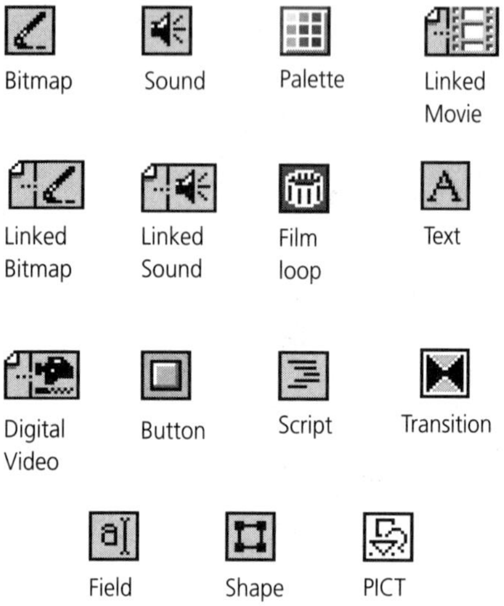

Figure 3. Cast member types are indicated by a small icon in the lower-right corner of each cast member.

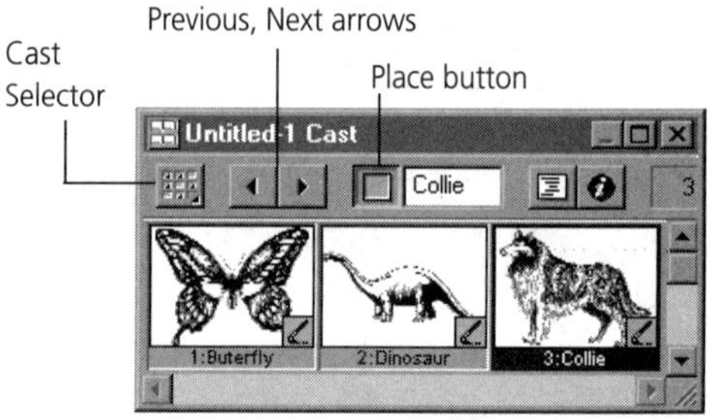

Figure 4. The **Place** button is used to move selected cast members to new positions in the cast window. Click the cast member you wish to move, such as cast member 1 depicted here.

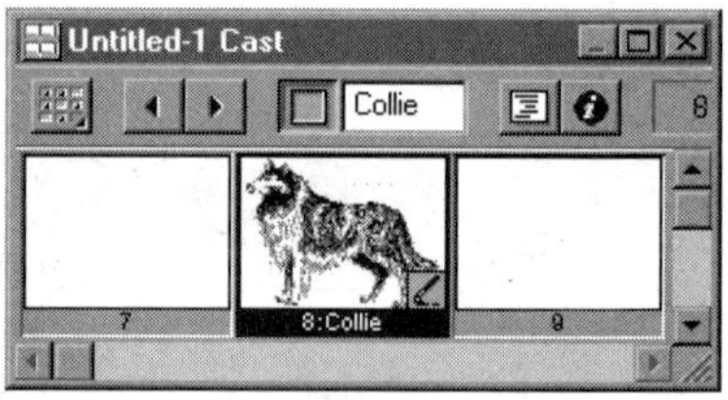

Figure 5. Drag the **Place** button to the new position in the cast window. Release the mouse button to move the selected cast member.

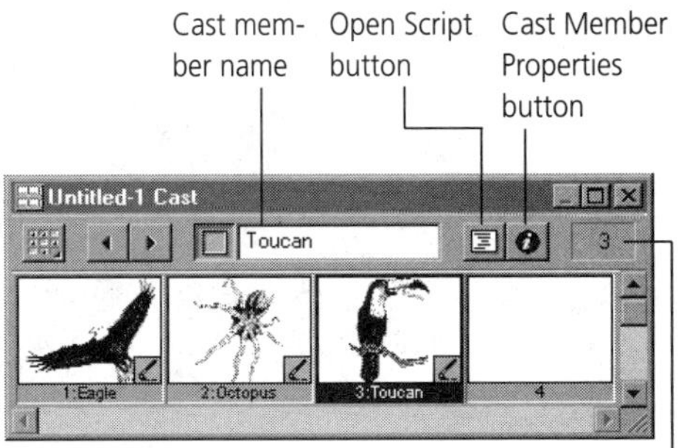

Figure 6. A cast window.

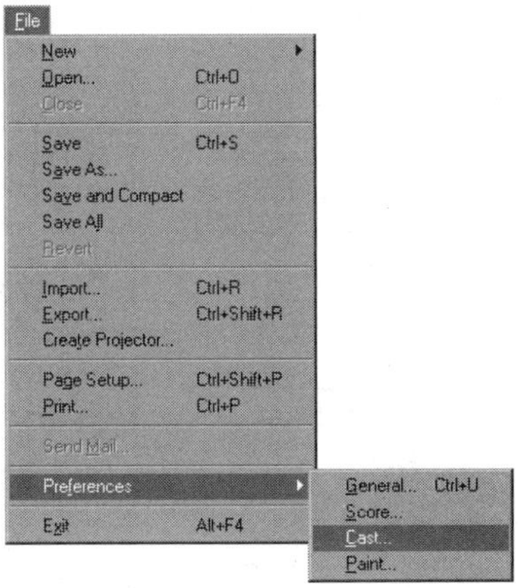

Figure 7. Choose **Preferences** from the **File** menu, and select **Cast** from the pop-up menu.

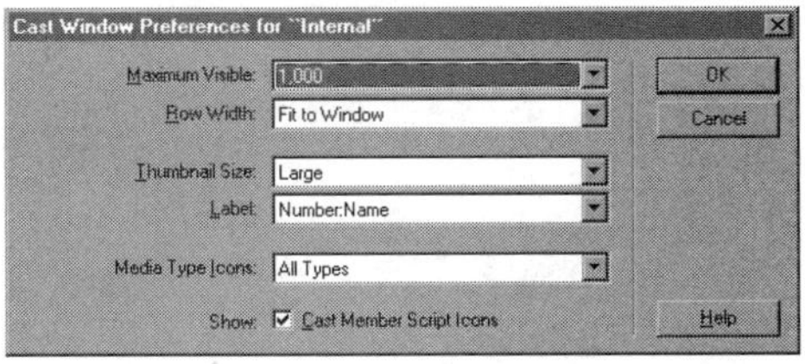

Figure 8. Use the pop-up menus in the **Cast Window Preferences** dialog box to change the appearance of a cast window.

Cast member name

Displays the name of the selected cast member assuming you have opted to assign one **(Figure 6)**. *(See page 39 for more about Cast member names)*

Open Script button

Click the Open Script button to open a script window for the currently selected cast member. *(See the Interactivity through Lingo chapter on page 204 for more about scripts)*

Cast Member Properties button

Click the Cast Member Properties button to display the Cast Member Properties dialog box for the currently selected cast member (you can also press Control-I). *(See page 34 for more about the Cast Member Properties dialog box)*

Cast member number

Displays the numerical position that the currently selected cast member occupies in the cast window. Positions are numbered left to right, and row by row in the window.

To change cast window preferences:

Director allows you to control how cast windows are displayed. You can change characteristics such as row width, thumbnail size, how labels are displayed, and which media type icons are visible.

1. Activate the cast window whose preferences you wish to change by clicking it.
2. Choose Preferences from the File menu, and select Cast from the pop-up menu **(Figure 7)**.
3. Use the pop-up menus in the Cast Window Preferences dialog box to make the desired changes **(Figure 8)**.

IMPORTING CAST MEMBERS

If you want your Director movie to incorporate graphics or sounds that have already been created in some other application (for instance, a background created in Photoshop, or a set of sound effects compiled in SoundEdit Pro), you'll first have to import those elements into a cast window.

You can import the following file types into Director for Windows: Bitmap files, JPEG files CompuServe GIF files, TIFF files, EPS files, Photo CD files, PC Paintbrush files, Window metafiles, Palettes, Sounds, Director movies, Cast files, video clips, FLC and FLI files, Macintosh PICT's, MacPaint files, and text files saved in the rich text (RTF) format.

To import a cast member:

1. Choose Import from Director's File menu (or press Control-R on the keyboard) **(Figure 9).**
2. In the Import dialog box, use the Files of type pop-up menu to indicate what kind of cast member you'd like to import **(Figures 10–11).** Only files in this selected format are displayed in the dialog box.
3. Use the Folders pop-up menu to navigate through your hard drive's file folders, and open the folder that contains the cast member you wish to import.
4. Click the desired cast member file, and then click the Add button to add it to the list of cast members you wish to import. Click the Add All button to add all the displayed cast member files to the list. Click the Import button to bring the added cast member(s) into the currently selected cast window.

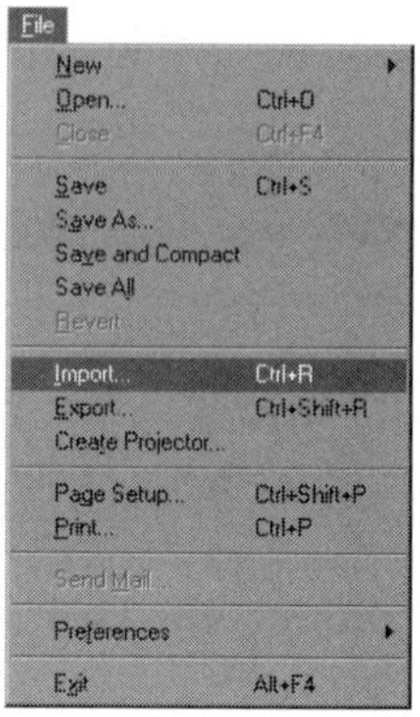

Figure 9. Choose **Import** from Director's **File** menu.

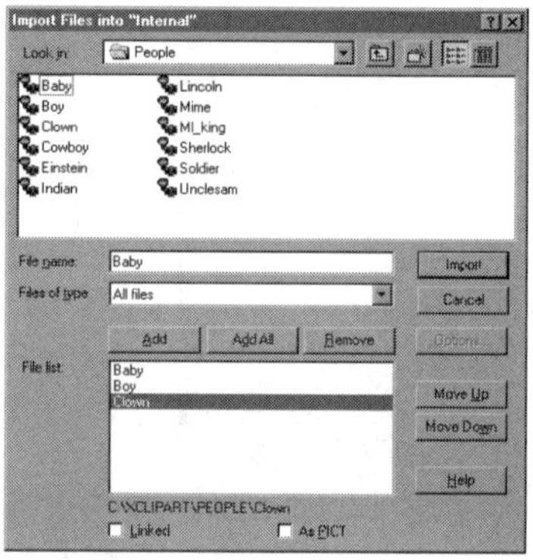

Figure 10. The **Import** dialog box.

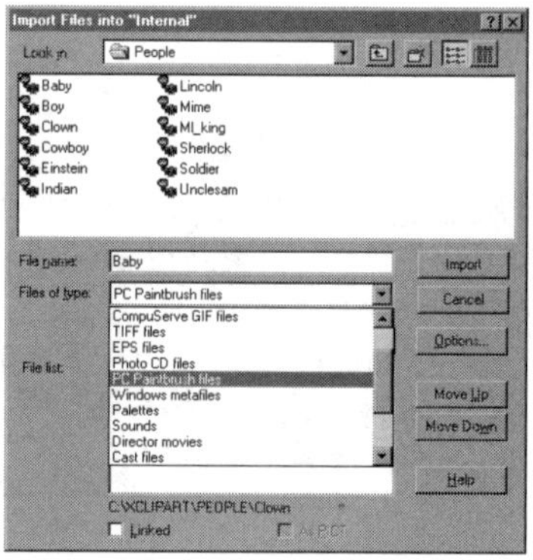

Figure 11. Use the **Files of type** pop-up menu to select a cast member type.

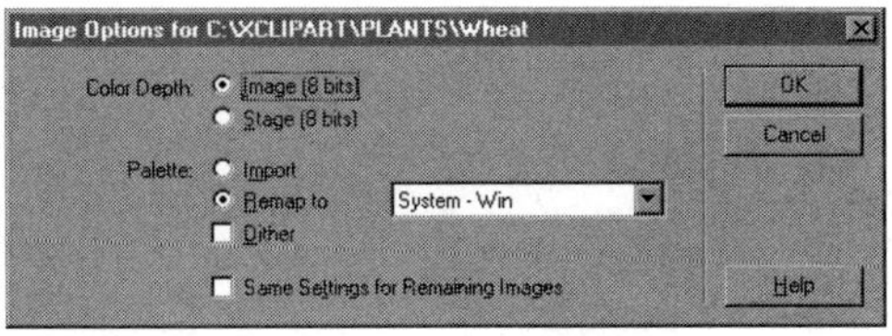

Figure 12. The **Image Options** dialog box allows you to set color depth and palette attributes for imported graphical cast members.

Image options for bitmap cast members

When you import a bitmap cast member with a color depth or palette different than the current movie's, an Image Options dialog box appears, which allows you to set color depth and palette attributes **(Figure 12)**.

The Color Depth option sets the desired color depth for the cast member. If you wish to import the image at its original color depth, click the Image option. Click the Stage option to import the image at the movie's color depth. (*See page 120 in the Color in Director chapter for details on movie color depth*)

The Palette option allows you to either import the image's original color palette (where it becomes installed as a cast member), or to remap the image to one of the currently available palettes in Director. By installing the cast member's palette into the cast window, you can ensure that the cast member will maintain its original colors when its palette is active. "Remap to" causes Director to replace the image's colors with the most similar colors from the palette you select in the pop-up menu.

Set the "Same Settings for Remaining Images" option if you wish to apply the same settings to all the files you have selected for importing.

Linking to a file

When you import a cast member file, Director actually copies the contents of that file into your movie, thus increasing its size. You can avoid this when you import PICT, sound, or Director movie files by linking to those files. Do so by checking the Linked checkbox in the import dialog box **(Figure 13)**.

If you check the Linked checkbox, Director will note the location of the original file on your hard drive and then refer to it when necessary. Not only does this approach keep your movie from bloating up in size, but also it means that if you ever change that linked cast member (for instance, if you use Photoshop to retouch an image file after it's been imported), Director will automatically reflect that change, and the updated cast member won't have to be imported again. Also different movies can share the same linked file. The drawback to linking Director to its cast member files is that those files must always be on hand when you play your movie. If Director cannot find a linked file, it will ask you to locate any missing files before going on.

Note: Director always links to digital video files when they are imported.

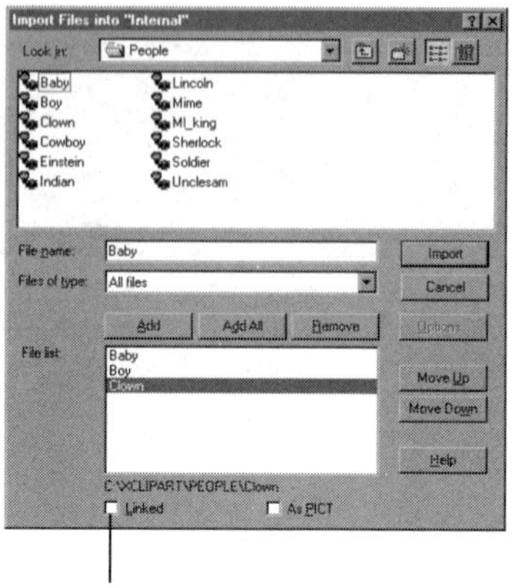

Figure 13. The Linked checkbox.

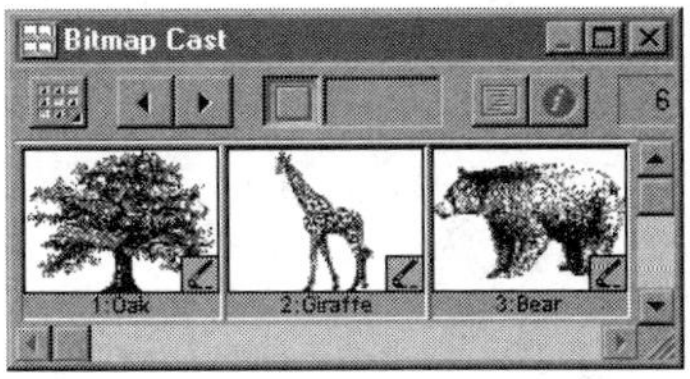

Figure 14. A cast window is shown, organized to hold bitmaps.

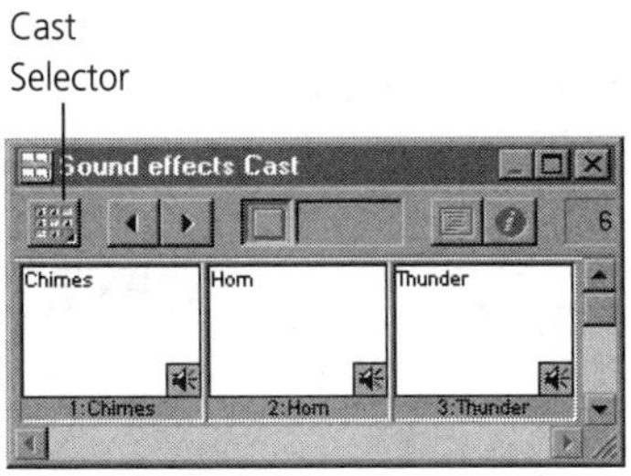

Figure 15. A cast window is shown, organized to hold sounds.

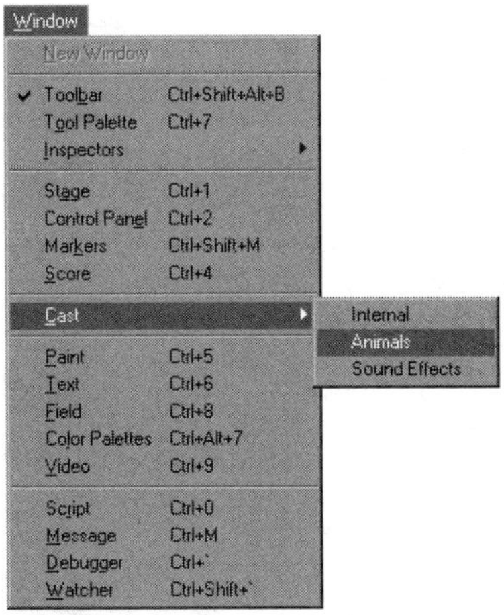

Figure 16. Choose **Cast** from the **Window** menu. If multiple casts are being used, select the cast you wish to view from the pop-up menu.

MULTIPLE CASTS

Director 5 supports the use of multiple casts in your movies. If your movie project involves a large number of cast members, it is helpful from an organizational standpoint to group together related cast members into separate casts. For example, you may choose to create two casts, one for storing bitmaps, and the other for sounds. Each cast is viewed in its own separate cast window **(Figures 14–15)**.

To open a specific cast window:

1. Choose Cast from the Window menu, and select the cast you wish to view from the pop-up menu **(Figure 16)**.

✓ Tip

- You can also use the Cast Selector **(Figure 15)** to choose which cast is displayed in the current cast window.

Internal and External casts

Casts in Director 5 are either internal or external. You can add as many internal or external casts as you wish to your movie. Director 5 automatically creates an **internal** cast for a new movie. Internal casts cannot be shared between Director movies. When you save your movie, all internal casts are automatically saved in the movie file. Internal casts are also stored directly in Projector files.

The advantage of using **external** casts is that they can be shared between Director movies. External casts are stored in separate files outside of the movie file. In order to incorporate cast members from an external cast in your movie, the external cast must first be linked to the movie (*see page 30*). After you link an external cast to the current movie, Director automatically opens that cast whenever you open that movie.

To create a new cast:

You can add as many internal or external casts as you wish to your movie.

1. Choose New from the File menu, and select Cast from the pop-up menu **(Figure 17)**.
2. In the New Cast dialog box (**Figure 18**), choose internal or external for the cast storage type by clicking the appropriate radio button. If the cast is external, check the "Use in Current Movie" checkbox if you want the cast linked to the current move.
3. Type a name for the cast in the text box.
4. Click the Create button.

✔ **Tip**

■ You can also create a new cast by clicking the Cast Selector in a cast window, and selecting New Cast from the pop-up menu.

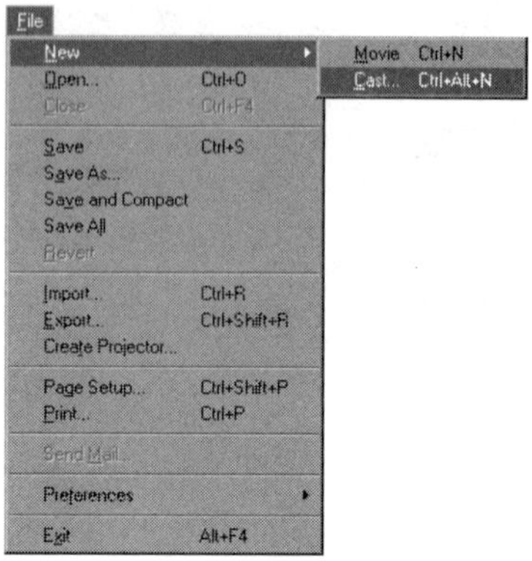

Figure 17. Choose **New** from the **File** menu, and select **Cast** from the pop-up menu.

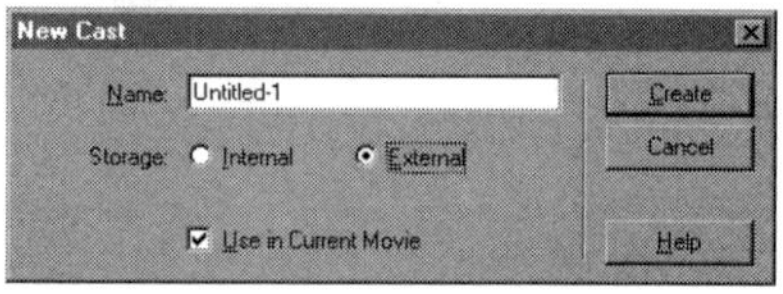

Figure 18. In the **New Cast** dialog box, choose internal or external for the cast storage type, and enter a name for the new cast.

To open an external cast:

External casts which are not linked to the current movie must be opened separately to access their cast members.

1. Choose Open from the File menu.
2. Select the external cast file you wish to open.
3. Click Open. The external cast is placed in its own cast window.

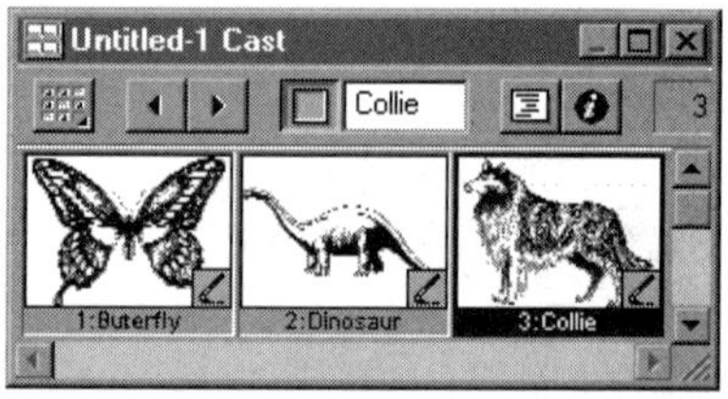

Figure 19. Activate the external cast that you wish to save by clicking its window.

To save an external cast:

1. Activate the external cast that you wish to save by clicking its window **(Figure 19)**.
2. Choose Save As from the File menu **(Figure 20)**.
3. Type a file name for the external cast and click Save.

Figure 20. Choose **Save As** from Director's **File** menu.

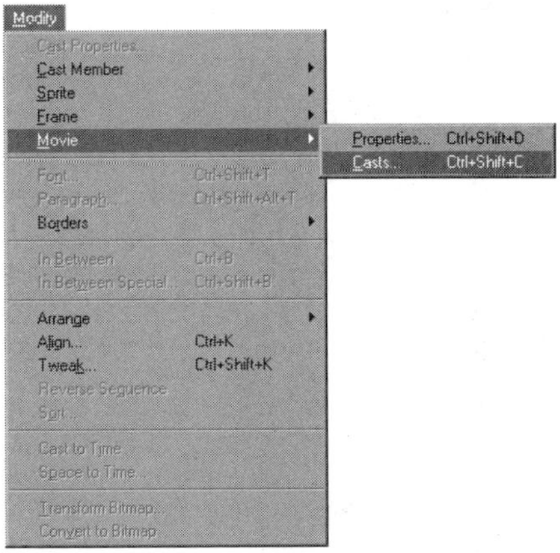

Figure 21. Choose **Movie** from the **Modify** menu, and select **Casts** from the pop-up menu.

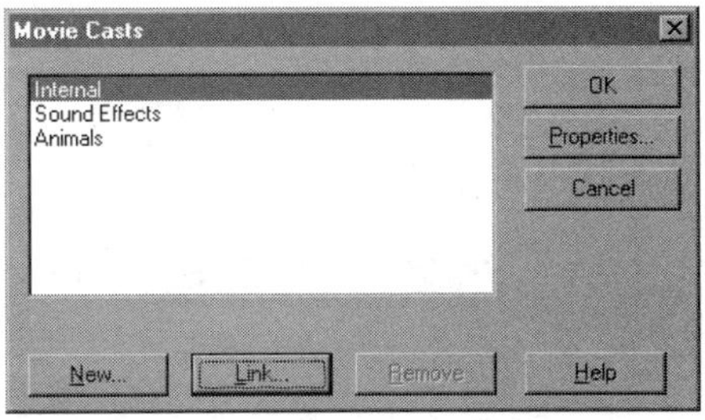

Figure 22. Click the **Link** button in the **Movie Casts** dialog box and select the external cast you wish to link to the current movie.

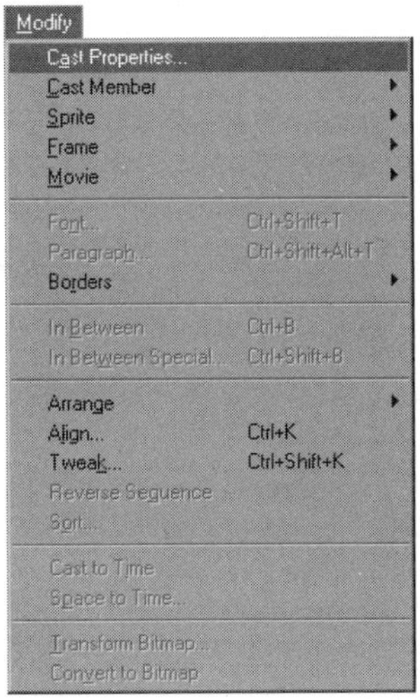

Figure 23. Choose **Cast Properties** from the **Modify** menu.

To link an external cast to the current movie:

1. Choose Movie from the Modify menu, and select Casts from the pop-up menu **(Figure 21)**.
2. Click the Link button in the Movie Casts dialog box **(Figure 22)**.
3. Select the External cast file you wish to link to the current movie.
4. Click OK.

To change and view properties of a cast:

Use the Cast Properties command to view and change settings for the currently selected cast. These settings include name, storage type (whether the cast is internal or external), size in kilobytes, and Preload (which determines when the cast is loaded into memory).

1. Activate the cast whose properties you wish to view or change by clicking in its window.
2. Choose Cast Properties from the Modify menu **(Figure 23)** to open the Cast Properties dialog box **(Figure 24)**.

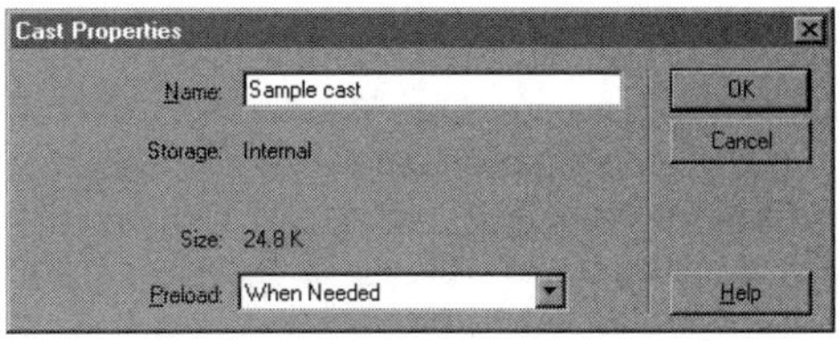

Figure 24. Use the **Cast Properties** dialog box to view and change settings for the currently selected cast.

MANAGING CAST MEMBERS

To get (and set) Cast Member Properties:

The Cast Member Properties command provides a variety of information regarding each cast member in your movie. For instance, you can use the Cast Member Properties command to find out how much memory a sound effect requires or what color palette is assigned to a cast member. Cast Member Properties also allows you to control a variety of cast member settings. You can turn on or off an accompanying sound in a film loop cast member or a linked movie. For a digital video cast member, you can specify the frame rate at which the video plays. You can also use the Cast Member Properties command to determine how Director will manage all your cast members within the memory limitations of your PC.

1. From a cast window, select the cast member whose properties you wish to see.
2. Choose Cast Member from the Modify menu and select Properties from the pop-up menu **(Figure 25)**. You can also click the Cast Member Properties button in a cast window.
3. The Cast Member Properties dialog box appears. The dialog box differs depending on the type of cast member you've selected—for instance, a bitmap graphic, a sound effect, a color palette, or a digital video **(Figures 26–27)**. This dialog box offers key information about the selected cast member, and lets you specify a variety of settings that control the cast member's behavior.
4. Click OK to save any settings you may have made to the cast member.

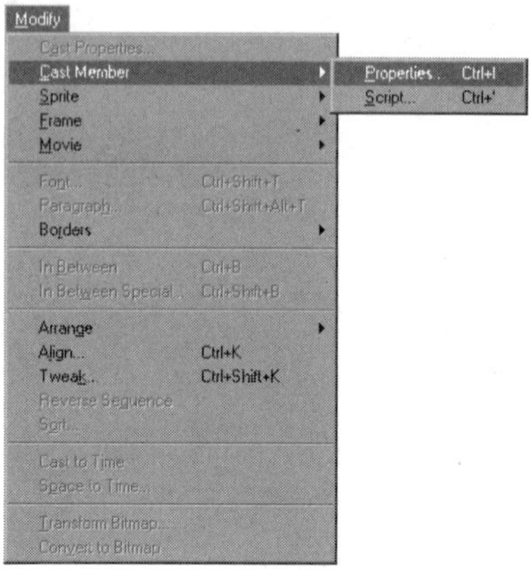

Figure 25. Choose **Cast Member** from the **Modify** menu and select **Properties** from the pop-up menu.

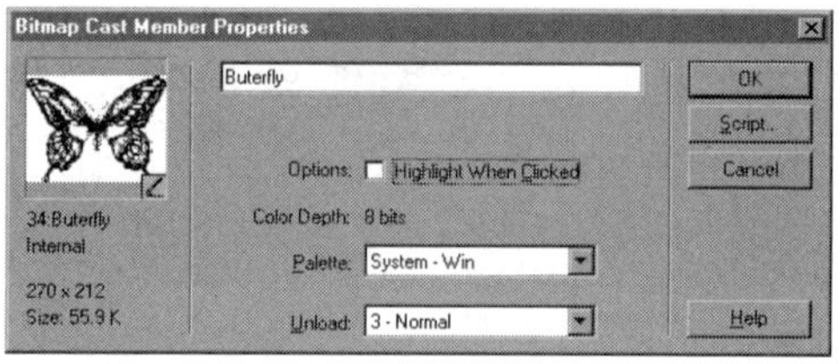

Figure 26. Cast Member Properties dialog box for a bitmap cast member.

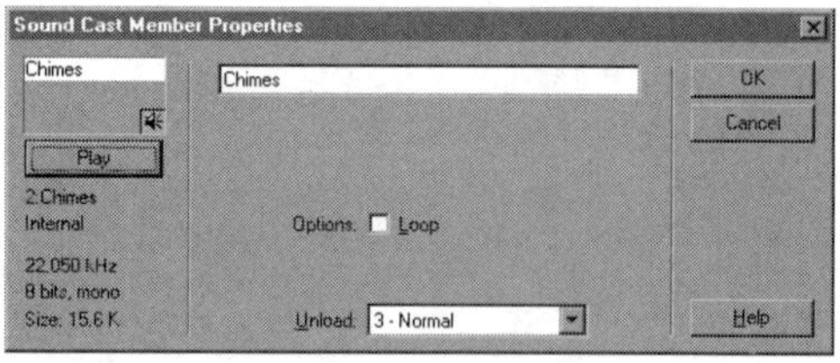

Figure 27. Cast Member Properties dialog box for a sound.

> **Unload setting.**
>
> Director allows you to set the following Unload values in the Cast Member Properties dialog box:
>
> **3** (Normal) Cast member is purged from memory as necessary.
>
> **2** (Next) Cast member is among the next group to be purged from memory.
>
> **1** (Last) Cast member is among the last group to be purged from memory.
>
> **0** (Never) Cast member is never purged from memory.

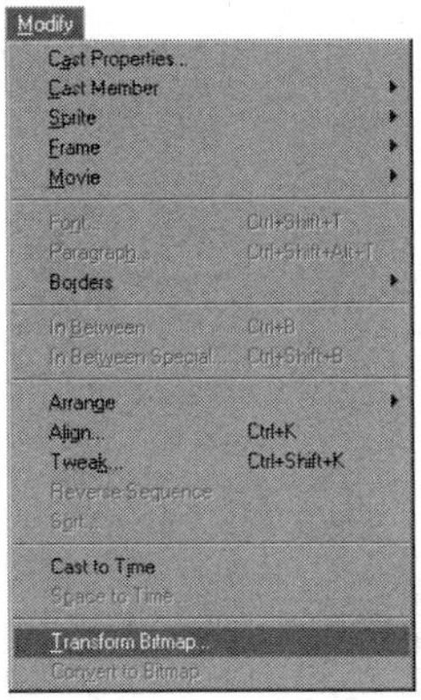

Figure 28. Choose **Transform Bitmap** from the **Modify** menu.

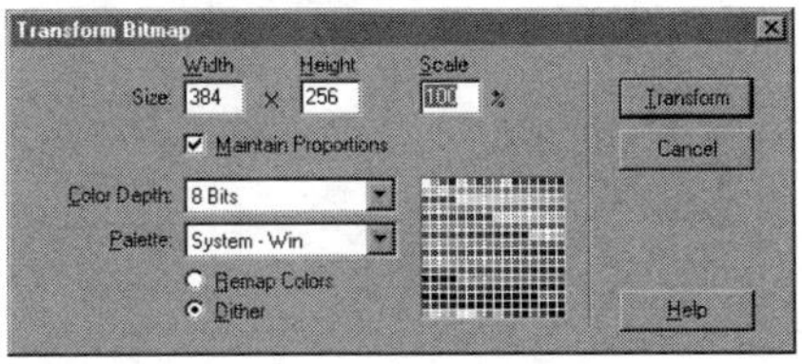

Figure 29. Change a cast member's size by entering new Width and Height dimensions, or a Scale percentage in the **Transform Bitmap** dialog box.

Note: The Cast Member Properties dialog box allows you to set the **Unload value** for the selected cast member. If your PC begins to run low on memory while playing your movie, Director tries to purge certain cast members from RAM to free more memory. If a purged cast member is required again, Director must load it back into memory from your hard disk, which can delay your movie's playback for a moment. For this reason you can manually set the Unload value for individual cast members, telling Director which cast members are least important to your movie and can be purged first in case memory is low, and which are really key and should not be purged at all.

To change a bitmap cast member's size:

1. From a cast window, select the bitmap cast member whose size you wish to change.
2. Choose Transform Bitmap from the Modify menu **(Figure 28)**.
3. In the Transform Bitmap dialog box, click the Width and Height fields and type in new values **(Figure 29)**. Check the Maintain Proportions option to maintain the cast member's original proportions, or enter a value in the Scale box to proportionately size your cast member.

Note: You cannot undo any changes made to a cast member using the Transform Bitmap command. Make sure you have a duplicate of the original cast member before making any changes.

Note: The Transform Bitmap command is also used to change a cast member's color depth, and the color palette it uses to display its colors. *(See the Color in Director chapter on page 119 for details on color depth and color palettes)*

To duplicate a cast member in a cast window:

Being able to duplicate a cast member is useful for a couple of reasons: If you wish to create a number of cast members that make up an animation sequence, you can base each distinctive frame on duplicates of one or more cast members, making minor changes to each duplicate. Also, if you wish to make changes to a cast member's color palette, it's a good idea to try your ideas on a duplicate. If you don't like the results, you can always go back to the original version.

1. From a cast window, click the cast member that you wish to duplicate (**Figure 30**).
2. Choose Duplicate from the Edit menu **(Figure 31)**. Director places a copy of the selected cast member in the next available position in the cast window.

✔ **Tip**

- You can also create a duplicate cast member by using the Copy and Paste commands under the Edit menu, and also by dragging a cast member in a cast window to a new location while holding the Alt key.

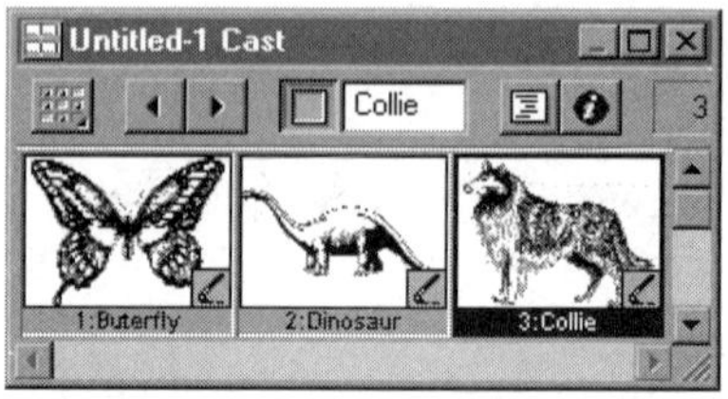

Figure 30. Click the cast member you wish to duplicate.

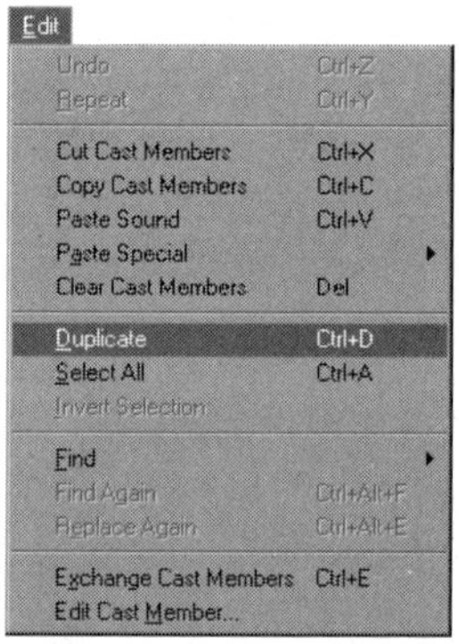

Figure 31. Choose **Duplicate** from the **Edit** menu.

To delete a cast member from a cast window:

1. In a cast window, click the cast member you wish to delete. Shift-click to select a range of cast members or hold down Control and click to select multiple non-adjacent cast members.
2. Choose Clear Cast Members from Director's Edit menu to remove the cast member(s) **(Figure 32)**. Even if the cast member has already been assigned to the score, it will no longer appear when you play your movie.

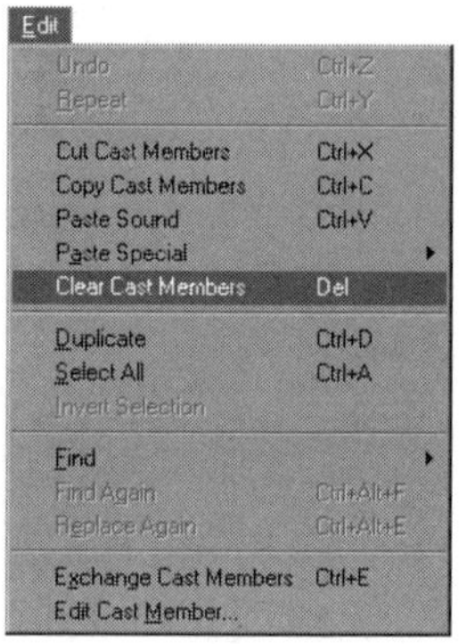

Figure 32. Choose **Clear Cast Members** from the **Edit** menu.

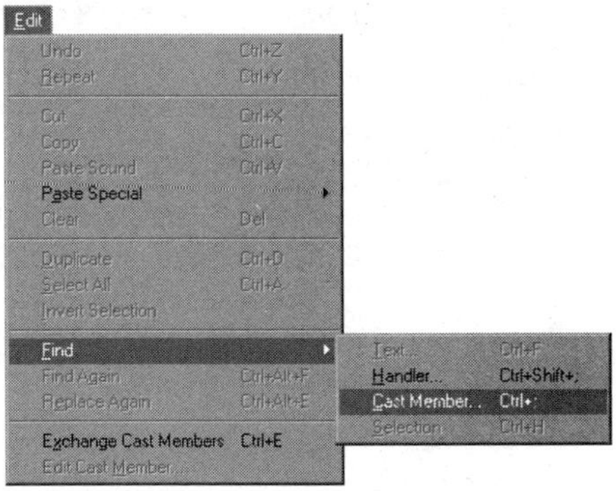

Figure 33. Choose **Find** from the **Edit** menu and select **Cast Member** from the pop-up menu.

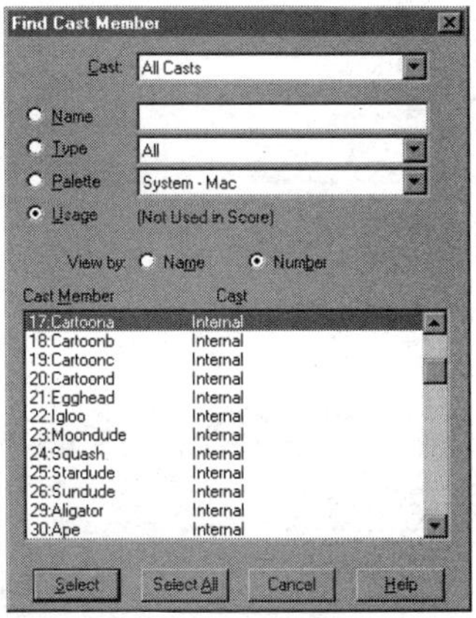

Figure 34. Click the fourth radio button in the **Find Cast Member** dialog box to find cast members not used in the score.

To delete cast members not used in the score:

You may find that you've imported a number of cast members into your movie that you never ended up using and want to delete. Director can find and delete them for you. Deleting unused cast members is wise since it frees memory.

1. Choose Find from Director's Edit menu and select Cast Member from the pop-up menu **(Figure 33)**.
2. Use the Cast pop-up menu in the Find Cast Member dialog box to select the cast whose unused cast members you wish to delete **(Figure 34)**.
3. Click the radio button labeled Usage **(Figure 34)**.
4. Click the Select All button and Director finds and selects all unused cast members in the selected cast. You may first need to click in the list to make the buttons selectable.
5. Choose Clear Cast Members from the Edit menu.

Note: Cast members may be incorporated into your movie by way of Lingo scripts, in which case certain cast members would not necessarily appear in the score. So before deleting the cast members that Director finds, make sure that they are not used in any scripts.

✔ Tip

- Once you've deleted a series of cast members, save your movie by using the Save and Compact command under the File menu. This operation reorders the cast and produces a more compact movie file as well as optimizing movie playback.

To reposition cast members in a cast window:

In some cases it's preferable to place all related cast members together in a cast window. For instance, suppose that you are building an animation sequence of a growling tiger. If you place the first frame of the animation in position 1 of a cast window, you'll want to place the next frame in position 2, the next in position 3, and so on **(Figure 35)**. Placing related cast members together is not only efficient from an organizational standpoint, but also helpful for creating film loop cast members.

Director makes it easy to reorder cast members within a cast window by dragging them from one position to another.

1. From a cast window, click to select the cast member you wish to reposition **(Figure 36).** You can Shift-click to choose multiple adjacent cast members or hold the Control key to select multiple non-adjacent cast members.
2. Drag the selected cast member (or one cast member in a multiple selection) to a new position in the cast window **(Figure 37)**.
3. Release the mouse button to place the cast member in its new location. If you were dragging multiple cast members, they will be positioned sequentially from that point.

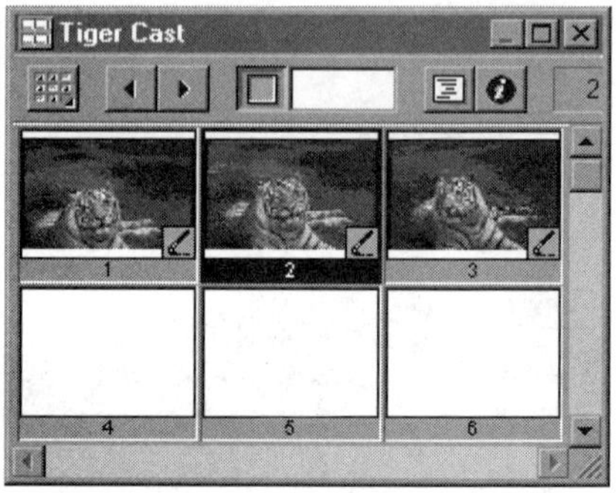

Figure 35. Related cast members, such as multiple frames in an animation, should be placed side by side in a cast window.

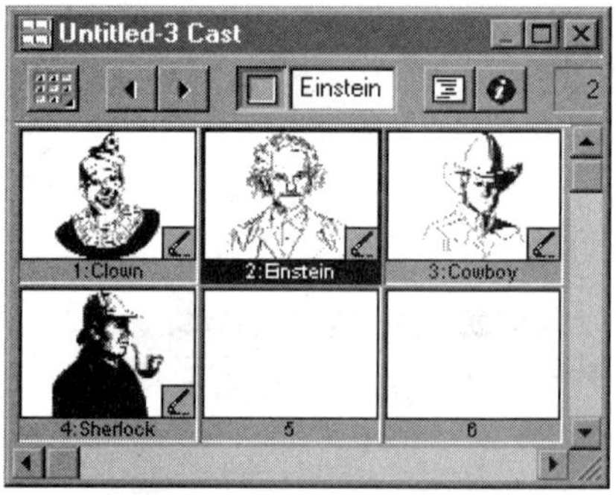

Figure 36. Click the cast member, such as Einstein in position 2.

Figure 37. Drag the selected cast member to its new location and release the mouse button.

Figure 38. Select the cast member you wish to name.

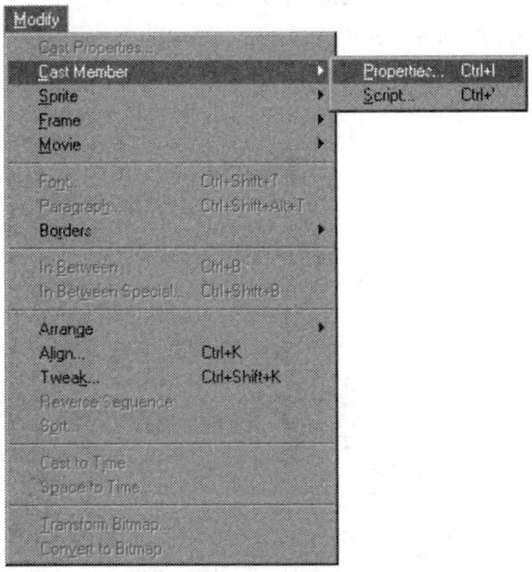

Figure 39. Choose **Cast Member** from the **Modify** menu and select **Properties** from the pop-up menu.

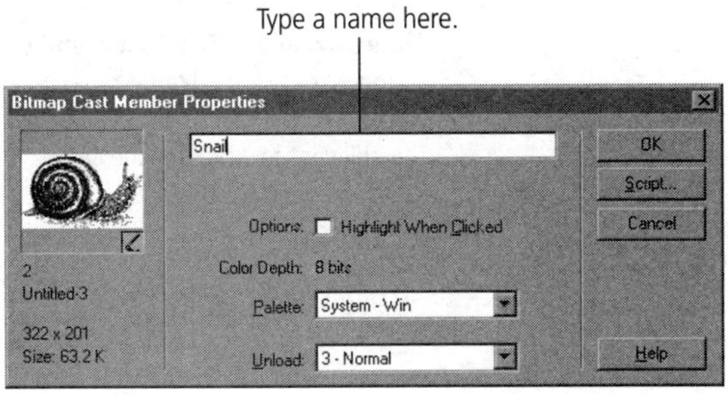

Figure 40. Enter a name in the **Cast Member Properties** dialog box.

To name a cast member in the cast window:

You can give cast members descriptive names (such as Sunset, Bird, Man 1 and Man 2) so that they're easier to find and manage in the cast window and throughout your entire movie.

1. In a cast window, click to select the cast member that you wish to name **(Figure 38)**.
2. Choose Cast Member from the Modify menu and choose Properties from the pop-up menu **(Figure 39)**.
3. In the Cast Member Properties dialog box, type the name you wish to assign the selected cast member **(Figure 40)**.
4. Click OK.

✔ Tip

- You can also enter a name for a selected cast member directly at the top of its cast window.

To find a cast member by its name:

If your movie contains a large number of cast members, it can become tedious to search through the casts manually to find one cast member out of potentially hundreds. If you've named your cast member, however, you can let Director find it for you automatically. It can also find a range of cast members that share common elements in their names, such as Man 1, Man 2, and Man 3.

1. Choose Find from Director's Edit menu and select Cast Member from the pop-up menu **(Figure 41)**.
2. In the Find Cast Member dialog box **(Figure 42)**, select which cast you wish to search from the Cast pop-up menu.
3. In the Find Cast Member dialog box, click the first radio button labeled "Name".
4. In the adjacent text box, type the name of the cast member(s) you'd like to find. You may type the name partially to find multiple cast members with similar names. For instance, you'd type "Man" to find cast members Man 1, Man 2, and so on.
5. Click Select and Director finds and selects the first cast member with a matching name in the specified cast. Click Select All if you wish to select all cast members with matching names. If the Select and Select All buttons are unselectable for some reason, click a cast member in the Find Cast Member dialog box list to make them selectable.

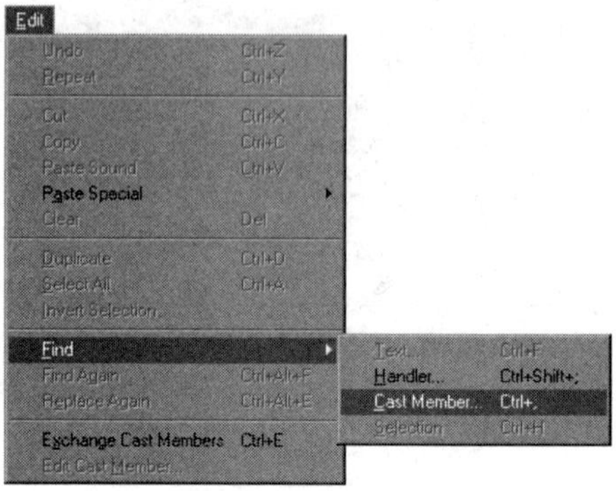

Figure 41. Choose **Find** from the **Edit** menu and select **Cast Member** from the pop-up menu.

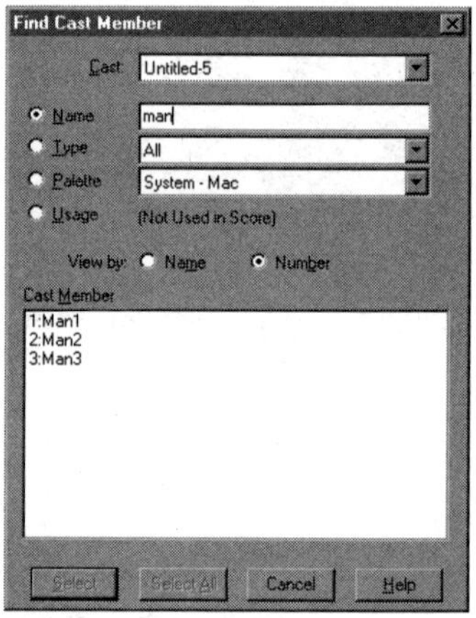

Figure 42. In the **Find Cast Member** dialog box, click the **Name** radio button and type a cast member name in the adjacent text box for the cast member you want to find.

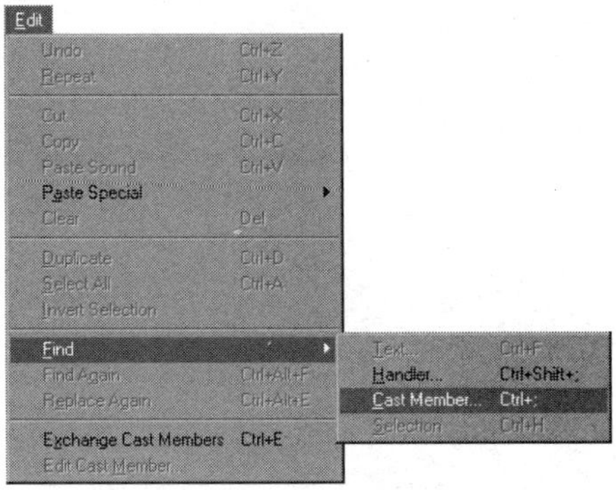

Figure 43. Choose **Find** from the **Edit** menu and select **Cast Member** from the pop-up menu.

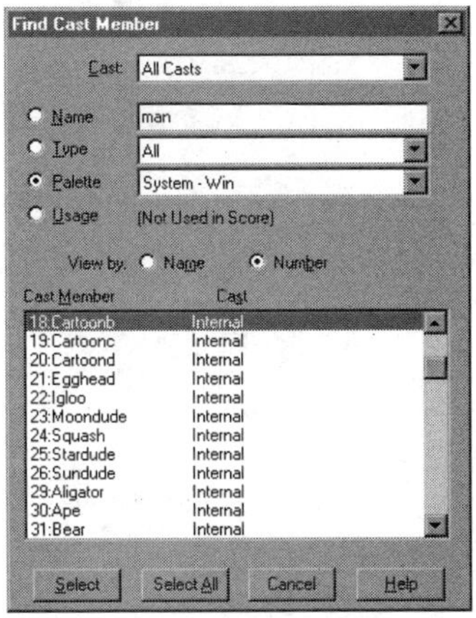

Figure 44. In the **Find Cast Member** dialog box, click the third option and choose a palette to search by from the pop-up menu.

To find a cast member by its color palette:

You can search and find cast members in your casts by the color palette they use. This is useful if you have a number of cast members that are mapped to one particular color palette, but must eventually be remapped to another one.

1. Choose Find from Director's Edit menu and choose Cast Member from the pop-up menu **(Figure 43)**.
2. In the Find Cast Member dialog box, select which cast you wish to search from the Cast pop-up menu.
3. In the Find Cast Member dialog box, click the third radio button and use the adjacent pop-up menu to select the palette used by the cast members you wish to find **(Figure 44)**.
4. Click the Select All button and Director finds and selects all the appropriate cast members in the specified cast. If the Select and Select All buttons are unselectable for some reason, click a cast member in the Find Cast Member dialog box list to make them selectable.

To sort cast members in a cast window:

Director can sort cast members by name, type, size, and the order in which they appear in your score. Being able to sort cast members is a great way to keep a large, unwieldy cast well organized. When Director sorts cast members, it also removes gaps in the cast window where you have cut or relocated earlier cast members.

1. Activate the cast window that you wish to sort.
2. Choose Select All from Director's Edit menu **(Figure 45)**.
3. Choose Sort from the Modify menu **(Figure 46)**.
4. In the Sort dialog box, select the method of sorting you wish to use **(Figure 47)**.
5. Click Sort.

✓ **Tip**

- When you sort a cast window, most or all cast members will be reassigned position numbers based on their new location in the window. However, if you have created Lingo scripts that refer to those cast members by number, rather than name, your scripts will no longer be able to find the proper cast members. To avoid this, refer to cast members by name in your scripts.

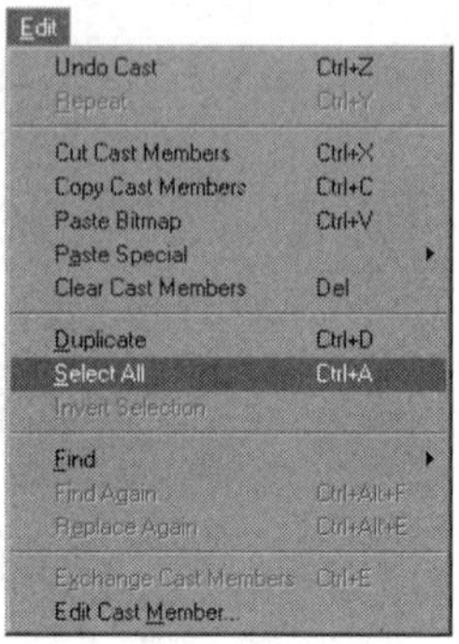

Figure 45. Choose **Select All** from the **Edit** menu.

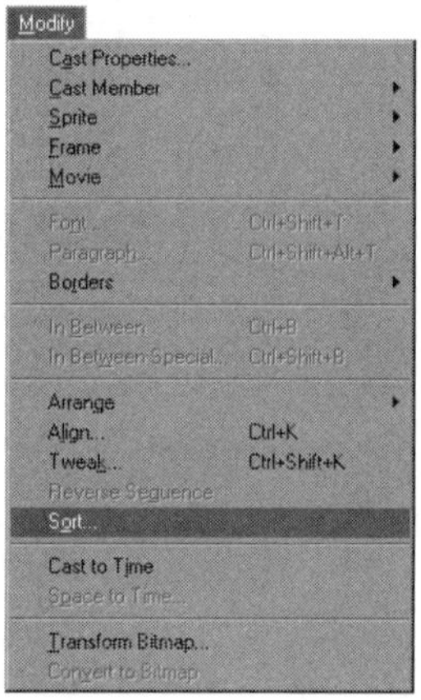

Figure 46. Choose **Sort** from the **Modify** menu.

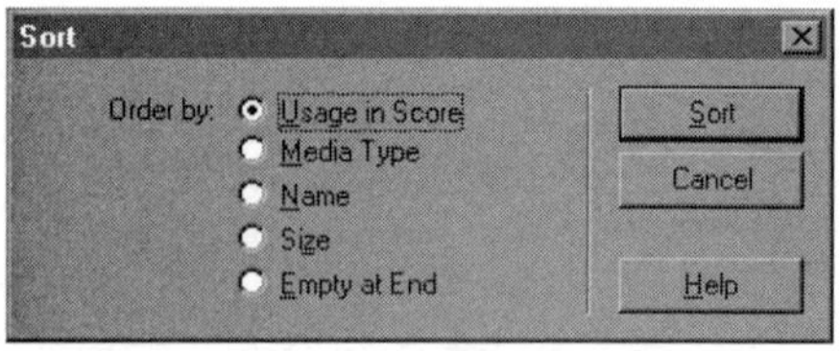

Figure 47. Select the method of sorting you wish to use.

SCORE, STAGE, AND SPRITES

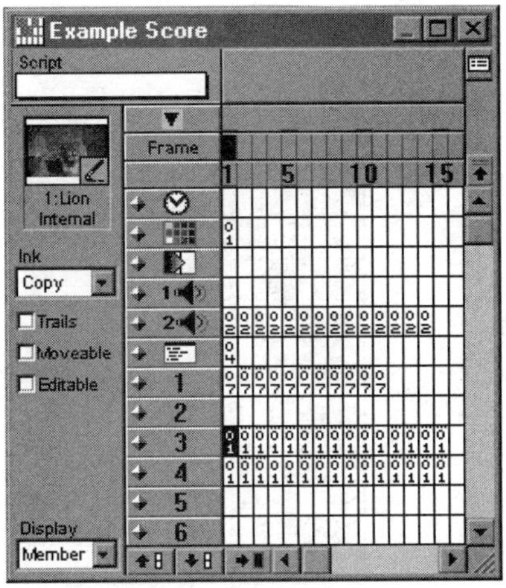

Figure 1. The score window provides a frame-by-frame record of all the components that form your Director movie.

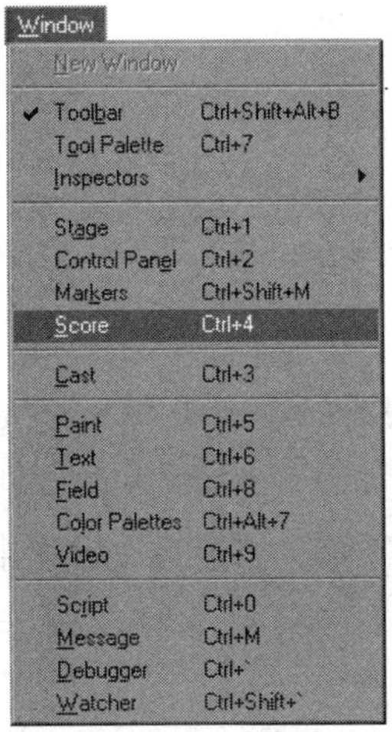

Figure 2. Choose **Score** from the **Window** menu.

Director's score **(Figure 1)** is similar to the script of a Hollywood movie. It describes what your cast members should do and when they should do it on the stage. Remember that the **Stage** is where your movie plays out. It usually takes up the full dimensions of your screen, and can be seen in the background behind Director's cast, score, and other windows.

A Director movie is assembled by assigning cast members, such as graphics and sounds, and events such as visual transitions and tempo changes, to various parts of the score, which represent various segments of time in your Director movie.

You can open the score window by choosing Score from the Window menu, or by pressing Control-4 **(Figure 2)**.

This chapter explains all the basics of working with the score, stage, and sprites—essential for building a Director movie. You will learn how to incorporate cast members into your movie by using the score and stage. You will learn about score notation, how to edit and manage the cells of the score, and what sprites are and how their properties can be changed.

Frames

The first thing to know about the score is that it is divided into small segments of time called frames. Each frame forms a column of cells and the frames are arranged horizontally across the score in sequential order **(Figure 3)**. Frames are numbered at the top of their columns. There's no limit to the number of frames you can have in a movie.

Frames in Director are just like the frames you find on a strip of celluloid film—where each frame provides the opportunity to change or continue the action taking place in the movie. For instance, a sound effect in your movie may begin playing at frame 1 but stop playing at frame 15. And in an animation sequence, frame 1 might feature a cast member graphic on the left most side of the stage. In frame 2, however, that cast member might move a little toward the right. It will appear to move even farther in frame 3, and so on. When a sequence of frames is played in rapid succession, animation occurs. How quickly Director plays the frames of a movie is known as **Tempo**, which you can set in frames per second. *(See page 191 in the Tempo chapter)*

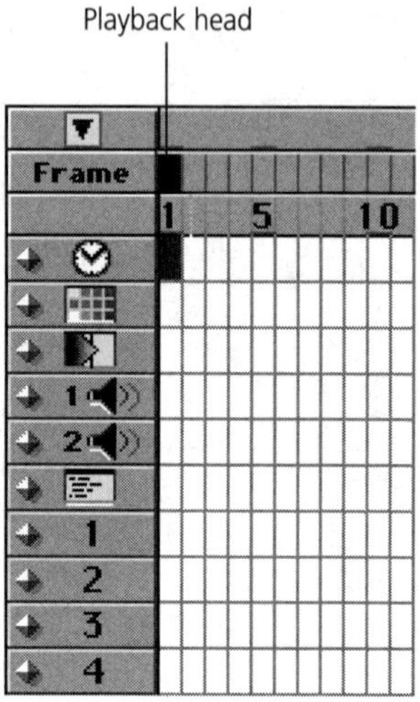

Figure 3. Each frame forms a column of cells and the frames are arranged horizontally across the score window in sequential order.

Playback head

The position of the **Playback head** in the score indicates which frame is currently displayed on the stage **(Figure 3)**. You can drag the playback head to display any frame of your movie on the stage.

✔ Tip

- Set the "Playback Head Follows Selection" option in the Score Window Preferences dialog box **(Figure 4)** and the playback head will move along with any cell selections you make. Disable the option and the playback head won't move unless you drag it. Choose Preferences from the File menu, and select Score from the pop-up menu to open the Score Window Preferences dialog box.

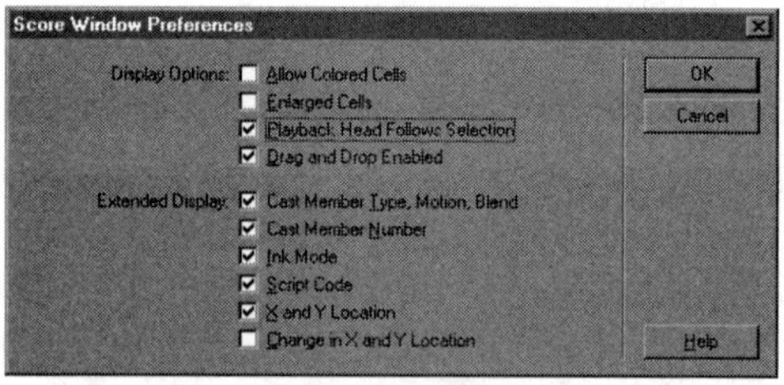

Figure 4. Set the **Playback Head Follows Selection** option in the **Score Window Preferences** dialog box, and the playback head will follow along with any cell selections you make in the score.

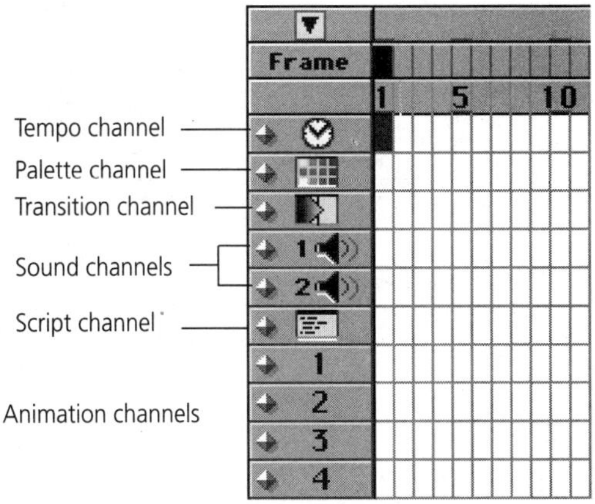

Figure 5. The channels run vertically along the left side of the score window. Each channel forms a row of cells.

Score channels

A large number of events can occur in any frame of Director's score. For instance, several cast member graphics can appear, a sound effect or two can play, and a transition to a new color palette can begin. You manage and direct these elements and events by placing them each into a **channel** of the score.

Director's channels run vertically along the left side of the score window **(Figure 5)**. Each channel forms its own row of cells extending through the frames. The following channel types are available, in this order:

- The tempo channel allows you to set the speed at which Director plays your entire movie, or just a sequence of frames.
- The palette channel allows you to set the color palette used to display your movie.
- The transition channel allows you to set video transition effects between scenes such as dissolves or wipes.
- Two sound channels allow you to incorporate sound effects, musical scores, and voice tracks.
- The script channel allows you to incorporate Lingo scripts (which are used to add interactive features to your movie).
- 48 animation channels are used to animate your cast member graphics. They are also called sprite channels.

Generally, you must place each new cast member or event that you wish to incorporate in a frame in a separate channel of the score. For instance, if you want to place a graphic into the score, you would place it in the first available animation channel. If you want a frame to feature two cast members on stage simultaneously, you add the second cast member to the next animation channel—say, channel 2 **(Figure 6)**. If you

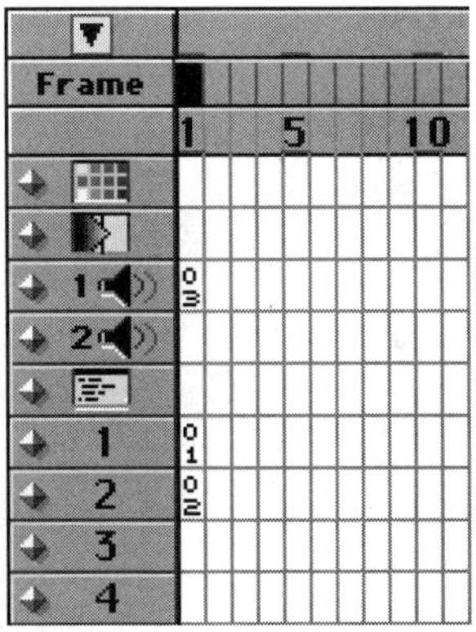

Figure 6. Frame 1 here contains two graphical cast members and a sound.

Score Channels

wish a sound effect to play as well, you place it in one of Director's two sound channels, at the same frame location where your graphics appear. And when you want to change the color palette currently used to display your Director movie, you set a new palette in the score's palette channel.

In summary, building the score of a Director movie is mostly a matter of assigning cast members to particular channels in the score, at particular frames or range of frames within each channel.

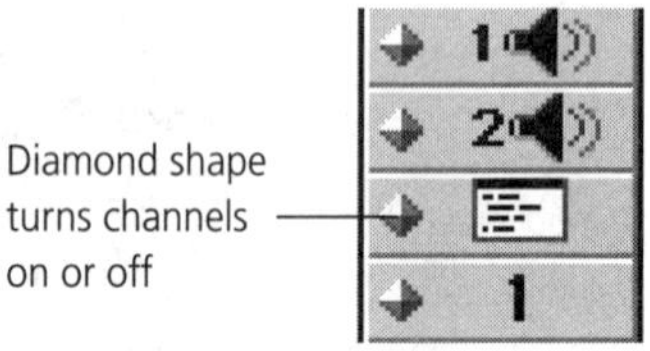

Figure 7. Turning a channel off causes Director to ignore it during movie playback.

To turn a channel on or off:

Click the diamond shape at the left side of a channel to turn the channel off during movie playback **(Figure 7)**. Doing so causes Director to ignore all information in that channel. This can improve playback performance. By default, all channels are turned on. Turning the script channel off causes Director to ignore all scripts during playback.

Figure 8. Five sprites are shown, each based on the same cast member seen in the cast window below. The properties of each sprite can be different, such as size.

Sprites

Sprite is the term used to describe one instance of a graphical cast member in one specific cell in an animation channel (graphical cast member types include bitmap, PICT, shape, text, field, button, and digital video). You create a sprite as soon as you drag a graphical cast member from a cast window onto the stage, or into the score.

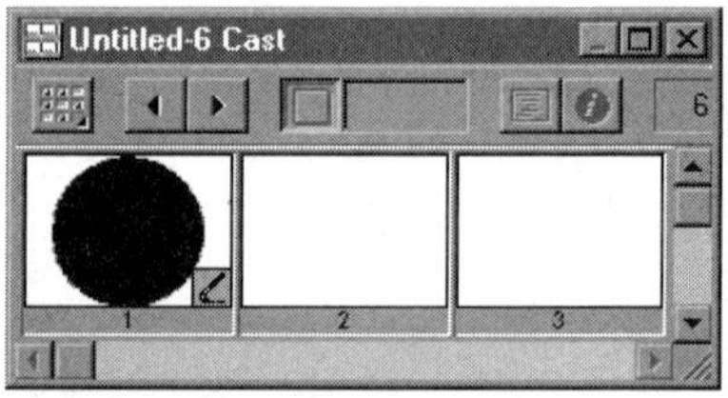

Figure 9. A single cast member can serve as the basis for many different sprites.

The function of a sprite is that you can change its properties, such as its size, blend percentage, and which ink effect it uses, and the original cast member it is based on will not change. This allows you to have many sprites in the score all based on the same cast member, yet each featuring different properties *(see pages 60-68 on setting sprite attributes)*. For example, you could have five sprites based on the same cast member, but each in a different size **(Figures 8–9)**. Arranging them in a sequence in the score **(Figure 10)** would create an animation of a growing image.

Figure 10. You can form an animation sequence by creating a series of unique sprites, each based on the same cast member, as represented here in the score.

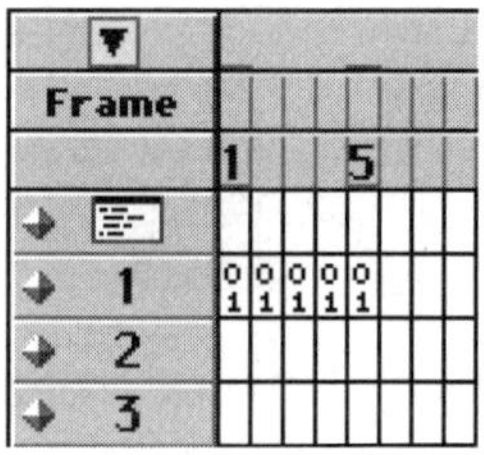

Turn a Channel Off, Sprites

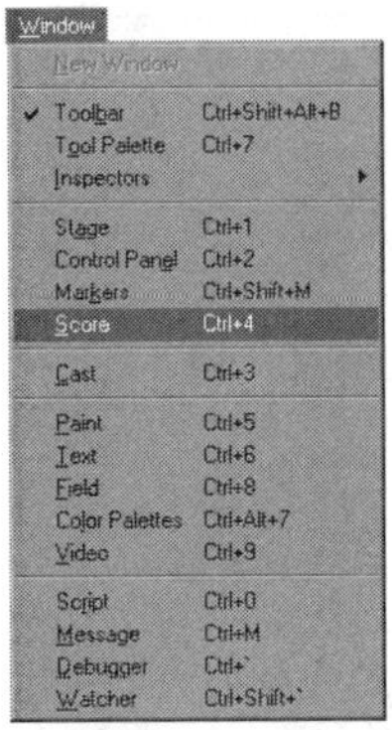

Figure 11. Choose **Score** from the **Window** menu.

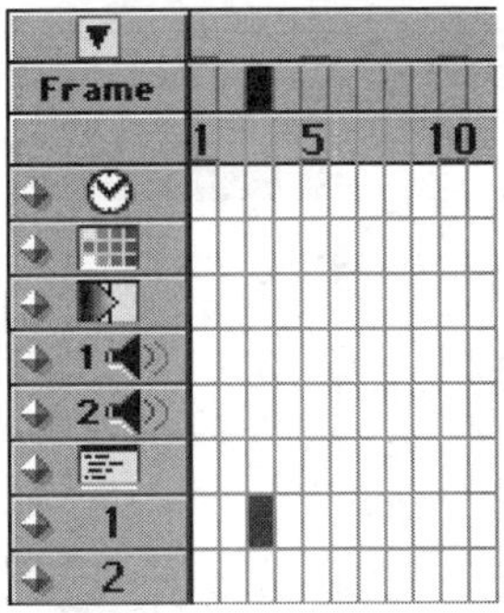

Figure 12. Click a particular frame in a particular channel where you wish to place your cast member.

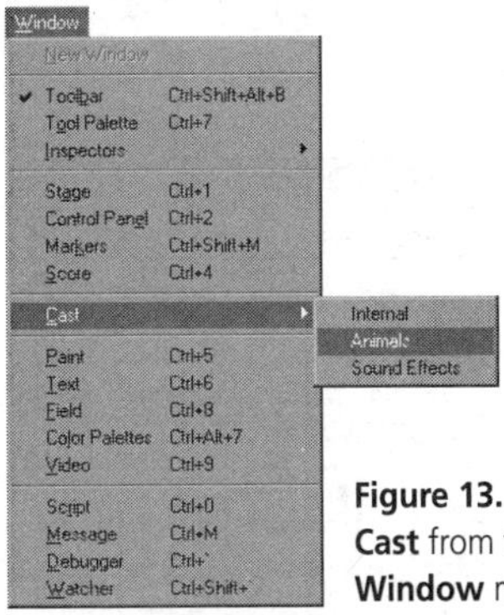

Figure 13. Choose **Cast** from the **Window** menu.

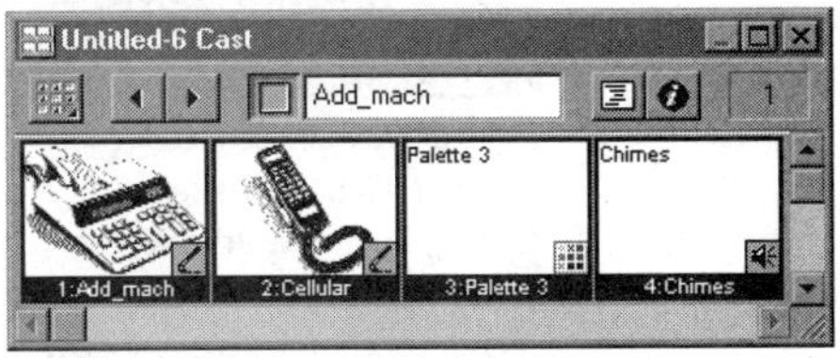

Figure 14. In the cast window, select the cast member(s) you wish to place on the stage. Cast members 1–4 are selected here.

PLACING CAST MEMBERS IN THE SCORE

A key step to creating any Director movie is assigning a cast member to a particular channel and frame in the score. You can do so by dragging a cast member from a cast window to Director's stage, or from a cast window to particular cells in the score window. Either method places the cast member in the score of your movie, although dragging to Director's stage is generally easier. Dragging in this manner is particularly expedient when you're incorporating graphical cast members, since you can immediately position them on the stage as they should appear in the frame. However, non-visible cast members, such as sounds, color palettes, or scripts are just as easily placed by dragging them to their destination cells in Director's score.

To place cast members on Director's stage:

1. Open the score window by choosing Score from Director's Window menu **(Figure 11)**.
2. In the score window, click the particular frame, in the particular channel where you wish to place your cast member. **(Figure 12)**.
3. Open a cast window by choosing Cast from the Window menu and selecting the appropriate cast from the pop-up menu **(Figure 13)**.
4. In the cast window, click the cast member that you wish to place on the stage. If you wish to place multiple cast members, select them together by Shift-clicking **(Figure 14)**.

5. Drag your cast member selection to the stage (the area outside the cast window). The selection appears as an outline **(Figure 15)**.

6. Release the mouse button to place the cast members on the stage. If you selected just one cast member, it is assigned to the frame and channel that you selected in step 2. If you dragged multiple cast members, they are all placed in the frame you selected in step 2, but each cast member is assigned to a different channel in the score window **(Figure 16)**, unless you held down the Alt key while dragging *(see the Tip below)*. Non-graphical cast members won't appear on stage, but will be entered into the score.

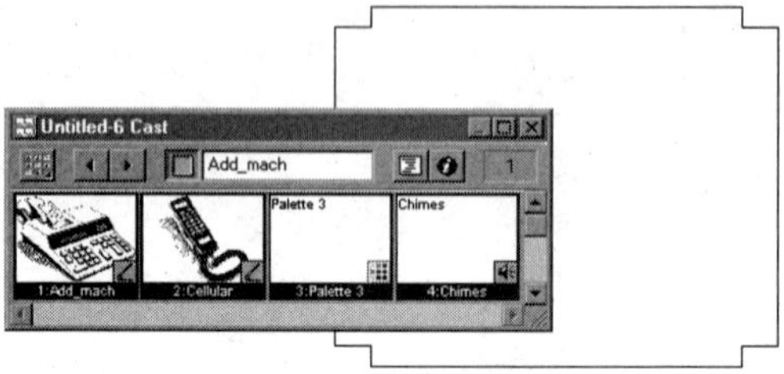

Figure 15. Drag your cast member selection to the stage. The selection appears as an outline while being dragged onto the stage.

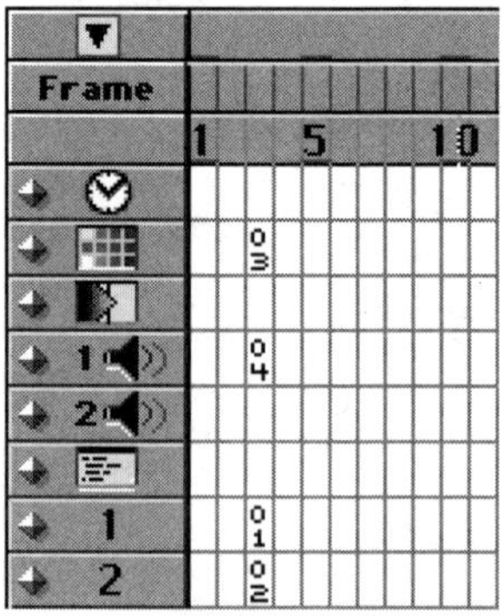

Figure 16. If you drag multiple cast members to the stage, each cast member is normally assigned to the same frame but a different channel in the score.

✔ Tip

- When you drag multiple cast members from the cast window to the stage, Director normally places each cast member in the same frame of your score, but in different channels of that frame **(Figure 16)**. Sometimes, however, you'll want a collection of cast members to be assigned to the same channel, but placed in separate frames of the score **(Figure 17)**. For instance, this would be desirable if you're placing a group of cast members that make up an animation sequence, where each cast member should be displayed one after the other in sequential frames. To place a collection of cast members into the score over time (into separate frames), follow steps 1–6 above, but hold down the Alt key as you drag the selected cast members from the cast window to the stage.

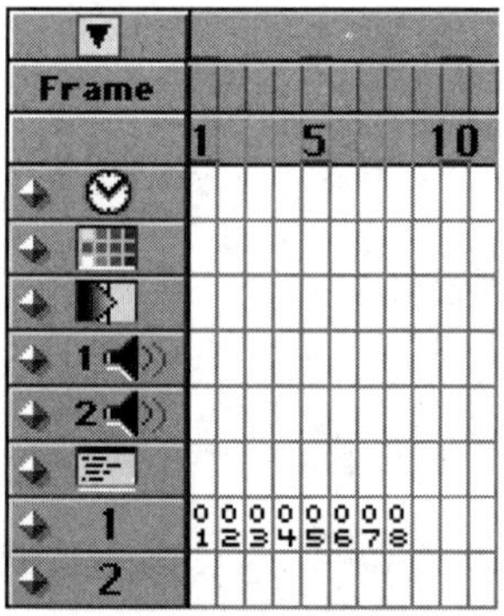

Figure 17. To place a collection of cast members in a series of frames, hold down the Alt key while dragging selected cast members from the cast window to the stage.

Place Cast Members on the Stage

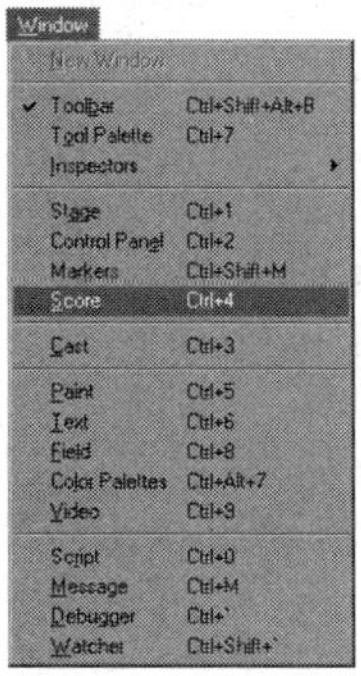

Figure 18. Choose **Score** from the **Window** menu.

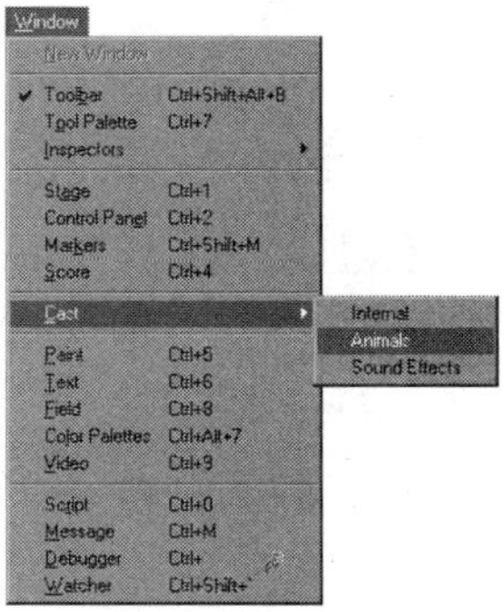

Figure 19. Choose **Cast** from the **Window** menu.

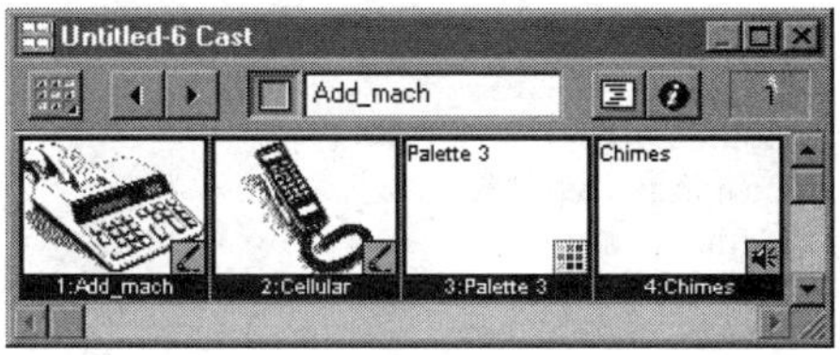

Figure 20. In a cast window, select the cast member(s) you wish to place in the score. Cast members 1–4 are selected here.

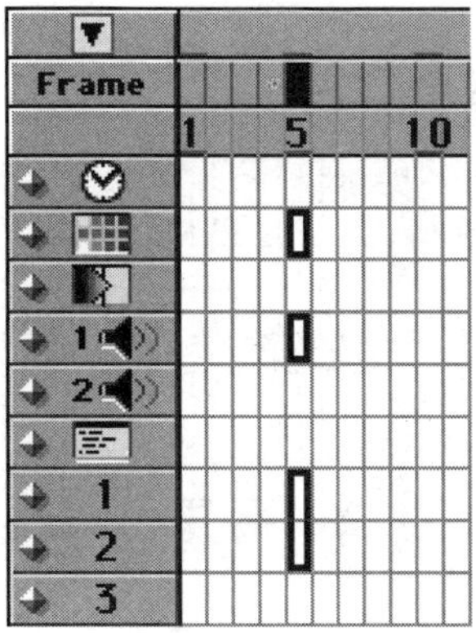

Figure 21. Director outlines the range of cells that your cast member selection will occupy in the score.

To drag a cast member directly to the score:

Rather than dragging cast members to the stage, you can place them directly into the score window.

1. Open the score window by choosing Score from Director's Window menu **(Figure 18)**.
2. Open a cast window by choosing Cast from the Window menu and selecting the appropriate cast from the pop-up menu **(Figure 19)**.
3. In the cast window, click the cast member that you wish to place in the score, so that it's selected. If you wish to place multiple cast members, you can select them together by Shift-clicking **(Figure 20)**.
4. Drag your cast member selection from the cast window to a cell in the score. As you drag, Director outlines the range of cells that your cast member selection will occupy **(Figure 21)**. Director outlines only cells that will accommodate your cast members (for instance, sounds can be dragged only to cells in the sound channels).
5. Release the mouse button to place the cast member(s) in the score. If you dragged just one cast member, it is assigned to the frame and channel that you dragged it to. If you dragged multiple cast members, they are all placed in the frame you dragged them to, but each cast member is assigned to a different channel in the score.

✔ Tip

- To place the cast members over time (into different frames of the same channel, rather than different channels of the same frame, which is the default), hold down the Alt key while dragging the cast members from the cast window to the score.

To exchange cast members in the score:

You can exchange a cast member in a cell or range of cells in the score with another cast member. If you are exchanging a graphical cast member, its positions on the stage throughout the frames are not changed.

1. Select a cell or range of cells where you want to switch the cast member **(Figure 22)**.
2. Select the new cast member in a cast window to replace the old cast member.
3. Choose Exchange Cast Members from the Edit menu **(Figure 24)**. The new cast member is placed into selected cells in the score **(Figure 23)**.

Note: Exchanging a graphical cast member may cause the new cast member to appear to shift from frame to frame. You may need to align the sprites on the stage. *(See page 67)*

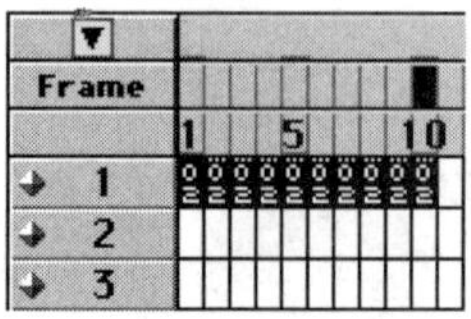

Figure 22. Select the cells where you want to switch the cast member.

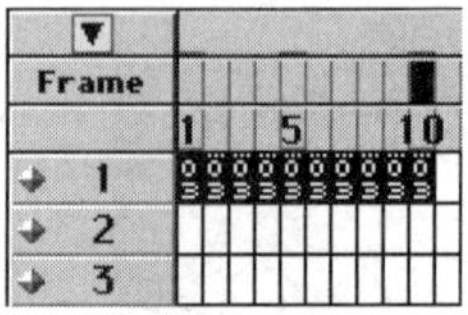

Figure 23. The new cast member is placed into the selected cells.

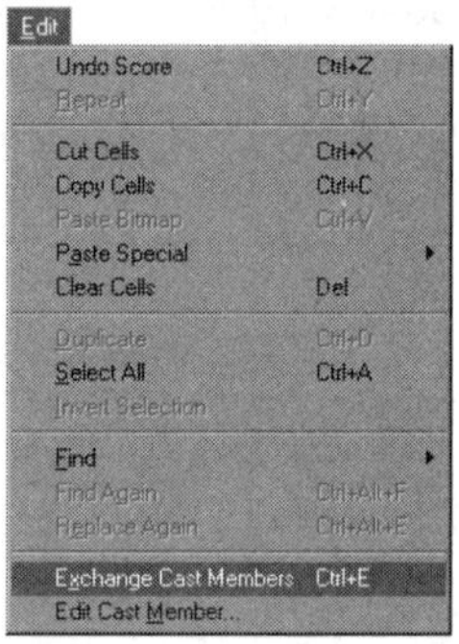

Figure 24. Choose **Exchange Cast Members** from the **Edit** menu.

To assign Lingo scripts to the score:

You can use the Script pop-up menu (located at the upper left-hand side of the score window) to assign score scripts to frames in the script channel, or to sprites. *(See page 204 in the Interactivity and Lingo chapter for details on scripts)*

1. Select the cells you wish to assign a score script to **(Figure 25)**.
2. Use the Script pop-up menu to select an existing script. Scripts are identified by their position number in the cast window **(Figure 25)**.
3. You can choose New from the Script pop-up menu to open a new script window. *(See page 208 for details on script windows)*

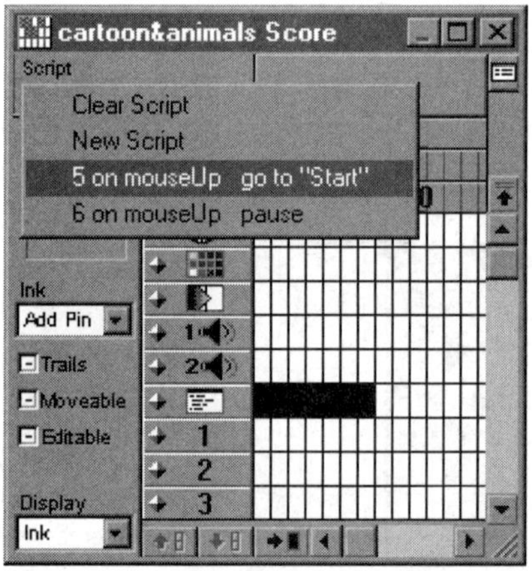

Figure 25. Select the cells you wish to assign a script to and choose an existing script from the **Script** pop-up menu.

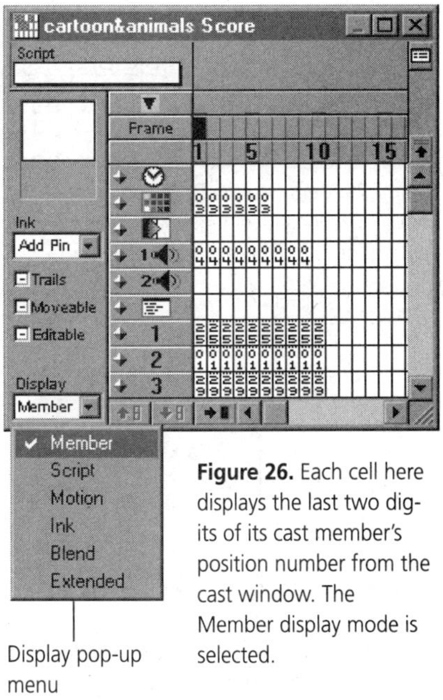

Figure 26. Each cell here displays the last two digits of its cast member's position number from the cast window. The Member display mode is selected.

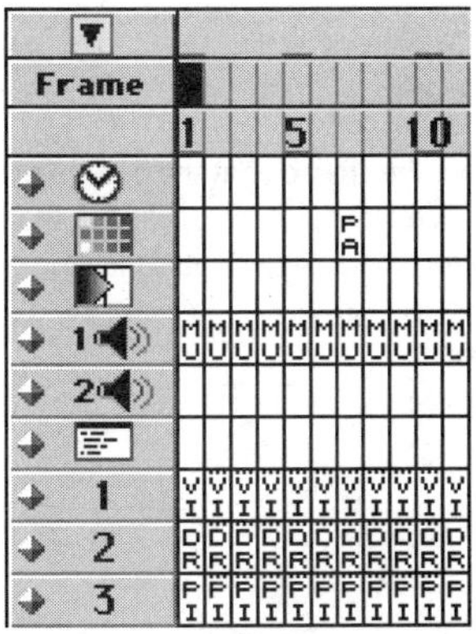

Figure 27. Each cell here displays the first two letters of the cast member's name.

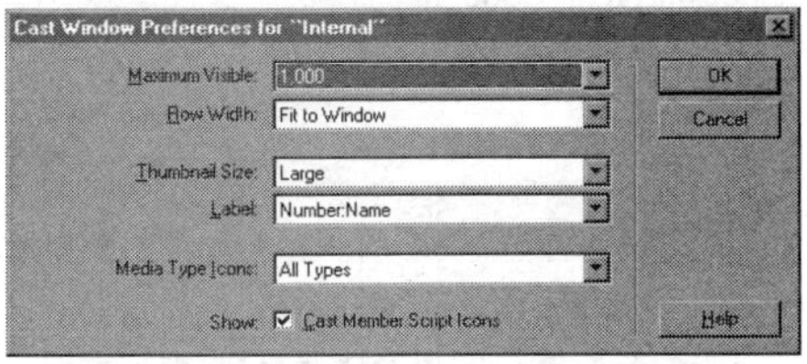

Figure 28. The **Label** setting in the **Cast Window Preferences** dialog box controls whether cells in the score display cast member names or numbers when the Member display mode is selected.

SCORE NOTATION

When you place cast members into the cells of the score, you'll notice that those cells become filled with small letters and numbers. These characters are called **cell notation** and they offer important information about what role the cells play in the overall score.

Director can display one of many different types of cell notation in its score, with each type offering different information about the cells' characteristics. You select which display mode Director uses by clicking the Display button in the lower-left corner of the score **(Figure 26)**, and choosing from the pop-up menu that appears.

Following are explanations of each type of cell notation that Director offers.

Member notation

Member notation is the default notation used in the score. In Member notation, each cell identifies the cast member that it contains. In this mode, each cell displays either the last two digits of its cast member's position number in the cast window **(Figure 26)**, or the first two letters of the cast member's name **(Figures 27)**. Which specific form is used depends on the Label setting in the Cast Window Preferences dialog box **(Figure 28)**. Open this box by choosing Preferences under the File menu, and selecting Cast from the pop-up menu.

Blend notation

Cells displayed in Blend notation show the blend percentage that's been assigned to the cell's cast member sprite *(see page 65 on setting the blend percentage of a sprite)*. For instance, a 35 refers to a 35% blend and two square symbols indicate a 100% blend **(Figure 29)**.

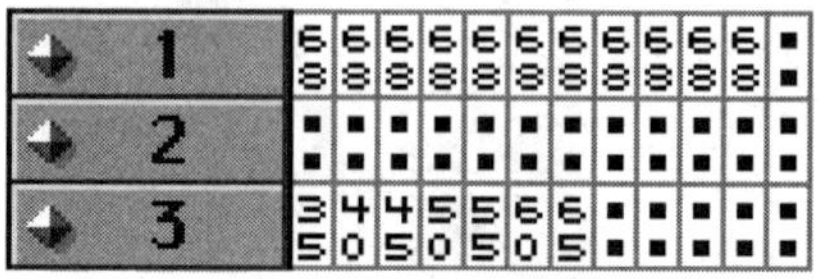

Figure 29. Cells displayed in Blend notation show the blend percentage that's been assigned to the cell's cast member sprite.

Ink notation

Cells displayed in Ink notation show which ink effects have been applied to sprites. The top character in the notated cell indicates the type of cast member contained—B is for bitmap cast members, Q stands for QuickDraw cast members (shapes), T for text cast members, P for PICT cast members, X, Y,and Z for button cast members, and a bullet symbol indicates a film loop, digital video, or embedded Director movie **(Figure 30)**. The bottom character in the cell indicates the type of ink effect at work. A small dotted line placed between the top and bottom characters indicates that trails have been turned on. *(See page 64 about trails)*

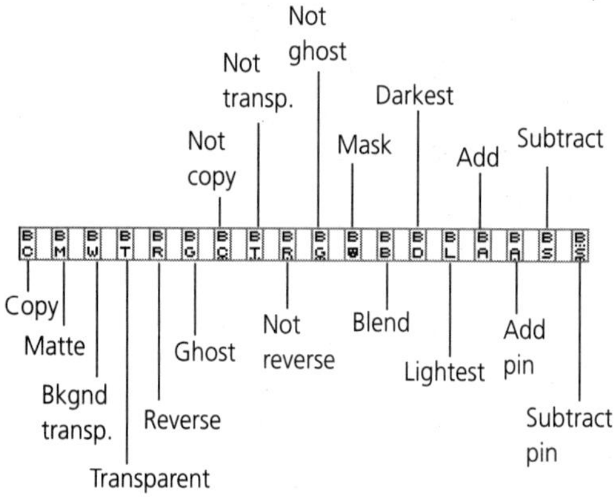

Figure 30. In Ink notation, the character at the bottom of the cell indicates which ink effect has been applied to the cast member sprite. The top character indicates the type of cast member contained as follows:

B - bitmap cast members.
Q - QuickDraw cast members.
T - text cast members.
P - PICT cast members.
X - button cast members.
Y - button cast members.
Z - button cast members.

A bullet indicates a film loop, digital video, or embedded Director movie.

Motion notation

Cells displayed in Motion notation show the direction in which their sprites are moving, if any **(Figure 31)**. The top character in the notated cell indicates the type of cast member contained—B is for bitmap cast members, Q stands for QuickDraw cast members (shapes), T for text cast members, P for PICT cast members, X, Y, and Z for button cast members, and a bullet symbol indicates a film loop, digital video, or embedded Director movie. A dash indicates that the cast member type is the same as in the previous frame. The bottom character in the notated cell indicates the direction in which the sprite is moving relative to the sprite's previous position. Small arrows denote the direction, while a square bullet symbol tells you that there is no movement for that cell.

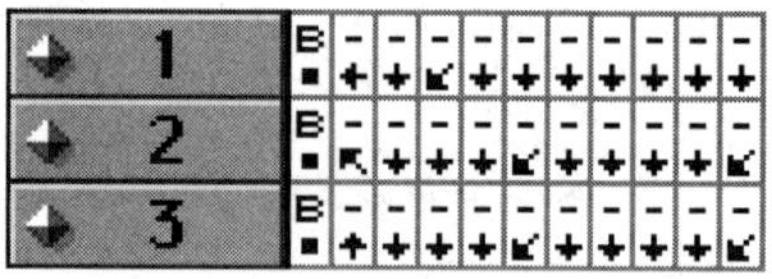

Figure 31. Cells displayed in Motion notation show the direction in which their sprites are moving.

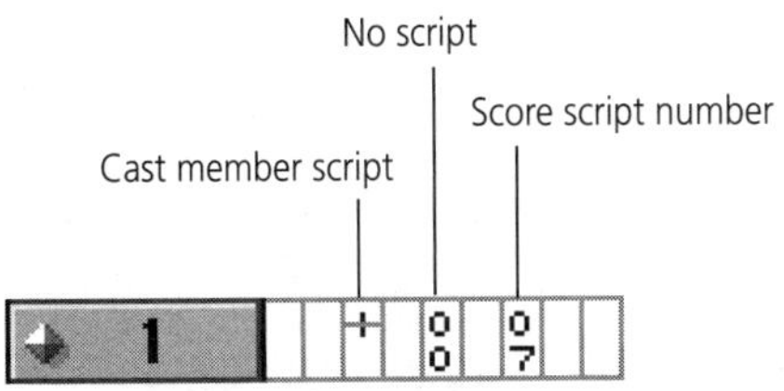

Figure 32. In Script notation, a number indicates the identifying number of the score script assigned to the cell. A plus sign indicates a cast member script is attached to the sprite's cast member, while 00 indicates that the cell has no script tied to it.

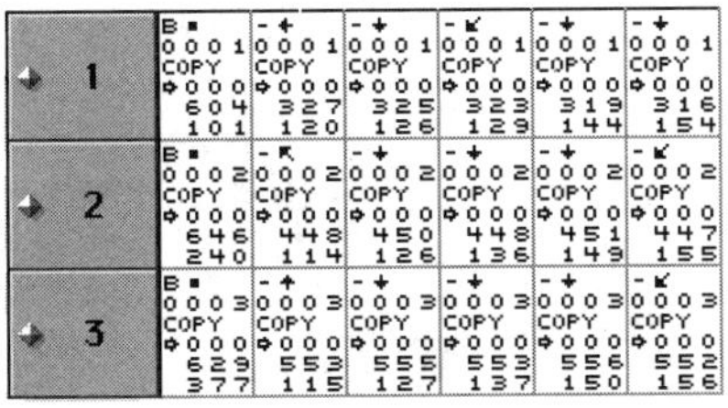

Figure 33. Score cells displayed in Extended notation.

Script notation

Cells displayed in Script notation show the number identifier of any score scripts that have been assigned to them **(Figure 32)** (this identifying number is based on the script's position in its cast window). Cells also display a plus sign when a sprite's cast member has a cast member script tied to it. A double zero symbol indicates a cell has no script tied to it.

Extended notation

Extended notation offers a wealth of detailed information about the characteristics of each cell in the score window **(Figure 33)**. In fact, this notation type is useful only for the most detailed and meticulous fine-tuning of your score, and is out of the scope of a Visual QuickStart Guide. For more information about Extended notation, see your Director documentation.

MANAGING AND ORGANIZING THE SCORE

Foreground and background priorities of sprites

If you plan to animate a number of sprites simultaneously on Director's stage, you'll need to control each sprite's **foreground/background priority**. For instance, in animating a character walking down a street, you may want the character to appear to walk in front of background buildings **(Figure 34)** but behind certain sprites such as parked cars, street lamps, and signposts.

The foreground/background priority of your sprites is determined by their order in the animation channels. Basically, sprites in higher numbered channels always appear in front of sprites in lower numbered channels (for instance, a sprite in channel 2 will appear in the background when overlapped by a sprite in channel 15).

As you build a scene in the score, you'll probably find it necessary to relocate certain sprites to earlier or later animation channels, to give them the proper foreground/background priorities. Director provides an easy way to do this by shuffling cells from one channel to the next.

Figure 34. A sprite's foreground/background priority is determined by its order in the 48 animation channels. Here, the person is in the foreground, while the city sprite is in the background.

To shuffle cells to an adjacent channel:

1. In the score, select the cells that you wish to interchange with cells from an adjacent channel **(Figure 35)**.
2. Click either the Shuffle forward or Shuffle backward button in the score **(Figure 36)** to interchange the selected cells with the cells in the channel below or above it. Shuffle forward brings the sprites in your cells one level closer to the foreground, while Shuffle backward pushes them one level closer to the background.

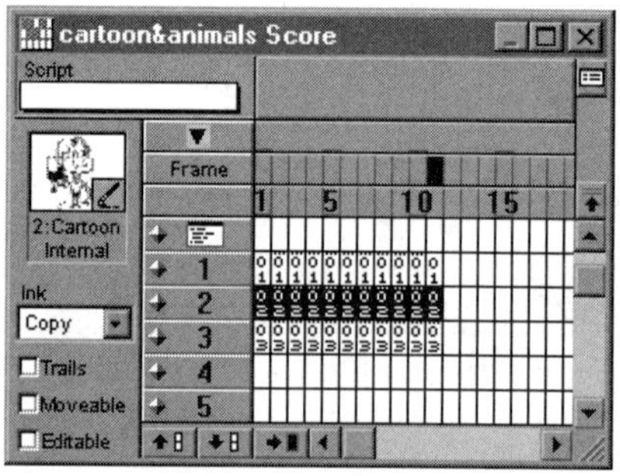

Figure 35. Select the cells that you wish to interchange with cells in an adjacent channel.

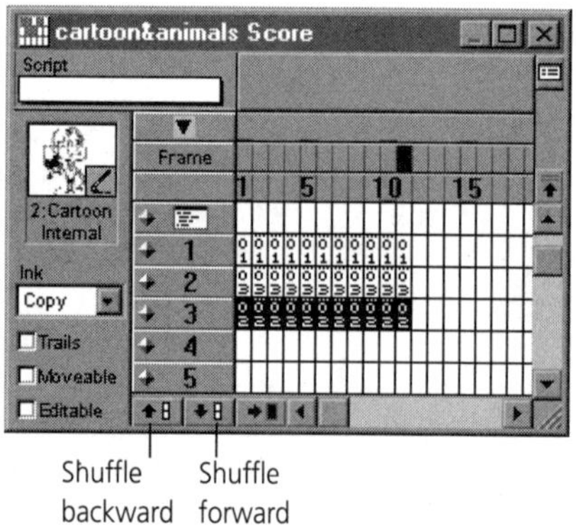

Figure 36. Click **Shuffle forward** or **Shuffle backward** to shift the selected cells one level closer to the foreground or background respectively.

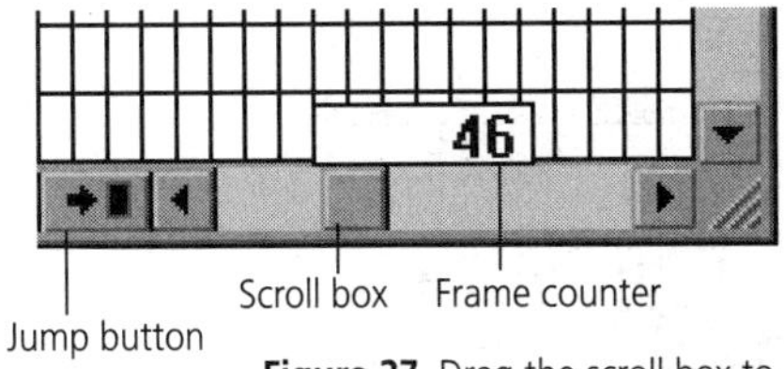

Figure 37. Drag the scroll box to move to a specific frame, or click the **Jump** button to move to the current frame on the stage.

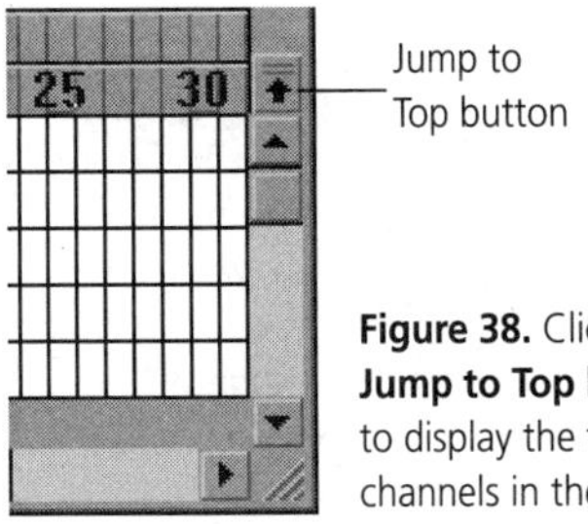

Figure 38. Click the **Jump to Top** button to display the first channels in the score.

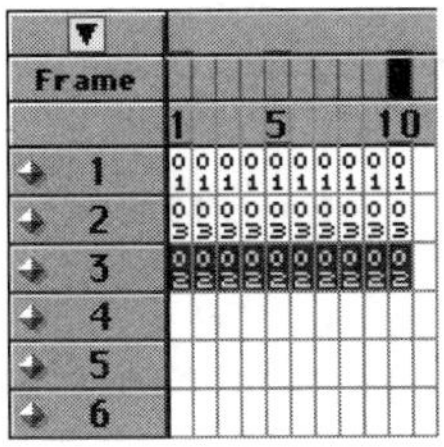

Figure 39. Select the cell or range of cells that you wish to move.

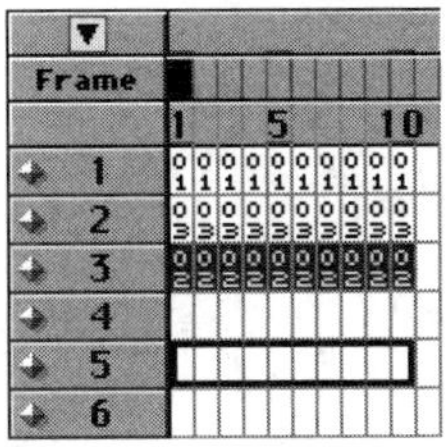

Figure 40. Drag the selected cells to a new position in the score.

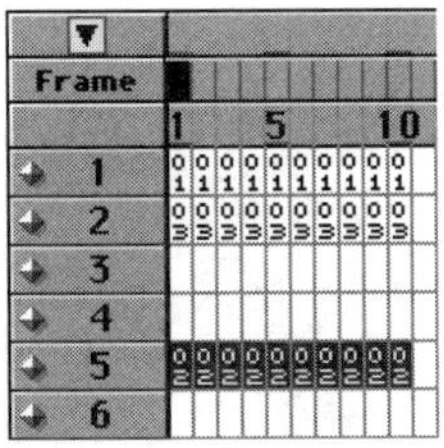

Figure 41. Release the mouse button, and the selected cells will be relocated.

To move within the score:

There are a number of ways to move within the score window:

- Move to a specific frame by dragging the horizontal scroll box and noting the value in its pop-up frame counter **(Figure 37)**.
- Click the Jump button to move the playback head to the frame that is currently displayed on the stage **(Figure 37)**.
- Click the Jump to Top button at the top right side of the score window to display the first channels in the score **(Figure 38)**.

To move cells within the score:

1. In the score window, drag to select the cell or range of cells that you wish to move **(Figure 39)**. Control-click to select a discontinuous selection of cells. Double-click a channel number to select all the cells in that channel. You can select a block of frames by dragging across the frame numbers at the top of the score.
2. Drag the selected cells to a new position in the score window **(Figure 40)**. If you wish to move a copy of the selected cells rather than the originals, hold down the Alt key while dragging the cells.
3. Release the mouse button, and Director moves the selected cells to the new location **(Figure 41)**. The contents of the selected cells automatically replaces whatever was present before.

✓ Tip

- You can also move cells within the score by using the Cut, Copy, and Paste commands. First select the cells you wish to move. Then choose Copy Cells or Cut Cells from the Edit menu. Select a new location in the score, and choose Paste Cells.

To insert new frames in the score:

Sometimes you'll find that you want to insert information into the score in a place where there are no empty cells to accommodate the new information. You can always use Director's cut and paste or drag cell features to shift existing cells to the right, leaving an empty region in the score, but this can become tedious, especially if you're not sure how many cells must be vacated. It's easier simply to insert new frames in the score.

1. In the score, select the cells that you wish to insert into another segment of the score **(Figure 42)**.
2. Use the Cut or Copy features (listed under the Edit menu) to place the selected cells into memory **(Figure 45)**.
3. Click the frame number in the score where you wish to insert the cells you've cut or copied **(Figure 43)**. An insertion line appears at the frame you've picked.
4. Choose Paste Cells from the Edit menu **(Figure 46)** to insert the cut or copied cells **(Figure 44)**. Notice that Director creates the necessary number of new frames in its channels to accommodate the selection.

✔ Tip

- If you've created Lingo scripts that refer to specific frame numbers in your movie, remember that inserting new frames can throw off the frame references made by your scripts, causing problems in your movie. To avoid such problems, consider using markers rather than numerical references in your scripts. *(See page 58 on Markers)*

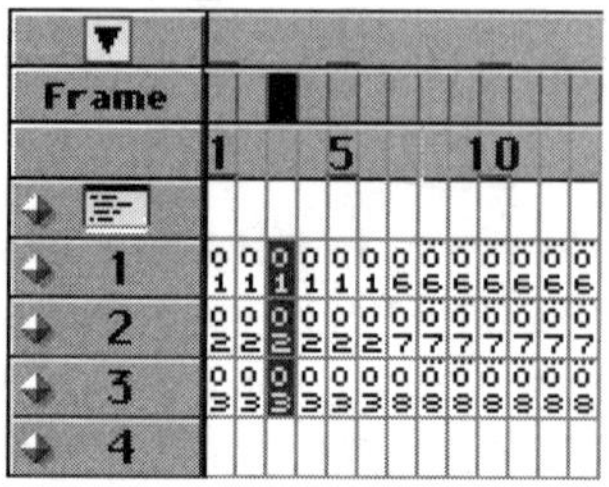

Figure 42. Select the cells that you wish to insert into another segment of the score.

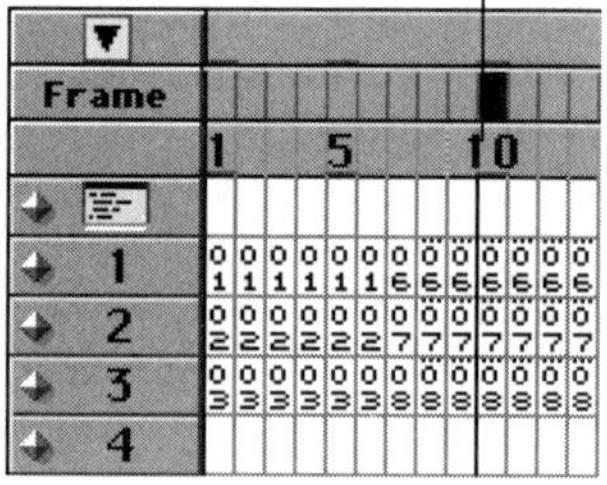

Figure 43. Click the frame number in the score where you wish to insert the cells you've cut or copied. An insertion line appears.

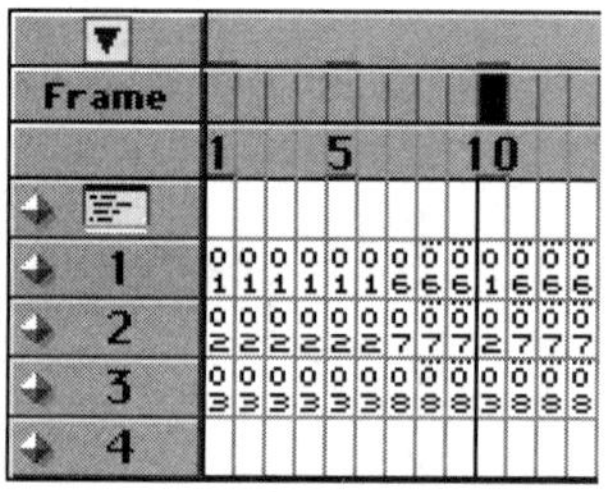

Figure 44. The selected cells have been inserted into frame 10.

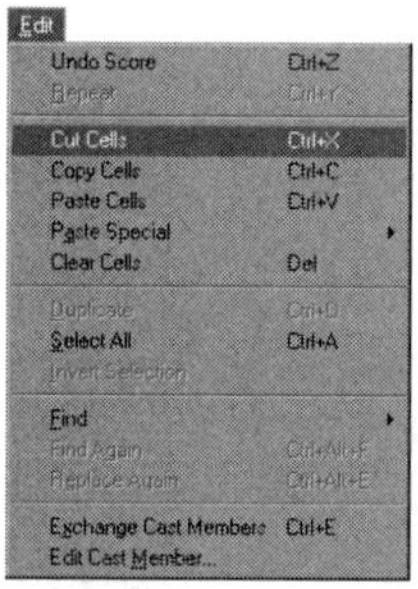

Figure 45. Choose **Cut** or **Copy Cells** under the **Edit** menu.

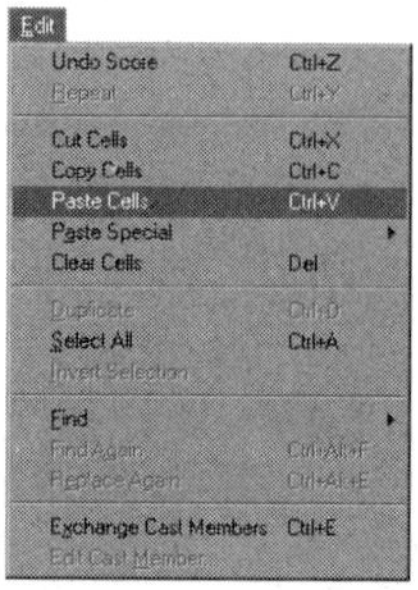

Figure 46. Choose **Paste Cells** from the **Edit** menu.

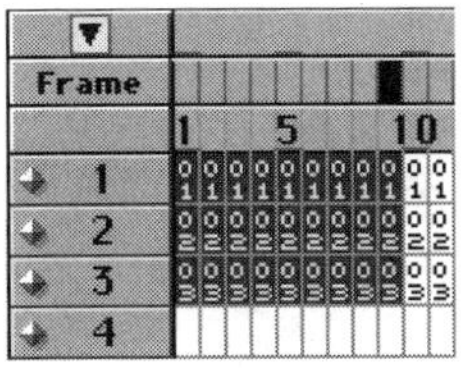

Figure 47. Drag across the cells you wish to cut from the score.

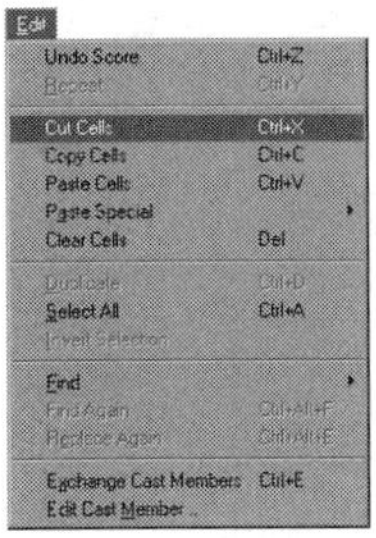

Figure 48. Choose **Cut Cells** from the **Edit** menu.

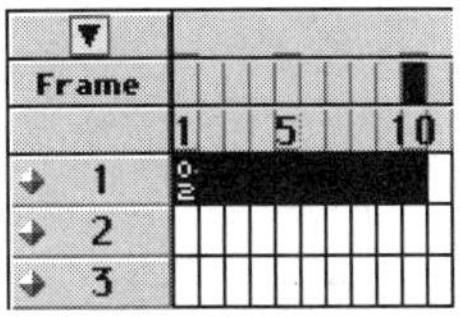

Figure 49. Select a cell and a range of frames.

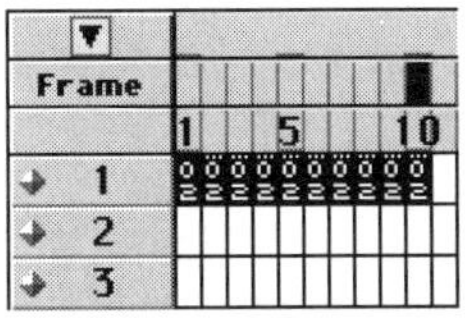

Figure 50. The cell is copied through the selected cells.

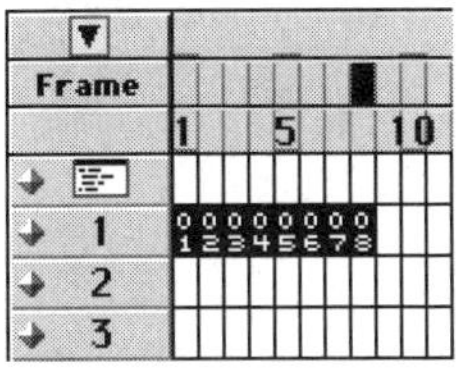

Figure 51. Select the range of cells you wish to reverse.

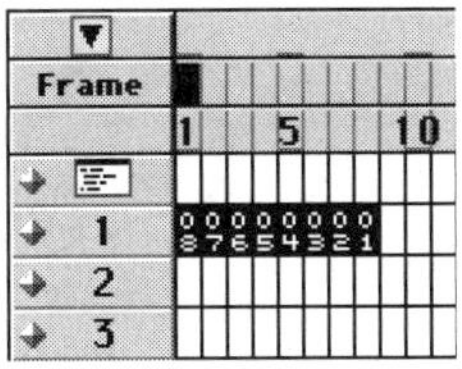

Figure 52. The order of the selected cells has been reversed.

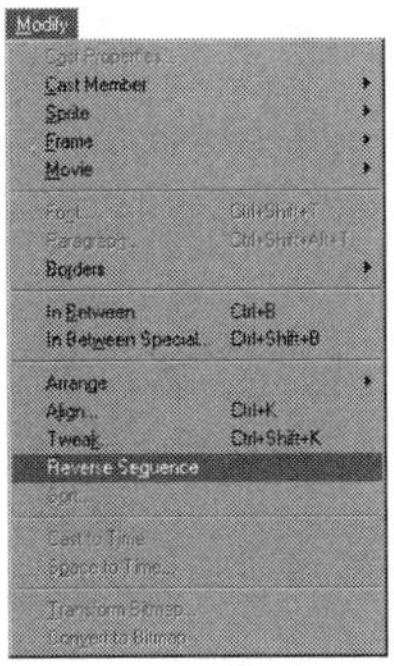

Figure 53. Choose **Reverse Sequence** from the **Modify** menu.

To cut or delete cells from the score:

1. In the score, drag across the cells you wish to cut or delete **(Figure 47)**.
2. Choose Cut Cells from the Edit menu to remove the cells from the score **(Figure 48)**. The cells are stored in memory and can be pasted back into the score. If you wish to delete the cells without storing them, press the Delete key, or choose Clear Cells from the Edit menu.

To fill cells with the same cell info:

You will often want the same cell information to occupy a range of frames in the score. Instead of copying and pasting a cell repeatedly, you can use the In Between command to fill a range of frames with the same cell information

1. Select a cell and a range of frames to the right of it through which you wish to copy it **(Figure 49)**.
2. Choose In Between from the Modify menu. The cell is copied through your range of selected cells **(Figure 50)**.

To reverse a sequence of cells:

1. In the score window, select the range of cells whose order you wish to reverse **(Figure 51)**. You can select cells in more than one channel.
2. Choose Reverse Sequence from the Modify menu **(Figure 53)**. The order of the selected cells is reversed **(Figure 52)**.

To add a marker to the score:

As the score of your movie grows to hundreds or even thousands of frames, it becomes harder to keep track of which frames do what.

The best way to manage a large score is to use special markers to label important sections. For instance, if you're creating an interactive business presentation, you could place a marker called "Main Menu" to mark the beginning of the frames that create the main menu of your presentation. Likewise, you could create "Sales" and "Marketing" markers to identify the frames that contain those respective sections of your movie **(Figure 54)**.

Also when it comes to writing scripts, referring to marker names instead of to changeable frame numbers ensures that Director will always know where to find a particular sequence of frames in your score. *(See the Interactivity through Lingo chapter on page 204 for details on scripts)*

1. In the score window, drag a marker from the marker well and position it above the desired frame **(Figure 55)**.

2. Type the name for your marker, and press Enter.

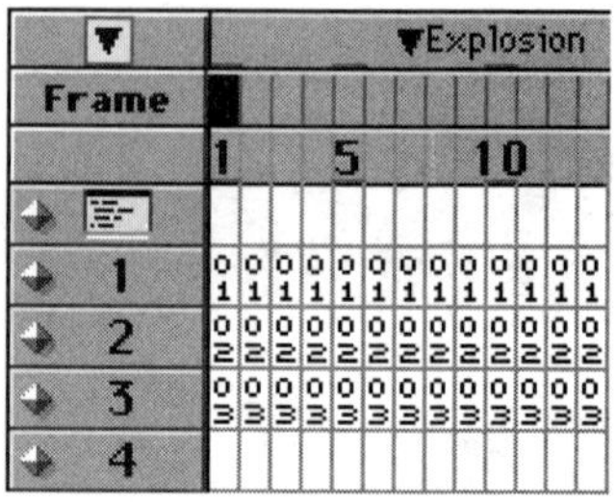

Figure 54. A marker is shown above frame 7 in the score.

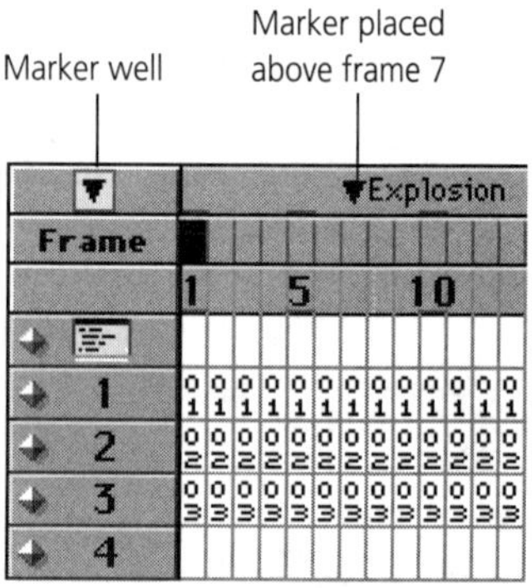

Figure 55. Drag a marker from the Marker well and position it above the desired frame. Type in a name.

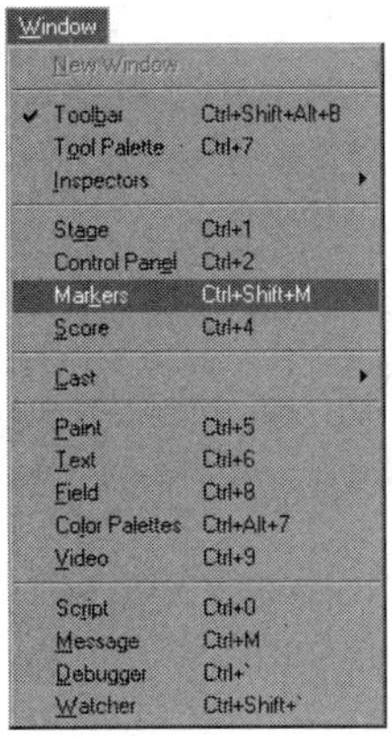

Figure 56. With the score window open, choose **Markers** from the **Window** menu.

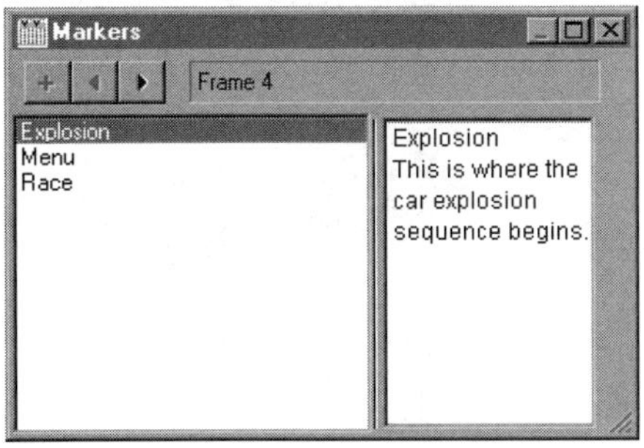

Figure 57. In the **Markers** window, click the marker name that you wish to find or annotate. You can add commentary on the right side of the **Markers** window.

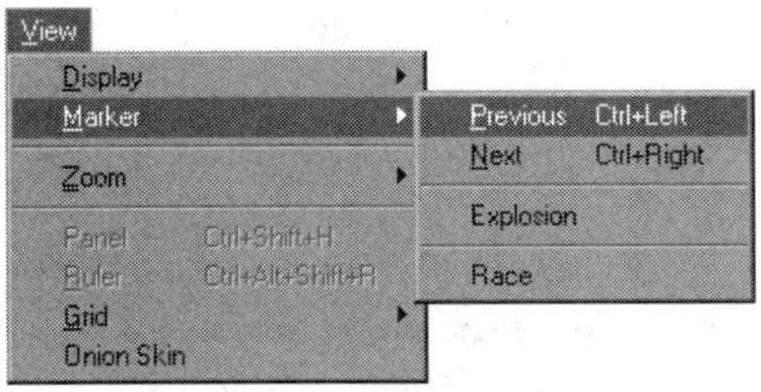

Figure 58. Choose **Marker** from the **View** menu and select the **Previous**, **Next**, or specific marker name to jump to in the score.

To find and annotate markers in the score:

Director features a Markers window that allows you to search for and jump to existing markers in your score. You can also use the window to add descriptive comments to markers—for instance, you might add scene descriptions or any other notes that might help someone understand what role the marked frames play in your movie's score.

1. With the score open, choose Markers from the Window menu **(Figure 56)**.
2. In the Markers window, click the marker name that you wish to find or annotate **(Figure 57)**. In the score window, Director immediately moves to the frame that contains the selected marker.
3. If you wish to add commentary to the selected marker, click the right half of the Markers window to first unselect the marker name that's repeated there. Make sure you then press Enter after the marker name before typing any commentary.

✓ Tip

- You can jump to the next or previous marker, or to a specific marker in the score, by choosing Marker from the View menu **(Figure 58)** and selecting the appropriate choice from the pop-up menu. Make sure the score is open.

To color cells in the score window:

You can add color to cells in the score window to help you identify its distinct parts. For instance, you might color all the cells of a particular animation sequence red, while another sequence blue. Having set up such a color code scheme, it's easy to see where each sequence begins and ends.

1. In the score window, select the cells that you wish to color **(Figure 59)**.
2. In the Cell color selector, click the color you'd like to apply to the selected cells **(Figure 59)**. *(If the Cell color selector is not visible in the score, see the Tip below)*

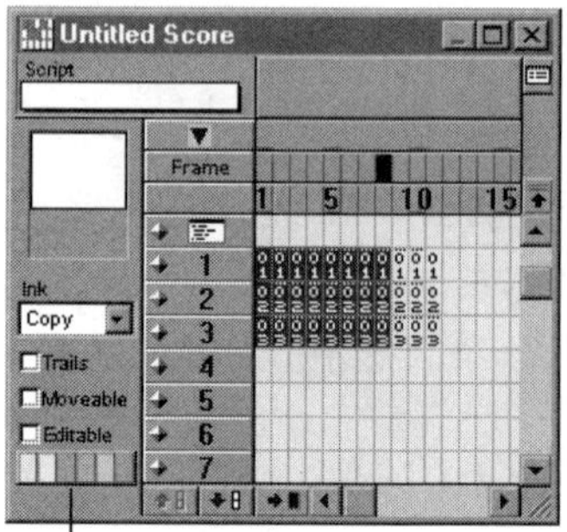

Cell color selector

Figure 59. In the score, select the cells that you wish to color and click on a color in the Cell color selector.

✔ Tip

- Colored cells can sometimes slow down scrolling performance of the score window. To avoid this, you can tell Director to show or hide colored cells. Choose Preferences from the File menu, and select Score from the pop-up menu. In the Score Window Preferences dialog box, select or deselect the Allow Colored Cells option **(Figure 60)**.

Allow Colored Cells option

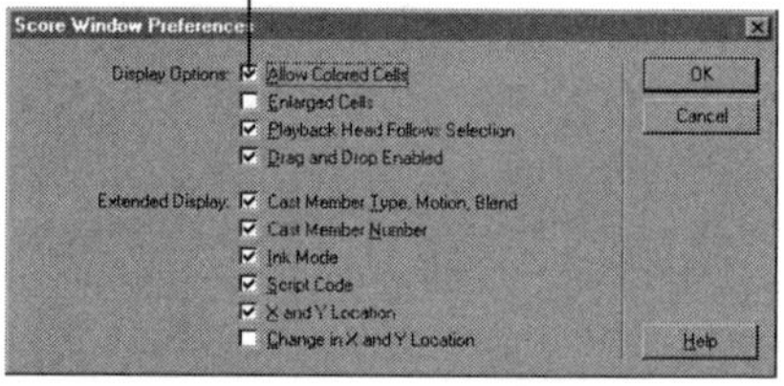

Figure 60. Select or deselect the **Allow Colored Cells** option in the **Score Window Preferences** dialog box to show or hide colored cells in the score.

SETTING SPRITE ATTRIBUTES

As defined on page 46, a sprite is an instance of a graphical cast member in a single cell of the score. You can have many sprites based on the same cast member, but each featuring its own unique properties. This can greatly reduce the number of cast members you need in your movie. You can change sprite attributes such as location, size, blend percentage, ink effect, trails, moveable, and editable. These attributes can be changed from the Sprite Properties dialog box **(Figure 61)**, and using the four options in the score **(Figure 62)**.

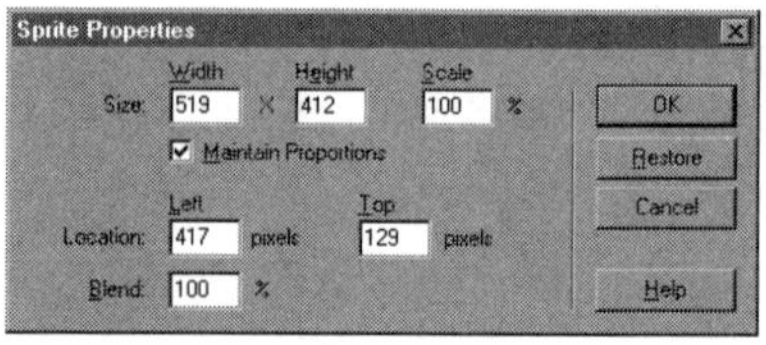

Figure 61. You can change the Size, Location, and Blend percentage properties of sprites in the **Sprite Properties** dialog box.

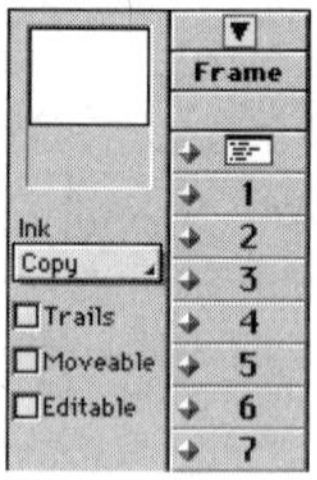

Figure 62. The score window allows you to set four attributes of a sprite. These are: Ink effect, Trails, Moveable, and Editable.

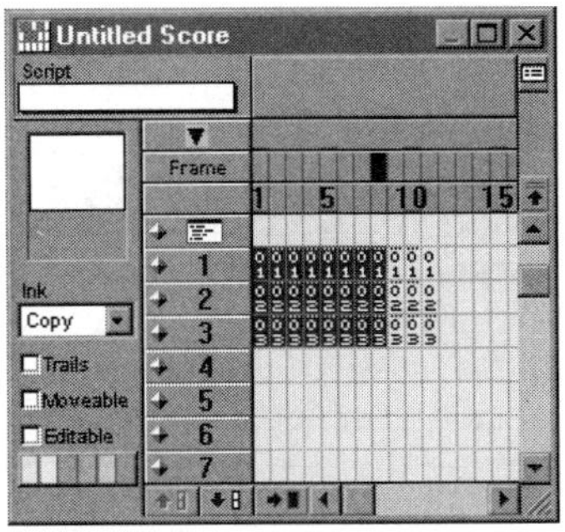

Figure 63. Select the cells in the score that contain the sprites to which you wish to apply a new ink effect.

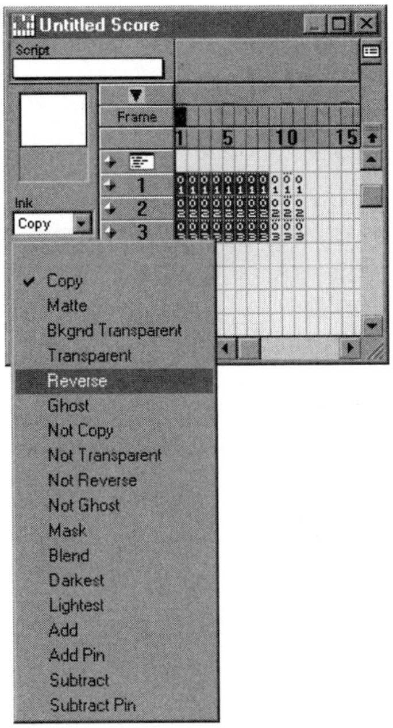

Figure 64. Use the **Ink** pop-up menu to select the desired ink effect.

To set an ink effect for a sprite in the score:

Director features a variety of ink effects that can be applied to sprites to change the way they appear on the stage. For instance, you can use ink effects to make sprites appear transparent, to darken or lighten sprites, and especially to determine how the colors of sprites should change when they overlap one another on the stage.

1. In the score window, select the cells that contain the sprites to which you wish to apply a new ink effect **(Figure 63)**.
2. Use the Ink pop-up menu on the left side of the score window to select the desired ink effect **(Figure 64)**.

The following list describes the effects that various inks have on your sprites. Although these explanations will help you determine the differences from one effect to another, the best way to understand them is through trial and error.

Copy This is the default ink effect. Sprites painted with this ink are surrounded by a rectangular bounding box. This box appears invisible on a white stage, but when the sprite is on a colored stage, or passes in front of another sprite, the bounding box is visible. Director animates sprites painted in the Copy ink more quickly than any other ink.

Matte Sprites appear without the white bounding box associated with the Copy ink effect. Sprites painted in this ink use more memory, and animate less quickly, than those in the Copy ink.

Bkgnd Transp.	Pixels in the sprite that were painted in the background colors are transparent, so you can see the background through them.
Transparent	Makes all colors transparent so that you can see any artwork behind them.
Reverse	White pixels in the sprite become transparent, so the background shows through.
Ghost	When two sprites overlap, any black pixels in the foreground sprite turn the pixels beneath of the sprite white. Any white pixels in the foreground sprite become transparent.
Not Copy **Not Transp.** **Not Reverse** **Not Ghost**	These inks act like the standard Copy, Matte, Transparent, and Ghost effects, except that they reverse foreground sprite's colors first.
Mask	Allows you to specify which parts of a sprite should be transparent and which opaque. For Mask ink to work, you need to design a special 1-bit mask cast member, which you place in the cast window in the position immediately following the cast member you wish to mask. *(See page 109 on creating masks)*
Blend	The colors of sprites painted in this ink will blend with the colors of the background sprite they pass over. This blend is created on the fly, which can significantly reduce Director's animation performance. Director creates the blend based on the percentage specified in the Sprite Properties dialog box.
Darkest	With this ink effect, Director compares the pixel colors of foreground and background sprites, and uses whichever pixels of the two are darker to color the foreground sprite. In other words, the darker colors of two overlapping sprites are made visible.
Lightest	Works like the Darkest ink effect, except that the lighter pixels of two overlapping sprites are visible.

Add When two sprites overlap, Director repaints that area in a new color that is created by adding the colors of the overlapping pixels together. If the value of the new color is greater than the maximum color value, then Director wraps the new color value around to the beginning of the color palette.

Add Pin Works the same way as the Add ink effect, except the new color value can't exceed the maximum color value.

Subtract Works the same way as the Add ink effect, except the new color for overlapping sprites is created by *subtracting* the foreground sprite's color value from the background sprite's color value. If the value of the two new colors is less than the minimum color value, Director wraps the new color value around to the top of the color palette.

Subtract Pin Works the same way as the Subtract ink effect, except the new color value can't be less than the minimum color value, and no wrap occurs.

✔ Tip

- Remember that using ink effects other than the default Copy ink can slow down your movie's animation performance. Try to use ink effects in strategic places, rather than across the board, if spry animation is important.

To apply trails to sprites:

You can set a sprite to leave a trail of images behind as it's moved around the stage from frame to frame **(Figure 65)**. This feature is wonderful for creating an animated hand-writing effect, where a trace is left wherever a cast member happens to move, as if someone were writing with a pencil.

1. In the score window, select the cells that contain the sprites to which you wish to apply trails **(Figure 66)**.
2. Click the Trails box on the left side of the score window to select it.

To make sprites moveable during movie playback:

It's possible to set Director to allow the sprites in your movie to be dragged on the stage while the movie is actually playing. An example where this might be useful would be in an educational game in Director, where children can rearrange a variety of items on the screen.

1. In the score window, select the range of cells that contain the sprites that you wish to render moveable by the user **(Figure 67)**. Remember that the sprites will be moveable only when Director is currently playing through the cells that you have selected in this step.
2. Click the score window's Moveable checkbox so that it's selected **(Figure 67)**.
3. If you wish to cancel the moveable effect, simply select the cells whose sprites have been rendered moveable, and deselect the Moveable checkbox.

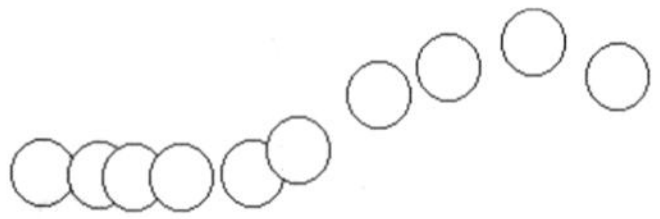

Figure 65. You can set a sprite to leave behind a trail of images as it's moved around, by selecting the Trails box in the score window.

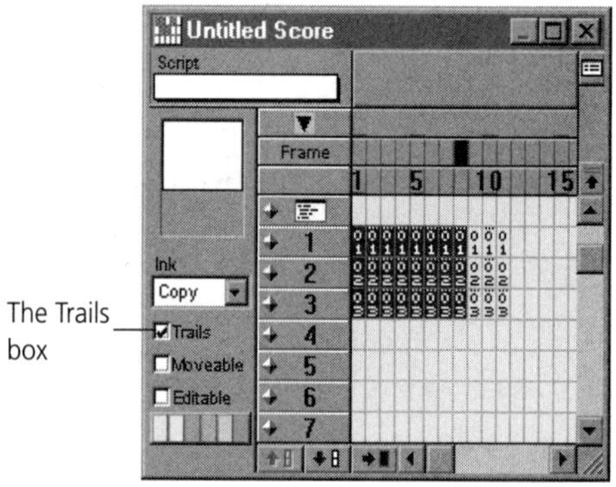

Figure 66. Select the cells in the score window that contain the sprites you wish to apply trails to, and click the **Trails** box.

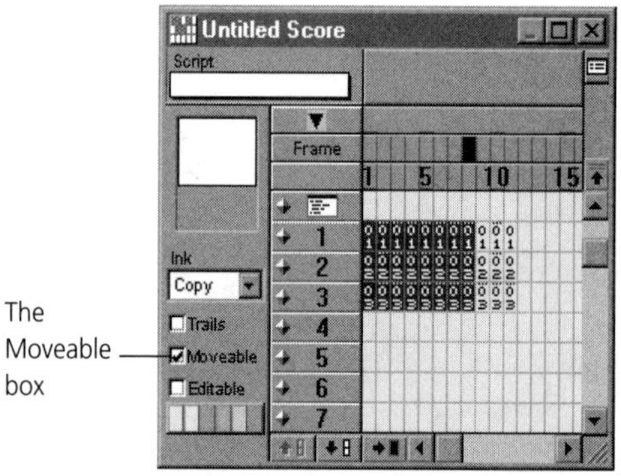

Figure 67. Select the range of cells in the score that contain sprites you wish to render moveable, and click the **Moveable** checkbox.

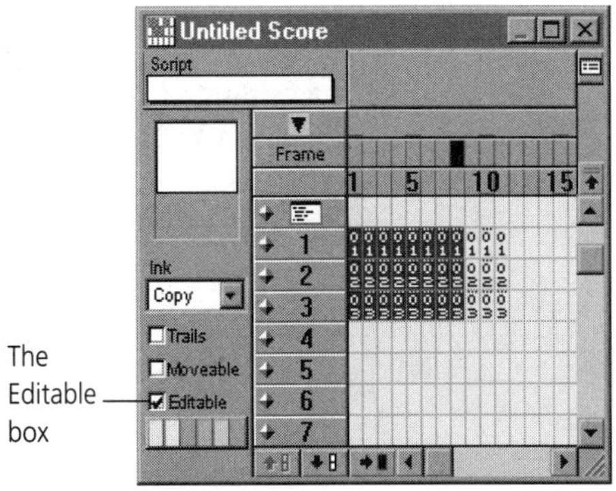

Figure 68. Select the range of cells in the score that contain the field sprites you wish to render editable, and click the **Editable** checkbox.

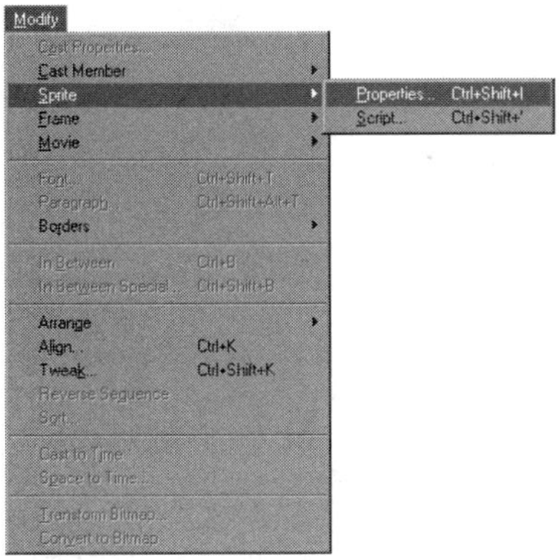

Figure 69. Choose **Sprite** from the **Modify** menu and select **Properties** from the pop-up menu.

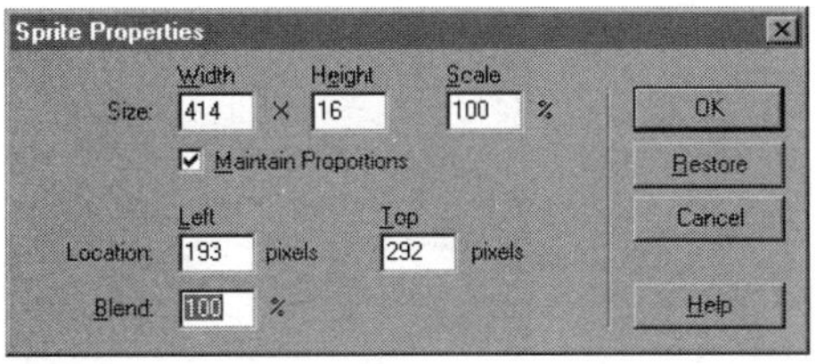

Figure 70. Double-click the Blend value in the **Sprite Properties** dialog box to set a new blend value for your selected sprite.

To make field sprites editable during movie playback:

Director allows you to select and edit the text of field sprites on the stage while the movie is actually playing. *(See page 179 in the Creating Text in Director chapter for details on field cast members)*

1. In the score window, select the range of cells that contain the field sprites that you wish to render editable by the user **(Figure 68)**. Remember that the sprites will be editable only when Director is currently playing through the cells that you have selected in this step.
2. Click the score window's Editable checkbox **(Figure 68)**.
3. If you wish to cancel the editable effect, simply select the cells whose sprites you've rendered editable, and deselect the Editable checkbox.

To set the blend percentage of a sprite:

The blend percentage of a sprite controls its transparency level. A 100% blend is completely opaque, while a 0% blend makes a sprite totally transparent to other sprites behind it.

1. Select a sprite or range of sprites whose blend setting you wish to change.
2. Choose Sprite from the Modify menu and select Properties from the pop-up menu **(Figure 69)**.
3. Double-click the Blend box in the Sprite Properties dialog box to set a new blend percentage **(Figure 70)**.

✔ Tip

- You can fade sprites it or out while animating by using the Blend setting in the In Between Special dialog box. *(See page 159 in the Animation Techniques chapter)*

To change the size of a sprite:

You can change the size and look of a sprite by stretching or squeezing it along either axis. Again, the change only affects the selected sprite; the original cast member in the cast window is not changed by this operation *(see page 35 to change a cast member's size)*. Stretching and squeezing sprites can lead to some interesting effects, especially when combined with Director's In-between animation capabilities *(see page 156 in the Animation Techniques chapter)*, which allow you to gradually change the size of sprites over multiple frames.

1. In the score, select the cell or range of cells that contain the sprites you wish to stretch or squeeze **(Figure 71)**. Director displays the sprites on the stage which are in the last frame of the selection you make. These sprites are each encased by a selection rectangle with handles at its corners and edges **(Figure 72)**.
2. Drag any of the selected sprite's handles to stretch or squeeze it **(Figure 73)**. If you selected just one cell in the score in step 1, only the sprite in that single cell will be affected. If the last frame of your cell selection has multiple sprites, you can stretch or squeeze any one of them, and all of them will be affected in the same way.

✔ Tip

- You can also stretch and squeeze a sprite by entering width and height dimensions in the Sprite Properties dialog box **(Figure 74)**. Open it by choosing Sprite from the Modify menu, and Properties from the pop-up menu. Check the Maintain Proportions option to maintain the sprites' original proportions while sizing, or enter a value in the Scale box to proportionately size your sprite.

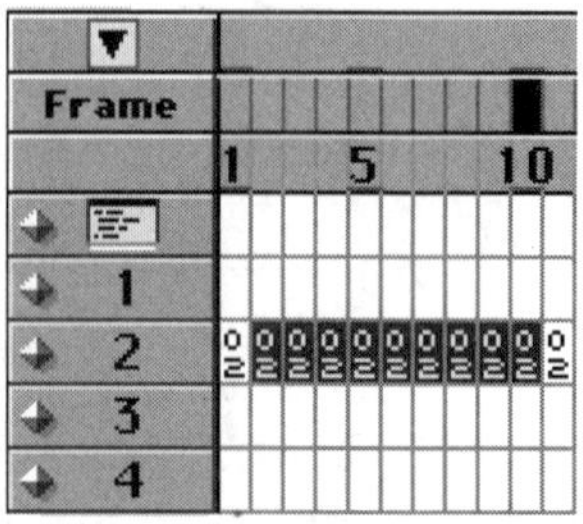

Figure 71. Select the cell or range of cells in the score that contain the sprites you wish to stretch or squeeze.

Figure 72. A sprite on the stage encased by a selection rectangle.

Figure 73. Drag any of the selected sprite's handles to stretch or squeeze it. The sprite has been stretched vertically here.

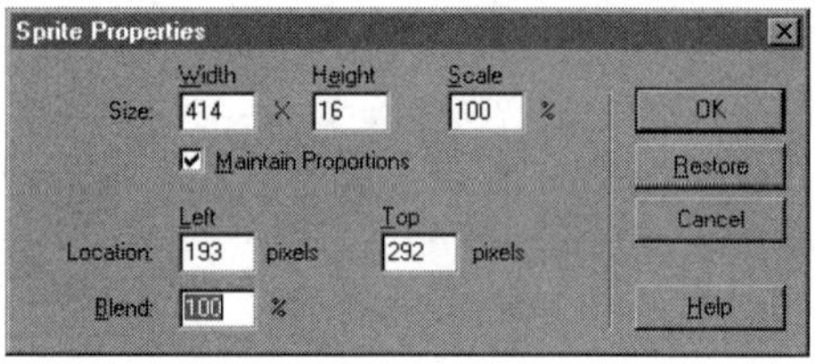

Figure 74. You can enter width and height dimensions in the **Sprite Properties** dialog box to stretch and squeeze your sprite.

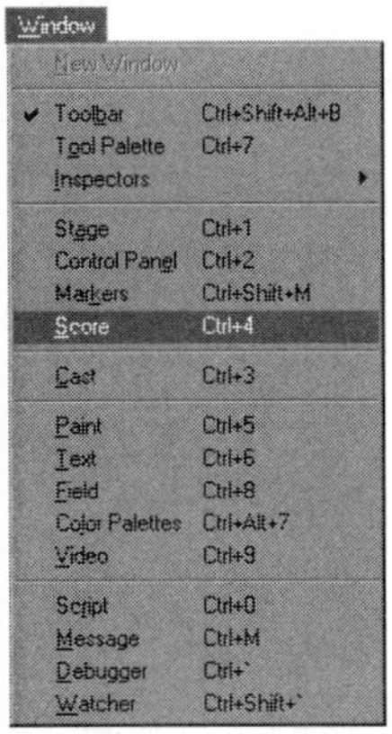

Figure 75. Choose **Score** from the **Window** menu.

Figure 76. Choose **Align** from the **Modify** menu.

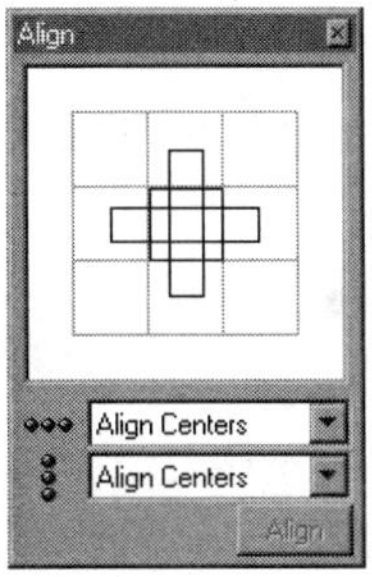

Figure 77. Use the **Align** dialog box to align the positions of selected sprites on the stage.

To change a group of sprites:

Once you have arranged a group of sprites in the score, you may decide you want to change a property of theirs. You can do so all at once for a group of sprites by selecting them in the score, and making the desired change. For instance, suppose you have ten sprites in one frame, and you want to move all of them by the same distance to the left. Just select them in the score, and move one of the sprites on the stage to the left. All the selected sprites will be affected in the same way.

To align sprites:

Sometimes you may need to align the positions of sprites on the stage so that they are all registered with respect to some reference. This is often necessary when building an animation sequence to ensure that the sprites do not appear to shift from one frame to the next.

You can align sprites on the stage by using the Align command under the Modify menu. Sprites can be aligned with respect to their centers, registration points (*see "To set a new cast member registration point" on page 82*), or with respect to any of the other eight points around the bounding box that encompasses each sprite. Aligning sprites does not change their cast members' registration points.

1. Choose Score from the Window menu **(Figure 75)**.
2. Select the cells containing the sprites that you wish to align.
3. Choose Align from the Modify menu **(Figure 76)**.
4. In the Align dialog box **(Figure 77)**, choose how you wish to align the sprites from the pop-up menus, and click Align. The sprites are aligned with respect to the last sprite you selected in step 2 above.

To align sprites to the grid:

You can use the grid in Director to align sprites on the stage **(Figure 78)**.

1. Choose Grid from the View menu, and select Show from the pop-up menu. The grid appears **(Figure 79)**.
2. If you wish your sprites to snap to the nearest grid line, choose Grid from the View menu, and select Snap To from the pop-up menu.
3. You can adjust the spacing and color of the grid lines in the Grid Settings dialog box **(Figure 80)**. Choose Grid from the View menu, and select Settings from the pop-up menu to open it.

To tweak sprites:

You can use the Tweak window to move sprites a precise number of pixels in the X and Y directions on the stage

1. Select the sprite(s) you wish to tweak on the stage or in the score. Shift-click to select multiple sprites on the stage.
2. Choose Tweak from the Modify menu **(Figure 81)**.
3. In the Tweak window, drag on its left side to visually specify the offset by which to move the selected sprites **(Figure 82)**. You can also click the up and down arrows to specify the X and Y offsets.
4. Click Tweak to move the sprites.

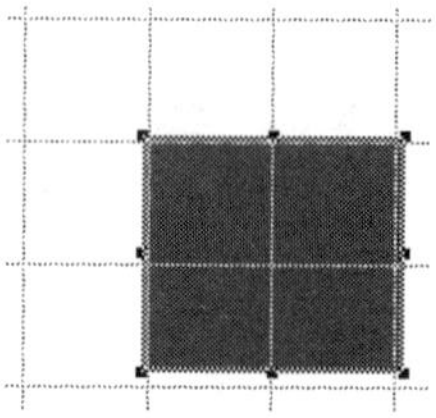

Figure 78. Use the grid to align sprites on the stage.

Figure 79. Choose **Grid** from the **View** menu, and select **Show** from the pop-up menu to display the grid on the stage.

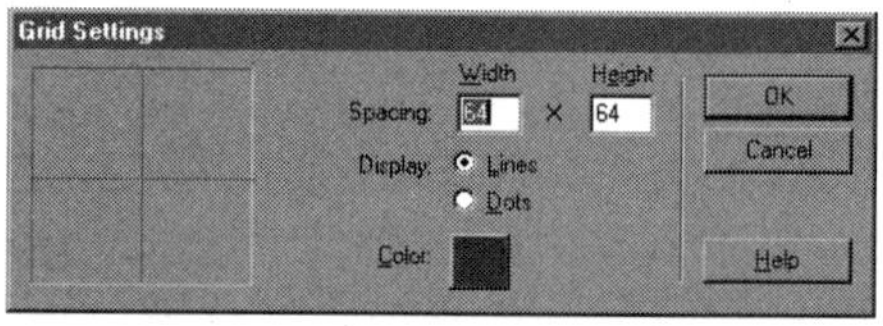

Figure 80. Use the **Grid Settings** dialog box to adjust the spacing and color of grid lines.

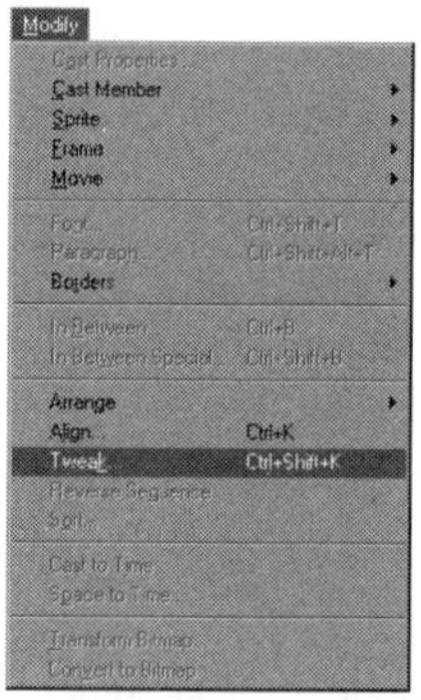

Figure 81. Choose **Tweak** from the **Modify** menu.

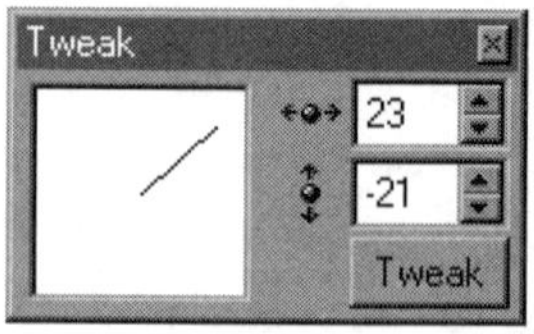

Figure 82. Use the Tweak window to move selected sprites by a precise pixel offset.

CONTROL PANEL 5

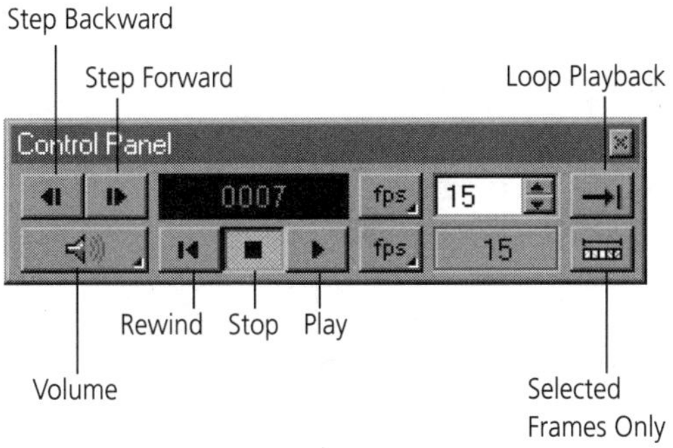

Figure 1. The Control Panel.

Director's Control Panel is used to control the playback of your movie **(Figure 1)**. Much like the controls on a VCR, you can play, rewind, step forward, or step backward through the frames of your movie. The Control Panel also allows you to adjust volume, and set loop playback. Open the Control Panel by choosing Control Panel from the Window menu **(Figure 2)** or by typing Control-2.

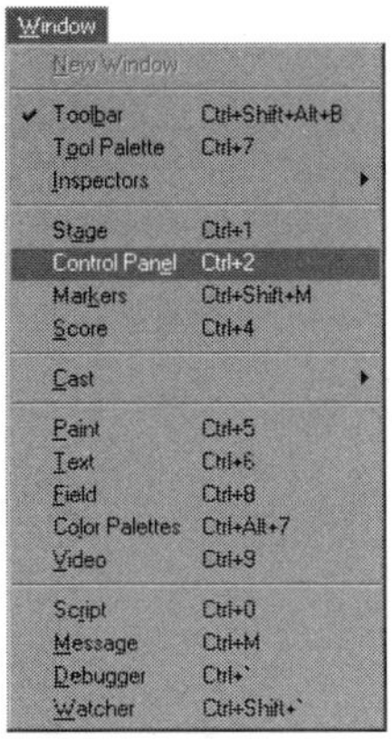

Figure 2. Choose **Control Panel** from the **Window** menu.

CONTROL PANEL BUTTONS

Rewind

Click the Rewind button (Control-Alt-R) to reset the movie to frame 1 **(Figure 3)**. Doing so during playback automatically stops the movie and rewinds to frame 1.

Figure 3. The **Rewind** button.

Step Backward

Step Backward (Control-Alt-Left Arrow) steps the movie back one frame at a time **(Figure 4)**. Holding down this button steps backward continuously.

Figure 4. The **Step Backward** button.

Stop

Stop (Control-.) stops the movie **(Figure 5)**.

Figure 5. The **Stop** button.

Step Forward

Step Forward (Control-Alt-Right Arrow) steps the movie forward one frame at a time **(Figure 6)**. Hold down this button to step forward continuously.

When a Score channel is in Step Recording mode, click Step Forward to copy the contents of the current frame to the next frame. *(See page 145 in the Animation Techniques chapter on Step Recording)*

Figure 6. The **Step Forward** button.

Play

Play (Control-Alt-P) starts the movie **(Figure 7)**. Press Control-1 to hide all open windows and the menu bar.

Figure 7. The **Play** button.

Volume

(Figure 8) (*See page 184 in the Sound chapter*)

Figure 8. The **Volume** button.

Loop Playback

Loop Playback (Control-Alt-L) controls whether your movie will repeat over and over **(Figure 9)**. If this button is selected, your movie will automatically start over from frame 1 each time it reaches the last frame. Loop is on by default.

Loop enabled (default)

Loop disabled

Figure 9.

Selected Frames Only

Selected Frames Only **(Figure 10)** allows you to play a portion of the current movie. First, open the score and select the frames you wish to playback. Then click the Selected Frames Only button. A green bar appears in the score above the selected frames. Now when you click the Play button, only these marked frames will play. Click the Selected Frames Only button again to remove the green bar and turn off the selection.

Selected Frames Only enabled

Selected Frames Only disabled

Figure 10.

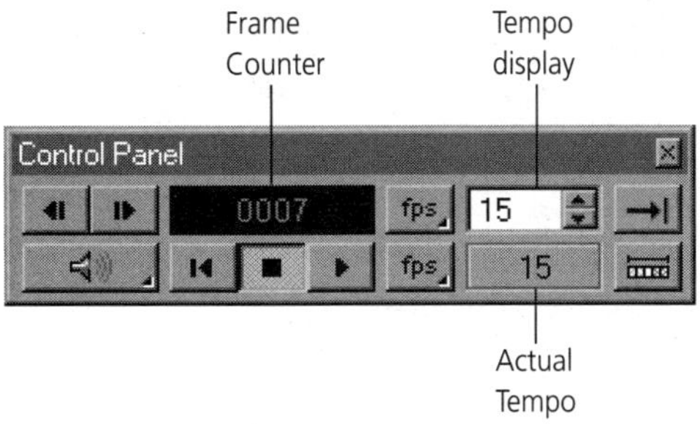

CONTROL PANEL INDICATORS

Frame Counter

The Frame Counter indicates which frame of your movie is currently displayed on the stage **(Figure 11)**. This corresponds to the Playback head indicator in the score window *(see page 44)*. You can enter a frame number to jump to by double-clicking the displayed frame number and typing a value.

Figure 11. The Frame Counter.

Tempo display

The Tempo display indicates the preset tempo that the current frame should play at, in frames per second **(Figure 12)**. Director will never play a given frame faster than this tempo, but may play slower because of performance limitations of your computer *(see the "Actual Tempo" section on page 72)*. You can change this target tempo setting for each frame by clicking the up or down arrows, or by double-clicking the displayed tempo number and typing a value. If a tempo setting has been entered in the tempo channel of the score at a certain frame, that setting takes precedence, and will be indicated here *(see page 191 in the Movie Tempo chapter for details on the Tempo channel)*. If no such tempo setting has been made, the Tempo display field displays a default value.

Figure 12. The Tempo display.

Actual Tempo

The Actual Tempo display **(Figure 13)** indicates the *actual* duration of the current frame in frames-per-second. The actual tempo of your frames can fall behind the set or desired tempo shown in the Tempo display, due to speed limitations of your computer.

Figure 13. The Actual Tempo display.

To compare the set tempo to the actual tempo:

You can step through a movie frame-by-frame and compare the set tempo in the Tempo display to the Actual Tempo. Since PC's vary in speed performance, some of them may not keep up with your set tempo. If you plan to run your movie on a wide range of PC's, comparing the set tempo to the actual tempo on a slower PC allows you to set appropriate tempo values for the frames, so that the actual tempo never falls below the set tempo. *(See the Movie Tempo chapter on page 194 for more details)*

1. Open the Control Panel by choosing Control Panel from the Window menu **(Figure 14)**.
2. Click Rewind to reset the movie to the first frame.
3. Click the Step Forward button and compare the number shown in the Tempo display to the number in the Actual Tempo display **(Figure 15)**.
4. Use the arrows in the Tempo display to set new tempo values for the frames.

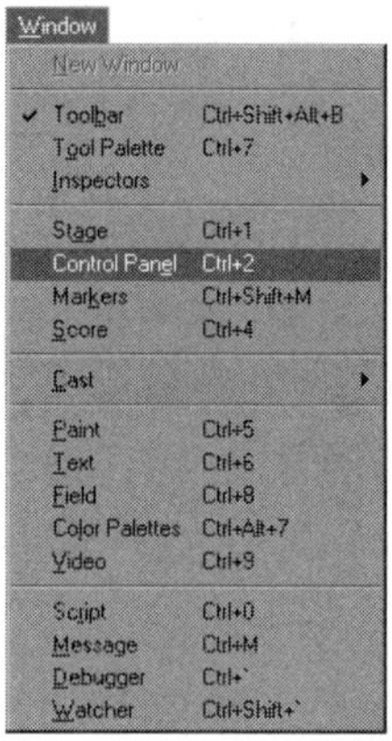

Figure 14. Choose **Control Panel** from the **Window** menu.

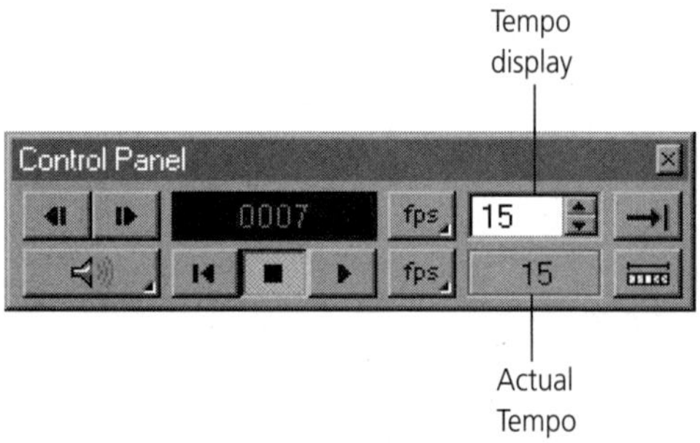

Figure 15. In the Control Panel, compare the set tempo value of each frame, shown in the Tempo display, to the Actual Tempo of each frame.

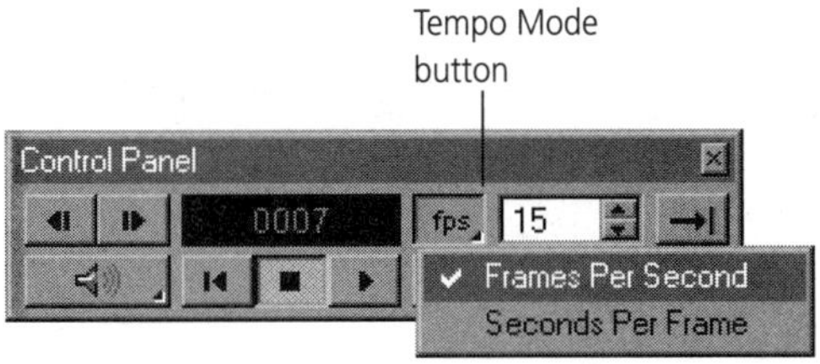

Figure 16. Use the **Tempo Mode** button to choose whether the Tempo display is shown in frames per second or seconds per frame.

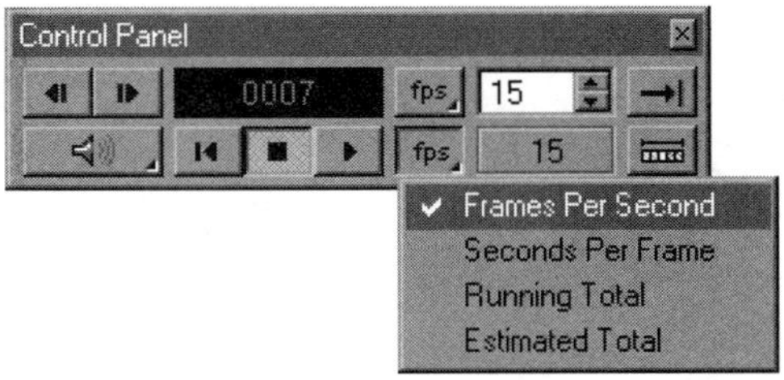

Figure 17. Click and hold the **Actual Tempo** mode button to display a pop-up menu which determines how the Actual Tempo is displayed.

Tempo Mode button:

Use the Tempo Mode button to choose whether the Tempo display value in the Control Panel is displayed in frames per second (FPS) or seconds per frame (SPF). Click and hold the Tempo Mode button and choose from the the pop-up menu **(Figure 16)**.

Actual Tempo Mode button:

Click and hold the Actual Tempo mode button **(Figure 17)** to display a pop-up menu of choices which determine how the Actual Tempo value is displayed. Your choices are Frames per Second, Seconds per Frame, Running Total, and Estimated Total. Running Total indicates the total elapsed time in seconds from the start of your movie to the current frame. Estimated Total is similar to Running Total, but is more accurate since it includes palette changes and transitions in its calculation of the frame durations.

✔ Tip

- Don't leave your Actual Tempo display in Estimated Total mode while playing back your movie, since this mode can lower playback speed due to its more intensive calculations.

PAINT WINDOW 6

Paint Window.
The paint window is used throughout this chapter. Choose Paint from the Window menu to open it **(Figure 1)** or press Control-5.

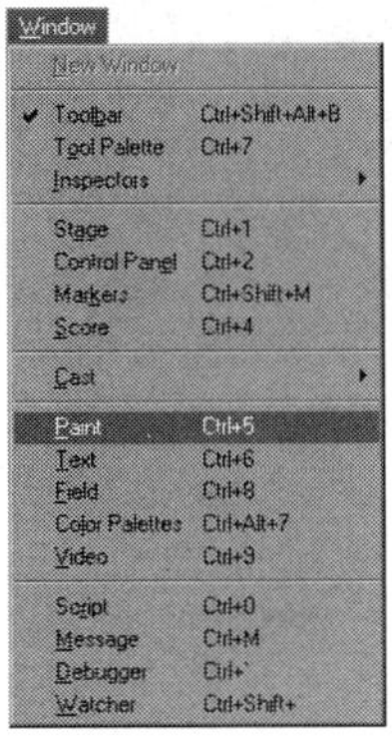

Figure 1. Choose **Paint** from the **Window** menu.

Figure 2. The paint window.

Director's paint window provides numerous tools such as the Air Brush, Paint Bucket, and Lasso for creating and editing bitmap cast member graphics **(Figure 2)**. While these tools aren't as elaborate as the Adobe Photoshop tools for example, they are robust enough to create many of the cast members you're likely to showcase in your movies.

The paint window also offers an **Effects** toolbar, which contains numerous special-effects commands that can be applied to your artwork, such as Rotate, Warp, Skew, and Perspective.

Director 5 provides a new feature called Onion Skinning, which allows you to create a cast member in the paint window while viewing one or more reference cast members that appear dimmed in the background. This technique is very useful for creating animated sequences. *(See page 111)*

Another new feature in Director 5 allows you to use image filters from Photoshop or Premiere to modify bitmap cast member graphics.

Shape or PICT cast members cannot be edited in the paint window. If you wish to create a shape cast member, use Director's Tool Palette. *(See page 115 in the Tool Palette chapter for details)*

This chapter covers the use of all tools and effects in the paint window. Ink masks, the Onion Skinning feature, and using image filters are covered in the last three sections of the chapter.

THE PAINT WINDOW

The link between the paint and cast windows

It's important to know that when you create a graphic in Director's paint window, that graphic also becomes a cast member in a cast window **(Figures 3–4)**.

In fact, the paint window shares a dynamic link with the cast window. From a cast window, you can double-click a bitmap cast member and it automatically opens in the paint window. And from the paint window, you can access all the bitmap cast members in a cast window by clicking the Previous and Next buttons in the paint window's upper left corner **(Figure 3)**. You specify which cast to work with by using the Cast selector pop-up menu in the upper right corner of the paint window.

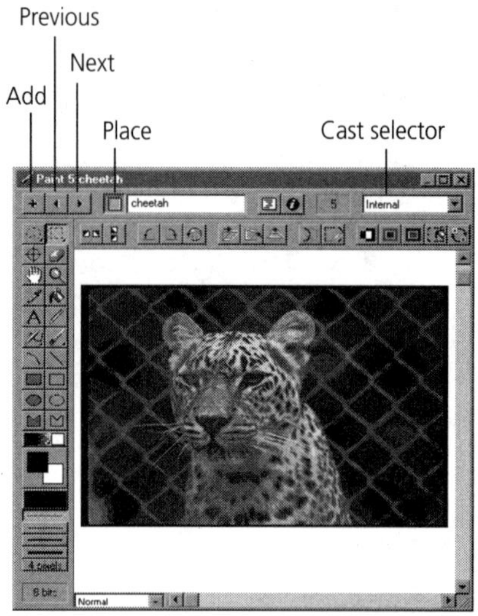

Figure 3. Objects drawn in the paint window automatically become new cast members, as shown below in the cast window.

To add a new cast member while using the paint window:

1. Click the Add button to create a new cast member **(Figure 3)**. Director displays an empty paint window and the image you draw becomes a cast member in the first available position in the cast window as soon as you close the paint window.

To place a graphic onto the stage from the paint window:

1. Drag the Place button onto the stage and Director places the image from the paint window onto the stage and into the score.

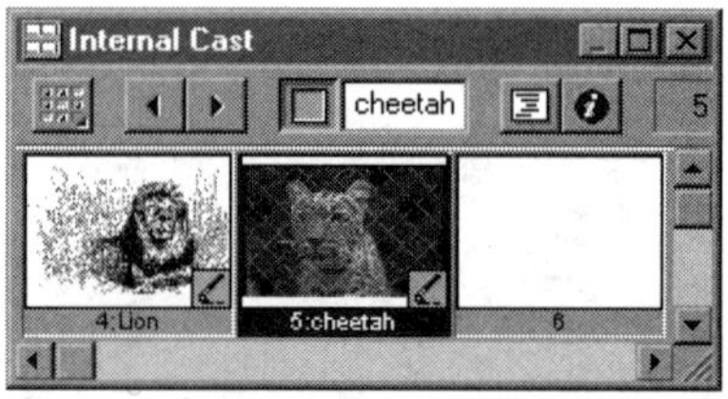

Figure 4. The cast window.

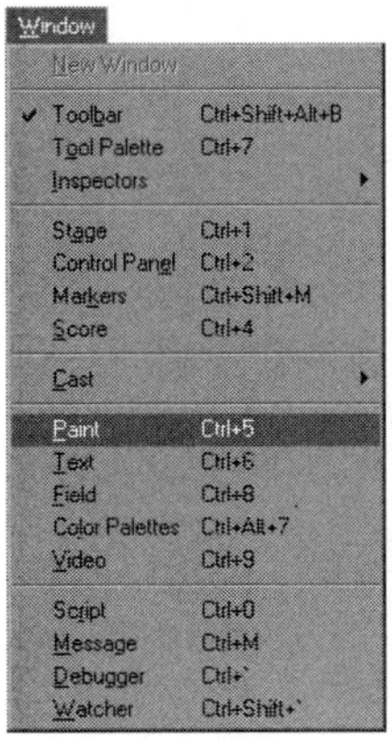

Figure 5. Choose **Paint** from the **Window** menu.

Figure 6. Choose **Ruler** from the **View** menu.

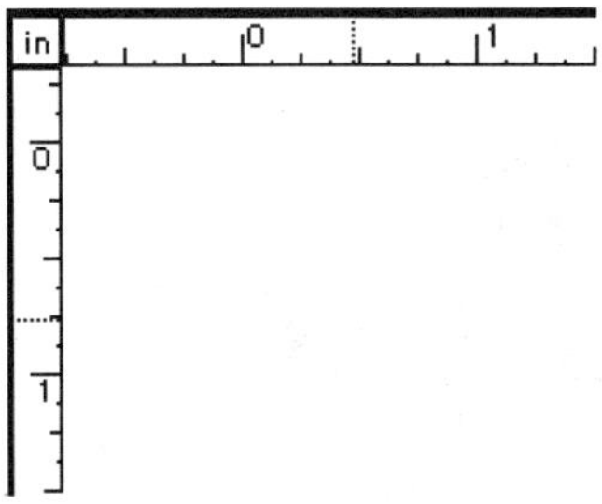

Figure 7. To change the ruler's units of measurement, click the upper- left corner of the ruler.

To show or hide rulers in the paint window:

You can display a set of horizontal and vertical rulers in the paint window to help you align and measure your artwork. The rulers can display their measurement values in either inches, centimeters, or pixels.

1. Choose Paint from the Window menu **(Figure 5)**.
2. Choose Ruler from the View menu. To hide the Ruler, choose it again **(Figure 6)**.

✔ Tips

- You can set a ruler's zero point by clicking the ruler and dragging to the point where you'd like the new zero point to be.
- To display the ruler's measurements in a new unit (inches, centimeters, etc.), click the upper-left corner where the horizontal and vertical rulers meet **(Figure 7)**.

To show or hide the paint tool palette:

If you need more space to work with in the paint window, you can hide the paint tool palette. Make sure to select the paint tool you wish to use first.

1. With the paint window open, choose Paint Tools from the View menu to show or hide the paint tool palette.

PAINT TOOL PALETTE

Director provides an assortment of painting tools used to create and modify bitmap cast members. These tools are located in the paint tool palette, which is found on the left side of the paint window **(Figure 8)**.

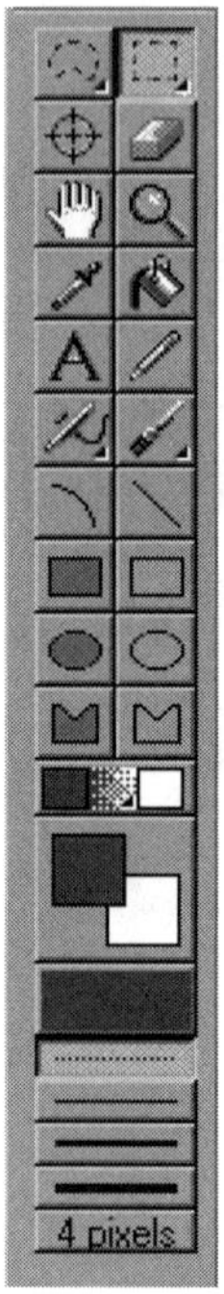

Figure 8. The paint tool palette is found on the left side of the paint window.

Lasso and Marquee tools

Like most PC paint programs, Director's paint window features a selection rectangle (called the Marquee), and a Lasso that allow you to select all or just parts of cast member artwork. Once artwork has been selected, you can use the other tools in the paint window to modify the selection—for instance, drag it to another region of the paint window, cut or copy it, rotate it, change its colors, warp it, and so on.

While the two tools work similarly, there is one important difference between them: The Marquee allows you to select rectangular regions of artwork, while the Lasso selects any region you "draw" with, giving you much greater flexibility in making artwork selections. Another difference is that some of Director's paint features work only with artwork selected by the Marquee, not by the Lasso (or vice versa). These instances are identified later in the chapter.

Figure 9. The Marquee tool.

To select artwork with the Marquee:

1. Click the Marquee tool in the paint tool palette **(Figure 9)**.
2. The mouse pointer becomes a crosshair. Position the crosshair wherever you want to begin your selection.
3. Drag the pointer up or down and to one side to outline a rectangular selection around your artwork **(Figure 10)**.

Figure 10. Drag the pointer to outline a rectangular selection or "marquee" around your artwork.

Figure 11. To stretch or compress an artwork selection, hold the Alt key, click anywhere in the selection and drag.

Figure 12. Click and hold the Marquee tool until the **Options** pop-up menu appears.

You'll see a dotted line called a "marquee" encase your artwork selection.

4. Release the mouse button to select the artwork within the marquee.

✓ **Tips**

- You can reposition your artwork selection by moving the mouse to the selection marquee (the crosshair becomes a pointer again) and dragging the artwork to a new area.
- Hold down the Alt key while dragging an artwork selection to drag a copy of it, leaving the original in place.
- To stretch or compress an artwork selection, hold down the Control key, click anywhere in the selection and drag **(Figure 11)**.
- To erase a selection, press the Backspace or Delete key.
- Double-click the Marquee tool to select the entire visible portion of the paint window.

To choose Marquee tool options:

You can control how the Marquee behaves when selecting artwork.

1. Click the Marquee tool in the paint tool palette. Hold the mouse button down until the Options pop-up menu appears **(Figure 12)**.
2. Drag to select one of the four options in the menu. Your choices are Shrink, No Shrink, Lasso, and See Thru Lasso.

Shrink makes the selection marquee tighten around whatever object you've selected, although the selection still keeps its rectangular shape. Director identifies an object's border by looking for color differences between pixels.

No Shrink selects all the artwork that you encased with the selection marquee.

Lasso makes the selection marquee tighten around whatever object you've selected but allows the selection area to take on an irregular shape, as if you had actually used the Lasso tool.

See Thru Lasso is similar to the Lasso option, but it makes all white pixels in your selection become transparent.

To select artwork with the Lasso tool:

1. Click the Lasso tool in the paint tool palette **(Figure 13)**.
2. The mouse pointer turns into a lasso when you move it inside the paint window. Position the Lasso wherever you want to begin your selection.
3. Drag the Lasso to draw a line around the art you wish to select **(Figure 14)**. Try to end your selection at the point where you started it.
4. Release the mouse button and Director highlights the selected area with the marquee. If you did not entirely encase your selection, Director automatically connects its starting and ending points.

✔ Tips

- You can use the Lasso tool to select a polygonal shape. Hold the Alt key while dragging the Lasso to create an anchor point and draw a straight selection line. Repeat this step to encase your artwork with such lines. double-click to end your selection.
- You can reposition your artwork selection by positioning the Lasso within the selection (the Lasso becomes a mouse pointer again), and dragging the artwork to a new location. If you hold down the Alt key, you drag a copy of the artwork, leaving the original in place.

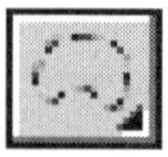

Figure 13. The Lasso tool.

Figure 14. Drag the Lasso to draw a line around the artwork you wish to select.

Figure 15. Click and hold the Lasso tool to display the **Options** pop-up menu.

To choose Lasso options:

You can control how the Lasso behaves when selecting artwork.

1. Click the Lasso tool in the paint tool palette. Hold the mouse button down until the Options pop-up menu appears **(Figure 15)**.
2. Drag to select one of the three options in the menu. Your choices are No Shrink, Lasso, and See Thru Lasso.

No Shrink selects all the artwork that you encase with the Lasso and does not fine-tune the selection.

Lasso makes the selection marquee tighten around whatever object you've selected. Director tries to identify an objects border by looking for color differences between pixels. The idea is to "fine-tune" the selection you made by hand.

See Thru Lasso makes all the white pixels in your selection become transparent.

Registration Points

A registration point is a fixed point of reference in a bitmap image. Every bitmap cast member in your movie has a default registration point, which is placed directly at its center **(Figure 16)**

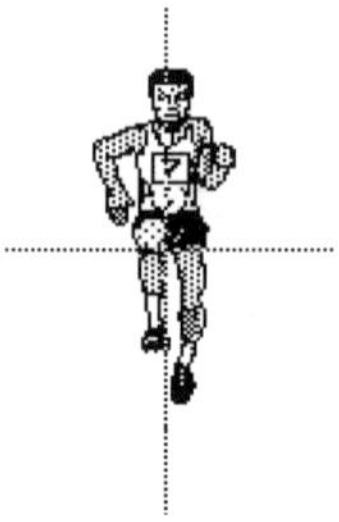

Figure 16. A cast member with its registration point shown in the paint window.

When you create cast members for an animation sequence, there's a chance that they may appear to jump and shift from one frame to the next when animated. To avoid this problem, you can adjust their registration points. For instance, if you were animating several frames of an athlete running, you could set a registration point where the character's feet touch the ground for each cast member in the sequence. This would ensure that the runner's feet never hit above or below ground level. *(Also see "To align Sprites" on page 67)*

You can view your cast member's registration point by opening the cast member in the paint window and clicking the Registration Point tool **(Figure 17)**

Figure 17. The Registration Point tool.

To set a new cast member registration point:

1. Open a cast member in Director's paint window.
2. Click the Registration Point tool in the paint tool palette to select it **(Figure 17)**. The current registration point assigned to the cast member appears at the intersection of the dotted lines.
3. Move the crosshair pointer to a new location in the paint window, and click to place the registration mark in this new location **(Figure 18)**.

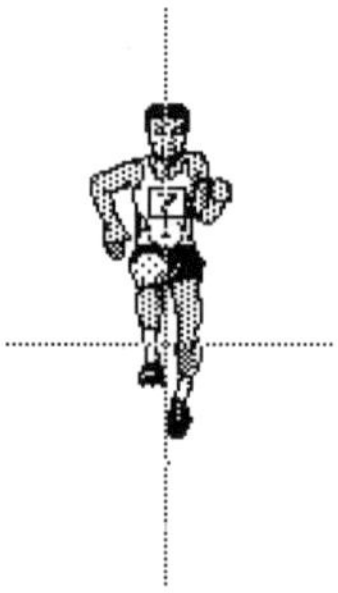

Figure 18. The Registration point here has been moved downward.

✔ **Tip**

- If you ever want to reset a registration point to its default position (that is, directly at the center of the cast member), double-click the Registration Point tool in the paint tool palette.

Registration Points

Figure 19. The Eraser tool.

Eraser

Erase a portion of an image by dragging the Eraser tool **(Figure 19)** across it. Double-click the Eraser tool to clear the entire image in the paint window.

Figure 20. The Hand tool.

Hand tool

The Hand tool is used to move an image around in the paint window **(Figure 20)**. Click the Hand tool then drag the image in the paint window to move it in any direction. Press the Spacebar in the paint window as a shortcut for selecting the Hand tool.

Figure 21. The Magnifying glass.

Magnifying glass

Select the Magnifying glass tool, and then click with it in the paint window to zoom in on your artwork **(Figure 21)**. Shift-click to zoom out.

Figure 22. The Eyedropper tool.

Eyedropper

The Eyedropper tool is used to "pick up" and match colors **(Figure 22)**. Click the Eyedropper anywhere in the paint window, and the color it is positioned on becomes the new foreground color. *(See page 91 on switching colors with the Eyedropper)*

Figure 23. The Paint Bucket tool.

Paint Bucket

Position the Paint Bucket **(Figure 23)** over empty space in your artwork and click to fill the space with the selected foreground color.

Figure 24. The Pencil tool.

Pencil

Drag the Pencil tool **(Figure 24)** to draw single pixels in the selected foreground color. Drawing over existing pixels in the foreground color will change the pixels to the selected background color.

Text tool

The Text tool allows you to enter bitmap text anywhere within the paint window **(Figure 25)**. Simply click the Text tool icon and then click the desired location in the paint window where text should be entered. A blinking cursor box appears. The text's font, size, and style can be modified in the Font dialog box, which is opened by choosing Font from the Modify menu, or by double-clicking the Text tool *(see the Creating Text in Director chapter on page 172)*. Once the bitmap text has been entered, there is no way of changing the font, size, or style of the text. Any effects or color changes can be applied to bitmap text just like to a regular bitmap image.

Figure 25. The Text tool.

Air Brush

Drag the Air Brush **(Figure 26)** to "spray" paint in the selected foreground color, and pattern if any. A variety of air brush settings allow you to specify the size and density of the Air Brush's spray. *(See page 103)*

Figure 26. The Air Brush tool.

Paint Brush

The Paint Brush tool **(Figure 27)** allows you to paint in the selected foreground color and pattern by dragging the mouse across the paint window. You can choose from a variety of brush shapes and design your own as well. *(See page 100)*

Figure 27. The Paint Brush tool.

Arc tool

The Arc tool **(Figure 28)** draws one quarter of an ellipse. Drag to preview the length and angle of your arc, and release the mouse button to draw it. Hold the Shift key while dragging to draw 45 degree arcs, and hold the Alt key while dragging to draw an arc in the currently selected pattern.

Figure 28. The Arc tool.

Figure 29. The Line tool.

Line tool

The Line tool **(Figure 29)** is used to draw straight lines. Drag to set any angle for your line. Hold the Shift key while dragging to draw 45 degree lines, and hold the Alt key while dragging to draw lines in the currently selected pattern. Use the Line Width Selector in the paint tool palette to change the thickness of the line.

Figure 30. The Filled Rectangle tool.

Filled Rectangle tool

Select the Filled Rectangle tool **(Figure 30)**, then drag the pointer to draw a solid rectangular shape in the selected foreground color, and pattern if any. The thickness of the border of the rectangle (visible only when a pattern is used) is set by the Line Width Selector located at the bottom of the paint tool palette. Hold down the Shift key while dragging to constrain the rectangle to a perfect square.

Figure 31. The Rectangle tool.

Rectangle tool

Select the Rectangle tool **(Figure 31)** then drag the pointer to outline a hollow rectangular shape of any size in the current foreground color.

Figure 32. The Filled Ellipse tool.

Filled Ellipse tool

Select the Filled Ellipse tool **(Figure 32)**, then drag to size the ellipse's solid shape. Hold down the Shift key while dragging to draw a circle. When you release the mouse button, the ellipse is drawn in the selected foreground color, and pattern if any.

Figure 33. The Ellipse tool.

Ellipse tool

Select the Ellipse tool **(Figure 33)** then drag the pointer to outline a hollow elliptical shape of any size in the current foreground color.

Filled Polygon tool

Select the Filled Polygon tool **(Figure 34)**, then click the mouse to draw straight lines that make up a polygon. Each mouse click draws a new line in the polygon, starting from the last line's ending point, and ending where the mouse pointer is positioned. Double-click to draw the polygon's final line segment that connects the first and last lines together. When the final segment of the polygon is drawn, its shape is filled with the selected foreground color, and pattern if any.

Figure 34. The Filled Polygon tool.

Polygon tool

Works just like the Filled Polygon tool, except the shape is hollow **(Figure 35)**.

Figure 35. The Polygon tool.

To set the width of a line or border:

You can change the width of a line or border drawn by the paint window's Line, Rectangle, Arc, Ellipse, and Polygon tools.

1. In the paint tool palette, click a line style in the Line Width Selector **(Figure 36)**. Click the dotted line item in the selector to draw filled shapes with no border. The bottom selection lets you use a custom line thickness. *(See Tip below)*
2. In the paint tool palette, select one of Director's shape tools (either the Line, Rectangle, Arc, Ellipse, or Polygon tool). When you draw with the tool, it will use the line thickness you just selected.

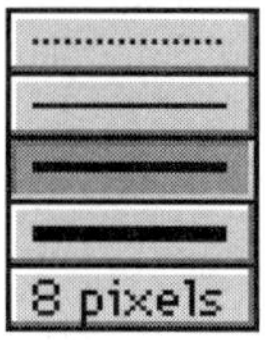

Figure 36. The Line Width Selector.

✔ Tip

- To create a custom line width, choose Preferences from the File menu, and select Paint from the pop-up menu. Use the scroll bar at the center of the dialog box to set the line thickness **(Figures 37–38)**. This value will be used when you choose the custom selection in the Line Width Selector.

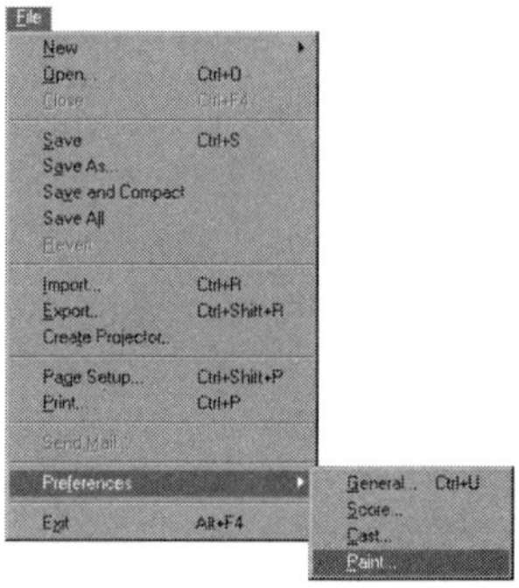

Figure 37. Choose **Preferences** from the **File** menu and select **Paint** from the pop-up menu.

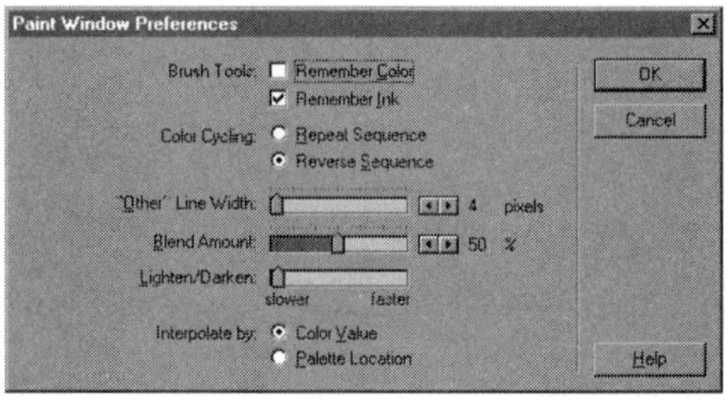

Figure 38. In the **Paint Window Preferences** dialog box, use the scroll bar at the center to set the custom line width.

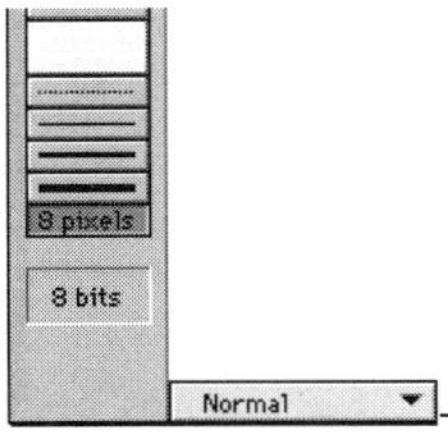

Figure 39. The Ink selector is located at the bottom-left side of the paint window.

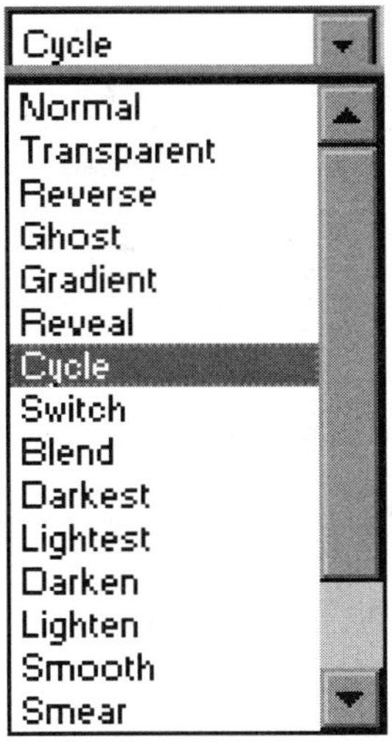

Figure 40. Click and hold the Ink selector to display the **Ink** pop-up menu.

INK EFFECTS

Director features a wide variety of **Ink effects** that can be applied to the artwork you create in the paint window (some of the effects include Reverse, Transparent, Smooth, Smear, Darken, and Lighten). These effects are applied with a specific paint tool (such as the Paint Bucket or Paint Brush). Director remembers which Ink effect you select for a specific tool to paint with.

To choose an Ink effect:

1. In Director's paint window, select the tool in the paint tool palette that you wish to apply an Ink effect with (for instance, the Paint Brush or Air Brush).
2. Click and hold the Ink selector at the bottom-left side of the paint window. The Ink pop-up menu appears **(Figures 39–40)**.
3. From the pop-up menu, choose the Ink effect that you wish to use with the selected paint tool and release the mouse button. *(See the following pages for a description of the various Ink effects available)*

Note: You can apply Ink effects to sprites via the score window. This is different from using Ink effects in the paint window, where you are actually modifying the original cast members. Applying Ink effects through the score only affects the cast members' sprites, and can create a very different visual effect. *(See page 61–63 about using Ink effects in the score window)*

Normal

Normal is the default ink setting. This ink is simply the current foreground color, and any selected pattern.

Transparent

Transparent ink makes the background color used in patterns transparent. When you paint with Transparent ink, you can see any artwork behind the pattern.

Reverse

Any color that you paint over using Reverse ink changes to its "mirror" color at the opposite end of the color palette. For example, a color ten spaces from the top of the palette changes to the color ten spaces from the bottom of the palette.

Ghost

Ghost ink paints with the current background color.

Gradient

Gradient allows you to paint with a blend of colors, ranging from the current foreground color to the current gradient destination color. The gradient options are set in the Gradient Settings dialog box.

Reveal

Reveal ink makes use of the previous cast member. As you paint with reveal ink, you uncover the previous cast member in its original foreground color.

Cycle

As you paint with Cycle ink, the color cycles through all the colors in the color palette between the current foreground color and destination color. Choose black and white for the foreground and destination colors to cycle through the entire color palette.

Switch

As you paint with Switch ink, any pixels in the current foreground color that you paint over are changed into the Gradient destination color.

Blend

Blend is a transparent ink. As you paint over your artwork, it will still be visible, but its colors are blended with the current foreground color. You can set the percentage of blend in the Paint Window Preferences dialog box.

Darkest

As you paint over an image with Darkest ink, Director compares the level of darkness of the foreground color to the pixels that you are painting over. If the foreground color is darker, the pixels of the image are replaced with its color.

Lightest

As you paint over an image with Lightest ink, Director replaces the pixels with the foreground color where the foreground color is lighter than the pixels of the image.

Darken

Darken ink reduces the brightness of artwork as you paint over it. You can set the rate of this Ink effect in the Paint Window Preferences dialog box.

Lighten

Lighten ink increases the brightness of artwork as you paint over it.

Smooth

Smooth ink blurs artwork as you paint over it. It is useful for smoothing out jagged edges. It only has an effect on existing artwork.

Smear

Smear ink causes the paint of your artwork to spread or smear as you drag the Paint Brush across it. The smear occurs in the direction you drag the Paint Brush.

Smudge

Similar to Smear ink, except the colors fade faster as they are smudged.

Spread

Spread ink works with the Paint Brush. As you drag the brush across your artwork, whatever image is originally under the brush is picked up and becomes the new shape for the Paint Brush.

Clipboard

Uses the contents of the clipboard as the pattern for your brush.

COLORS, PATTERNS, AND GRADIENTS

Color Basics

There are three color specifications that you can set in the paint window which are used in coloring your cast member artwork. **Foreground** color is Director's primary color specification: Whatever color is selected as your foreground color will be used to color all the artwork you create with Director's paint tools (for instance, the Paint Brush, the Air Brush, and the Pencil). The foreground color is also used to color solid patterns, and used as the primary color in multicolored patterns. Director's **Background** color, on the other hand, is used as the secondary color in multicolored patterns. Finally, the **Gradient destination** color is used in conjunction with the foreground color to create a blended color spectrum.

The current foreground color, background and gradient destination colors, and the pattern selector are all displayed in the paint tool palette **(Figure 41)**.

Note: The colors available to you in the paint window depend on the color depth setting of your movie, and the current color palette. *(See the Color in Director chapter on pages 120-122 for details on color depth and the current palette)*

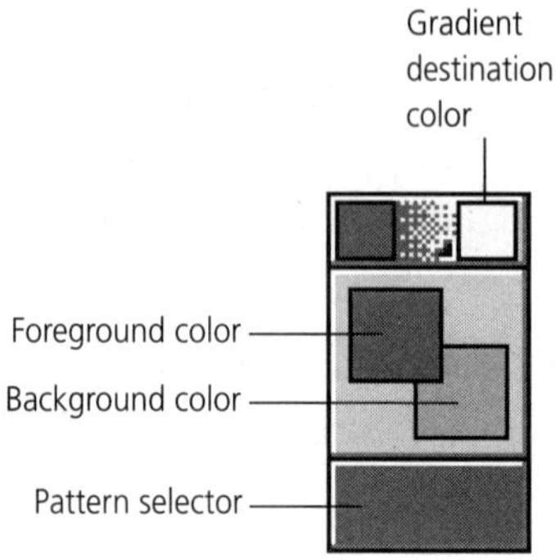

Figure 41. The three color specifications and the Pattern selector are displayed in the paint tool palette.

To choose the foreground color:

1. Click and hold the Foreground color chip in the paint tool palette. A pop-up color palette appears **(Figure 42)**.
2. Drag to the desired color and release the mouse button. The highlighted color becomes the new foreground color.

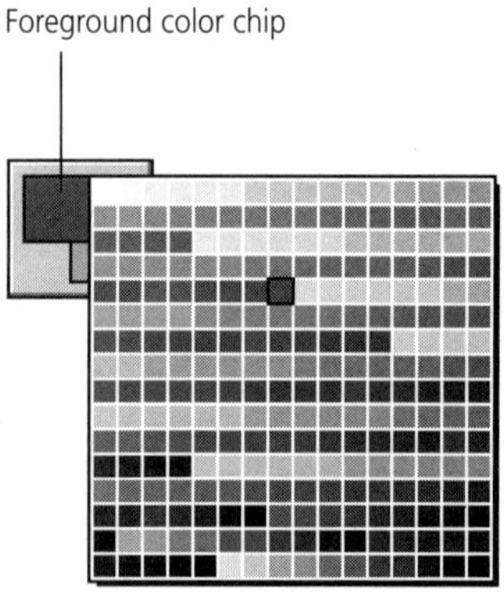

Figure 42. Click and hold the Foreground color chip until the pop-up color palette appears.

✔ **Tip**

- Double-click the Foreground or Background color chip to open the Color Palettes window.

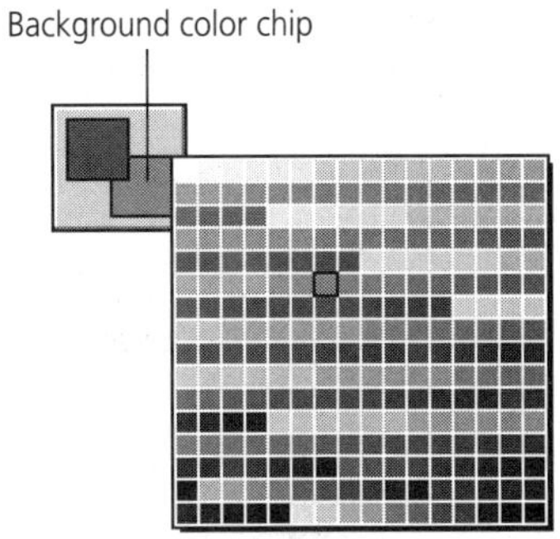

Figure 43. Click and hold the Background color chip until the pop-up color palette appears.

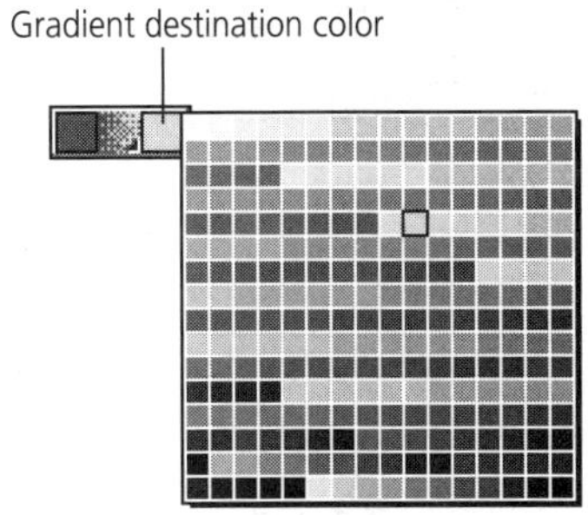

Figure 44. Click and hold the Gradient destination color until a pop-up color palette appears.

Figure 45. The Eyedropper tool

Figure 46. Place the Eyedropper over the particular color that you wish to switch and click the mouse.

Figure 47. Click the **Switch Colors** button in the Effects toolbar in the paint window.

To choose the background color:

1. Click and hold the Background color chip in the paint tool palette. A pop-up color palette appears **(Figure 43)**.
2. Drag to the desired color and release the mouse button.

To choose the Gradient destination color:

1. In the paint tool palette, click and hold the Gradient destination color. A pop-up color palette appears **(Figure 44)**.
2. Drag to the desired color and release the mouse button.

To switch a particular color in a cast member:

Director makes it easy to isolate a particular color in a cast member and then switch that color with any color of your choice.

1. Make sure that your cast member is displayed in Director's paint window.
2. Click the Eyedropper in the tool palette **(Figure 45)**.
3. Move the Eyedropper over the particular color in your cast member that you wish to switch and click the mouse **(Figure 46)**. The color the Eyedropper "picks up" becomes the new foreground color.
4. In the paint tool palette, click and hold the Gradient destination color. A pop-up color palette appears.
5. Drag the pointer to the new color you wish to switch to.
6. Use the Marquee or Lasso tool to select the portion of your image where the color switch should take place.
7. Click the Switch Colors button in the Effects toolbar **(Figure 47)**.

Switch a Color in a Cast Member

To choose a pattern:

You can use some of Director's paint tools (such as the Paint Bucket, Paint Brush, and Air Brush) to paint with a specific pattern instead of with a solid color.

1. Click and hold the Pattern chip in the paint tool palette. A pop-up pattern palette appears **(Figure 48)**.
2. Drag to the desired pattern and release the mouse button.

✔ **Tip**

- Double-click the Pattern chip to open the Pattern Settings dialog box, where you can edit patterns or select a different pattern palette to work with. There are four different pattern palettes you can choose from.

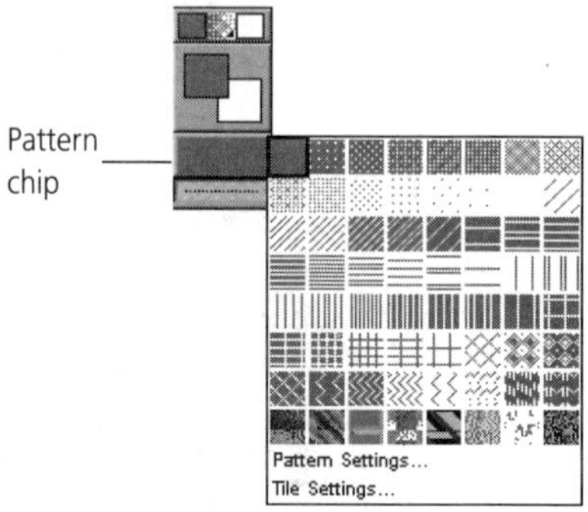

Figure 48. Click and hold the Pattern chip to display the pop-up **Pattern** palette.

To edit or create a pattern:

1. With Director's paint window open, click and hold the Pattern chip and select Pattern Settings at the bottom of the pop-up palette.
2. In the Pattern Settings dialog box, click the pop-up menu and select the Custom menu item **(Figure 49)**. Director features four sets of patterns: The custom set can be edited, while the other three sets—Grays, Standard and QuickDraw—are always available to you and cannot be changed.
3. Click a custom pattern that you wish to edit. An enlarged version of the selected pattern appears in the pattern edit box **(Figure 50)**.
4. In the pattern edit box, click any open space to place a black pixel in the pattern. Click an existing pixel to make it white.
5. Click the directional arrows to move the pattern shape up, down, and sideways.
6. When you're happy with your custom pattern, click OK, and Director adds it to its custom pattern library.

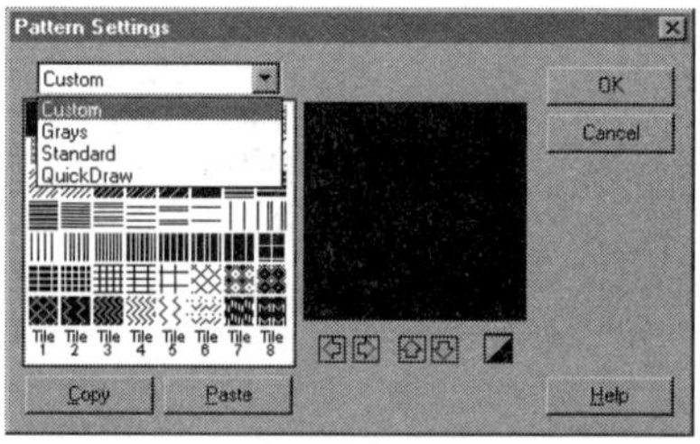

Figure 49. In the **Pattern Settings** dialog box, click the pop-up menu and select the Custom menu item.

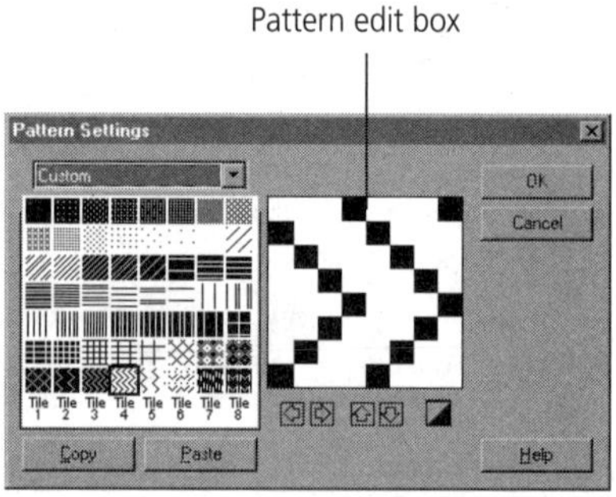

Figure 50. Click the custom pattern that you wish to edit. An enlarged version of the pattern appears in the pattern edit box.

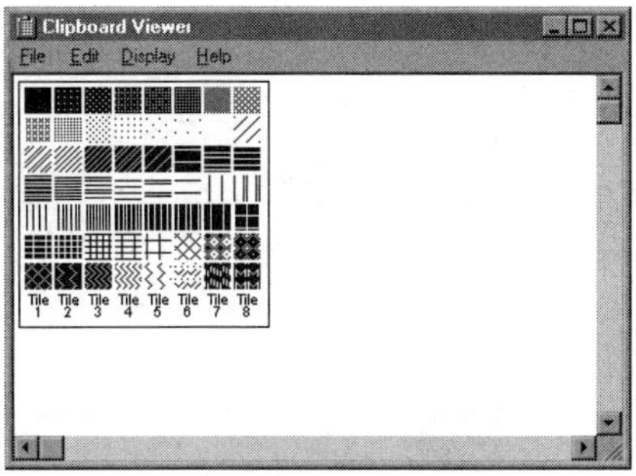

Figure 51. Your custom patterns can be stored in the Windows Clipboard Viewer.

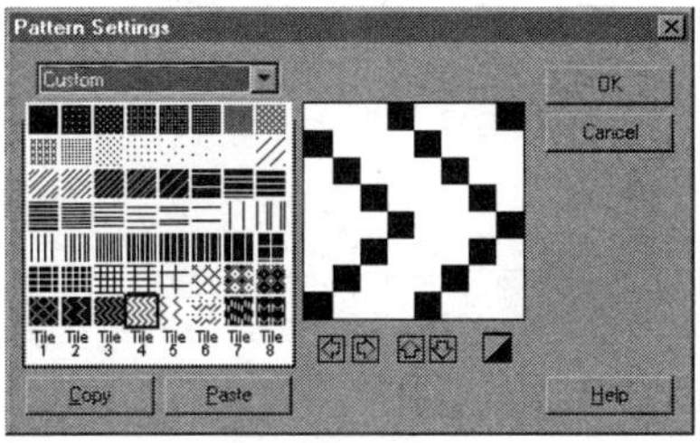

Figure 52. Click the **Copy** button in the **Pattern Settings** dialog box.

To copy your custom pattern library to the Clipboard Viewer:

You can store sets of custom patterns by copying them to and from the Windows Clipboard Viewer **(Figure 51)**.

1. Click the Copy button in the Pattern Settings dialog box **(Figure 52)**; this stores the pattern information in the Clipboard.
2. Click Cancel.
3. Open the Windows Clipboard Viewer.
4. Choose Save As from the File menu in the Clipboard Viewer to save your custom patterns.

To reinstall stored patterns from the Clipboard Viewer:

1. Open the Clipboard Viewer and open the file that contains the desired patterns.
2. Return to Director's paint window, open the Pattern Settings dialog box, and click the Paste button to install the copied pattern set.

✔ Tips

- Even though you can't directly edit the patterns contained in Director's Grays, Standards, and QuickDraw patterns, you can copy those predefined patterns into Director's Custom set, and edit them from there. From the Pattern Settings dialog box, use the pattern pop-up menu to select one of Director's noneditable pattern sets, and then click the Copy button. Choose the Custom pattern set from the pattern pop-up menu and click the Paste button.
- Director lets you "pick up" a pattern displayed in its paint window, and edit it in the Pattern Settings dialog box. To do so, open the Pattern Settings dialog box and click on your artwork in the paint window.

To create a gradient:

You can paint your bitmap artwork with a **gradient**, which is a blend of colors that you define. Setting up a gradient is simple: You set the foreground color, which is the color that Director begins the blend with, and choose the Gradient destination color, which is the color that the foreground color will be blended through. Director can then automatically blend the two colors to display a range of colors in between **(Figure 53)**. A good use of a gradient would be to create a sunset, where colors blend from red to yellow.

Figure 53. A sample gradient.

Gradient colors can be used with a number of Director's paint tools, including the Paint Brush, Paint Bucket, Ellipse, Rectangle, and Polygon tools.

1. In Director's paint window, select the painting tool that you wish to apply the gradient color to (for instance, the Paint Brush or Paint Bucket).
2. Click the Foreground color chip in the paint window and select a color from the pop-up color palette **(Figure 54)**. This will be the color that the gradient begins with.

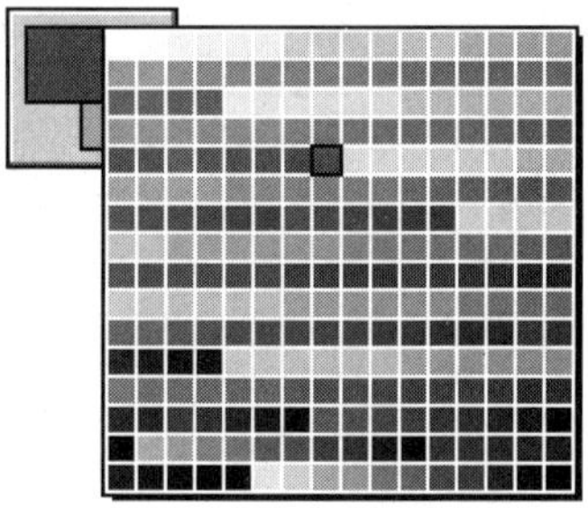

Figure 54. Click the Foreground color chip and select a color to begin the gradient with.

3. Click the Gradient destination color and choose a color from the pop-up color palette. This is the color that your gradient will blend to **(Figure 55)**.

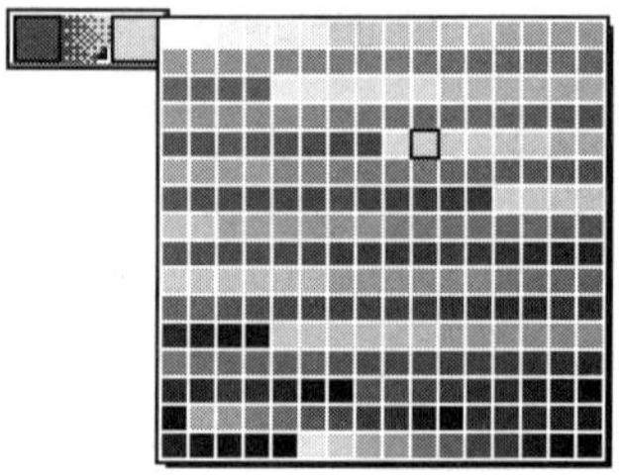

Figure 55. Click the Gradient destination color, and choose the color that your gradient will blend to.

4. Click the Ink selector in the paint window, and choose Gradient from the pop-up menu **(Figure 56)**. The paint tool that you selected in step 1 will now paint with a gradient rather than a solid color.

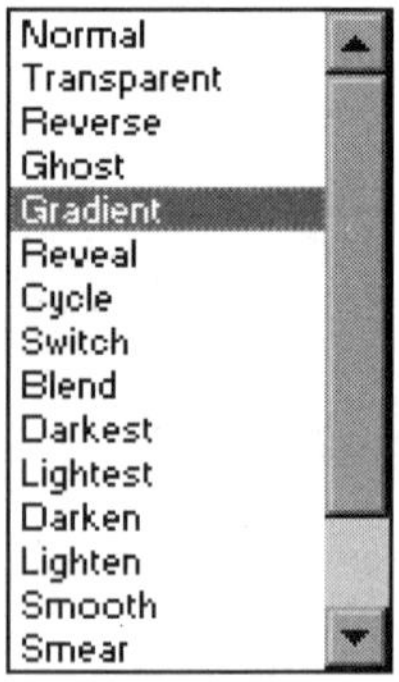

Figure 56. Click the Ink Selector and choose **Gradient** from the pop-up menu.

✔ **Tip**

- To stop painting with a gradient, simply choose the Normal Ink effect from the Ink pop-up menu.

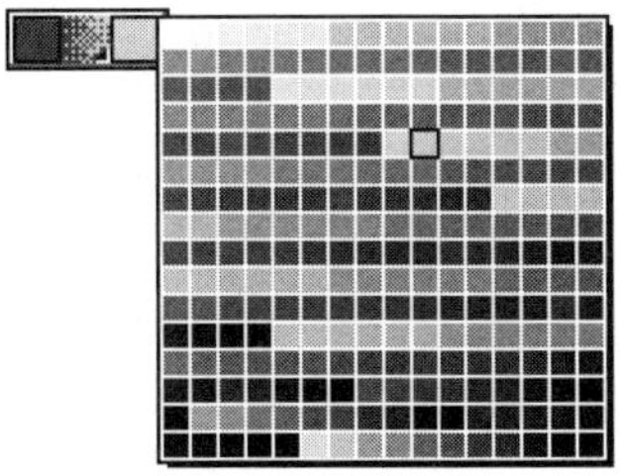

Figure 57. Double-click the Gradient destination color to open the **Gradient Settings** dialog box.

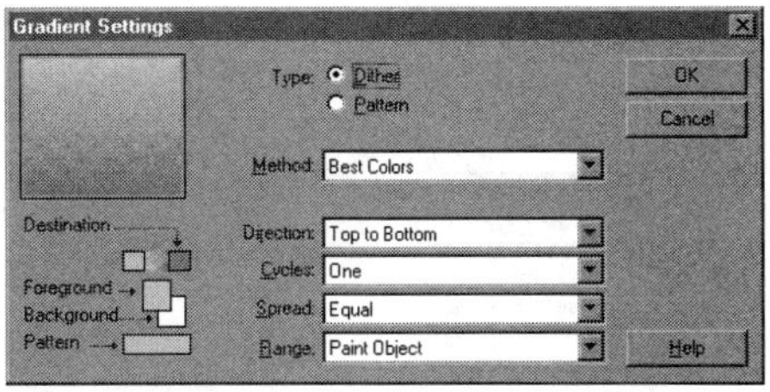

Figure 58. The **Gradient Settings** dialog box.

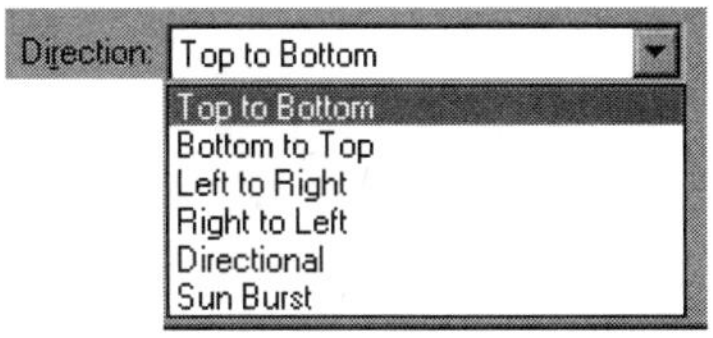

Figure 59. The **Direction** pop-up menu.

Figure 60. A Top to Bottom gradient.

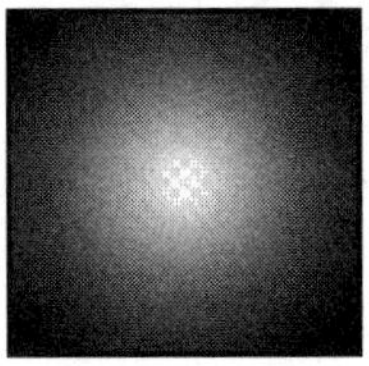

Figure 61. A Sun Burst gradient.

To change gradient settings:

Director allows you to customize a color gradient. For instance, you can control the direction in which the gradient fills a given area (from the top, the bottom, and so on), and the "spread" of the gradient (whether the colors are spread evenly, or concentrated in certain areas).

1. In the paint window, double-click the Gradient destination color to open the Gradient Settings dialog box **(Figure 57)**.
2. In the Gradient Settings dialog box, use the Foreground color chip and Gradient destination color to select the colors used to create your gradient **(Figure 58)**.
3. Use the dialog box's pop-up menus to fine-tune the characteristics of your gradient. Gradient options are described below:

Direction

Use the Direction pop-up menu to control the direction in which your gradient fills a particular area **(Figure 59)**. The directional possibilities include straightforward selections such as **Top to Bottom (Figure 60)** and **Bottom to Top**, as well as two unique options: **Directional** allows you to set a custom direction for the gradient with whatever paint tool you are using to apply the gradient. For instance, if you are using the Paint Bucket to fill an area with a gradient, a directional line appears as soon as you click the Paint Bucket in the paint window. Move the directional line in the desired direction, and click to begin your gradient fill.

Sun Burst begins a gradient at the outer edges of an area, and moves toward the center in concentric circles **(Figure 61)**.

Cycles

Use the Cycles pop-up menu to specify how many times a gradient repeats within an area **(Figure 62)**. You can set the gradient to cycle through its color spectrum up to four times in a given area. You also specify whether the gradient is sharp, meaning the gradient cycles from foreground to destination color, and then again from foreground to destination **(Figure 63)**, or smooth **(Figure 64)**, which makes the gradient cycle from foreground to destination color, and then in the next cycle, from the destination color to the foreground color.

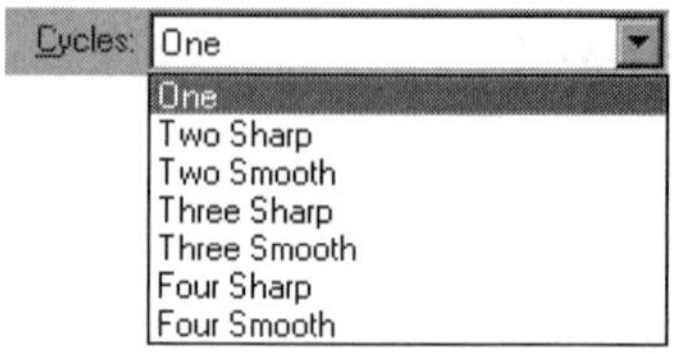

Figure 62. The **Cycles** pop-up menu.

Method

Use the Method pop-up menu together with the Type selector to control how Director blends colors to create its gradient **(Figure 65)**.

Following are the Method selections for the Dither type gradient:

Best Colors ignores the arrangement of colors in the current color palette, and uses only colors that create a continuous blend between your foreground and destination colors, using a dithered pattern.

Adjacent Colors creates the gradient blend by using all the colors in the selected color palette that occur between the foreground and destination colors, even if those in-between colors do not create a smooth blend.

Two Colors blends only the foreground and destination colors with a dithered pattern.

One Color simply fades the foreground color with a dithered pattern.

Standard Colors blends the foreground and destination colors, ignoring the colors between them and adds several blended colors having a dithered pattern.

Multi Colors—similar to Standard Colors, but the dithered pattern is randomized.

Figure 63. A Two Sharp gradient.

Figure 64. A Two Smooth gradient.

Figure 65. The **Method** pop-up menu and **Type** selector.

Following are the Method selections for the Pattern type gradient:

Best Colors ignores the arrangement of colors in the palette you're using, and uses only colors that create a continuous blend between your foreground and destination colors. The gradient is drawn with whatever pattern has been selected. The **Transparent** version of this option makes any white pixels in this blend transparent.

Adjacent Colors creates the gradient blend by using all the colors in the selected palette that occur between the gradient's foreground and destination colors, even if those in-between colors do not create a smooth blend. The **Transparent** version of this option makes any white pixels in this blend transparent

Spread

Use the Spread pop-up menu to control how Director distributes the colors of your gradient within an area **(Figure 66)**. **Equal** spaces the gradient's colors evenly throughout an area, while **More Foreground (Figure 67)** or **More Destination (Figure 68)** increases the amount of foreground or destination color in a gradient. **More Middle** devotes more space to the gradient's middle colors.

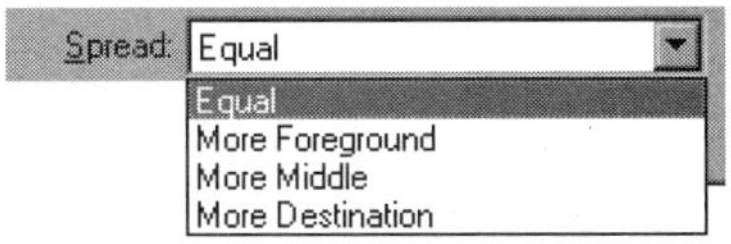

Figure 66. The **Spread** pop-up menu.

Figure 67. A More Foreground gradient.

Figure 68. A More Destination gradient.

Range

Use the Range pop-up menu to decide whether the full range of blended colors in your gradient should be applied over a cast member, a paint object, or over the entire paint window **(Figure 69)**. Choosing **Paint Object** ensures that the full range of the gradient's colors will be seen in any sized brush stroke or fill area **(Figure 70)**, while the full range of colors may not be seen with the **Cast Member** or **Window** options **(Figure 71)**.

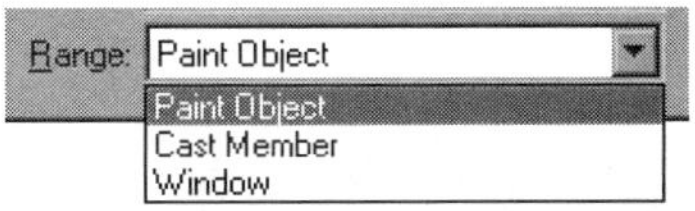

Figure 69. The **Range** pop-up menu.

Figure 70. A Paint Object gradient.

Figure 71. A Window gradient.

TILES AND BRUSH SHAPES

Tiles are similar to patterns in that you can apply them as textures or "fillers" to artwork created in Director. The difference between a tile and a pattern is that the tile is created from an existing cast member in your movie. For instance, if you have a cast member of a brick, you can turn it into a tile that can be used to paint a brick wall. Since tiles are based on an existing cast member, they can feature more than the simple foreground/background color combination that limits traditional patterns. A tile features as many colors as the cast member it's based on.

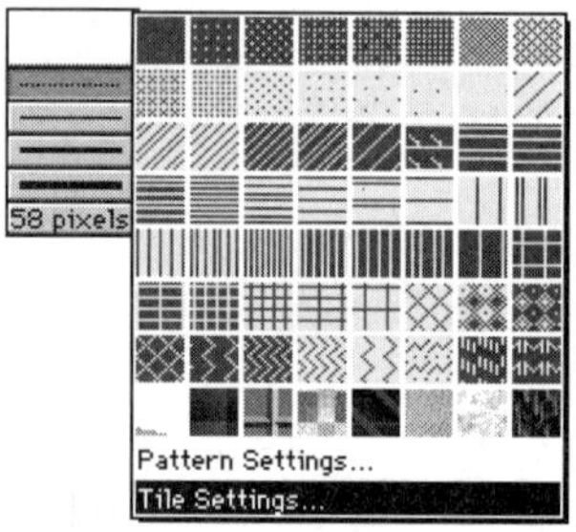

Figure 72. Choose **Tile Settings** from the **Pattern** pop-up menu.

To create a tile from a cast member:

1. Make sure that the cast member you wish to base your tile on has already been placed in a cast window. Creating the tile will have no effect on the cast member.
2. In the paint window, click and hold the Pattern chip. Choose Tile Settings from the Pattern pop-up menu **(Figure 72)**.
3. In the Tile Settings dialog box, click the Cast member radio button to select it **(Figure 73)**. The Cast member radio button will be dimmed if your Director movie has no color cast members. You can also choose from a set of built in tiles by clicking the Built-in radio button. Cast members must be saved in at least two bits of color (four colors total) to be turned into a tile.
4. Click the left and right arrows next to the Cast member radio button to cycle through the cast members and choose the particular cast member you wish to turn into a tile. All the cast members appear in the left side of the Tiles dialog box. The right side of the box displays what the particular cast member will look like in tiled form.

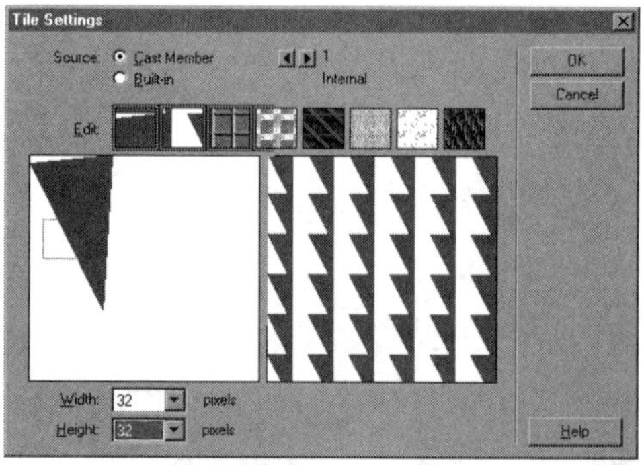

Figure 73. Click the **Cast Member** radio button in the **Tile Settings** dialog box.

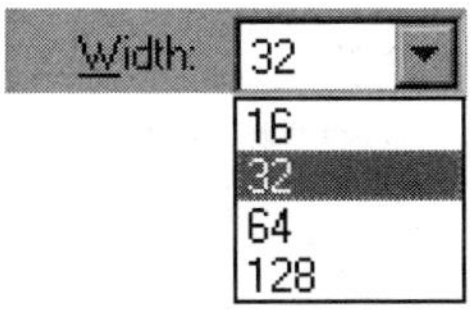

Figure 74. The **Width** pop-up menu.

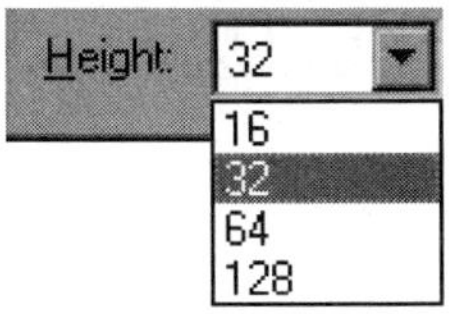

Figure 75. The **Height** pop-up menu.

5. Use the Width and Height pop-up menus to determine the pixel dimensions that the cast member should conform to as a tile **(Figures 74–75)**. The range of dimensions goes from 16 by 16 to 128 by 128 pixels.
6. Drag the dotted border on the left side of the Tile Settings dialog box to encompass the portion of the cast member you wish to turn into a tile.
7. Click OK to create a new tile based on the selected cast member. Your new tile will now be displayed at the bottom of the paint window's Pattern palette, which is displayed by clicking the Pattern selector chip.

To choose a Paint Brush shape:

Director's Paint Brush offers five different shapes—labeled Brush 1 through Brush 5—you can choose from each time you select the brush tool. You can change and customize these brush shapes through Director's Brush Settings dialog box. *(See page 101 for details)*

1. Click the Paint Brush tool in the paint tool palette, and do not release the mouse button. A pop-up menu appears, listing the different brush shapes that you can choose from **(Figure 76)**.
2. Drag to select the brush shape you wish to use. Director will now paint with this particular brush shape.

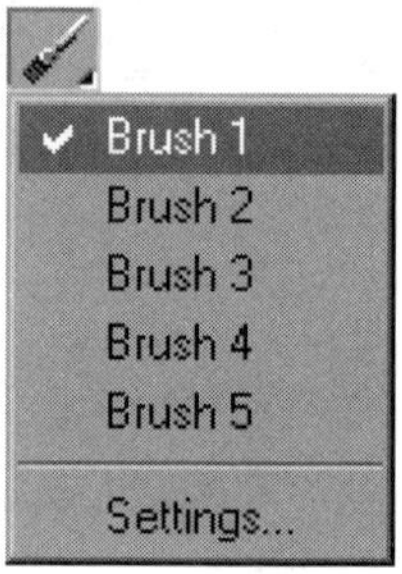

Figure 76. Click and hold the Paint Brush tool in the paint tool palette to display the pop-up menu.

Optional

Only five brush shapes can be selected from the brush's pop-up menu, while Director can actually store a much wider variety of shapes. You can assign different shapes (probably ones that you have customized yourself) to the pop-up menu, replacing the default styles that are initially assigned. To do so, first follow steps 1 and 2 above to select a brush shape that you wish to replace from the pop-up menu.

3. Once you've selected a brush shape (Brush 1 through Brush 5), click the Paint Brush tool and select Settings from the pop-up menu **(Figure 77)**.
4. In the Brush Settings dialog box, select the new brush shape that you wish to substitute **(Figure 78)**.
5. Click OK and Director will remember to use this new brush shape whenever you select the respective brush number (Brush 1 through Brush 5) from the pop-up menu.

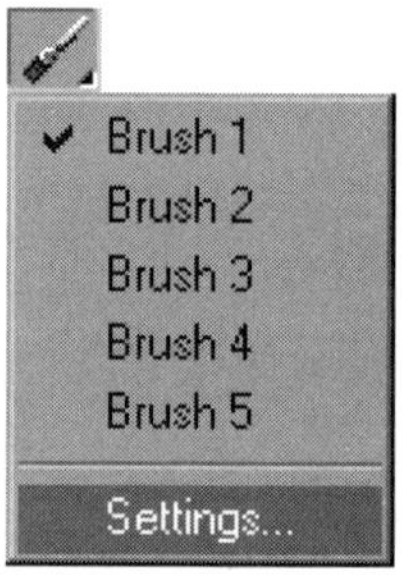

Figure 77. Click the Paint Brush tool and select **Settings** from the pop-up menu.

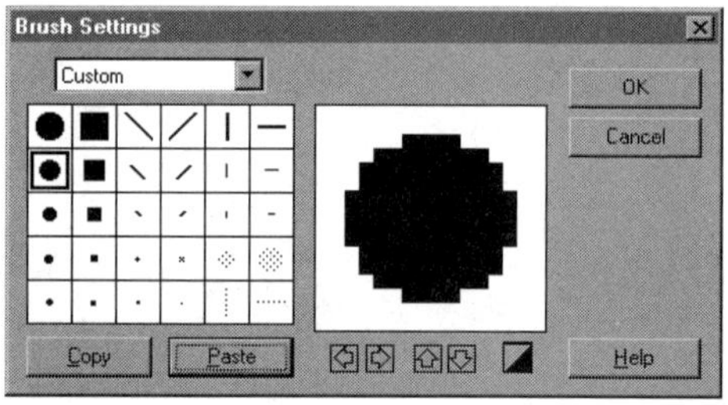

Figure 78. In the **Brush Settings** dialog box, select a new brush shape to use.

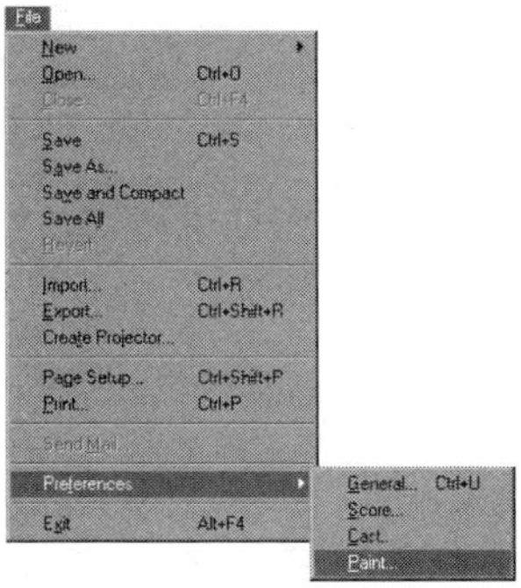

Figure 79. Choose **Preferences** from the **File** menu and select **Paint** from the pop-up menu.

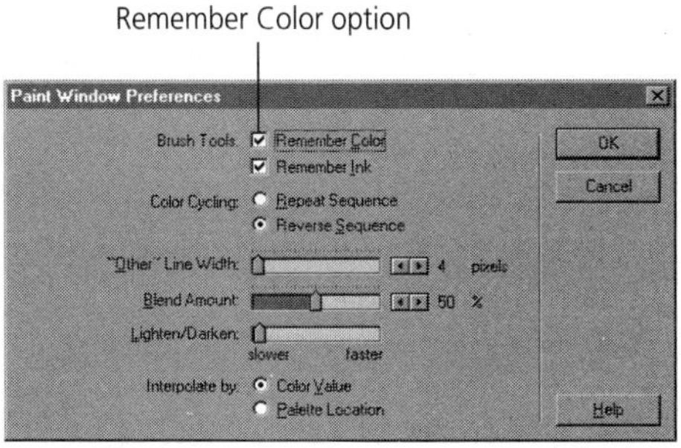

Figure 80. In the **Paint Window Preferences** dialog box, check the **Remember Color** option.

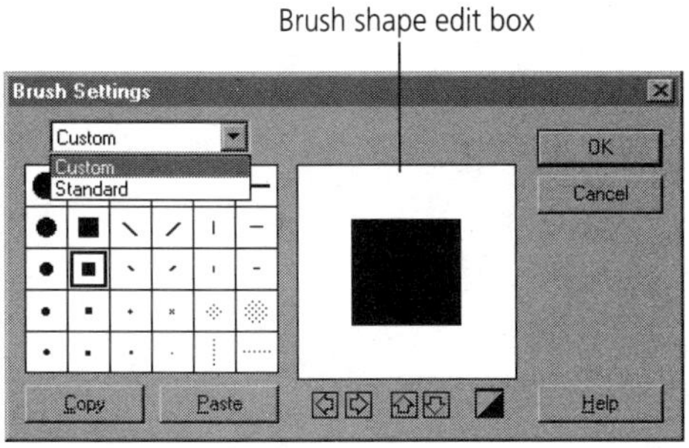

Figure 81. In the **Brush Settings** dialog box, click the pop-up menu and select the Custom menu item.

✔ Tips

- Double-click the Paint Brush tool to open the Brush Settings dialog box.
- You can tell Director to automatically select a particular color when you paint with a particular brush—for instance, red for Brush 1, green for Brush 2, and so on. To make Director remember the particular color settings you've associated with each brush shape, choose Preferences from the File menu, and select Paint from the pop-up menu **(Figure 79)**. In the Paint Window Preferences dialog box, check the Remember Color option **(Figure 80)**.

To edit a Paint Brush shape:

While Director features a variety of existing Paint Brush shapes, you can edit them to form your own custom brush styles. Editing is a matter of rearranging the individual pixels that make up the brush's shape.

1. With Director's paint window open, double-click the Paint Brush tool.
2. In the Brush Settings dialog box, click the pop-up menu and select the Custom menu item **(Figure 81)**. Director recognizes two varieties of brush shapes: Standard shapes, which are always available to you and cannot be changed, and Custom shapes, which you can edit.
3. Click the custom brush shape that you wish to edit. An enlarged version of the selected brush appears in the brush shape edit box.
4. In the brush shape edit box, click any open space to place a new pixel in the brush. Click on a pixel to erase it.

5. Click the directional arrows in the Brush Settings dialog box to move the brush shape up, down, and sideways.
6. When you're happy with your new brush design, click OK, and Director adds the new brush to its custom brush library.

✔ **Tips**

- You can store and retrieve sets of custom brush shapes by copying them to and from the Windows Clipboard Viewer **(Figure 82)**. To store your custom brush set, first click the Copy button in the Brush Settings dialog box; this stores the brush information in the Clipboard. Now leave the dialog box (click Cancel), open the Windows Clipboard Viewer, and choose Save As under the File menu to save the brush shapes. To reinstall these stored brushes, open the Clipboard Viewer, and open the file that contains the desired brush set. Return to Director's paint window, open the Brush Settings dialog box, and click the Paste button to install the copied brush set.
- Director lets you "pick up" any pattern displayed in the paint window and use it as a brush shape. To do so, open the Brush Settings dialog box, and click any pattern outside the dialog box to pick it up.

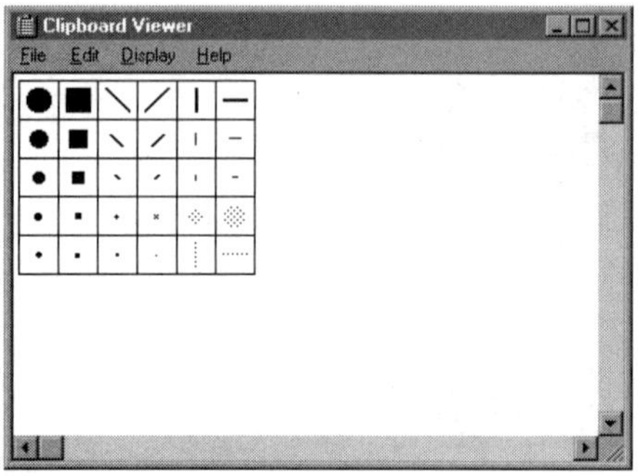

Figure 82. You can store and retrieve your custom brush shapes from the Windows Clipboard Viewer.

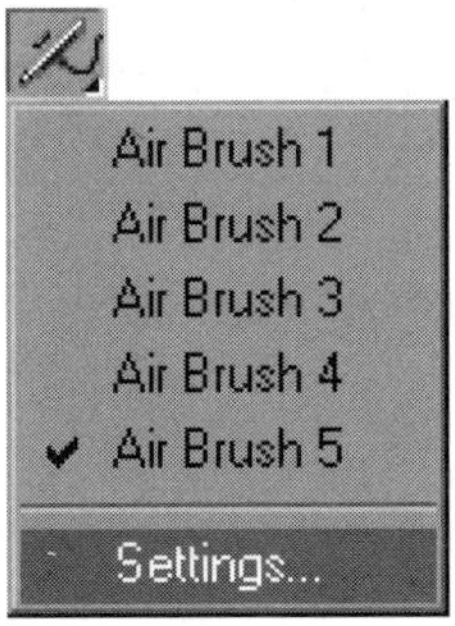

Figure 83. Click and hold the Air Brush tool and select **Settings** from the pop-up menu.

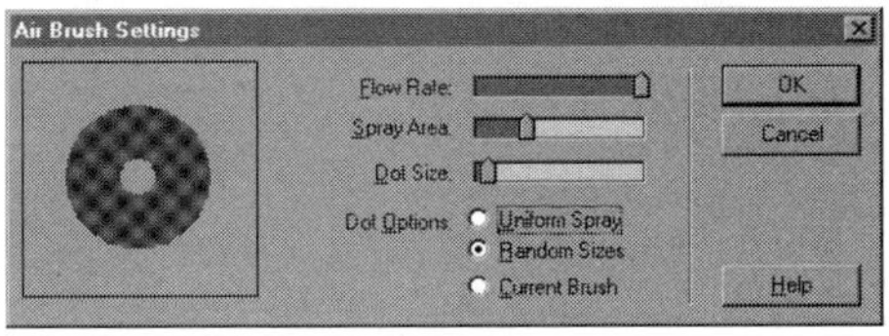

Figure 84. In the **Air Brush Settings** dialog box, drag the Flow Rate, Spray Area, and Dot Size scroll bars to adjust the Air Brush.

Figure 85. The Uniform Spray Air Brush setting.

Figure 86. The Random Sizes Air Brush setting.

Figure 87. The Current Brush setting of the Air Brush.

To adjust the Air Brush spray pattern:

Director lets you adjust the size of the Air brush's spray area, the size of the ink dots it sprays into that area, and the speed at which it sprays them.

1. With Director's paint window open, click and hold the Air Brush tool and select Settings from the pop-up menu that appears **(Figure 83)**.
2. In the Air Brush Settings dialog box, drag the Flow Rate, Spray Area, and Dot Size scroll bars to adjust the speed at which it sprays the dots, the size of the Air Brush's spray area, and the size of the dots it sprays into the area **(Figure 84)**. As you adjust the scroll bar values, Director displays a preview of how your new settings will affect the Air Brush tool. The gray circle indicates the current size of the Air Brush's spray area, while the white circle inside represents the size of the dots themselves.
3. Click either the Uniform Spray, Random Sizes, or Current Brush radio buttons to indicate how the Air Brush should spray. With the Uniform Spray setting, your Air Brush sprays dots of identical size, while the Random Sizes setting randomly varies the size of dots sprayed. The Current Brush settings causes the Air Brush to spray in the shape that's currently selected for the Paint Brush tool **(Figures 85–87)**.
4. Click OK so that your new Air Brush settings take effect.

To choose an Air Brush shape:

Director remembers five different Air Brush settings—labeled Air Brush 1 through Air Brush 5—for you to choose from when you select the Air Brush tool. You can change and customize these settings through the Air Brush Settings dialog box.

1. Click and hold the Air Brush tool in the paint tool palette. A pop-up menu appears **(Figure 88)**, listing the different brush settings that you can choose from.

2. Drag to the setting you wish to use, and release the mouse button. Director will now paint with this particular Air Brush setting.

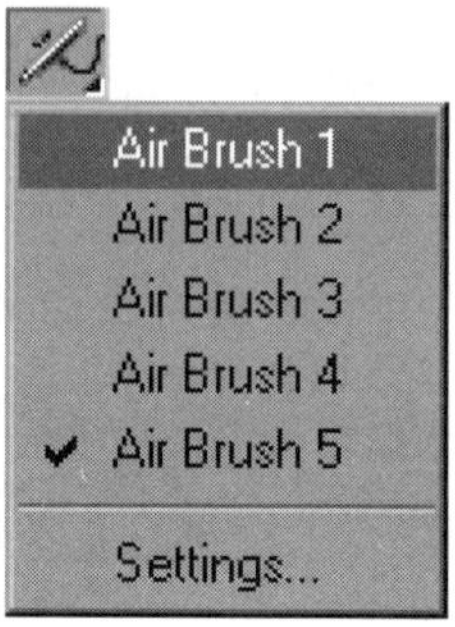

Figure 88. Click and hold the Air Brush tool in the paint tool palette to display the pop-up menu.

Optional

You can replace each of the five Air Brush settings with your own custom ones. To do so, first follow steps 1 and 2 above to select the Air Brush setting that you wish to customize.

3. Double-click the Air Brush tool.

4. In the Air Brush Settings dialog box, change the brush's Flow Rate, Spray Area, and Dot Size settings **(Figure 89)** to the new desired values. *(See page 103 for more about these settings)*

5. Click OK, and Director will remember to use these new settings whenever you select the same brush setting from the Air Brush tool's pop-up menu.

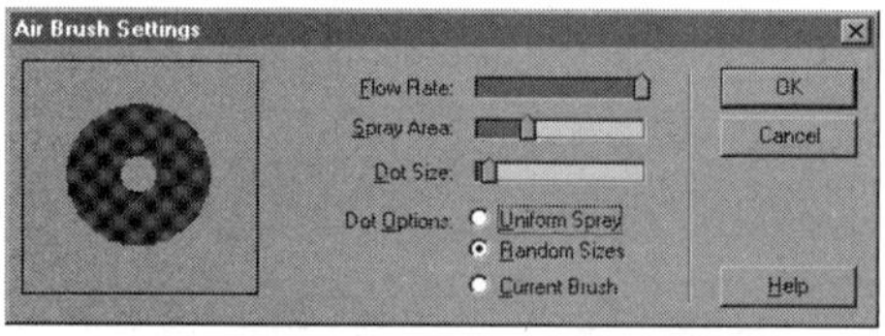

Figure 89. In the **Air Brush Settings** dialog box, drag the Flow Rate, Spray Area, and Dot Size scroll bars to adjust the Air Brush.

EFFECTS TOOLBAR

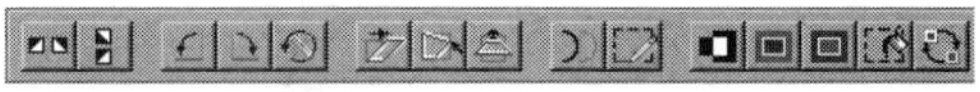

Figure 90. The **Effects** toolbar.

Director's Effects toolbar **(Figure 90)** offers a variety of effects and functions that can be applied to existing artwork. These features include flips and rotations of cast members, edge traces, color switches, and image distortions such as warp and perspective. You can perform an effect on any portion of an image, rather than the whole thing. For most of these effects, you must use Director's Marquee tool, not its Lasso, to make the selection.

Figure 91. Select the artwork that you wish to rotate with the Marquee tool.

To rotate artwork left and right by 90-degrees:

Director lets you rotate entire images or parts of images in 90-degree increments.

1. In Director's paint window, click the Marquee tool and use it to select the artwork that you wish to rotate **(Figure 91)**.
2. Click either Rotate Right or Rotate Left in the Effects toolbar **(Figure 92)** to rotate the selected artwork 90 degrees **(Figures 93–94)**.

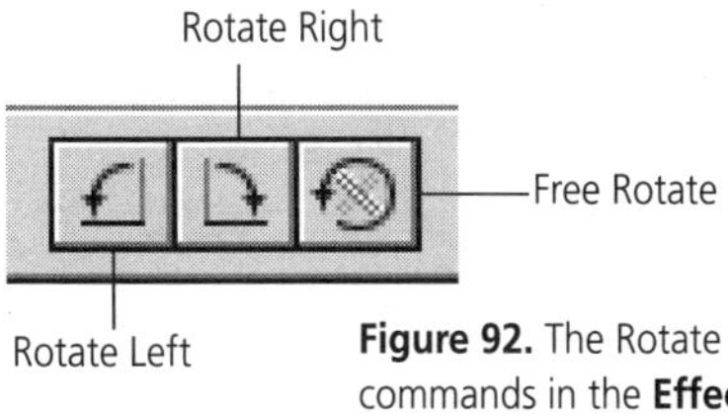

Figure 92. The Rotate commands in the **Effects** toolbar.

Figure 93. The artwork after using **Rotate Right**.

Figure 94. The artwork after using **Rotate Left**.

To freely rotate artwork in 1-degree increments:

The Free Rotate command lets you rotate artwork in 1-degree increments.

1. In Director's paint window, click the Marquee tool and use it to select the artwork that you wish to rotate.
2. Click Free Rotate in the Effects toolbar. Notice that Director places little "handles" at each corner of your selection.
3. Drag one of the handles to rotate your art selection in 1-degree increments **(Figure 95)**.

Figure 95. Using **Free Rotate**, drag one of the handles to rotate your art selection in 1-degree increments.

To flip artwork horizontally or vertically:

Director lets you "flip" an artwork selection to create a mirror-image **(Figure 96)**.

1. In Director's paint window, click the Marquee tool and use it to select the artwork that you wish to flip.
2. Click either Flip Horizontal or Flip Vertical in Director's Effects toolbar **(Figure 97)**.

Figure 96. You can "flip" an artwork selection to create a mirror-image.

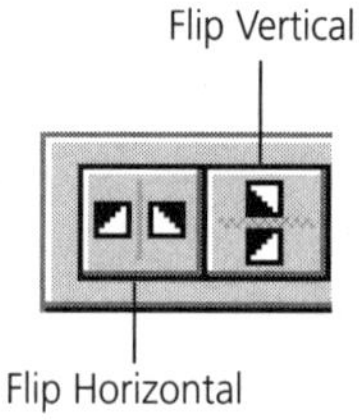

Figure 97. Click either **Flip Horizontal** or **Flip Vertical** in the **Effects** toolbar.

To distort artwork:

You can alter the shape and dimensional appearance of artwork using Director's Skew, Warp, and Perspective commands **(Figures 98–102)**. Skew slants the artwork while maintaining a parallelogram shape; Warp allows you to bend and stretch artwork; and Perspective makes the artwork seem as if it is being viewed from a particular vantage point, with one part of the image appearing to be closer than the other.

1. In the paint window, click the Marquee tool, and use it to select the artwork that you wish to alter.
2. Choose Skew, Warp, or Perspective from Director's Effects toolbar. Notice that Director places little "handles" at each corner of your selection.
3. Drag one of the handles to apply the desired effect to the artwork.

✔ Tip

- You may want to make a copy of your artwork before distorting it. To do so, select the image with the Marquee tool, move the mouse pointer within the selection marquee, hold down the Alt key, and drag to copy the artwork to a new location.

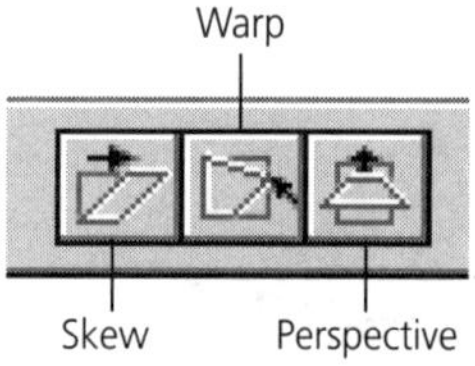

Figure 98. Skew, Warp, and **Perspective** in the **Effects** toolbar.

Figure 99. Unaltered artwork.

Figure 100. The Skew effect.

Figure 101. The Warp effect.

Figure 102. The Perspective effect.

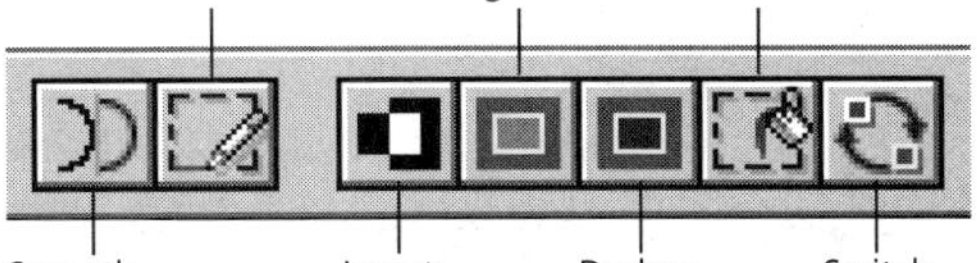

Figure 103. The **Effects** toolbar.

Figure 104. The **Smooth** command softens the edges of your artwork.

Figure 105. The **Trace Edges** command creates an outline around the edges of your selected artwork.

Figure 106. The **Invert Color** effect reverses the colors of an image.

To apply other special effects to artwork:

Smooth, Trace Edges, Invert Colors, Lighten, Darken, Fill, and Switch Colors are additional commands in the Effects toolbar that you can apply to your artwork.

1. In Director's paint window, click the Marquee or Lasso tool, and use it to select the artwork that you wish to affect (note that you cannot use the Lasso tool with the Trace Edges command).
2. Choose Smooth, Trace Edges, Invert Colors, Lighten, Darken, Fill, or Switch Colors from Director's Effects toolbar **(Figure 103)**.

The **Smooth** command softens the edges of your artwork **(Figure 104)** by adding pixels that blend the colors between edges.

The **Trace Edges** effect creates an outline around the edges of the artwork you've selected **(Figure 105)**. Select Trace Edges repeatedly to increase the number of outlines in the trace.

The **Invert Color** effect reverses all the colors in the selected artwork. If the artwork is black and white, white pixels turn to black, and vice versa, which creates a negative image **(Figure 106)**. If the artwork uses more than two colors, Director reverses the order in which the colors are displayed. The artwork's color palette is effectively flipped, so that the colors that were assigned to the top of the palette are placed at its bottom. *(See the Color in Director chapter on page 122 for details on palettes)*

The **Lighten** and **Darken** commands respectively increase and decrease the brightness of the selected artwork.

The **Fill** command fills the selected area in the paint window with the foreground color and pattern.

Switch Colors *(See page 91)*

To create a sequence of in-between images of an artwork selection:

Director's **Auto Distort** command creates a number of in-between images for artwork that you transform with the Skew, Warp, Perspective, or the Rotate commands. Let's say you use the Free Rotate command to rotate a picture by 350 degrees—almost a full circle. You can then use Auto Distort to create versions of the artwork in a number of rotated positions between 0 and 350 degrees—for instance, at 60 degrees, 120 degrees, 180, 240, and so on **(Figure 107)**. Director then places each of these in-between images into the current cast window, where they can be incorporated in your movie as an animation sequence.

1. In the paint tool palette, click the Marquee tool, and use it to select the artwork that you wish to Auto Distort.
2. Click Skew, Warp, Perspective, or the Rotate commands in the Effects toolbar. Notice that Director places little "handles" at each corner of your selection.
3. Drag one of the handles to rotate or distort the selected art.
4. While the Marquee is still active, choose Auto Distort from the Xtras menu **(Figure 108)**.
5. In the Auto Distort dialog box, type the number of in-between cast members you wish to create **(Figure 109)**. In other words, how many new cast members should be created to transform the original artwork to the altered state created in step 3 above.
6. Click Begin. Director creates the new in-between cast members and adds them into the next available positions in the cast window.

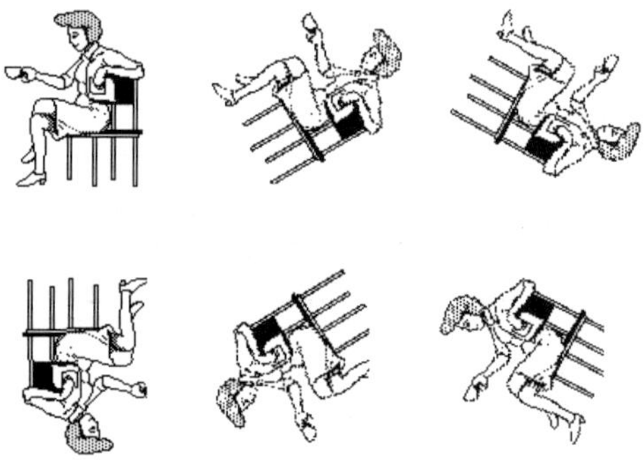

Figure 107. The **Auto Distort** command has been used here in combination with the **Free Rotate** command to create a series of in-between rotated images.

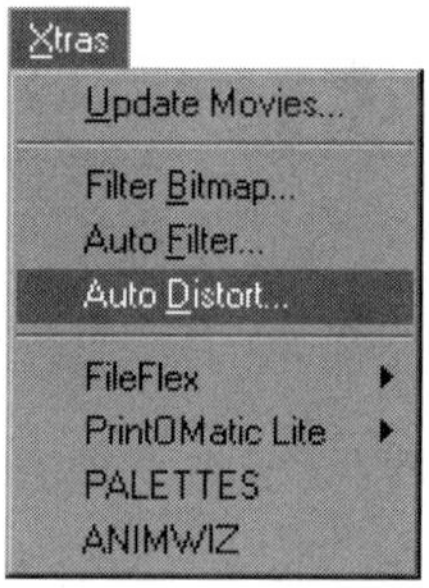

Figure 108. Choose **Auto Distort** from the **Xtras** menu.

Figure 109. In the **Auto Distort** dialog box, enter the number of in-between cast members you wish to create.

INK MASKS

Figure 110. The windows of this house cast member are transparent, allowing you to see the characters behind them.

An ink mask allows you to make certain parts of a cast member appear transparent—in other words, you can see through it to other artwork in the background—while other parts of the cast member remain opaque. Why would you ever want a cast member to behave that way? Imagine creating a scene in which a house is viewed from outside, and animated characters can be seen through its windows **(Figure 110)**. In such a scene, the house itself would be opaque but the windows transparent, allowing you to see the characters behind them. Another good example is a scene of a moving car. The car is opaque, but its windows are transparent so that you can see the passing scenery.

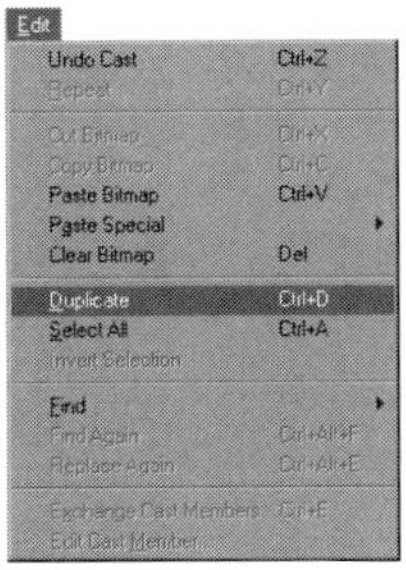

Figure 111. Choose **Duplicate** from the **Edit** menu.

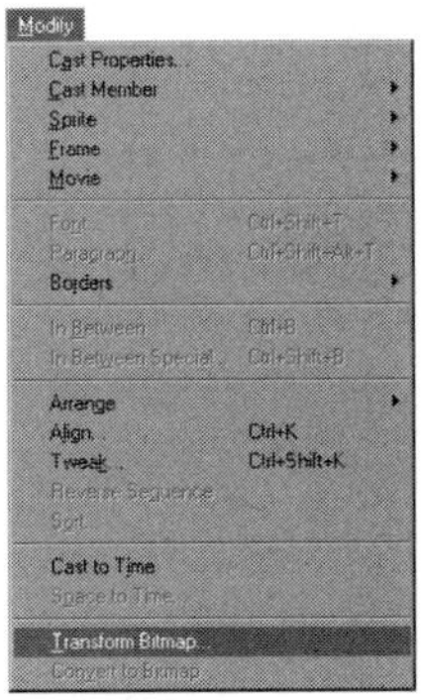

Figure 112. Choose **Transform Bitmap** from the **Modify** menu.

To create a mask:

1. Open the cast member you wish to mask (make transparent in certain parts) in the paint window. A quick way to do this is to double-click it in the cast window.
2. Choose Duplicate from the Edit menu **(Figure 111)**.
3. While viewing the cloned cast member, choose Transform Bitmap from the Modify menu **(Figure 112)**.
4. In the Transform Bitmap dialog box, select 1-Bit in the Color Depth pop-up menu **(Figure 113)**. You are changing the cloned cast member to black and white (1-bit color depth), which is required to make a mask.
5. Click Transform.
6. From the paint tool palette, select either the Paint Bucket or Paint Brush tool.

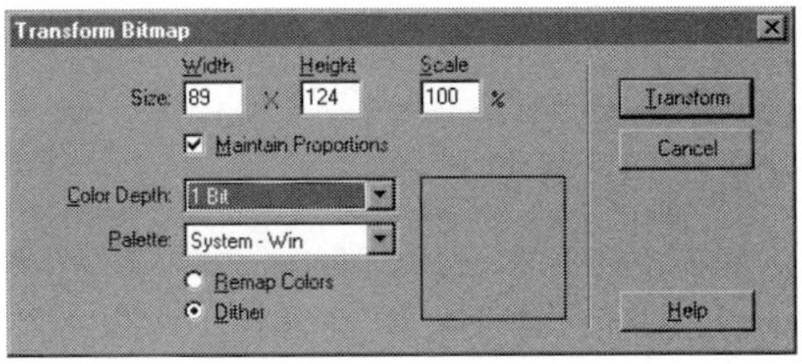

Figure 113. Select 1-Bit in the **Color Depth** pop-up menu in the **Transform Bitmap** dialog box.

Ink Masks

7. Fill in the parts of the cloned cast member that should be opaque (that is, that should not be seen through). Be sure not to paint outside the borders of the cloned cast member; doing so could create a ghosting effect when you place the mask in your movie.
8. In the cast window, make sure that the cloned cast member you've created is positioned immediately following the original version of the cast member **(Figure 114)**. If it is not already there, drag the clone to the appropriate location.
9. Choose Score from the Window menu.
10. Place the cast member you wish to mask in Director's score.
11. Select the frames in the score that contain the cast member you wish to mask.
12. In the score, click and hold the Ink selector to display a pop-up menu, and choose Mask. **(Figure 115)**. Director displays your masked cast member in the selected frames.

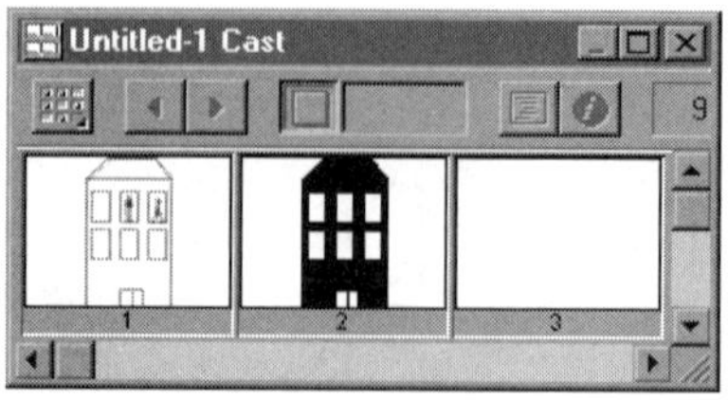

Figure 114. In the cast window, make sure the cloned cast member is positioned immediately following the original cast member.

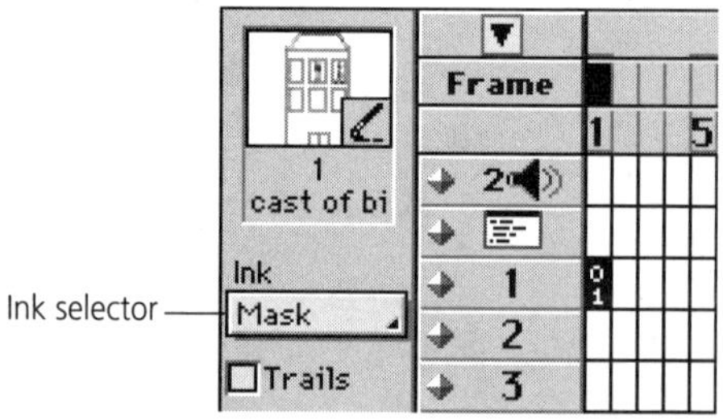

Figure 115. In the score window, choose **Mask** in the **Ink** pop-up menu.

Ink Masks

ONION SKINNING

Figure 116. Open the cast member you wish to use as the background reference image in the paint window.

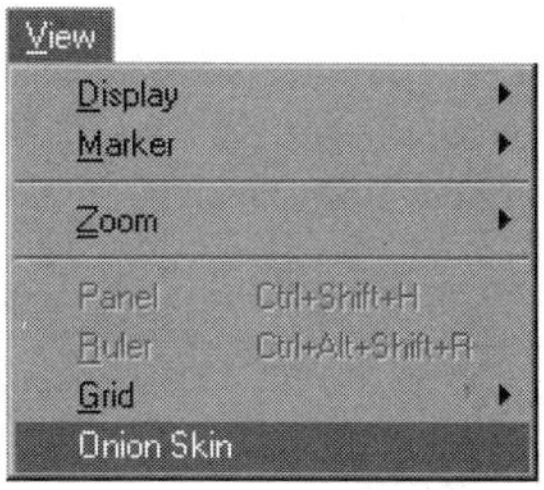

Figure 117. Choose **Onion Skin** from the **View** menu.

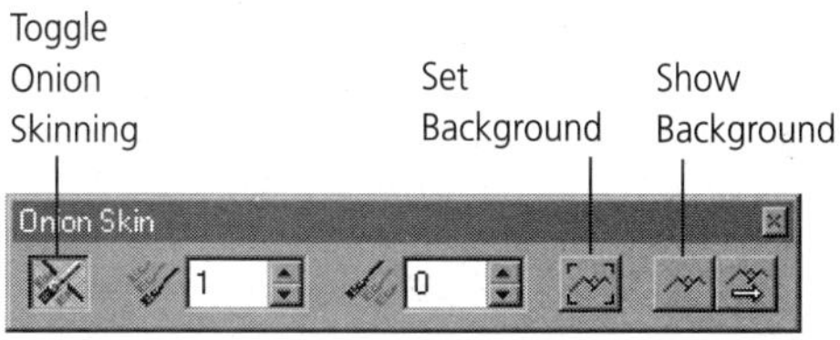

Figure 118. The **Onion Skin** toolbar.

Figure 119. The reference cast member appears dimmed in the paint window. Draw your new cast member on top of this image.

Onion Skinning is a technique which allows you to create a cast member in the paint window while viewing one or more reference cast members which appear dimmed in the background. You effectively draw on top of these reference images, tracing the parts of their features that will carry over to the new cast member. The reference cast members are not altered in the process.

The term onion skin refers to the very thin paper traditional animators use to trace over one or more previous images.

Onion Skinning is extremely useful for creating sequences of closely related cast members, which would be hard to generate without viewing reference images.

To use Onion Skinning:

Follow the steps below to create a new cast member while viewing one other previously rendered cast member as a background reference image:

1. Open the cast member you wish to use as the background reference image in the paint window **(Figure 116)**. You can do so by double-clicking it from its cast window.
2. Choose Onion Skin from the View menu **(Figure 117)**.
3. Click Toggle Onion Skinning in the Onion Skin toolbar **(Figure 118)**.
4. Click Set Background **(Figure 118)**.
5. Click the New Cast Member button in the paint window.
6. Click Show Background in the Onion Skin toolbar. The reference cast member appears dimmed in the paint window **(Figure 119)**. You now draw your new cast member on top of this image. The reference cast member is not altered by doing so.

To create a cast member while viewing a sequence of reference cast members:

As you create a cast member that is part of an animation sequence, it is very helpful to view several preceding frames of the sequence at the same time, so that your new cast member will fit in appropriately. With this technique, your reference cast members appear on top of each other in the paint window, with decreasing levels of brightness **(Figure 123)**. This allows you to create your new cast member in precise relation to the entire sequence.

1. Open the cast window that contains the reference cast members you wish to use. Make sure the reference cast members are grouped together.
2. In the cast window, create an empty position immediately following or preceding your reference cast members, and select it **(Figure 120)**.
3. Choose Media Element from the Insert menu and select Bitmap from the pop-up menu **(Figure 121)**. The paint window is opened.
4. Choose Onion Skin from the View menu.
5. Click Toggle Onion Skinning in the Onion Skin toolbar to turn it on **(Figure 122)**.
6. Click the arrows in the Preceding or Following Cast Members setting in the Onion Skin toolbar **(Figure 122)** to display your reference cast members. You can display as many of them as you have by setting the appropriate value. They are displayed on top of each other in the paint window **(Figure 123)**. The further away your reference cast members are from your new cast member in the cast window, the dimmer they appear.
7. Draw your new cast member on top of your reference images.

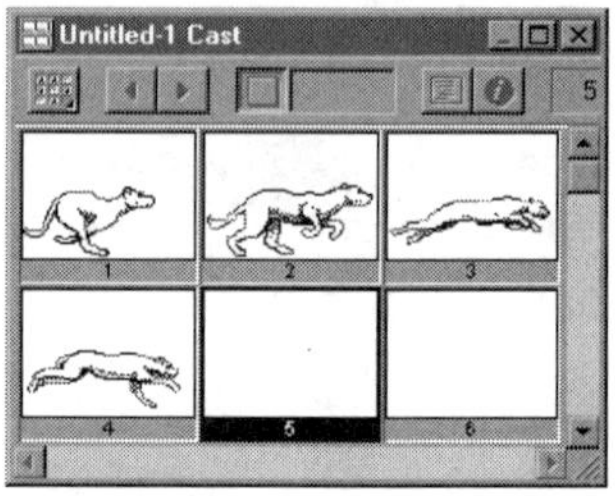

Figure 120. Create an empty position in the cast window immediately following or preceding your reference cast members. Select it.

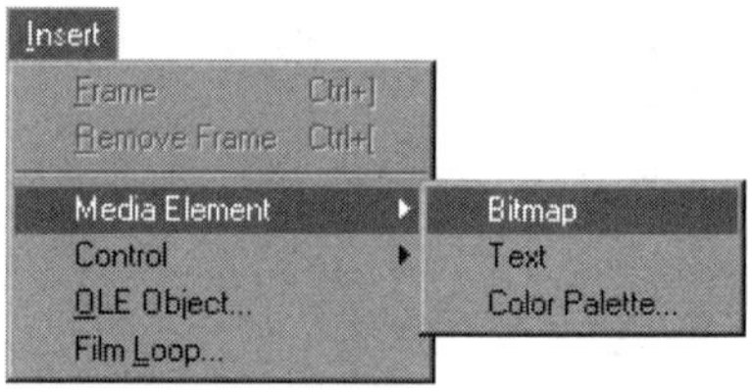

Figure 121. Choose **Media Element** from the **Insert** menu and select **Bitmap** from the pop-up menu.

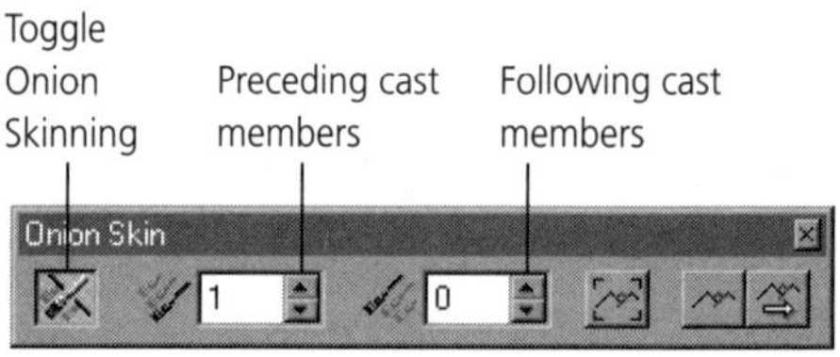

Figure 122. The **Onion Skin** toolbar.

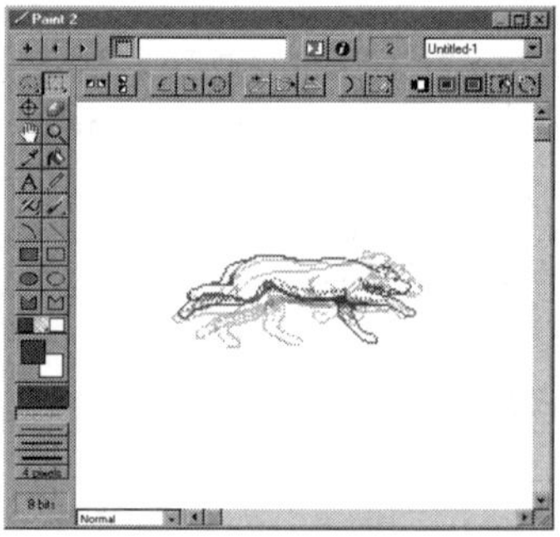

Figure 123. Your reference cast members appear on top of each other in the paint window

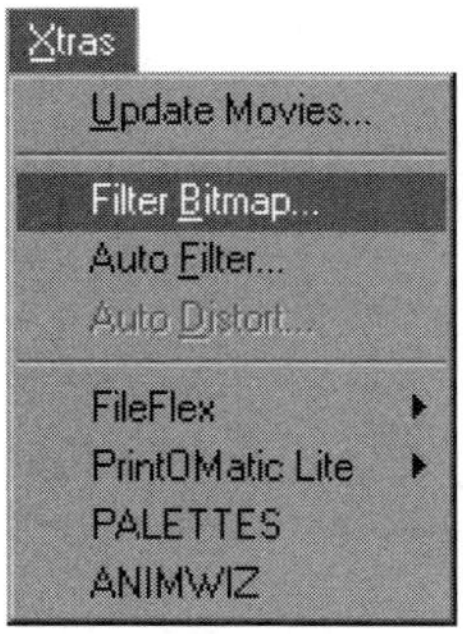

Figure 124. Choose **Filter Bitmap** from the **Xtras** menu.

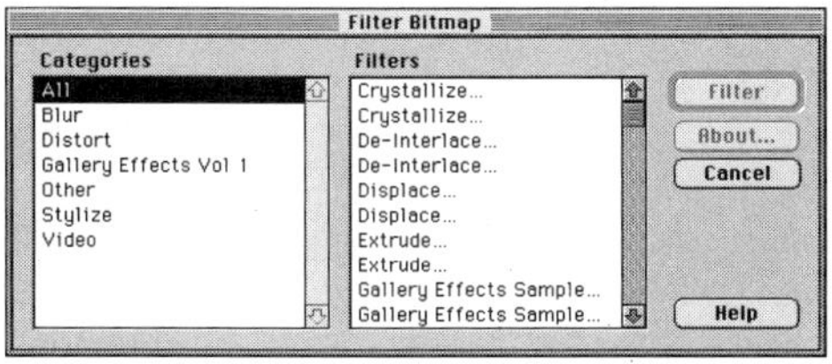

Figure 125. On the left side of the **Filter Bitmap** dialog box, select the category of filters you wish to view. On the right side, select the filter you wish to apply to your cast member and click **Filter**.

IMAGE FILTERS

Director allows you to apply Photoshop or Premiere image filters to your bitmapped cast members. In order for Director to have access to such filters, you must first place them in the Xtras folder in the Director application folder *(see page 225 in the Xtras chapter for more details on installing Xtras)*. You can then apply a filter to modify a portion of a bitmapped cast member, or to modify multiple cast members at once. Image filters are applied in either the cast window or paint window.

To apply a filter to a portion of a bitmapped cast member:

1. Open the cast member in the paint window.
2. Use the Marquee or Lasso tool to select the part of the cast member you wish to modify.
3. Choose Filter Bitmap from the Xtras menu **(Figure 124)**.
4. On the left side of the Filter Bitmap dialog box, select the category of filters you wish to view **(Figure 125)**. Select All to view every available filter.
5. On the right side of the Filter Bitmap dialog box, select the filter you wish to apply to your cast member and click Filter. At this point, your filter will most likely display its own custom dialog box which allows you to enter filter settings. Make the appropriate selections and apply the filter. If your filter doesn't have a custom dialog box, it will be immediately applied after you click Filter.

✔ Tip

■ You can apply a filter to a multiple cast member selection in a cast window. Select the appropriate cast members in a cast window and choose Filter Bitmap from the Xtras menu.

TOOL PALETTE 7

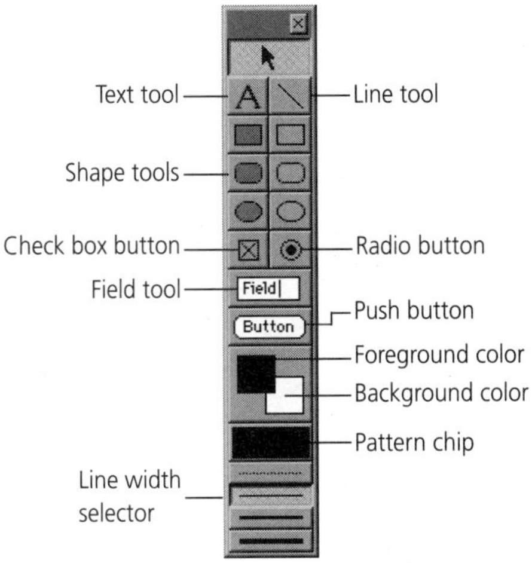

Figure 1. The Tool Palette.

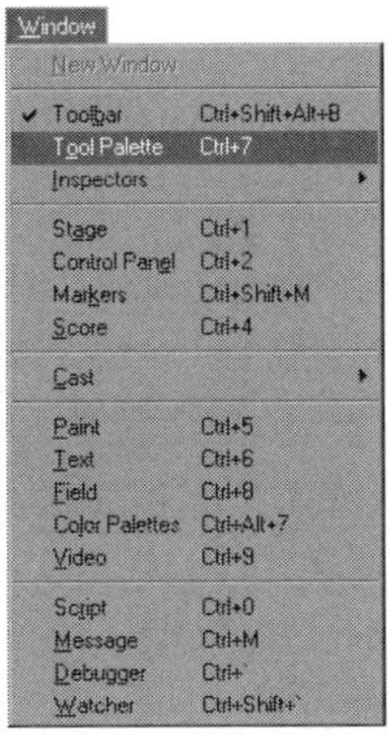

Figure 2. Choose **Tool Palette** from the **Window** menu.

Figure 3. The Text tool.

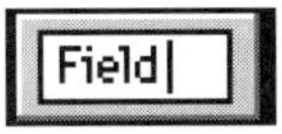

Figure 4. The Field tool.

Director's Tool Palette allows you to create text, shapes, and buttons directly on the stage **(Figure 1)**. These objects are automatically placed in the cast and score windows. Open the Tool Palette by choosing Tool Palette from the Window menu **(Figure 2)**.

Shapes created with the Tool Palette are called **QuickDraw** graphics. They offer several advantages over bitmap graphics created in Director's paint window: QuickDraw shapes (including lines) can be resized and edited on the stage. They consume a lot less memory than bitmap images, and print much better to laser printers. On the down side, QuickDraw graphics animate slower, so if speed is an issue, use bitmaps. You cannot edit QuickDraw graphics in the paint window.

Text tool

Use the Text tool **(Figure 3)** to create text as an alternative to using the text window under the Window menu. Text created with the Text tool is visible in the text and cast windows.

Select the Text tool, then click the stage where you wish to create and position some text. Click the arrow in the Tool Palette to select text on the stage that you wish to edit. *(See pages 174–177 in the Creating Text in Director chapter for more information on the Text tool and creating text with the text window)*

Field tool

The Field tool **(Figure 4)** also allows you to create text on the stage, except this text has the feature of being editable during movie playback. *(See page 179 for more information about using the Field tool)*

Line tool

Use the Line tool to draw lines on Director's stage **(Figure 5)**. Drag it to size your line. The line width can be changed by using the Line width selector at the bottom of the Tool Palette.

Figure 5. The Line tool.

Shape tools

The shape tools in the Tool Palette work very much like the shape tools in the paint window **(Figure 6)**. Click a hollow shape tool to draw an outline of that shape on the stage by dragging (you can set the thickness of the outline by using the Line width selector at the bottom of the Tool Palette). The shaded shape tools produce solid shapes using the current foreground color and pattern.

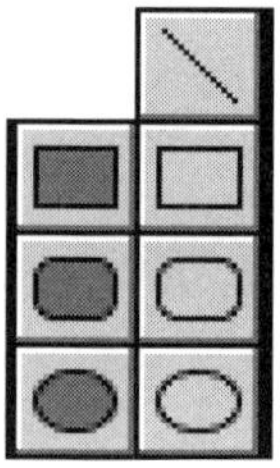

Figure 6. The shape tools.

✔ Tip

- Hold the Shift key while dragging a shape tool on the stage to constrain it to a perfect square or circle. Hold the Shift key while dragging the Line tool to constrain it to 45-degree lines.

Button tools

Director allows you to create push buttons, check boxes, and radio buttons by using the button tools provided in the Tool Palette **(Figure 7)**. Select the appropriate button tool, then drag a rectangle on the stage where the button should be placed. You can then type in the text that should appear on or next to your button. The font, size, and style of the button text can be set in the Font dialog box (choose Font from the Modify menu), or by using the Text Inspector *(see page 177 for info about the Text Inspector)*. Once placed onto the stage, a button cast member is created. Button text can be edited directly on the stage.

Figure 7. The button tools.

During movie playback, buttons appear to respond when clicked, but cause no special action unless they have a Lingo script attached to them. *(See page 204 for information on scripts)*

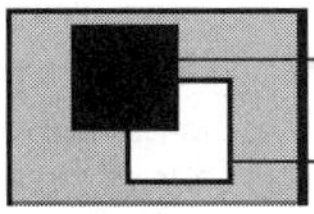

Figure 8. The Foreground and Background color chips.

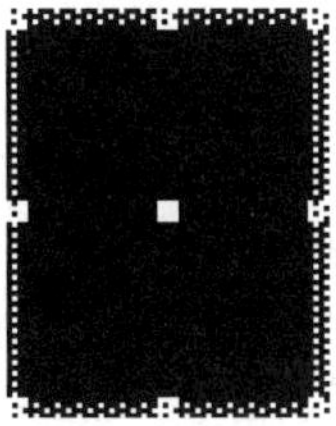

Figure 9. Select a QuickDraw line or shape on the stage.

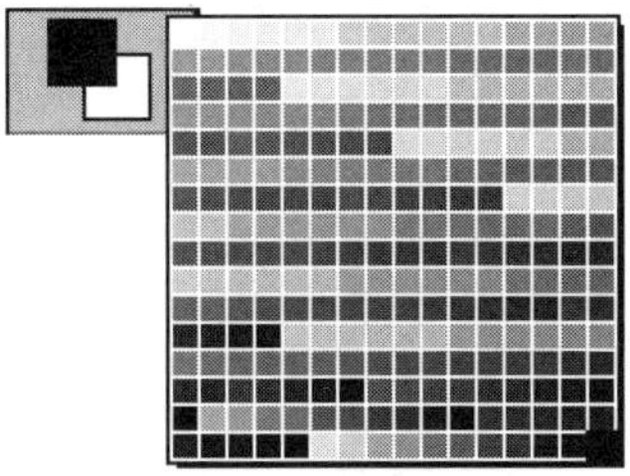

Figure 10. Click and hold the Foreground or Background color chips to select a new color from the pop-up menu.

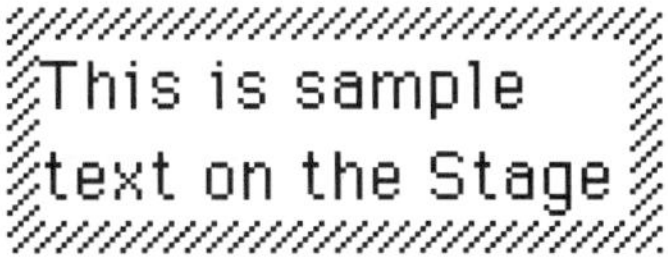

Figure 11. Double-click a text cast member on the stage.

FOREGROUND AND BACKGROUND COLOR CHIPS

Use the Foreground and Background color chips in the Tool Palette **(Figure 8)** to set the colors of QuickDraw lines, QuickDraw shapes, and sprites. Use them to also set the color of text on the stage, as well as text in text and script windows.

To set the color of QuickDraw lines or shapes:

1. Select a QuickDraw line or shape on the stage. A thick border appears around the image **(Figure 9)**.
2. Click and hold the Foreground or Background color chips in the Tool Palette to select a new color from the pop-up menu for the foreground or background colors **(Figure 10)**. The background color has no effect on a QuickDraw line, but does effect the color of solid QuickDraw shapes if a pattern for them is selected.

To set the color of text on the stage:

1. In the score, select the frame that contains the text cast member whose color you wish to change. Double-click the text cast member on the stage (a thick border appears around it) **(Figure 11)**.
2. Select a foreground color using the Foreground color chip **(Figure 10)**. Additional text now typed will have this color, but to change existing text color, select the actual text first by dragging across it, and then click the Foreground color chip.
3. Select a background color for the text block by using the Background color chip.

To set the color of text in text and script windows:

1. Select a text or script window so that it is the active window **(Figure 12)**.
2. Select a foreground color using the Foreground color chip in the Tool Palette **(Figure 13)**. Additional text now typed will have this color, but to change the color of existing text, select the actual text first by dragging across it and then click the Foreground color chip.
3. Select a background color for the text or script window by using the Background color chip in the Tool Palette.

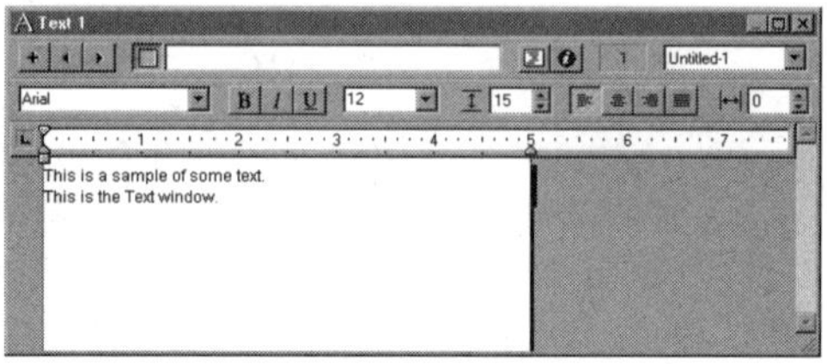

Figure 12. Make a text or script window active.

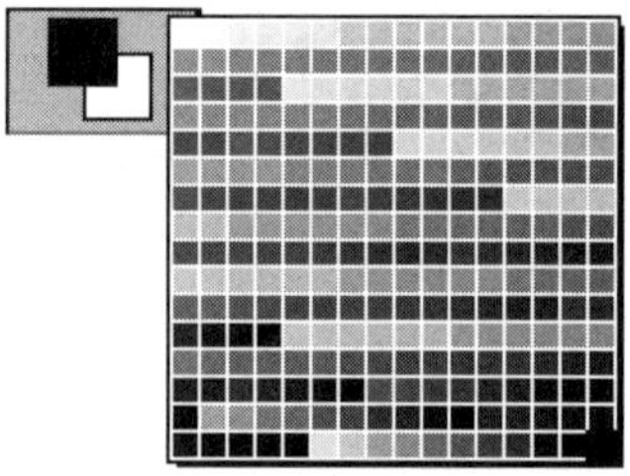

Figure 13. Click and hold the Foreground or Background color chips to select a new color from the pop-up menu.

To set the color of sprites:

1. Select a sprite on the stage or in the score.
2. Choose a new foreground or background color using the Foreground and Background color chips in the Tool Palette **(Figure 13)**. Unless the foreground color of the sprite is originally black, changing its foreground color in this manner can result in unpredictable colors.

Pattern chip

Click and hold the Pattern chip to select a new pattern from the pop-up menu **(Figure 14)**.

Figure 14. The Pattern chip.

Line width selector

Allows you to set the line width that's used with the Line tool and hollow shape tools **(Figure 15)**.

Figure 15. The Line width selector.

COLOR IN DIRECTOR 8

Color Palette.

The Color Palette is used throughout this chapter. Choose Color Palettes from the Window menu to display it (**Figure 1**).

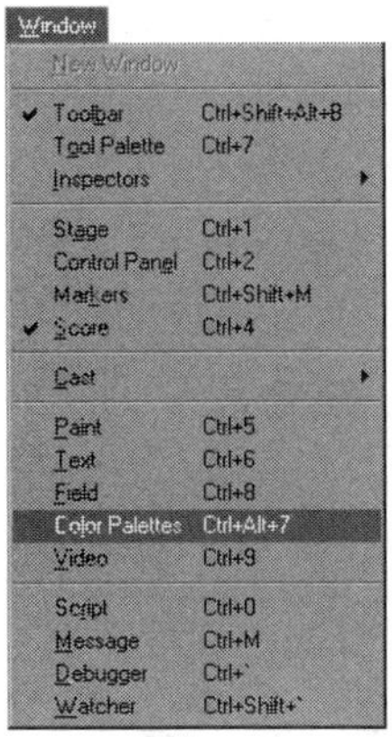

Figure 1. Choose **Color Palettes** from the **Window** menu.

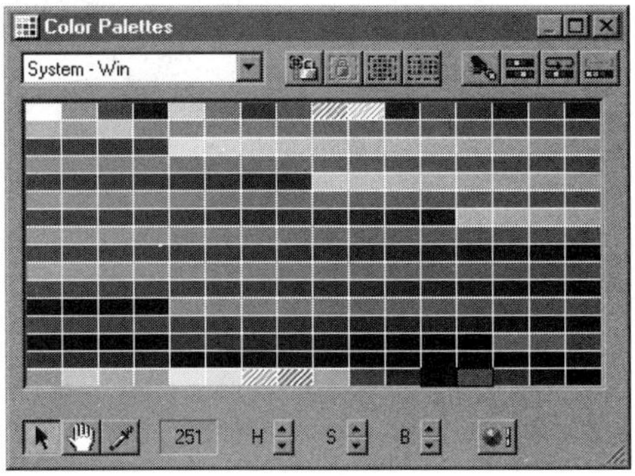

Figure 2. The color palettes window.

If you plan on creating Director movies that use 8-bit color depth or less *(see Color Depth on the next page)*, it is especially important to understand the nature of color palettes in Director and how to work around their limitations. This knowledge will enhance your ability to create visually pleasing movies.

In this chapter you'll learn about movie and cast member color depth and how these settings relate to color palettes. You will learn how to create and edit color palettes using the color palettes window **(Figure 2)**. And you'll learn how to take the most commonly used colors from a variety of cast members and arrange them into a new "optimal" palette that all cast members can use simultaneously. You will also discover how to create impressive visual effects through palette transitions and a special technique called "color cycling" that makes cast members appear to animate and pulse.

COLOR DEPTH

The first thing to know about color in Director is color depth. Color depth generally refers to the number of colors that your computer can display on the screen at the same time. The maximum depends on the type of video card installed in your PC.

Color depth is expressed in bits per pixel. 1-bit color depth corresponds to black and white, 2-bit is 4 colors, 4-bit is 16 colors, 8-bit is 256 colors, 16-bit is 32,768 colors, and 32-bit is 16.7 million colors.

In Director, there are two types of color depth settings. The first is the color depth of your overall movie. The second is cast member color depth. Each bitmap cast member has its own color depth setting.

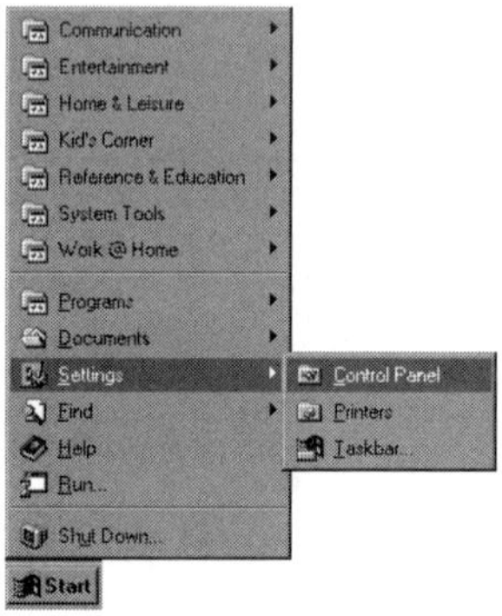

Figure 3. Click **Start** and choose **Control Panel** from the **Settings** menu.

Movie color depth

Your movie's color depth corresponds to the color depth setting of your monitor. Movie color depth (also referred to as stage color depth) determines the maximum number of colors that can be displayed by any image in Director. This setting takes precedence over cast member color depth. For example, if your movie is set to 8-bit color depth, a 16-bit or 32-bit cast member will be displayed in 8-bit color (256 colors).

To change movie color depth:

1. Open the Control Panel folder and double-click the Display icon. For Windows 95, Click Start and choose Control Panel from the Settings menu **(Figure 3)**, and double-click the Display icon.
2. In the Display Properties dialog box, click the Settings tab at the top.
3. Set your monitor to display the number of colors you wish to have available in Director **(Figure 4)**. This affects all other open applications.
4. Save your movie and restart Director.

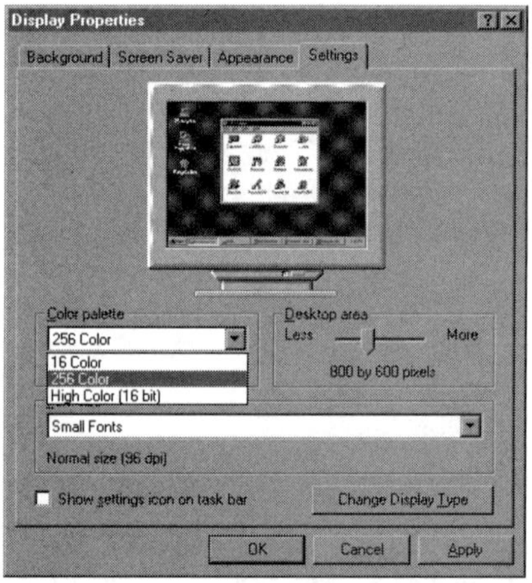

Figure 4. In the **Display Properties** dialog box, select a new color depth for your monitor from the **Color palette** menu. This setting is also the new color depth for your Director movie.

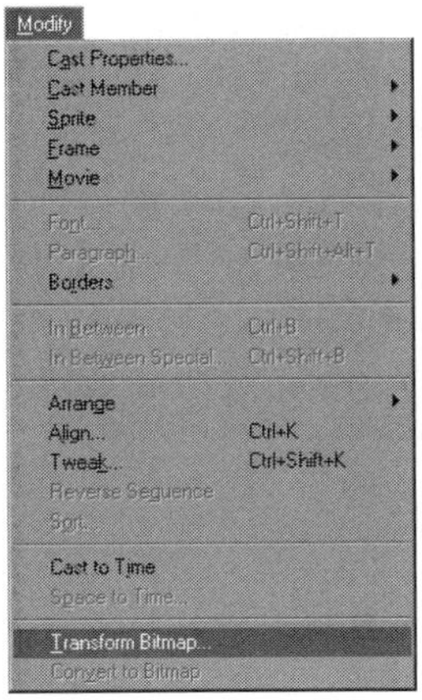

Figure 5. Choose **Transform Bitmap** from the **Modify** menu.

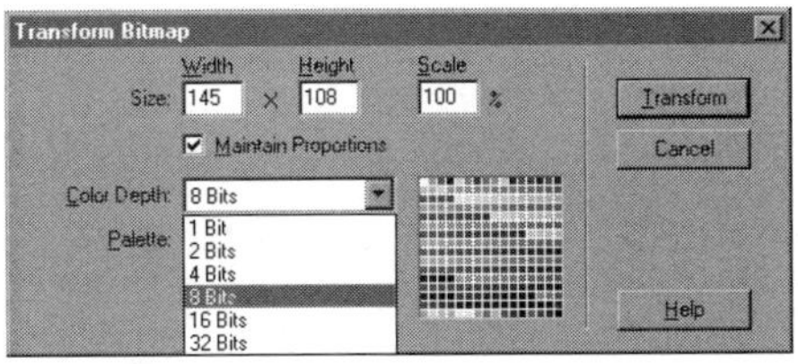

Figure 6. In the **Transform Bitmap** dialog box, use the **Color Depth** pop-up menu to select the desired cast member color depth.

Cast member color depth

Each bitmap cast member in Director has its own color depth setting, which can differ from the movie color depth. You can view this setting for any bitmap cast member by selecting it in a cast window, and choosing Transform Bitmap from the Modify menu, or by clicking the Cast Member Properties button.

The larger a cast member's color depth, the more memory it requires, and the slower it animates. If your movie will be playing on a wide variety of systems, 8-bit color depth is still the safest choice.

In order for a cast member to display its entire range of colors in your movie, the movie color depth setting must be set at least as high as the cast member color depth. For example, if you want to accurately display a 16-bit cast member (32,768 colors), the movie color depth setting must be at least 16-bits.

Note: If your cast members have higher color depth settings than your movie, the extra colors will not be displayed, but they will still animate slowly, as if all their colors were being displayed. In most cases, you should transform these cast members to the color depth setting of your movie, or lower.

To change a cast member's color depth:

You cannot undo this operation. Make sure you have a copy of the original cast member before proceeding.

1. Select the cast member in the cast window whose color depth you wish to change.
2. Choose Transform Bitmap from the Modify menu **(Figure 5)**.
3. In the Transform Bitmap dialog box, use the Color Depth pop-up menu to select the new depth for the cast member **(Figure 6)**.
4. Click Transform.

COLOR PALETTES

A **color palette** is a collection of all possible colors that can be displayed on the screen at any one time **(Figure 7)**. When your movie color depth is set to 8-bits (256 colors) or lower, the colors that Director can display (including colors in its user interface) are limited to those which are contained in color palettes. On the other hand, colors you can display in 16-bit or higher movies are not restricted to limited choices in color palettes since Director has a continuous spectrum of colors to work with (in such movies, you use color palettes only for the purpose of selecting colors to paint with).

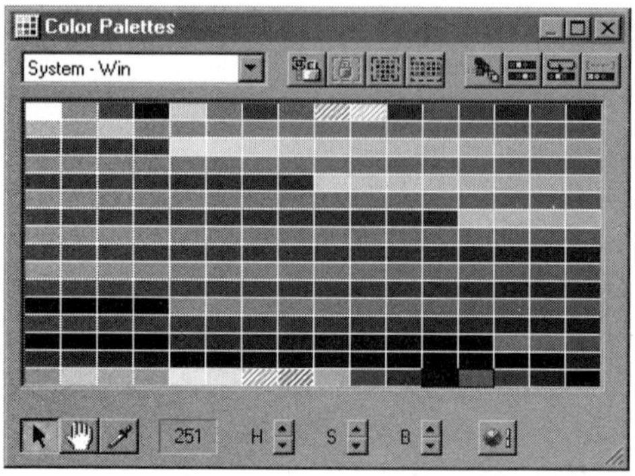

Figure 7. This is an 8-bit (256 colors) color palette.

Director has a number of standard built-in 8-bit color palettes you can choose from *(see page 125)*, or you can create your own color palettes. You can also import color palettes into Director *(see page 128)*. Palettes you create or import become cast members.

The current color palette

Only one color palette is active in any single frame of your movie and this palette is called the **current color palette**. All cast members are displayed in the colors of the current palette. A different current palette can be set for each frame of your movie by using the score's palette channel **(Figure 8)** *(see page 125)*. The colors that can simultaneously appear in any single frame of your movie must be in the current color palette set for that given frame. An 8-bit Director movie can display more than 256 unique colors, but not in any single frame. It can do so over a range of frames, by switching the current palette in those frames.

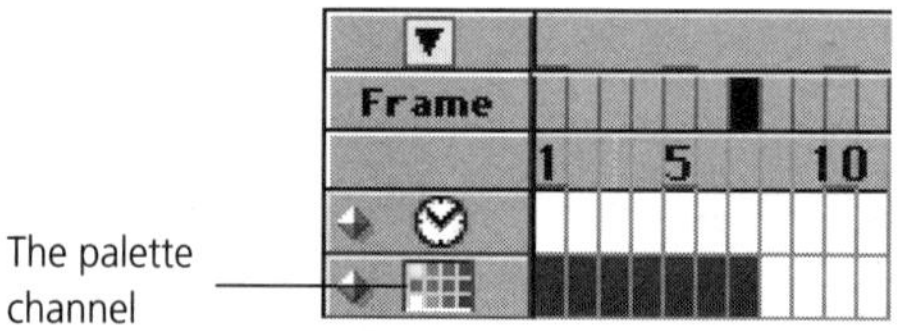

Figure 8. Use the palette channel to set the current color palette for any frame.

Figure 9. This is an 8-bit cast member. Its colors are identified by referencing color positions in the current palette.
In this example, the color of pixels in the labeled section are all the same and correspond to the color in the seventh position in the current color palette (shown in Figure 10).

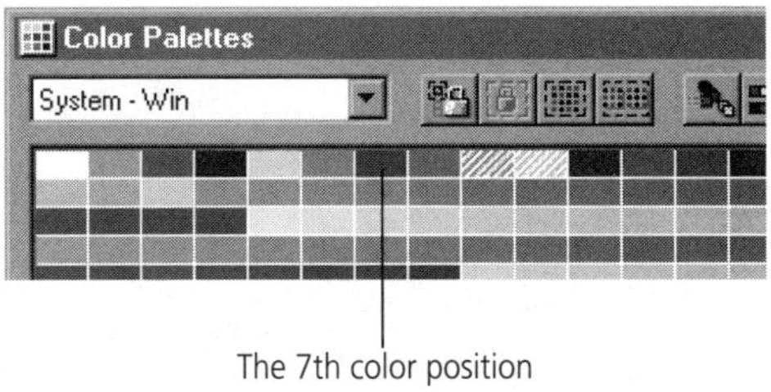

Figure 10. The color mapping of the cast member in Figure 9 is such that its small labeled section is mapped to the seventh color palette position. If you change the seventh color position in the current palette to green in this example, the small section in figure 9 will turn green.

Cast members and color palettes

When you create a 2-, 4-, or 8-bit image in any graphics application such as Photoshop, a color palette is used to describe all colors in that image. This color palette is linked to the image file. When you import such an image into Director, you can import its linked color palette *(see page 128)*. In order for Director to display any 2-, 4-, or 8-bit cast member in its proper colors, the color palette used to create the original image should be set as the current palette. Another way to ensure that a cast member's colors are displayed accurately is to remap it to a new color palette that has similar colors to its original palette *(see page 129)*, and then use that palette as the current palette.

Each 2-, 4-, and 8-bit bitmap cast member in Director is mapped (or assigned) to a particular color palette. This means that each pixel in a cast member is assigned to the specific color position in the cast member's mapped palette which holds the corresponding color that the pixel is painted in. For example, if a section of a cast member is red, the pixels in that section are assigned to the color position which holds the same color in the palette the cast member is mapped to. If you display a cast member using a current palette that's different from its assigned palette, the cast member will probably be displayed in the wrong colors. This is because the cast member's pixels are still mapped to its assigned palette, but this mapping is used to reference the colors in the current palette, and this results in improper colors being shown.

You can see which palette a cast member is mapped to and remap the cast member to a new palette by using the Transform Bitmap command (see page 129).

Figures 9–10 give an example as to how a set of pixels in a cast member is mapped to a specific color position.

ASSIGNING COLOR PALETTES TO FRAMES AND CAST MEMBERS

To set a default color palette:

You can set a default color palette that is used automatically when you create a new Director movie. This default palette is used as the current color palette in your frames until a new palette is set in the palette channel. *(See page 125)*

1. Choose Movie from the Modify menu and select Properties from the pop-up menu **(Figure 11)**.
2. Use the Default Palette pop-up menu to select the palette you wish to use as your movie's default palette **(Figure 12)**.
3. Click OK.

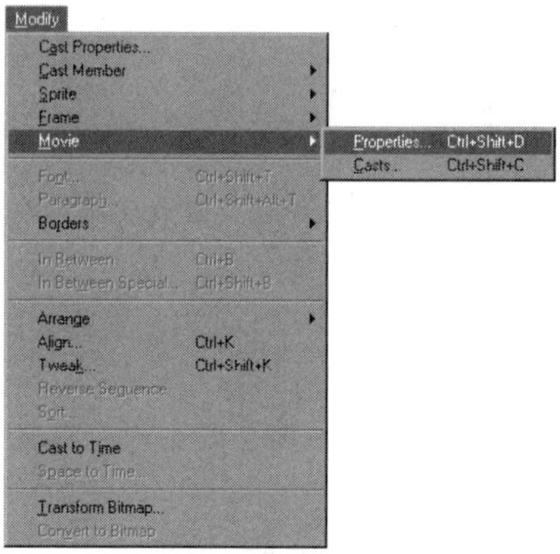

Figure 11. Choose **Movie** from the **Modify** menu and select **Properties** from the pop-up menu.

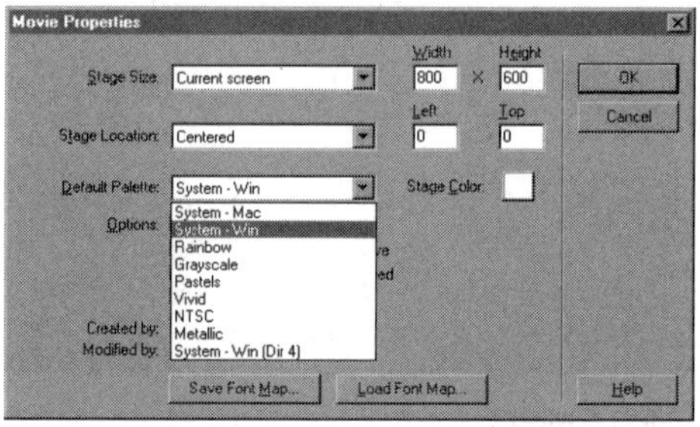

Figure 12. Select your movie's default palette from the pop-up menu.

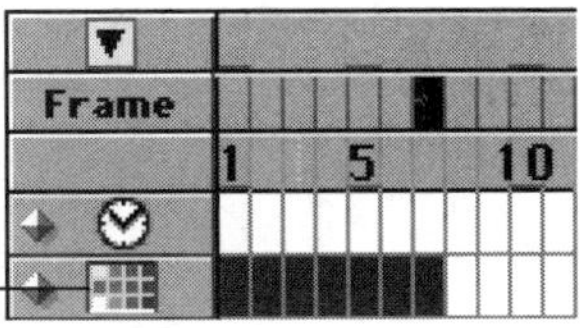

Figure 13. In the palette channel, select the frame or series of frames whose palette you would like to set.

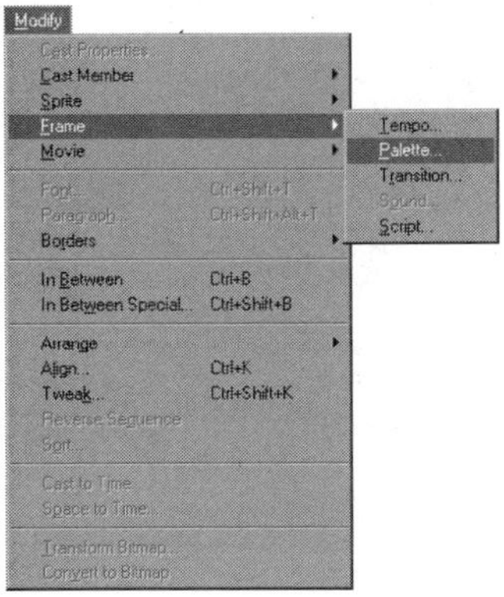

Figure 14. Choose **Frame** from the **Modify** menu and select **Palette** from the pop-up menu.

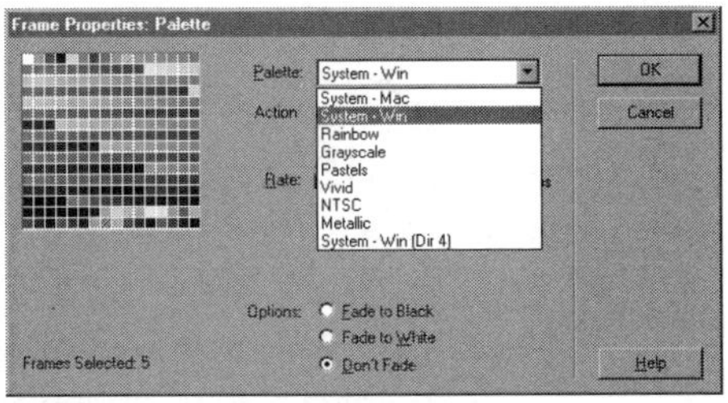

Figure 15. In the **Frame Properties** dialog box, use the **Palette** pop-up menu to choose a palette you wish to apply to the selected frames.

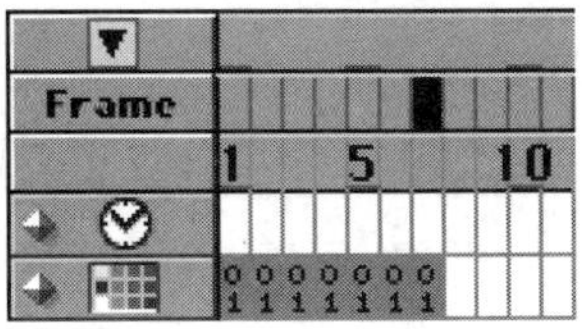

Figure 16. Click OK in the **Frame Properties** dialog box and Director sets the new palette in selected frames.

To set the current color palette in the palette channel:

When Director plays a movie, it displays its cast members using a color palette specified in the palette channel of the score. These settings override any default palette set through the Movie command *(see page 124)*. Like all of Director's score channels, the palette channel **(Figure 13)** can be controlled on a frame-by-frame basis—for instance, frame 1 can employ palette A to display cast members, while frame 5 switches to palette B, and frame 15 switches to palette C. By swapping palettes like this, you can display a sequence of distinct cast members in their original palettes, and create unique visual effects by changing between palettes over time.

When you are placing a cast member on the stage that uses a palette different from the currently active palette, Director automatically assigns that cast member's palette to the palette channel and uses it for all subsequent frames until a new palette is set in the channel. Setting a new palette in the palette channel is easy.

1. In the palette channel, select the frame or frames where you wish to set a new color palette **(Figure 13)**.
2. Choose Frame from the Modify menu and select Palette from the pop-up menu **(Figure 14)**.
3. In the Frame Properties dialog box, use the Palette pop-up menu to choose the palette you wish to apply to the selected frames. Your choices include all of Director's core palettes (System, Rainbow, Pastels, etc.), plus any you've created **(Figure 15)**.
4. Click OK. Director sets the new palette in the selected frames **(Figure 16)**. Don't be surprised if the cast members in those frames suddenly change colors—they are now displayed in the colors of your new palette.

✔ **Tip**

- You can double-click a frame in the palette channel to open the Frame Properties dialog box.

To set a color palette transition over a single frame:

Switching palettes in a scene can be a little jarring: You see a particular set of colors in one frame, and in the next frame the set is entirely different. Director lets you use a palette transition to control the speed at which colors change, smoothing the switch from one palette to the next.

1. In the palette channel of the score window, select the cell where you would like your palette transition to take place **(Figure 17)**.
2. Choose Frame from the Modify menu and select Palette from the pop-up menu **(Figure 18)**.
3. In the Frame Properties dialog box, use the Palette pop-up menu to choose the palette to which you wish to make a transition **(Figure 19)**. Remember that the palette you set in this frame should be different from the palette used in the channel's previous frames.
4. In the Frame Properties dialog box, adjust the Rate scroll bar to determine how fast the transition between the old and new palettes will be. The speed can be set anywhere between 1 and 30 frames per second **(Figure 20)**. During playback, your movie will pause in this frame while the transition takes place.
5. Click OK to apply the new palette with its transition.

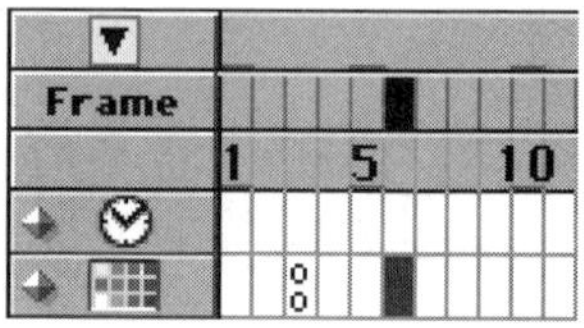

Figure 17. Select the cell in the palette channel where the palette transition should take place.

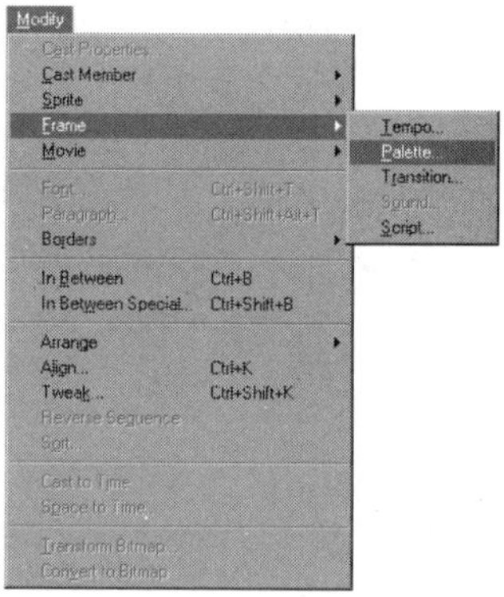

Figure 18. Choose **Frame** from the **Modify** menu and select **Palette** from the pop-up menu.

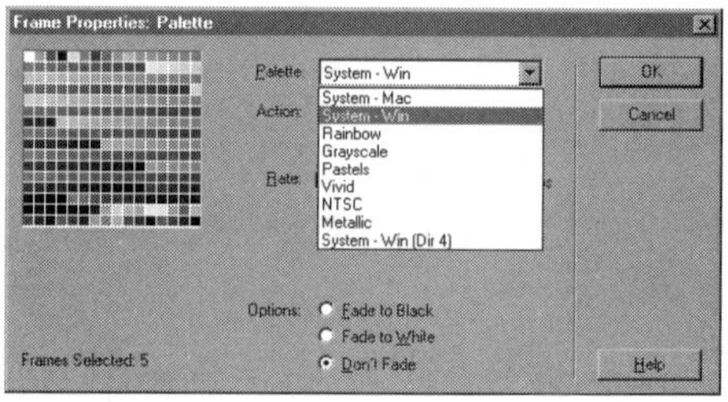

Figure 19. Use the **Palette** pop-up menu in the **Frame Properties** dialog box to choose the palette to transition to.

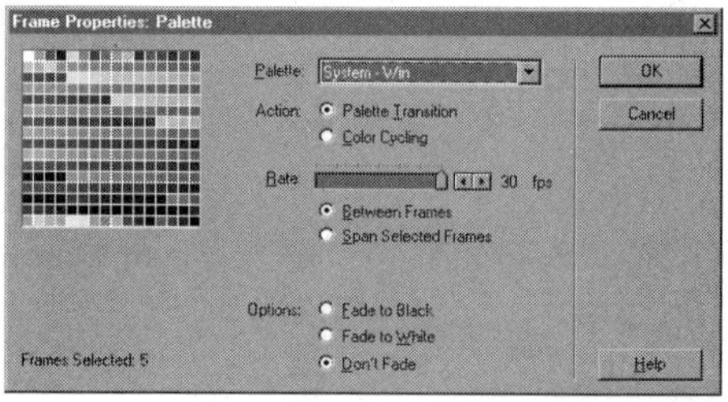

Figure 20. Adjust the Rate scroll bar to set how fast the transition between the palettes should be.

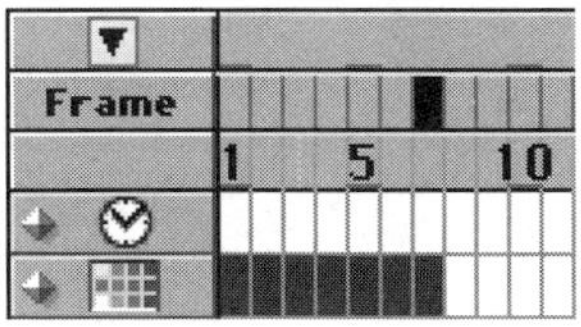

Figure 21. Select a series of cells in the palette channel in which your palette transition will occur.

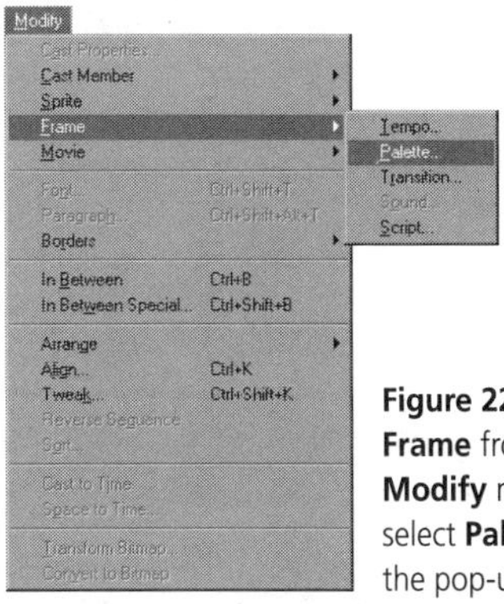

Figure 22. Choose **Frame** from the **Modify** menu and select **Palette** from the pop-up menu.

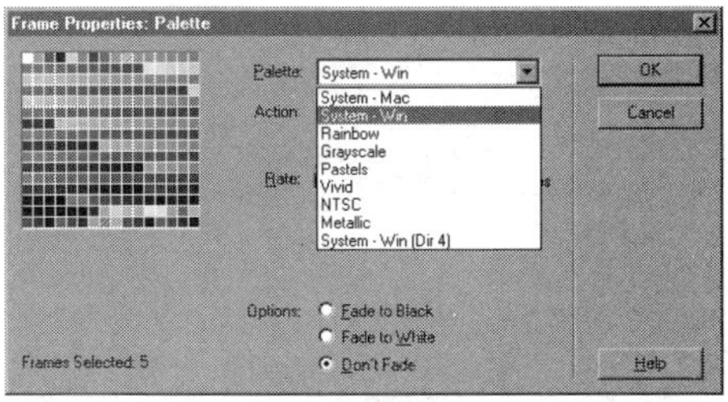

Figure 23. In the **Frame Properties** dialog box, select the transition palette in the **Palette** pop-up menu.

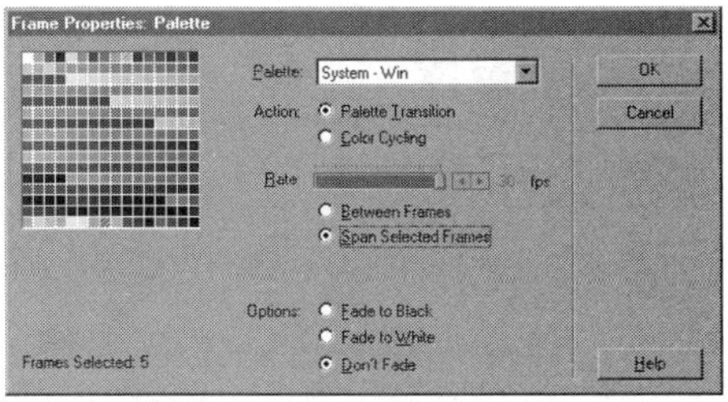

Figure 24. Select the **Span Selected Frames** option.

To set a color palette transition over a series of frames:

Just as you can set a smooth palette transition over one frame, you can set a transition to last over a series of frames. This will make the transition between color palettes more subtle, and your animation can continue without interruption.

1. In the palette channel, select the series of cells in which your palette transition will occur **(Figure 21)**.
2. Choose Frame from the Modify menu and select Palette from the pop-up menu **(Figure 22)**.
3. In the Frame Properties dialog box, use the Palette pop-up menu to select the palette to which you want to make a transition **(Figure 23)**.
4. Select the Span Selected Frames option **(Figure 24)**.
5. Click OK to apply the new palette with its transition.

To import a new color palette into Director:

You import a color palette into Director for Windows in one of two ways: The first is by importing an image that was created with the desired palette (the palette is linked to this image and can be imported). The second is by directly importing a palette file.

1. Choose Import from the File menu **(Figure 25)**.
2. In the Import dialog box, select the image file that uses the color palette you wish to import and click Import **(Figure 26)**. The Image Options dialog box appears if the image's color palette is different from the currently active color palette.
3. Click the Import radio button **(Figure 27)** in the Image Options dialog box and click OK to import the image's color palette. The color palette is placed into the active cast window. *(See page 29 in the Cast Windows chapter for more details on the Image Options dialog box)*

or

1. Choose Import from the File menu **(Figure 25)**.
2. In the Import dialog box, choose Palettes in the Files of type pop-up menu, and select the palette file to import.

Figure 25. Choose **Import** from the **File** menu.

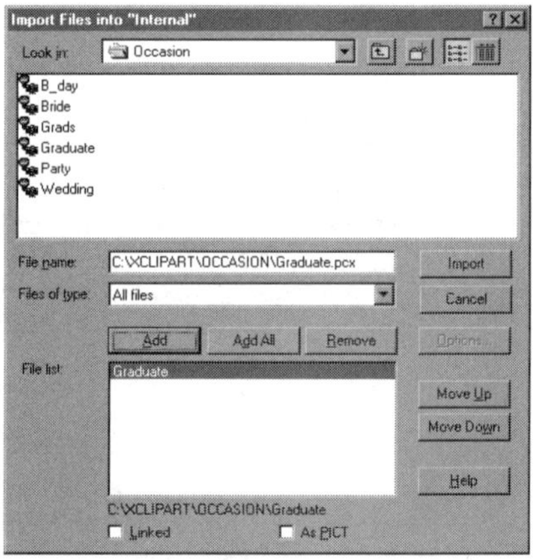

Figure 26. Select the desired cast member and click Import.

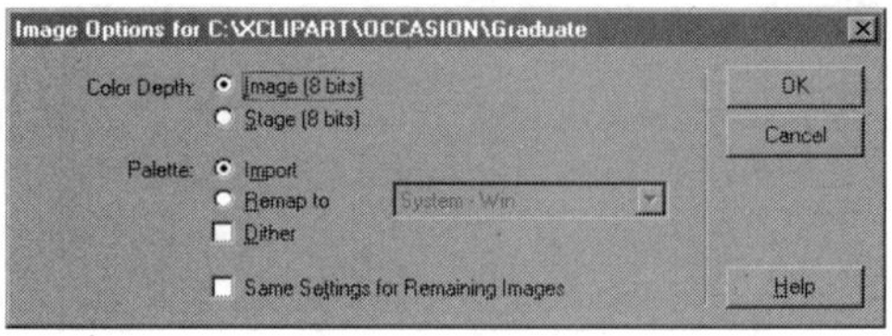

Figure 27. Click the **Import** radio button in the **Image Options** dialog box, then click **OK** to import the image's original color palette.

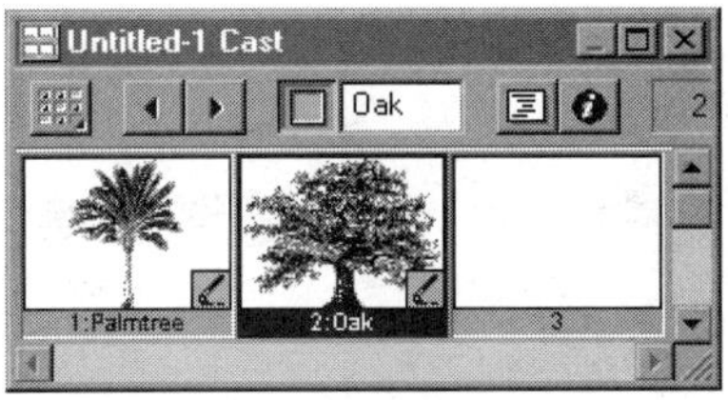

Figure 28. Select the cast member you'd like to remap.

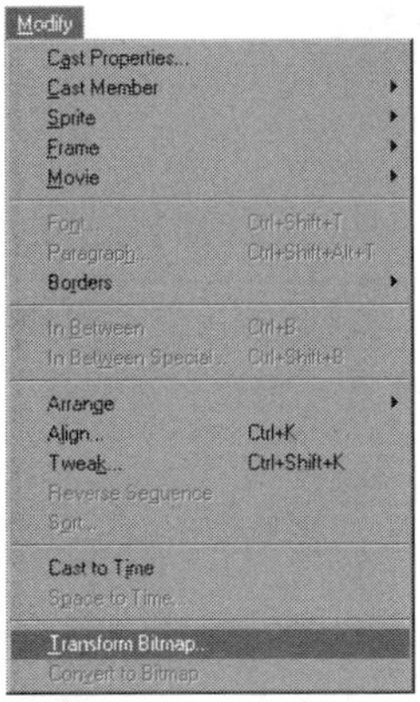

Figure 29. Choose **Transform Bitmap** from the **Modify** menu.

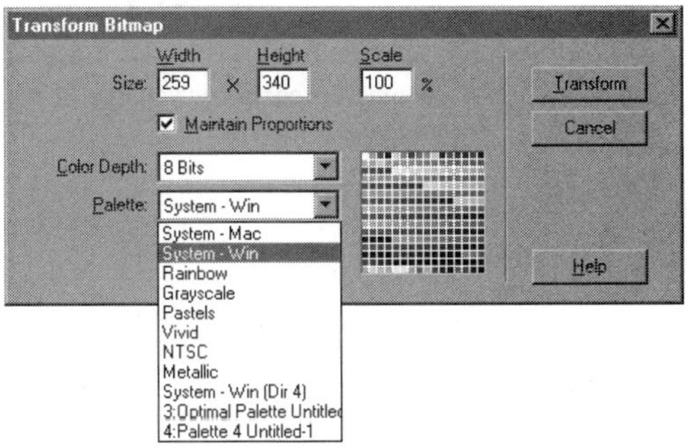

Figure 30. In the **Transform Bitmap** dialog box, select a palette from the **Palette** pop-up menu to which the cast member should be remapped.

To remap a cast member to a different color palette:

Director lets you "remap" a cast member to a different palette. When you remap a cast member to a new palette, Director examines the cast member's original colors (actually examines which color each pixel is currently mapped to), and remaps its pixels to new color positions in the new palette which contain colors that best match the original. This often leads to a close, but not identical match of colors. To improve results, the palette you are remapping to should have a similar set of colors compared to the cast member's currently assigned palette.

1. In a cast window, select the cast member you would like to remap **(Figure 28)**.
2. Choose Transform Bitmap from the Modify menu **(Figure 29)**.
3. In the Transform Bitmap dialog box, use the Palette pop-up menu to choose the palette to which the cast member should be remapped **(Figure 30)**.
4. Click the Remap Colors radio button in the Transform Bitmap dialog box.
5. Click Transform to remap the cast member to the new palette. Now play your movie back to see how the cast member looks in its new color scheme, or examine the cast member more closely in Director's paint window.

✔ **Tip**

- Since remapping a cast member can distort its colors, it's a good idea to perform your first remap on a copy of the cast member. This way, you can still revert to an earlier color scheme. To copy a cast member, select it in the cast window, and choose Copy from the Edit menu; then select an empty cast member position and choose Paste from the Edit menu.

To remap cast members on the stage to the current palette:

When you have cast members on the stage that are assigned color palettes different from the current palette, these cast members will not appear in their accurate colors. Director can automatically remap all such cast members on the fly to the current color palette. Note that this feature only affects the appearance of cast members on the stage, and does not permanently remap the actual cast members.

1. Choose Movie from the Modify menu and select Properties from the pop-up menu **(Figure 31)**.
2. In the Movie Properties dialog box, check the Remap Palettes When Needed box **(Figure 32)**.
3. Click OK.

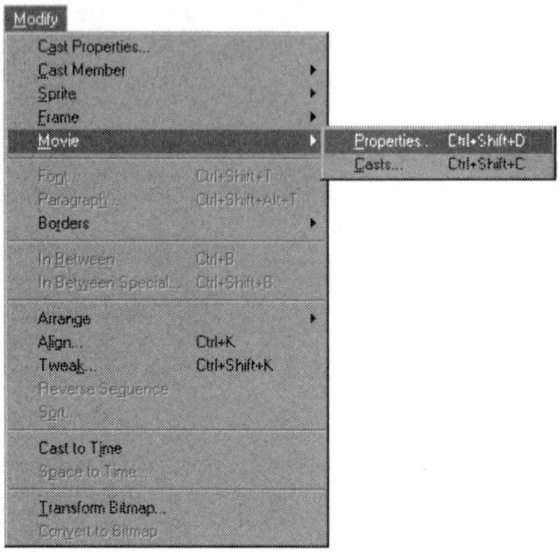

Figure 31. Choose **Movie** from the **Modify** menu and select **Properties** from the pop-up menu.

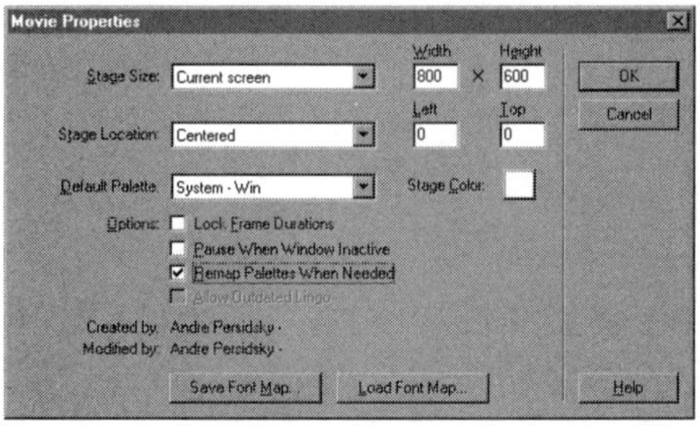

Figure 32. In the **Movie Properties** dialog box, check the **Remap Palettes When Needed** box.

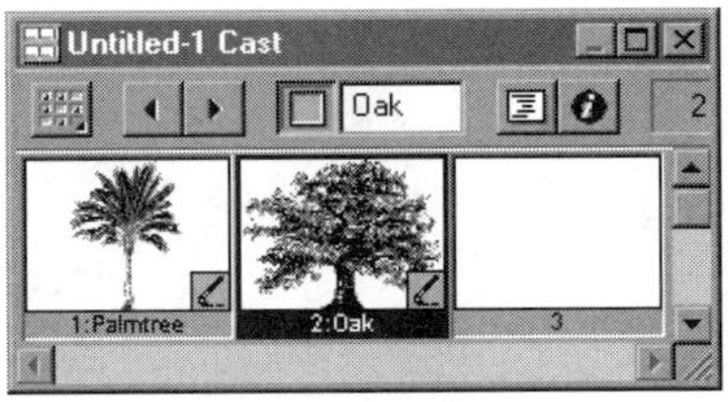

Figure 33. Select the cast member whose palette you wish to use as the basis for your optimal palette.

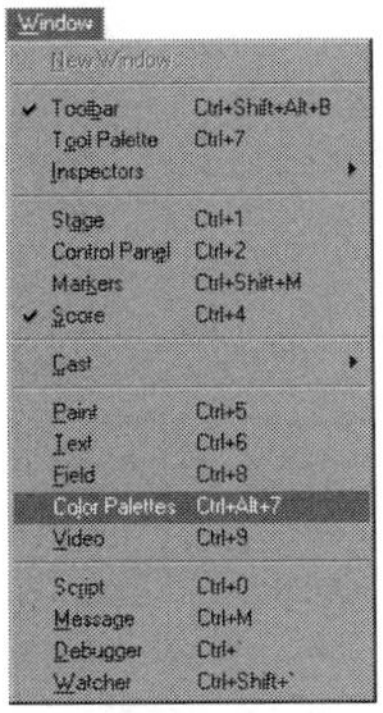

Figure 34. Choose **Color Palettes** from the **Window** menu.

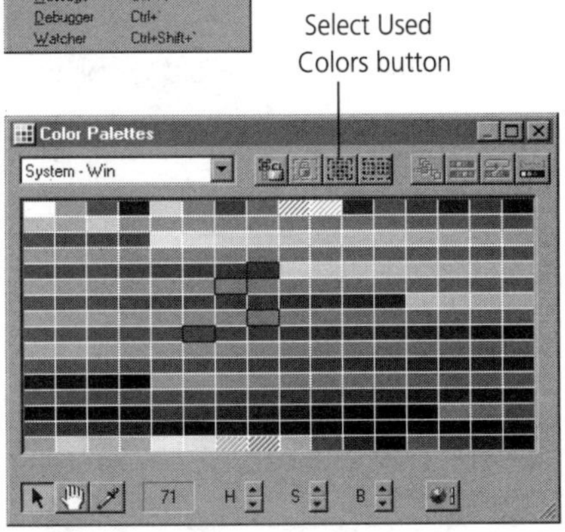

Figure 35. Click the **Select Used Colors** button in the color palettes window.

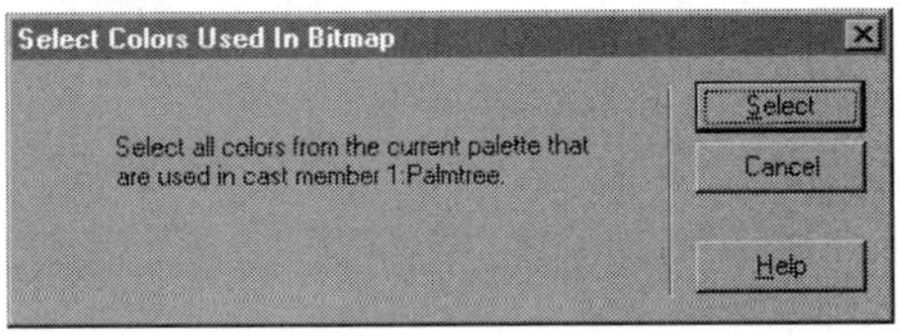

Figure 36. In the **Select Colors Used in Bitmap** dialog box, click the **Select** button to highlight all colors used by the selected cast member.

CREATE AN OPTIMAL COLOR PALETTE

It's possible to create a single, specialized palette that incorporates many of the same colors, or similar ones, shared by your entire cast. Once you've created this "optimal" palette, you can remap all of your cast members to it using the steps outlined on page 129. This approach allows your movie to operate from a single common palette, keeping colors consistent throughout.

Remember, however, that remapping a cast member to a new palette—even an optimal one—often leads to a close but not identical match of colors. So don't be surprised if your cast members are colored a little differently once they've been remapped to an optimal palette.

To create an optimal color palette for all cast members:

1. In a cast window, select a cast member whose assigned palette you wish to use as the basis for your optimal palette **(Figure 33)**. It's preferable to choose a cast member that uses only a small number of the colors available in its palette. For instance, a cast member that uses only three colors from a palette of 256 would be ideal.
2. Choose Color Palettes from the Window menu **(Figure 34)**.
3. In the color palettes window, click the Select Used Colors button **(Figure 35)**.
4. In the Select Colors Used in Bitmap dialog box, click the Select button **(Figure 36)**. Director will highlight all the colors used by the cast member you selected earlier. It's often difficult to tell which of the palette's colors are selected. Selected colors have a thin black border, while unselected colors have thin white borders **(Figure 35)**.

5. Choose Duplicate from the Edit menu **(Figure 37)**. By copying the original palette, you're free to work without disturbing the cast member's current coloring.

6. In the Create Palette dialog box, type the name you wish to give this palette **(Figure 38)**. You might want to use something descriptive, such as "Optimal Palette". Click OK.

7. With all the used colors still highlighted in the color palettes window, click the Hand tool and then drag one of the highlighted colors to the second color position in the first row of colors (the position immediately to the right of white). Director rearranges the selected colors into a continuous range **(Figure 39)**.

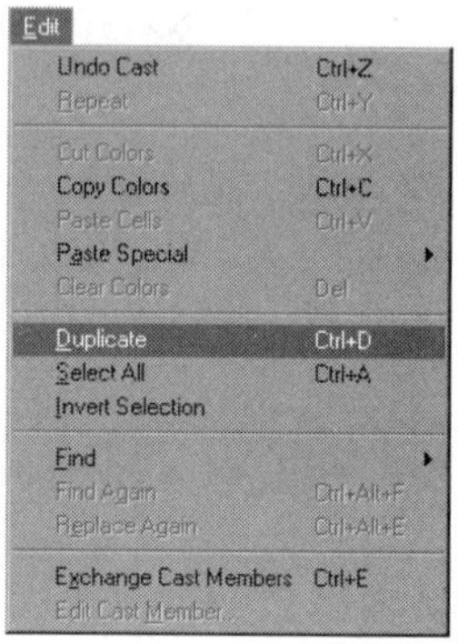

Figure 37. Choose **Duplicate** from the **Edit** menu.

Figure 38. Type the name you wish to give this duplicated palette in the **Create Palette** dialog box.

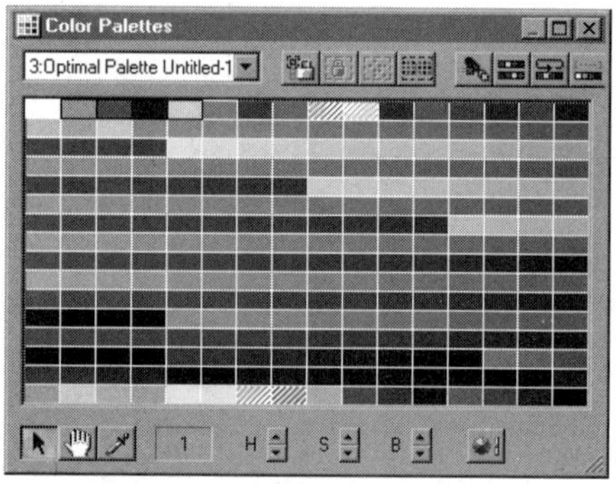

Figure 39. Drag one of the highlighted colors to the second position in the first row. Director rearranges the selected colors into a continuous range.

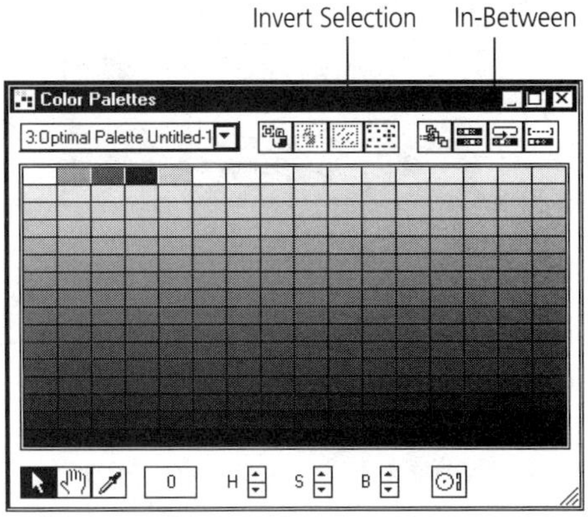

Figure 40. In-Betweening a range of colors changes them into a continuous blend of similar colors, so you can easily tell them apart from the used colors.

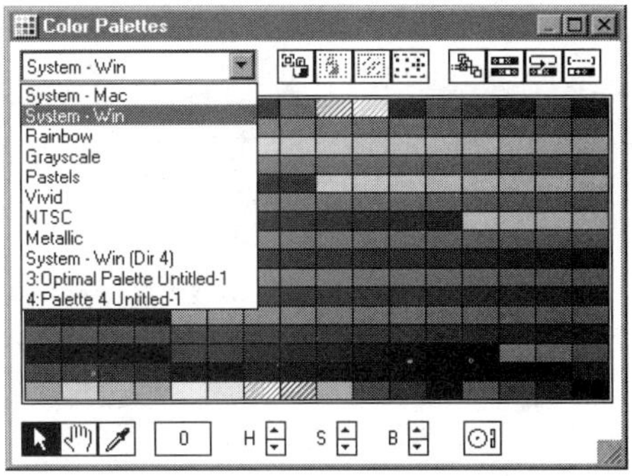

Figure 41. In the color palettes window, click the **Palette** pop-up menu and select another palette used by other cast members in your movie.

8. Click the Invert Selection button in the color palettes window. This selects all the *unused* colors in the palette.
9. Click the In-Between button in the color palettes window **(Figure 40)**. Director changes all unused colors into a continuous blend of similar colors so you can easily tell them apart from the used colors that will be the backbone of your optimal palette **(Figure 40)**. In this area of blended colors (which you don't need, since these colors are not used by the cast member selected in step 1) you can paste additional colors from other color palettes.
10. You're now ready to collect additional colors used by your cast members from other color palettes. In the color palettes window, click the Palette pop-up menu and select another palette used by other cast members in your movie **(Figure 41)**.

11. In the color palettes window, click each color chip that you'd like to add to your optimal palette **(Figure 42)**. Hold down the Control key to make multiple, discontinuous selections, or the Shift key to select a range. You can also select a cast member in the cast window that uses this palette and then click the Select Used Colors button in the color palettes window to highlight all the colors the cast member uses. Try to select a handful of colors that best represent the color range of the palette. For instance, pick a couple of reds, a couple of blues, a few grays, greens, and so on.
12. Choose Copy Colors from the Edit menu **(Figure 43)**.
13. In the color palettes window, click the Palette pop-up menu and select the optimal palette you created earlier **(Figure 44)**.

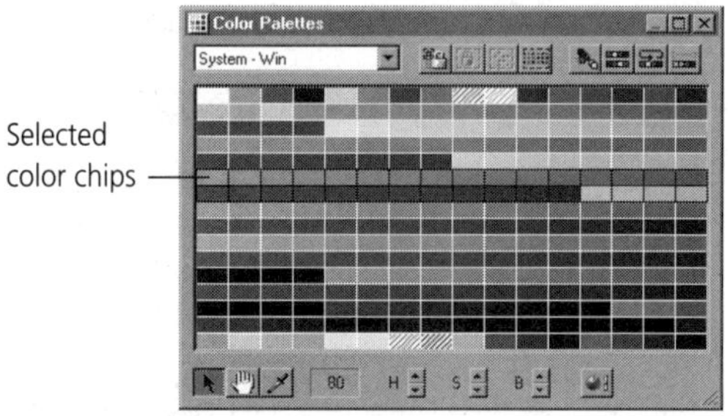

Figure 42. In the color palettes window, select the color chips to be added to your optimal palette.

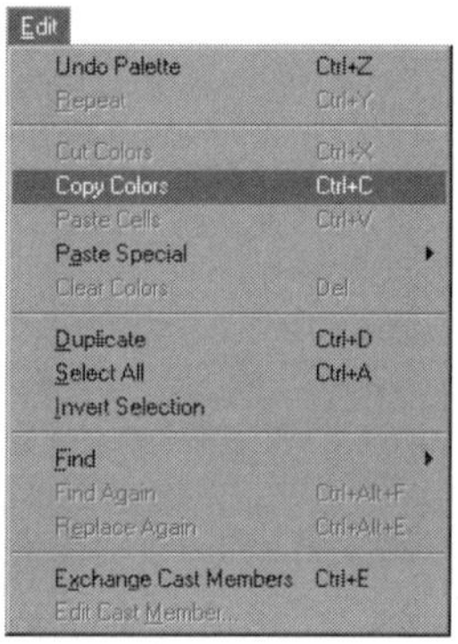

Figure 43. Choose **Copy Colors** from the **Edit** menu.

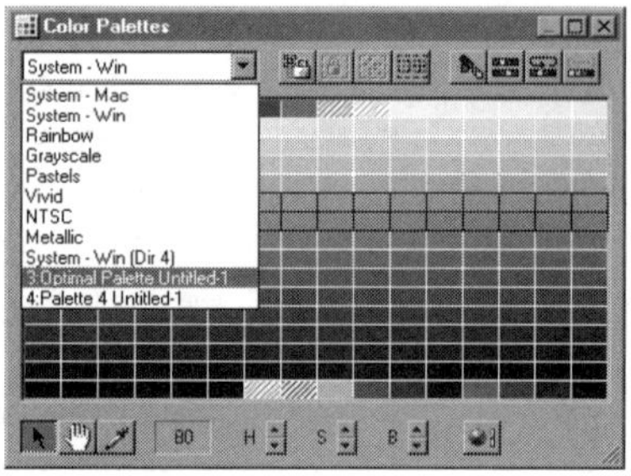

Figure 44. In the color palettes window, click the **Palette** pop-up menu and select the optimal palette you created earlier.

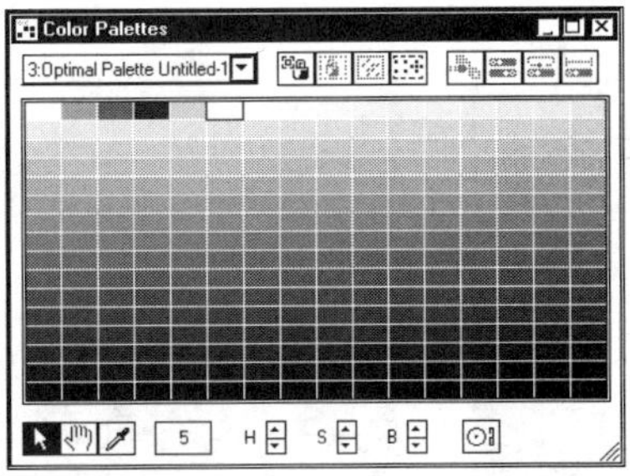

Figure 45. In the optimal palette, highlight one of the blended, unused color chips.

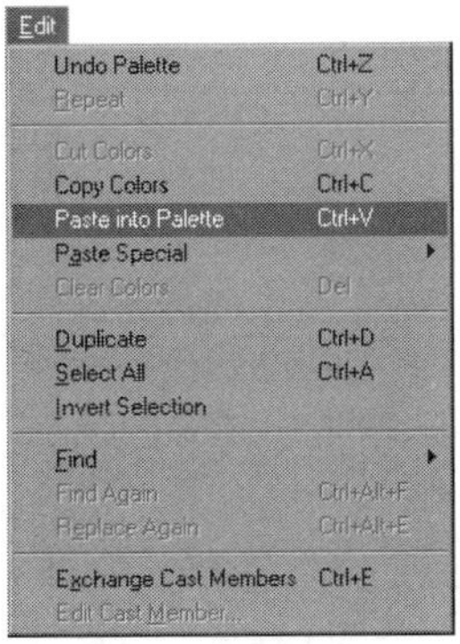

Figure 46. Choose **Paste Into Palette** from the **Edit** menu.

14. In the optimal palette **(Figure 45)**, select the first blended chip that immediately follows the last used color in the palette. Make sure that you have enough blended, unused color chips to accommodate the new colors.

15. Choose Paste Into Palette from the Edit menu to add the new colors to your optimal palette **(Figure 46)**.

16. Repeat steps 10 through 15 to continue adding colors from other color palettes.

17. Close the color palettes window when you've filled up your optimal palette.

18. Now you're ready to remap your movie's cast members to the optimal palette you've just created. To do so, follow the steps outlined on page 129, under the heading "*To remap a cast member to a different palette*".

✓ Tip

- Creating an optimal palette can sometimes require a lot of trial and error. After your first attempt, you may find that the optimal palette's colors are still not true enough to your cast member's original colors. In that case, simply open the optimal palette (choose Color Palettes from the Window menu) and adjust or replace the colors that affect your cast members. *(See page 136 for more details about editing the colors in a palette)*

CREATING CUSTOM COLOR PALETTES

If you wish to create a custom color palette, the first step is to create a duplicate of one of Director's standard palettes, since they cannot be modified. You are then free to edit any color in this duplicate palette, or even replace the colors all together.

To duplicate a color palette:

1. Choose Color Palettes from the Window menu **(Figure 47)**.
2. In the color palettes window, use the Palette pop-up menu to select the color palette you'd like to duplicate **(Figure 49)**.
3. Choose Duplicate from the Edit menu **(Figure 48)**.
4. In the Create Palette dialog box **(Figure 50)**, type a name for the duplicate palette and click OK. The palette is placed in the active cast window.

To edit colors in the color palettes window:

1. Choose Color Palettes from the Window menu **(Figure 47)**.
2. In the color palettes window, use the Palette pop-up menu to select the color palette you'd like to edit **(Figure 49)**. Since you cannot modify the standard preset Director palettes, you will be prompted with the Create Palette dialog box when you try to change a standard palette.
3. With the pointer tool click the color chip you want to edit. The chip is highlighted by a black border.

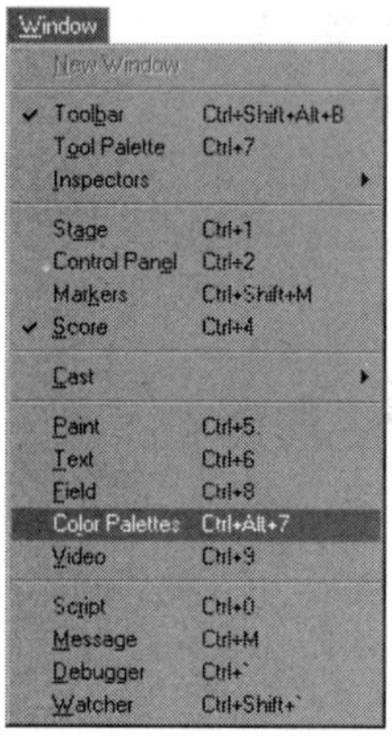

Figure 47. Choose **Color Palettes** from the **Window** menu.

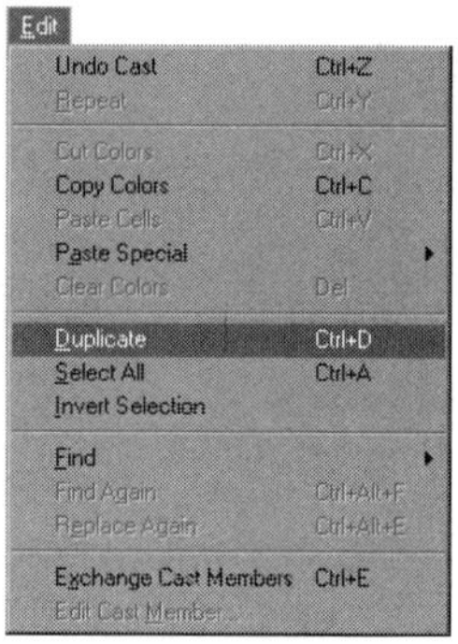

Figure 48. Choose **Duplicate** from the **Edit** menu.

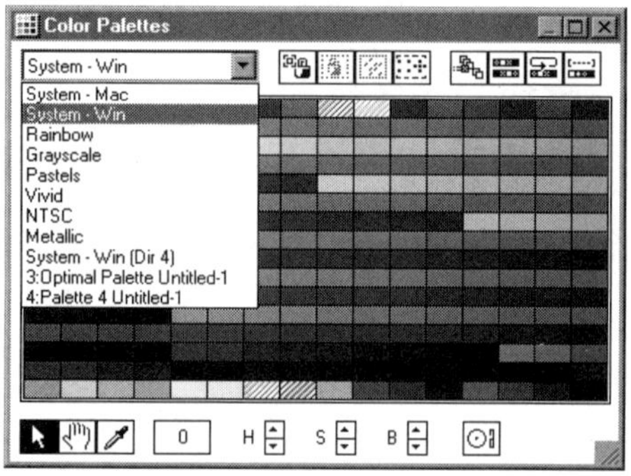

Figure 49. In the color palettes window, select a palette from the **Palette** pop-up menu.

Figure 50. Type the name you wish to give this duplicate palette in the **Create Palette** dialog box.

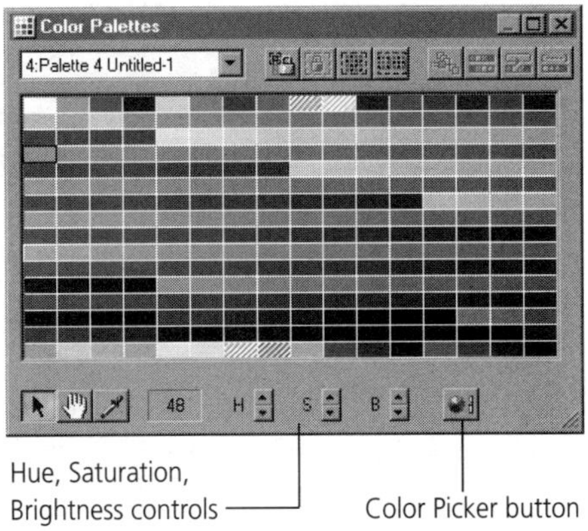

Figure 51. Click the color chip you want to edit.

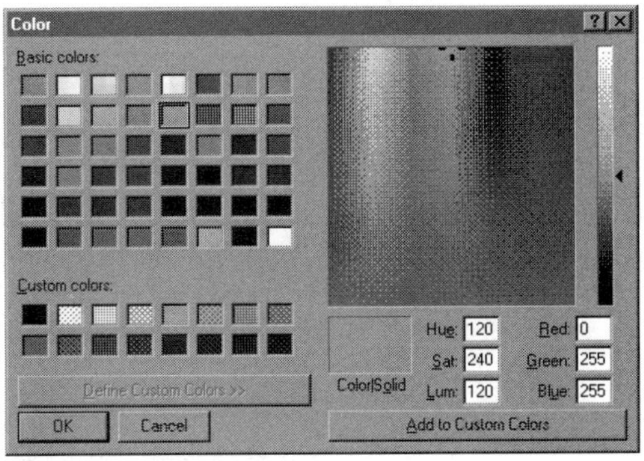

Figure 52. In the **Color Picker** dialog box, click inside the color box to select a color, or type values into the Hue, Saturation, Brightness, or Red, Green, Blue boxes for a precise selection.
In the **HSB** color model, **hue** refers to the basic color that is created by mixing two primary colors, such as red and green. **Saturation** refers to the amount of white that's mixed into any given color—a fully saturated color is vivid, containing no white, while a less saturated color appears lighter, more pastel. **Brightness** measures how much black is mixed into a color. Lowering the brightness value adds more black, making the color darker and muddier. A brightness value of 0 makes a color solid black.
The **RGB** model is simpler, defining colors by mixing varying degrees of red, green, and blue. Each color has over 65,000 possible degrees.
You can create one of the more than 16 million colors that your PC can display with either of these color models.

4. Use the hue, saturation, and brightness controls (labeled H, S, and B, respectively) at the bottom of the color palettes window to adjust the color. Clicking the up and down arrows steps through new values for the color **(Figure 51)**.

or

4. For greater accuracy in your color selection, use the Color Picker. The Color Picker allows you to describe a new color by using precise numeric values or simply by clicking the color box. With a color chip selected in the color palettes window, click the Color Picker button **(Figure 51)**.
5. In the Color Picker dialog box, click a desired color in the color box **(Figure 52)**. Use the Color Picker's scroll bar to control brightness. To make a precise selection, type values in the Hue, Saturation, and Brightness boxes, or the Red, Green, and Blue boxes.
6. When you're satisfied with the selected color, click OK. Director places the new color in the palette.

✔ **Tip**

- When editing a color chip, you may want to work with a copy of it. This way you can easily return to the original color if you have to, since only its copy will have been changed. To copy a color, select it in the palette and choose Copy Colors from the Edit menu. Then select an unused color chip in the palette and choose Paste into Palette from the Edit menu.

To copy and paste colors in a palette:

You can use Director's Copy and Paste features to move colors from one palette to another or to rearrange colors within a single palette.

1. Choose Color Palettes from the Window menu.
2. In the color palettes window, use the pointer or hand tool to select the color chips you wish to copy. Hold down the Control key to make multiple, discontinuous selections, or Shift-click to select a range between two color chips **(Figure 53)**.
3. Choose Copy Colors from the Edit menu **(Figure 54)**.
4. If you are copying the colors to a new palette, use the Palette pop-up menu in the color palettes window to choose the destination palette.
5. Click the new color chip position in which to paste the copied colors **(Figure 55)**.
6. Choose Paste into Palette from the Edit menu to place the copied colors **(Figure 56)**.

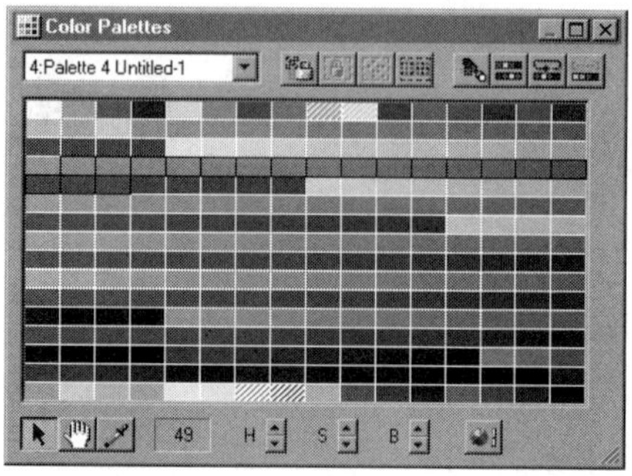

Figure 53. In the color palettes window, use the pointer or hand tool to select the color chips you wish to copy.

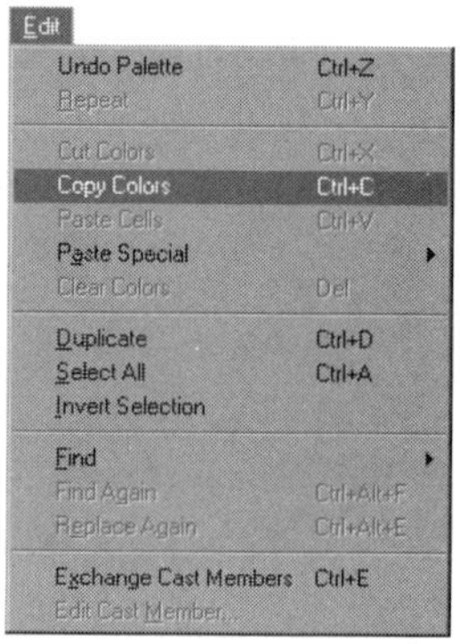

Figure 54. Choose **Copy Colors** from the **Edit** menu.

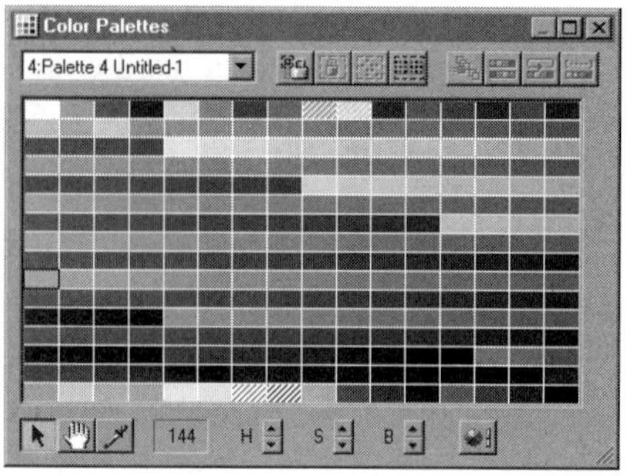

Figure 55. Click the new color chip position where the copied color(s) will be pasted.

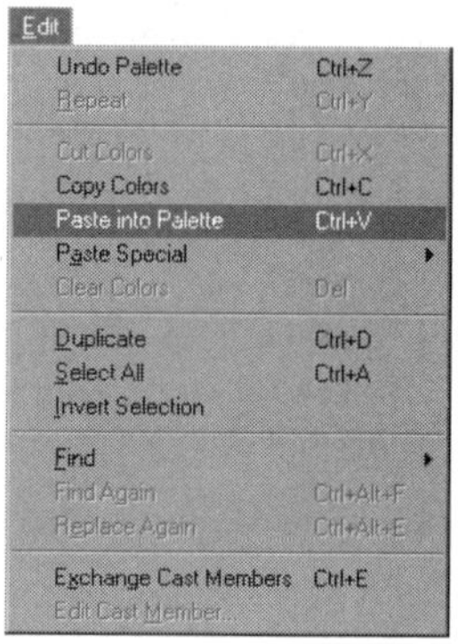

Figure 56. Choose **Paste Into Palette** from the **Edit** menu.

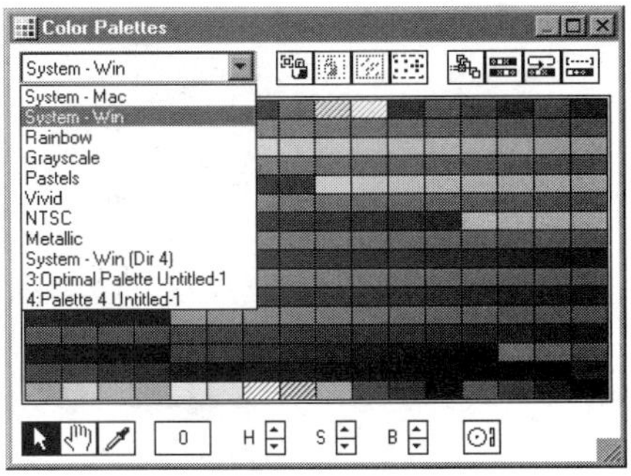

Figure 57. In the color palettes window, use the **Palette** pop-up menu to select the desired palette.

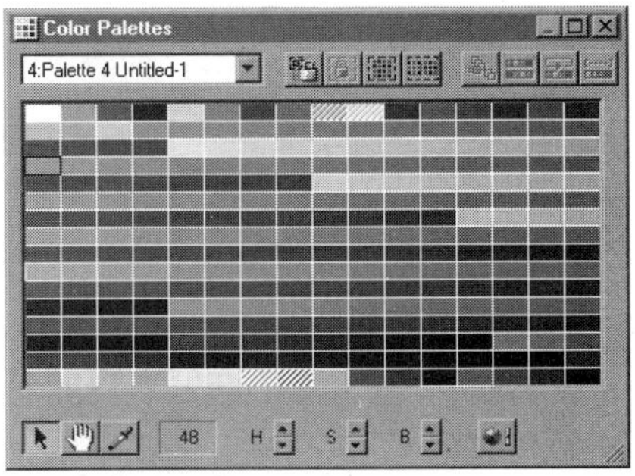

Figure 58. With the pointer tool, select the first color in your blend.

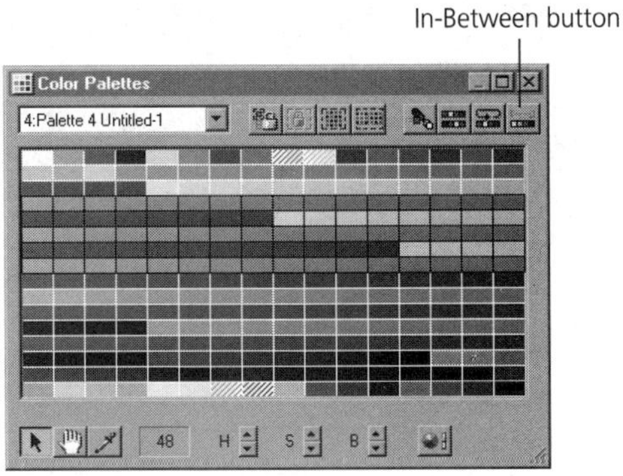

Figure 59. Hold down the Shift key and select your blend's destination color to highlight all colors in this range.

To blend colors within a palette:

You can create a range of colors that blends from one color to a second color. For example, if you were creating a sunset backdrop, you might need a blend of colors from red to yellow. Blending colors is especially useful for creating subtle gradient fills and smooth color cycling.

1. Choose Color Palettes from the Window menu.
2. In the color palettes window, use the Palette pop-up menu to select the desired palette **(Figure 57)**.
3. With the pointer tool, select the first color in your blend **(Figure 58)**. For instance, if you want to blend the palette from red to yellow, you would first click the red color chip.
4. Hold down the Shift key and select your blend's destination color **(Figure 59)**. If blending from red to yellow, you'd select the yellow color chip.
5. Click the In-Between button in the color palettes window **(Figure 59)**. The palette will blend in a continuous tone from the first selected color to the second.

✔ Tip

- Sometimes you'll want to control the number of color chips over which your blend occurs—for instance, you may want a blend to occupy only fifteen or twenty color chips, rather than taking up a hundred valuable chips in an already limited palette. To do this, you may have to move the two blended colors closer together in their palette so that they are separated by the desired number of color chips. To move a color chip, use the palette window's hand tool to drag it to a new position in the palette.
- You may want to work with a duplicate of your original palette, since creating a blend can radically change it.

To sample colors directly from artwork:

Director's Eyedropper tool makes it easy to identify specific colors that appear in a cast member on the stage. With the Eyedropper, you can click any color you see on the stage, and Director automatically highlights that color in the color palettes window. This is especially useful when you want to isolate certain colors, either for modification or for copying into another custom palette that you're building, such as an optimal palette.

1. In the score, select the cell that contains the cast member sprite whose colors you'd like to identify with the Eyedropper. The sprite should appear on the stage **(Figure 60)**.
2. Choose Color Palettes from the Window menu **(Figure 61)**.
3. In the color palettes window, select the Eyedropper tool **(Figure 62)**.
4. With the Eyedropper tool, click the sprite on the stage to sample its color at any point **(Figure 60)**. This color becomes highlighted in the color palettes window **(Figure 62)**. You can now modify the color or copy it to a new palette.

Figure 60. Use the Eyedropper tool to sample the colors of a cast member sprite on the stage.

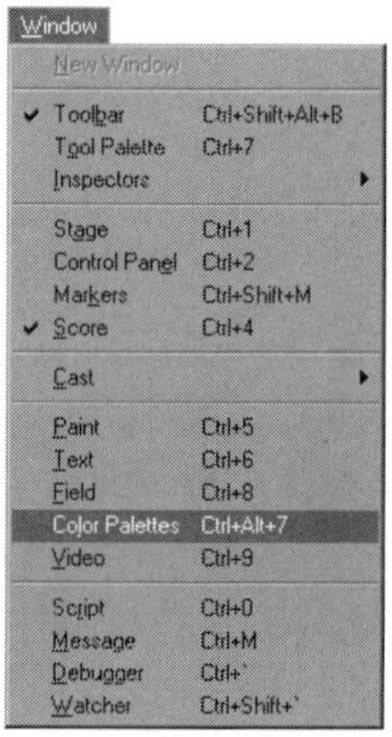

Figure 61. Choose **Color Palettes** from the **Window** menu.

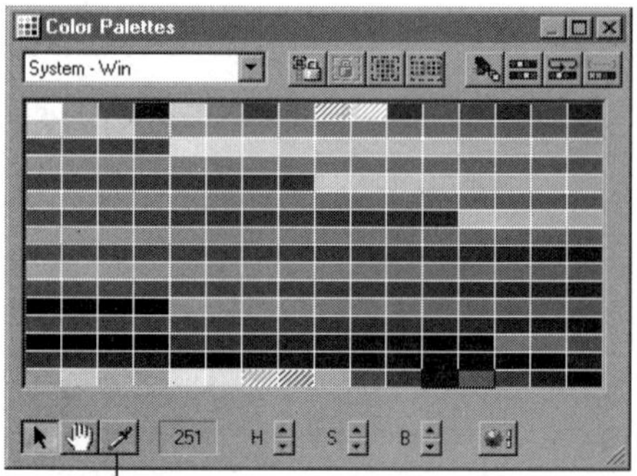

The Eyedropper tool

Figure 62. In the color palettes window, select the Eyedropper tool.

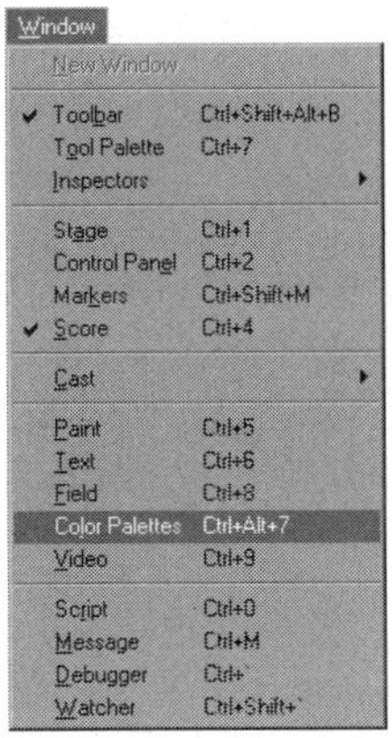

Figure 63. Choose **Color Palettes** from the **Window** menu.

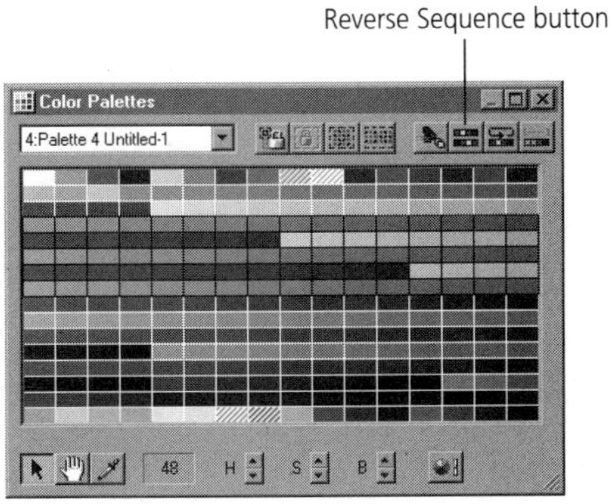

Figure 64. In the color palettes window, select a range of colors to be reversed.

To reverse the order of a palette's colors:

You can reverse the order of all the colors in a palette, or just within a select range. Reversing colors causes the chips positioned toward the end of the palette to be moved toward the palette's beginning. Doing so can change the coloring of cast members that are based on that particular palette.

1. Choose Color Palettes from the Window menu **(Figure 63)**.
2. In the color palettes window, select the first color chip in the range **(Figure 64)**.
3. Hold down the Shift key and select the last color chip in the range. All color chips between the two colors will be selected.
4. Click the Reverse Sequence button in the color palettes window. Director reverses the order of all the colors selected **(Figure 64)**.

✓ Tip

- Reversing the color order in a palette will adversely affect the coloring of cast members using that palette. Consequently you may want to work with a duplicate of the palette, and then apply the new palette to cast members selectively.

To sort colors in a palette:

Director can sort the colors in a color palette by their hue, saturation, or brightness values. This feature is helpful when you would like to compare related colors in a palette.

1. Choose Color Palettes from the Window menu.
2. In the color palettes window, select a range of colors to sort **(Figure 65)**. Using the pointer tool, select the first color chip in the range.
3. Hold down the Shift key and select the last color chip in the range. All color chips between the two selections will be selected.
4. Click the Sort button in the color palettes window **(Figure 65)**.
5. In the Sort Colors dialog box, click either Hue, Saturation, or Brightness to indicate which color attribute you'd like to sort by **(Figure 66)**. Sorting by hue is recommended, since it arranges similar colors together in the palette.

✔ **Tip**

- Like most other changes to a color palette, sorting the color order will affect the coloring of cast members using that palette. Consequently you may want to create a duplicate of the palette, sort your colors in the copied palette, and then apply the new palette to cast members selectively.

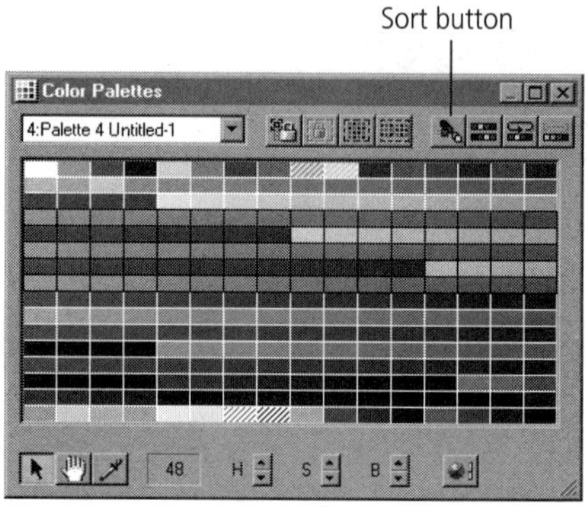

Figure 65. In the color palettes window, select a range of colors to sort.

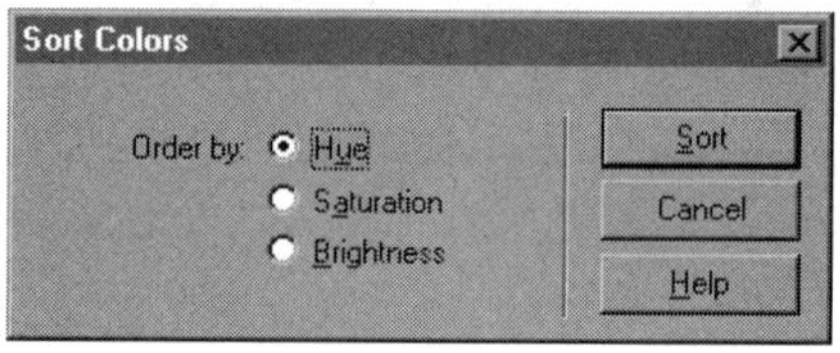

Figure 66. In the **Sort Colors** dialog box, click Hue, Saturation, or Brightness to indicate which color attribute to sort by.

COLOR CYCLING

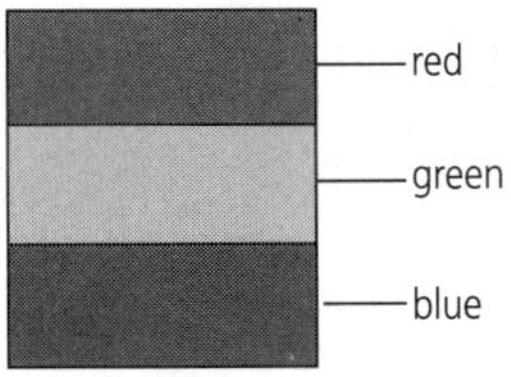

Figure 67. Color cycling, initial colors.

The technique known as **color cycling** achieves the illusion of animation by rotating a selected range of colors in a palette over time. For instance, let's take a cast member that is painted red on top, green in the middle, and blue at its base **(Figure 67)**. Let's assume these three colors are grouped sequentially in a color palette, and that they have been selected for color cycling. Color cycling rotates these colors so that in the first step of the cycle, the red color will shift to the cast member's middle, the green to its base, and the blue to its top. In the next step of the cycle, the red will shift to the cast member's base, the green to its top, and blue to the middle **(Figures 68–69)**.

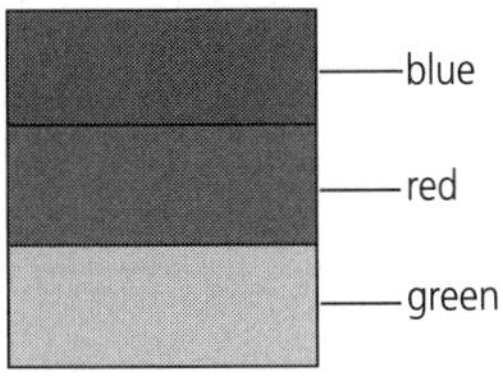

Figure 68. Color cycling, first step.

Cycling colors is the process used to animate TV weather maps, where a storm front appears to pulsate through a range of dark and light shades of blue. It's also handy for effects such as fire and explosions, where color pulses through a series of reds, yellows, and oranges.

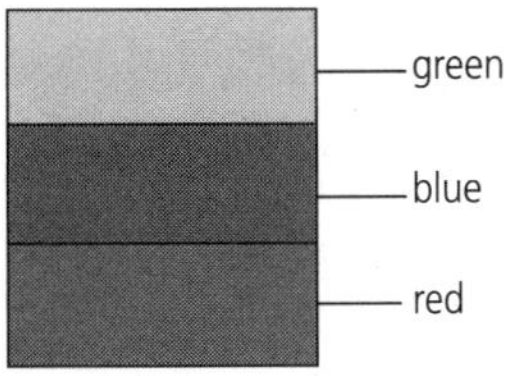

Figure 69. Color cycling, last step.

Color cycling in Director is applied to a selected range of colors over a series of frames. Within those frames, any cast members painted in the selected colors will be cycled.

To cycle colors in a palette:

1. Place the cast members that you wish to color cycle in the desired animation channels and frames of Director's score.
2. In the score's palette channel, select the frame or series of frames that contain the sprite(s) you wish to color cycle **(Figure 70)**. You can select a single frame if you would like to color cycle a stationary sprite (in other words, one that won't move while being cycled). You can cycle throughout an animation by selecting a range of sprites.

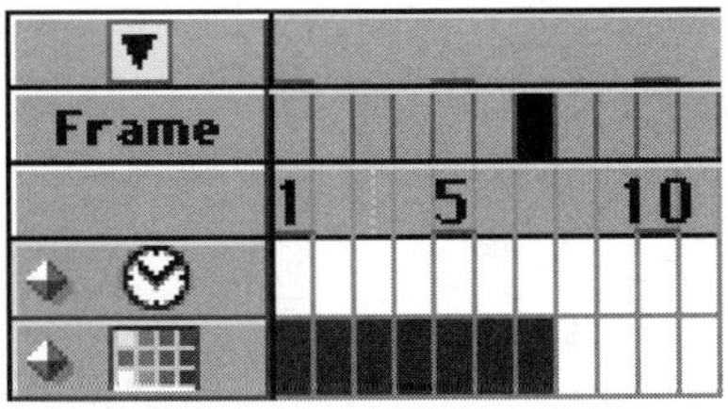

Figure 70. In the score's palette channel, select the frame or series of frames that contain the sprite(s) you wish to color cycle.

3. Choose Frame from the Modify menu and select Palette from the pop-up menu **(Figure 71)**.
4. In the Frame Properties dialog box, click the Color Cycling radio button to select it **(Figure 72)**.
5. Use the Palette pop-up menu to select the palette you wish to apply and cycle in the frames selected in the score.
6. In the Frame Properties dialog box, select a range of colors in its palette that you wish to cycle. You can Shift-click two color chips to select the range of colors between them **(Figure 72)**.
7. Type the number of cycles in the Cycles box if you wish to make complete color cycles per frame. A cycle is achieved each time Director rotates through all the colors selected in step 6.
8. Click the Loop radio button if you want the color cycle to start from the beginning when it reaches the end.

or

8. Click the Auto Reverse radio button if you wish the color cycling to reverse itself at the end of a cycle—for instance, to cycle colors from red to blue in the first cycle, and then from blue to red in the second.
9. Click OK to apply your color cycling to the selected frames in the score.

Note: Color cycling can occur only over a continuous range of colors in a palette. If you wish to cycle only through several colors that are scattered throughout the palette, you will have to group them first in the palette. *(See page 138 on "To copy and paste colors in a palette")*

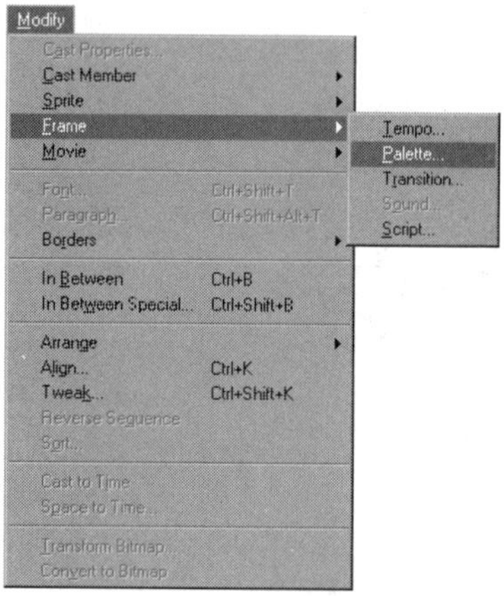

Figure 71. Choose **Frame** from the **Modify** menu and select **Palette** from the pop-up menu.

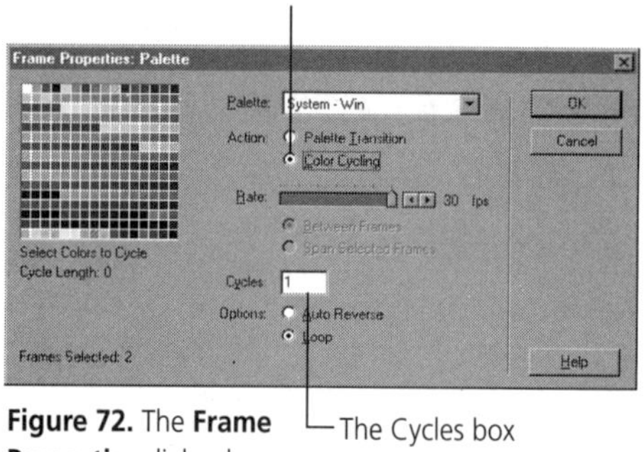

Figure 72. The **Frame Properties** dialog box.

ANIMATION TECHNIQUES 9

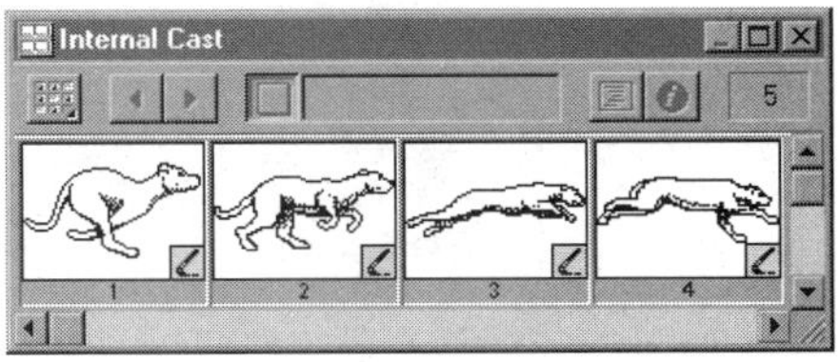

Figure 1. **Cast to Time**, **Space to Time**, and the **Paste Relative** commands are used to place a sequence of cast members over successive frames in your movie.

There are two basic ways of creating animation in Director: the first is by changing the positions of sprites on the stage over successive frames (translation); the second is by arranging an alternating sequence of sprites over successive frames. Both methods are often combined at the same time. An example of this would be the dog in **Figure 1** moving across the stage while its frames are cycling through the sequence.

The first animation method (translation) is supported by the following techniques in Director: Step Recording, In-betweening, and Real-Time recording. The second method (arranging a sequence of sprites over successive frames) is supported by the Cast to Time, Space to Time, and the Paste Relative commands. This chapter covers the basics of using both groups of techniques.

Film loops are covered at the end of the chapter.

Step Recording

Step recording is the most precise method of creating animation in Director—you arrange each frame of an animation by hand. Step recording is also the most labor-intensive method for the same reason: First you arrange your sprites in a given frame, then record the frame, then rearrange the sprites slightly, then record the next frame, then rearrange, then record, and so on **(Figure 2)**. This process of creating a series of frames, all of which feature small differences in the size or position of sprites, is what makes animation possible.

Figure 2. With **Step Recording**, animation is created by manually adjusting and recording sprite positions on a frame-by-frame basis. Above, the frames of an animation are shown all at once. Each successive frame features a cyclist slightly shifted to the left on the stage.

If you're looking to perform quick and painless animation, Step recording is not the method to use. You'd be better served by techniques such as In-betweening,

Real-time recording, Cast to time, or Space to time, which are also detailed in this chapter. But if you want complete, hands-on control over the behavior of sprites from one frame to another, Step recording is the method of choice. Also, if you're new to animation in general, you'll find it useful to learn this fundamental technique.

To Step-Record an animation:

1. In the score window, click the desired frame in the desired animation channel to indicate where your Step recording will begin. If you don't select a frame, Director will probably start with frame 1 in channel 1 **(Figure 3)**.
2. Drag a cast member onto the stage. As soon as you do this, a recording indicator appears beside the channel number to which you have assigned this cast member **(Figure 4)**. The Step Record indicator signifies that the current frame of your animation is being recorded to the score.
3. Position the sprite as it should appear in the first frame of your animation. Once in position, click the Step Forward button in Director's control panel window **(Figure 5)** to record the first frame to the score, and move the playback head to the second frame of your animation.
4. Position the sprite as it should appear in the next frame (again, you will probably want to move it slightly or change its shape). Once in position, click the Step Forward button in the control panel window to record this new frame to the score.

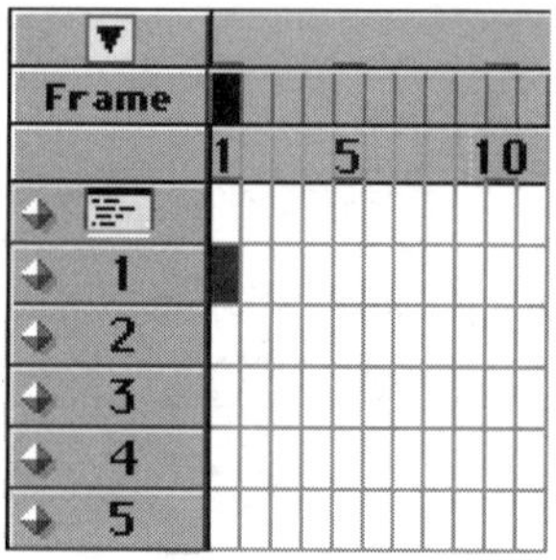

Figure 3. Select the cell in the score where your Step recording should begin.

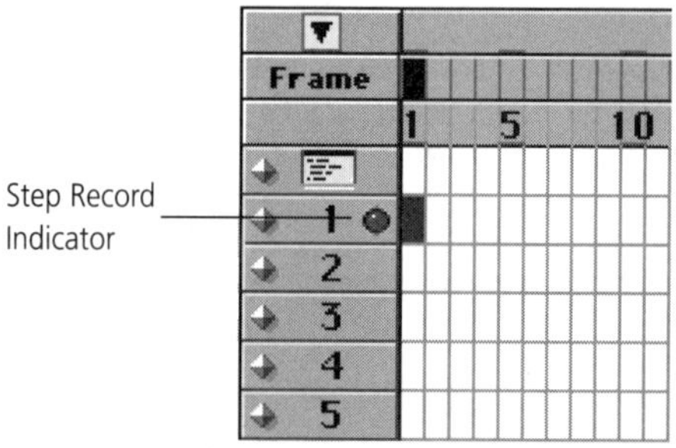

Figure 4. When you drag a cast member onto the stage, a recording indicator automatically appears beside the channel number to which the cast member is assigned.

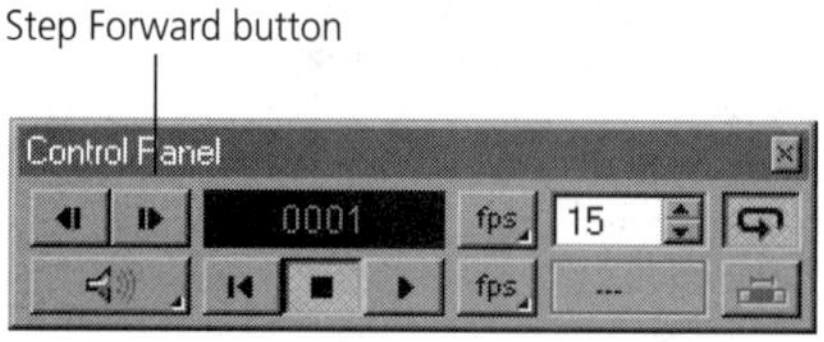

Figure 5. Click the **Step Forward** button in the control panel to record a frame of your animation, and advance to the next frame.

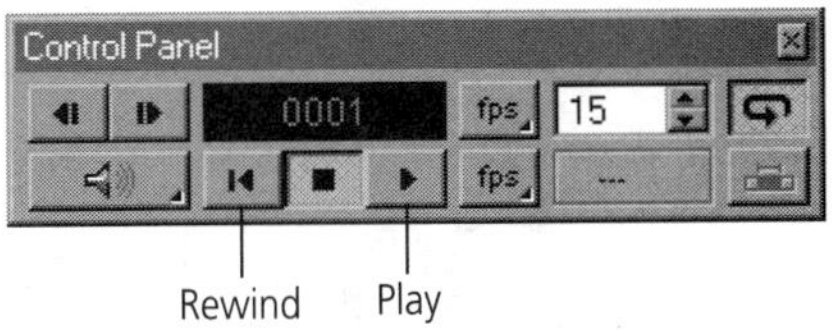

Figure 6. Click **Rewind**, then click **Play** in the control panel to play back your full sequence of frames.

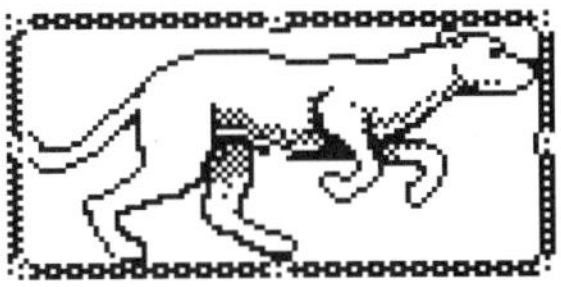

Figure 7. By Alt-clicking a sprite on the stage, you turn on Step recording for the channel that contains this sprite. The sprite is highlighted by a thick border indicating that it's being recorded.

5. Repeat Step 4 as many times as necessary to complete the animation. When you are finished, you can use the control panel to rewind and play back the full sequence of frames **(Figure 6)**.

✔ Tips

- You can turn step recording on or off for a particular channel by holding down the Alt key and clicking the channel number to the left of the channel cells.
- You can record a sprite that's already on the stage by clicking it while holding down the Alt key. A thick selection border appears surrounding the sprite, indicating that it is being recorded **(Figure 7)**. Step recording is turned on in the channel that contains this sprite.
- You can turn on Step recording for multiple sprites on the stage by Alt-clicking each of them. The Step record indicator appears in each of the channels containing these sprites.

ANIMATING CAST MEMBER SEQUENCES

To place cast members into sequential frames using Cast to Time:

The Cast to Time command offers a convenient way to create an animation by moving a series of cast members from a cast window into sequential frames in Director's score. Suppose you have four cast members that form an animation sequence, such as a dog running **(Figure 9)**. By placing these four cast members into sequential frames in the score, an animation sequence is created. You still need to arrange the positions of the sprites on the stage.

Normally when you drag a multiple cast member selection from a cast window into the score, the cast members are all placed into the same frame, but each into a separate channel. Use the Cast to Time command to place cast members of a multiple cast member selection into sequential frames in the same channel.

1. In the score window, click a cell to indicate the starting point where your cast members should be placed **(Figure 8)**.
2. In the cast window, select the cast members that you want to move onto the stage and into your score **(Figure 9)**. You can select a sequential range of cast members by clicking the first member in the sequence and while holding down the Shift key, clicking the last member in the sequence. To select cast members in a non-sequential order (for instance, the first, third, and seventh members), hold down the Control key while clicking.

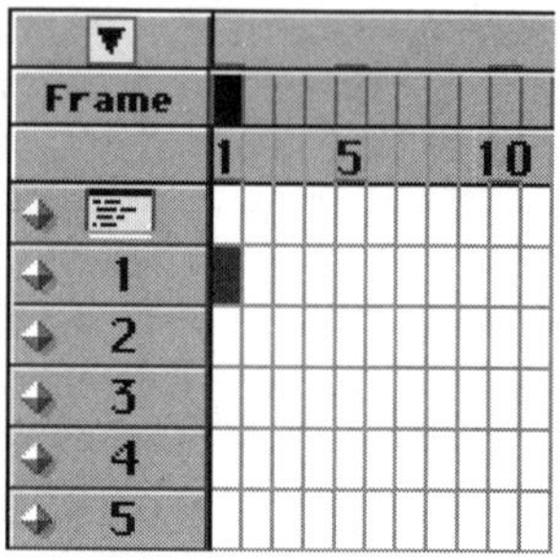

Figure 8. Select the cell in the score to indicate the starting point where your cast members should be placed.

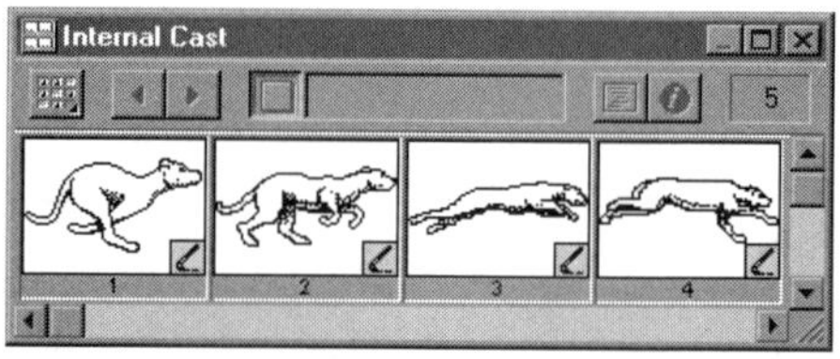

Figure 9. In a cast window, select the cast members that you want to move onto the stage and into sequential frames in the same channel in the score.

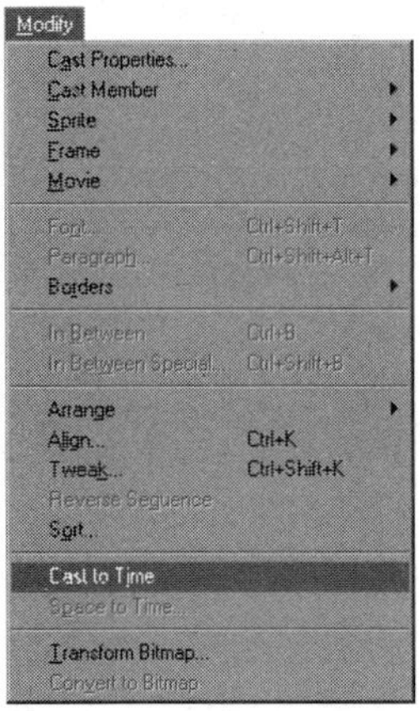

Figure 10. Choose **Cast to Time** from the **Modify** menu.

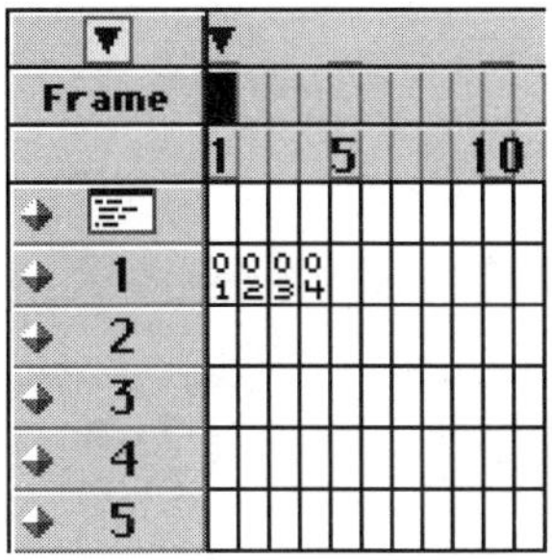

Figure 11. Four selected cast members have been placed into sequential frames in the score using **Cast to Time**.

3. With the cast window still active, choose Cast to Time from the Modify menu **(Figure 10)**. Director places the selected cast members onto the stage, and into their respective frames (for instance, if you selected 4 cast members, they will be placed into 4 sequential frames of Director's score) **(Figure 11)**. You can now rewind and play your new animation using the control panel window.

✓ Tips

- As a shortcut, you can place selected cast members across frames in the score by holding the Alt key while dragging them from the cast window.
- Before using Cast to Time, make sure that the order of cast members in your selected sequence corresponds to the order the cast members should have in the frames.
- To reposition an entire sequence of cast members that was placed on the stage using the Cast to Time command, select all the cells that contain the cast members you'd like to move, and drag the cast member that appears on the stage to a new position. Although it seems like you've only moved one cast member, Director moves the entire sequence of cast members in the frames that you selected in the score.

Space to Time

You will find it convenient to initially place cast members that form an animation sequence, such as a dog running across the stage, into a single frame in the score, so you can view all of them at once on the stage for proper positioning. After positioning these cast members, you will probably want to transfer them from the single frame in the score to multiple frames occupying a single channel, to form an animation sequence. The Space to Time command allows you to do just that.

1. Select a cell in the score where you wish your animation sequence to begin.
2. Drag the cast members that comprise your animation sequence one by one from the cast window onto the stage area, and arrange their positions as they should appear in the animation sequence. Director automatically places these cast members into sequential channels in the score, all in the same frame **(Figure 12)**. Be sure to drag them in the order in which your animation sequence takes place.
3. Select the cells in the score that comprise your animation sequence, and choose Space to Time from the Modify menu to rearrange the cells into a single channel **(Figure 13)**.
4. In the Space to Time dialog box, enter the Separation value that indicates how many frames apart the cast members should be placed **(Figure 14)**. Director rearranges your sprites so that they occupy a single channel, instead of a single frame **(Figure 15)**.

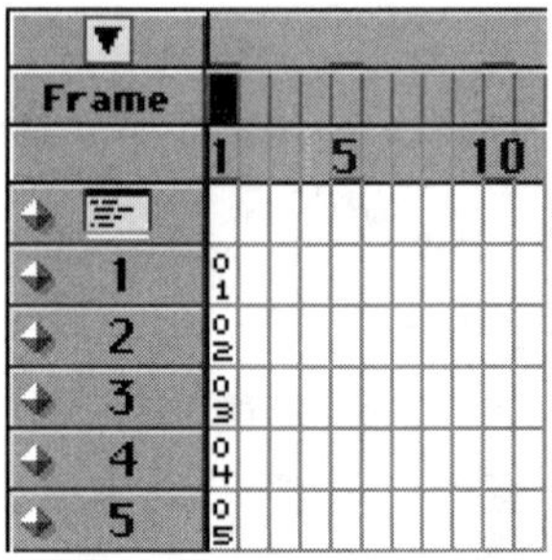

Figure 12. Cast members dragged from a cast window onto the stage are automatically placed into sequential channels in the score.

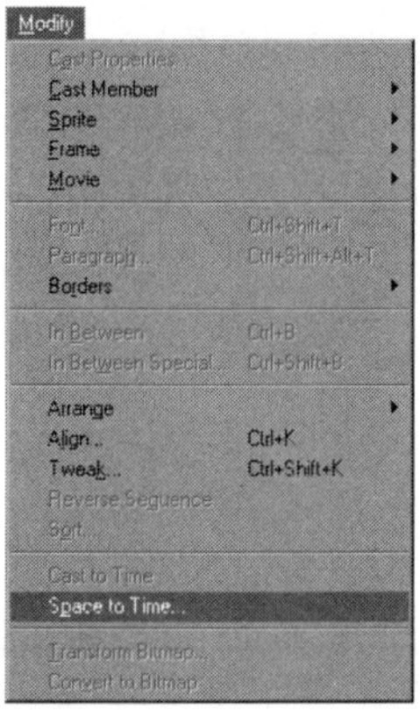

Figure 13. Choose **Space to Time** from the **Modify** menu.

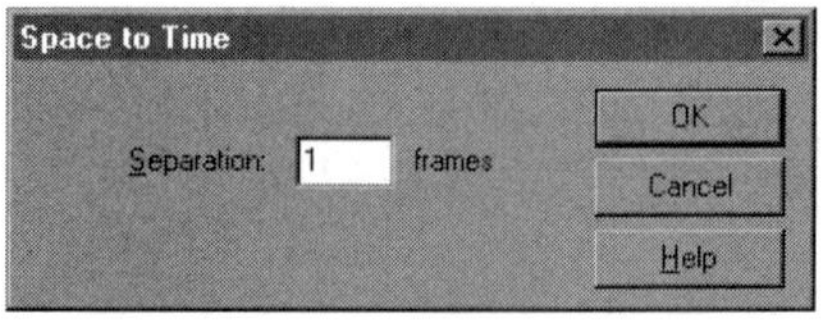

Figure 14. The Separation value in the **Space to Time** dialog box determines how many frames apart sprites will be placed in the score.

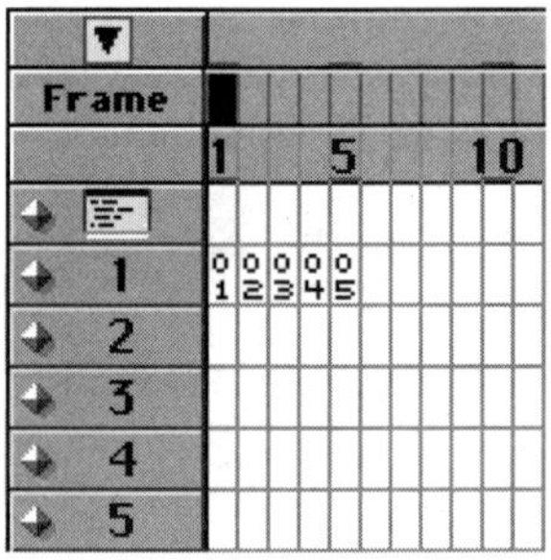

Figure 15. Sprites are shown rearranged into a single channel using **Space to Time**.

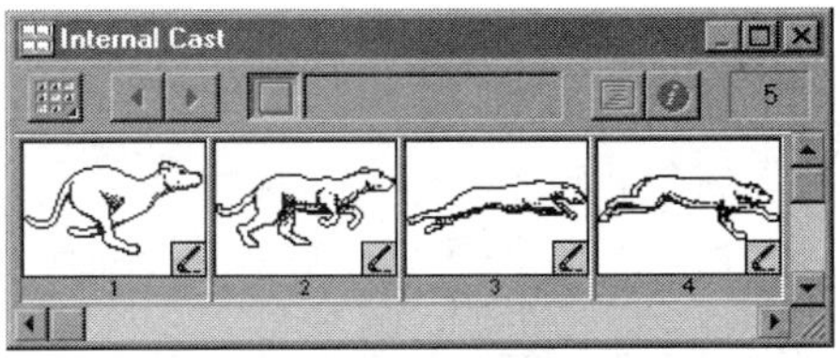

Figure 16. The cast window here shows four cast members that comprise the animated sequence of a running dog.

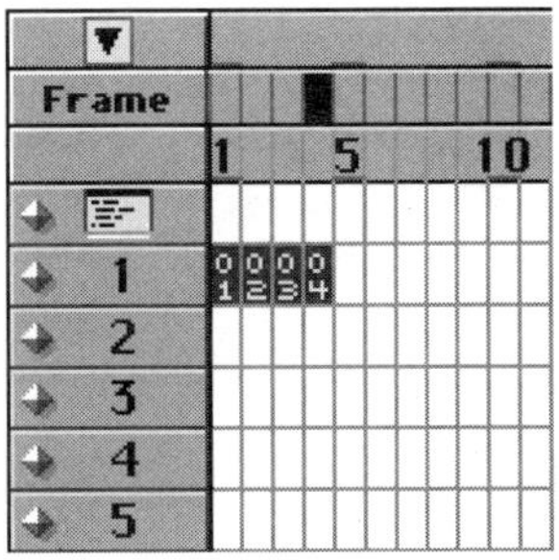

Figure 17. Select the cells in the score that make up your animated sequence.

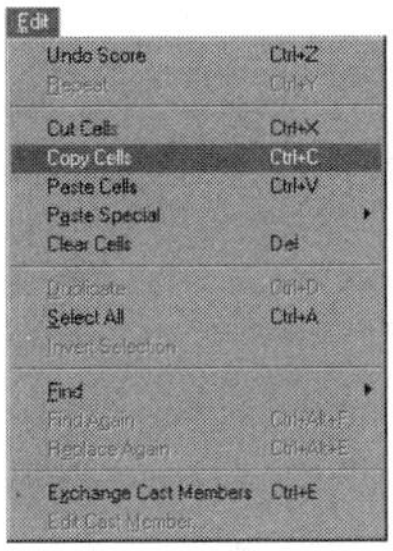

Figure 18. Choose **Copy Cells** from the **Edit** menu.

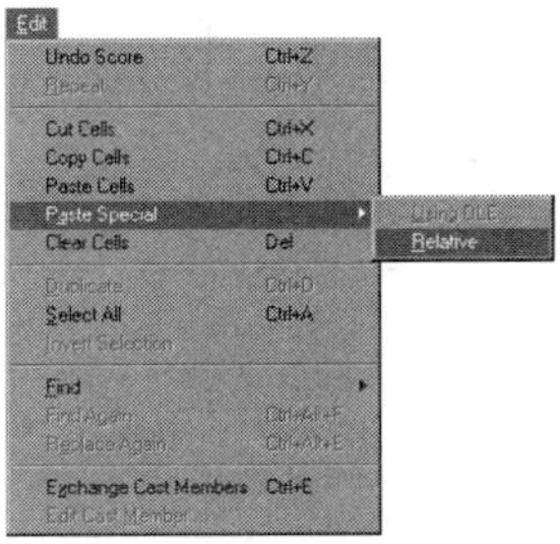

Figure 19. Choose **Paste Special** from the **Edit** menu, and select **Relative** from the pop-up menu.

Figure 20. Using **Paste Relative**, a copy of an animated sequence (such as a running dog in this case) is placed on the stage exactly where the previous sequence ends. The first six frames are shown.

✔ **Tip**

■ Space to Time is a convenient way to set up the points used with the curved In-between feature *(see pages 154-155)*. Place your cast member into the key points on the stage all in a single frame. Then use Space to Time to transfer these key points into multiple frames. In the Space to Time dialog box, enter a value of 10 to 20 for the Separation so that your in-between curve consists of enough frames to appear smooth.

To paste an animated sequence relative to another:

A useful technique for creating a long animated sequence involves repeating a shorter sequence over and over again while moving it across the stage. Take for example a running dog, with only four distinct cast members in its sequence **(Figure 16)**. You can create the illusion of a long animation by playing this short sequence repeatedly while moving it across the stage. Paste Relative allows you to link together a series of short sequences to achieve this effect.

1. In the score, select the cells that make up your animated sequence **(Figure 17)**.
2. Choose Copy Cells from the Edit menu **(Figure 18)**.
3. Select the cell in the score immediately following the last cell of your sequence.
4. Choose Paste Special from the Edit menu, and select Relative from the pop-up menu **(Figure 19)**. A copy of your sequence is placed onto the stage beginning exactly where the previous sequence ends **(Figure 20)**.

IN-BETWEEN ANIMATION

Of the various animation techniques that Director supports, **In-between** animation is probably the most practical and convenient to use. That's because the In-between feature automatically creates frames for you. All you need to do is specify the starting and ending frames, called **key frames**, and Director generates the rest.

The In Between command allows you to animate a sprite along a straight line. This is done by setting up the first frame of the animation in which a sprite is in location A, and then setting up the last frame in which the sprite is in location B **(Figure 21)**. Once you've created these key frames, you can use the In Between command to automatically draw all the intermediary frames necessary to move the sprite from the first frame to the last **(Figure 22)**. The more empty frames you set up between your key frames, the smoother your animation will be.

The In Between Special command extends the capabilities of the standard In Between *(see pages 154-160)*. Use it to generate animations along curved and circular paths; Add acceleration and deceleration to the motion of your sprites; And use it to In-between the sizes, colors, and blend values of your sprites. In Between Special lets you In-between several attributes of your sprite at the same time. For example, you can In-between the position of your sprite on the stage, while In-betweening its size, color, or blend setting (even all at the same time).

To create an In-between animation along a straight path:

1. In the score, click the desired frame in the desired channel to indicate where to begin your In-between animation **(Figure 23)**.

Figure 21. Locations A and B represent the **key frames** that are used with the In Between command.

Figure 22. The In Between command fills in all the frames *in between* your **key frames**. Ten separate frames are shown here all at once.

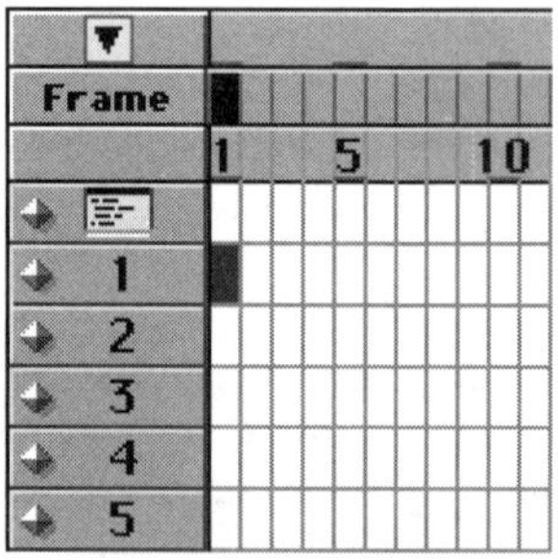

Figure 23. Select the cell in the score where your In-between animation should begin.

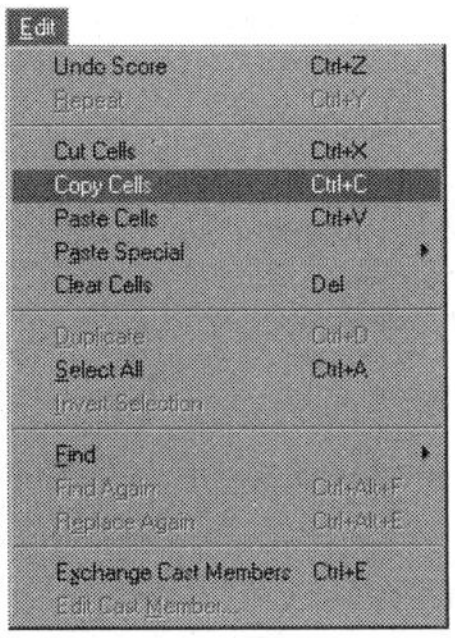

Figure 24. Choose **Copy Cells** from the **Edit** menu.

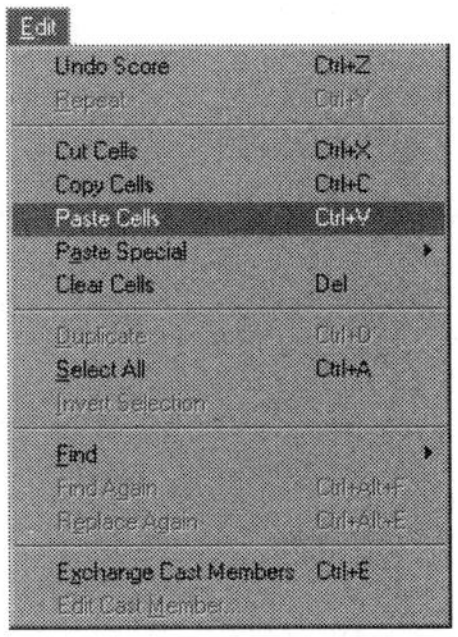

Figure 25. Choose **Paste Cells** from the **Edit** menu.

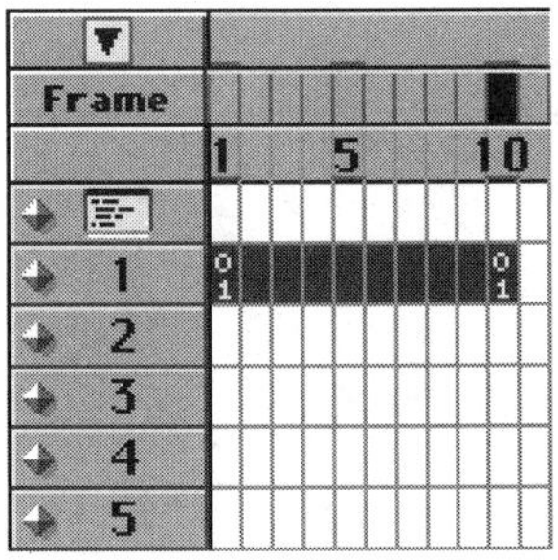

Figure 26. In the score, select the **key frames** and all the frames between them.

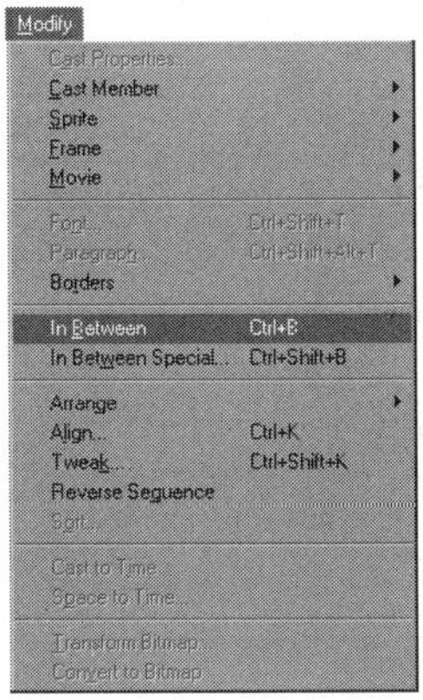

Figure 27. Choose **In Between** from the **Modify** menu.

2. Drag the cast member you wish to animate from the cast window onto Director's stage to create the first key frame of the animation. Be sure to position it at the location where your animation should begin.
3. Click the score window to make it active, and select the cell that contains the cast member you just positioned on the stage. Choose Copy Cells from the Edit menu **(Figure 24)**.
4. In the score, select a later frame in the same channel that the first key frame occupies to set up your second key frame. The more empty frames that are between the first key frame and the second, the smoother your animation will be.
5. Choose Paste Cells from the Edit menu **(Figure 25)** to place your sprite into this second key frame, and onto Director's stage. Now, on the stage, move the sprite to the location where your animation should end.
6. In the score, select all the frames from the starting point to the ending point of your animation by dragging across them **(Figure 26)**. Be sure to include the key frames in this selection.
7. Choose In Between from the Modify menu **(Figure 27)**. Director fills in all the *in between* frames to create your animation.

✓ Tip

- You can change the path of your In-between after it has been generated by simply adjusting the positions of the sprites in the key frames, reselecting the cells between them, and choosing the In Between command. Cells in the score which are generated by an In-between have dotted lines at the top. This is helpful when you wish to redo an In-between since you can easily identify the key frame cells which don't display these lines.

To create In-Between animations that curve:

The In Between Special command can be used to animate a sprite along a curved path. The process is similar to the one used to animate a sprite in a straight line, but instead of creating only two key frames, you create at least three to describe your sprite's curved path.

1. In the score window, click the desired frame in the desired channel to indicate where your In-between animation will begin.
2. From the cast window, drag the cast member you wish to animate onto the stage to create the first key frame. Be sure to position it at the location where your animation should begin.
3. From the cast window, drag the same cast member as you did in step 2 onto the stage, so that the two sprites share the stage **(Figure 28)**. Position it in a new location to set the second key frame of the curved In-between animation.
4. Repeat step 3 as many times as necessary to set all the key frames that define your curved path **(Figure 29)**.
5. In the score window, select all the sprites that make up the key frames of your curved animation sequence. These cells should all lie in the same frame **(Figure 30)**.

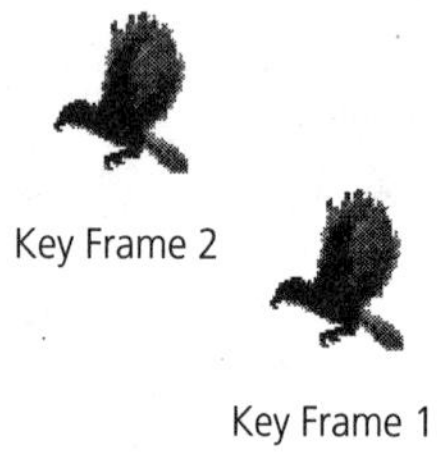

Figure 28. Drag your cast member onto the stage to a new location to create key frame 2.

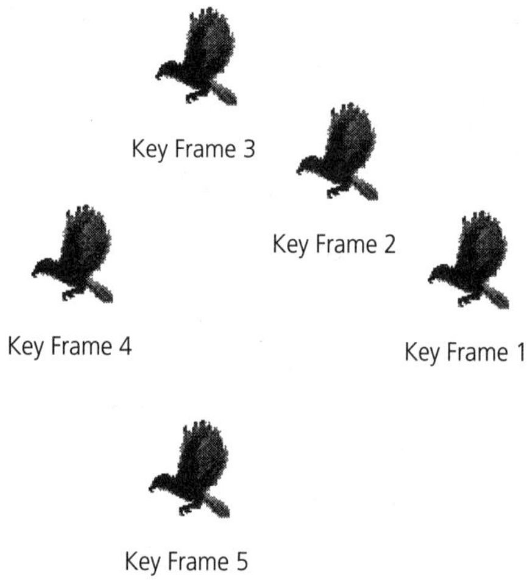

Figure 29. Five key frames here have been positioned on the stage to define a curved path for an In-between Special animation.

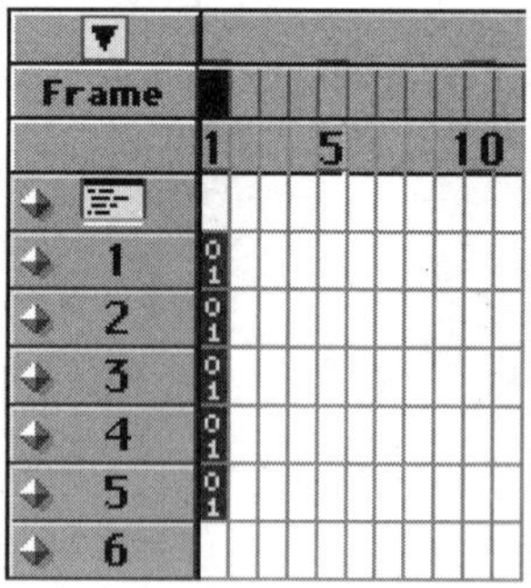

Figure 30. In the score, select all the key frames of your curved animation sequence.

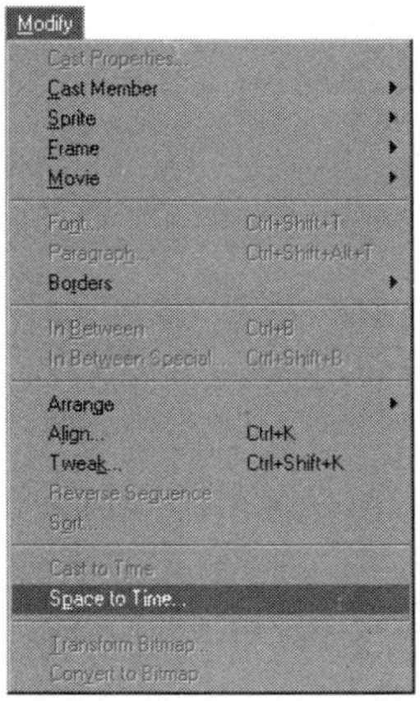

Figure 31. Choose **Space to Time** from the **Modify** menu.

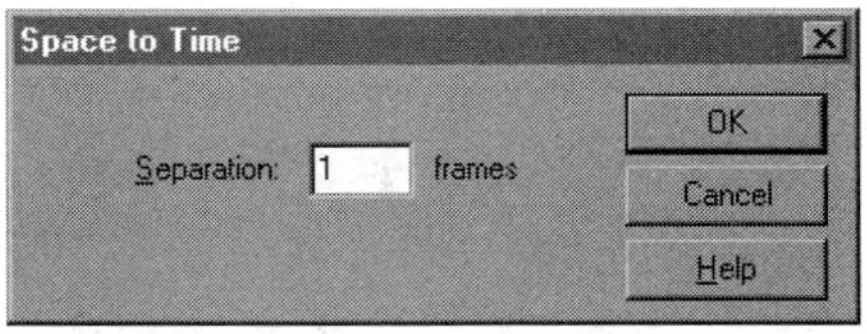

Figure 32. The Separation value in the **Space to Time** dialog box determines how many frames apart sprites will be placed in the score.

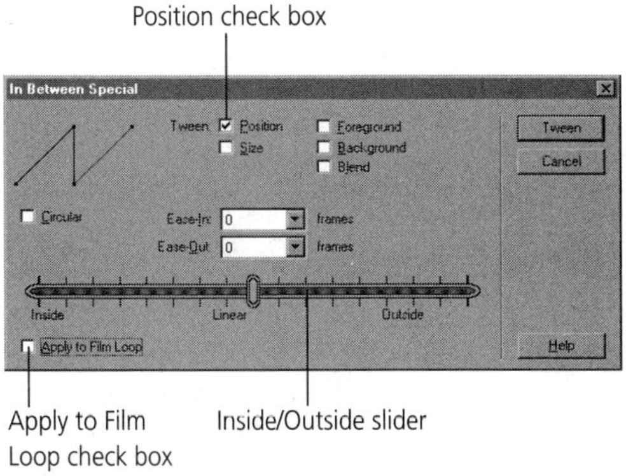

Figure 33. The **In Between Special** dialog box.

6. Choose Space to Time from the Modify menu **(Figure 31)**, which transfers the cast members into the same channel, while assigning each cast member to a different frame in that channel.
7. In the Space to Time dialog box, type the number of empty frames for Director to place between each of the key frames you created **(Figure 32)**. Remember, the more empty frames you place between the key frames, the smoother your animation will be.
8. Click OK.
9. Choose In Between Special from the Modify menu while the key frames are still selected in Director's score.
10. In the In Between Special dialog box, click the Position checkbox to indicate that the In-between operation will apply to the location of the sprites you selected in the score **(Figure 33)**.
11. If the cast member you're animating is a film loop *(see page 166)*, click the Apply to Film Loop checkbox.
12. In the In Between Special dialog box, drag the Inside/Outside slider to fine-tune how your sprite moves within its curved path. Setting the bar to the left (Inside) causes your sprite to stay inside the boundaries defined by the positions of the key frames you've created for its path. Setting it in the center (Linear) causes your sprite to move in straight lines between the key frame positions, while setting the bar to the right (Outside) creates a curved path which passes through each key frame position on the outside.
13. Click Tween in the In Between Special dialog box to place the animation into the score.

To accelerate and decelerate with In-betweening:

When you set up an In-between animation along any type of path (straight or curved), you can add acceleration and deceleration to the motion of your sprites using the In Between Special command. This adds a touch of realism to how your sprites appear to behave.

1. Set up the key frames of your in-between animation for either a straight line or curved path as described on pages 152-154.
2. Select the range of cells in the score which include your key frames and all the cells between them.
3. Choose In Between Special from the Modify menu **(Figure 34)**.
4. In the In Between Special dialog box, use the **Ease-In** and **Ease-Out** pop-up menus to set the number of frames in which the sprite will speed up at the beginning of its animation, and slow down at its end **(Figure 35)**.
5. Check the Position check box in the In Between Special dialog box.
6. Click Tween to create the animation.

To stretch or squeeze a sprite with In-betweening:

You can use In-betweening to create a sequence of frames that show your sprite gradually stretching or squeezing. Once again, all you need to do is set up the key frames of your In-between animation. In this case, your first key frame would show your sprite in its original state. The second key frame would show the sprite as it would appear in its final stretched or squeezed form.

1. In the score window, click the desired frame in the desired channel to indicate where to begin your In-between animation.

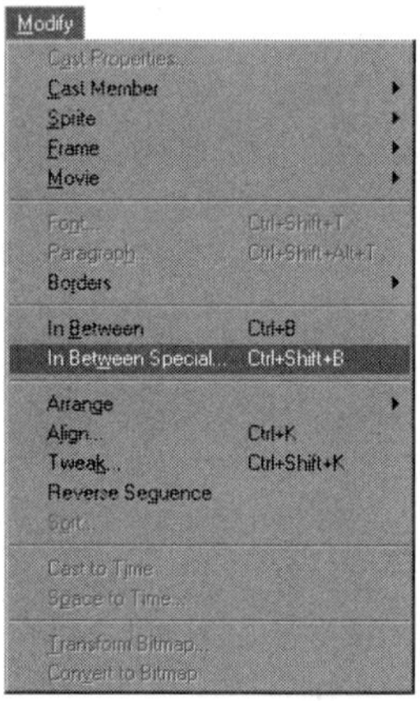

Figure 34. Choose **In Between Special** from the **Modify** menu.

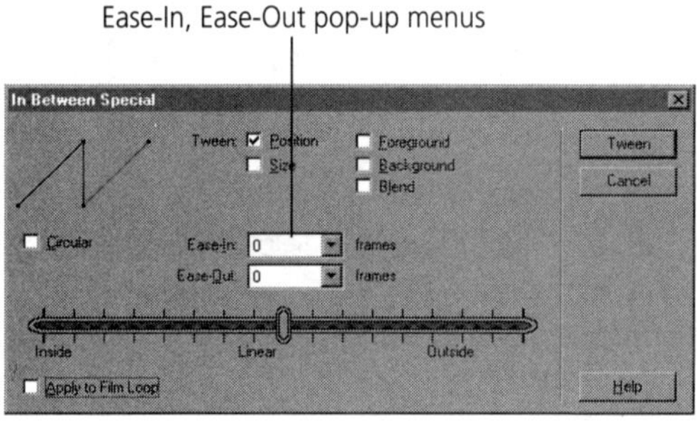

Figure 35. Use the **Ease-In** and **Ease-Out** pop-up menus in the **In Between Special** dialog box to accelerate and decelerate your In-between animation.

Figure 36. Drag the cast member you wish to stretch or squeeze from the cast window onto the stage.

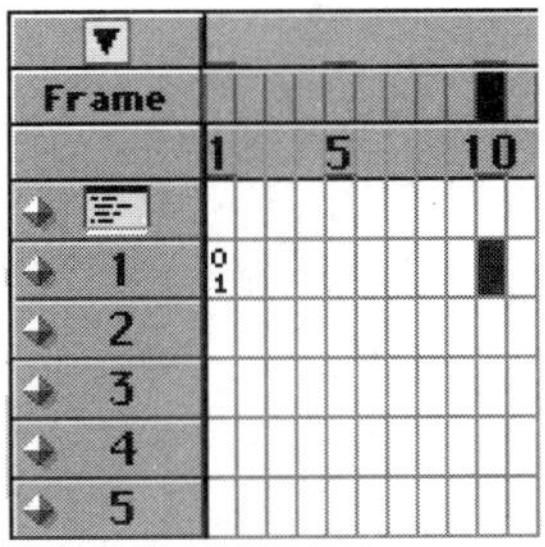

Figure 37. In the score, select a later frame in the same channel that the first key frame occupies. This frame will be your second key frame.

Figure 38. Drag the handles on the selection rectangle surrounding your sprite to stretch or squeeze it.

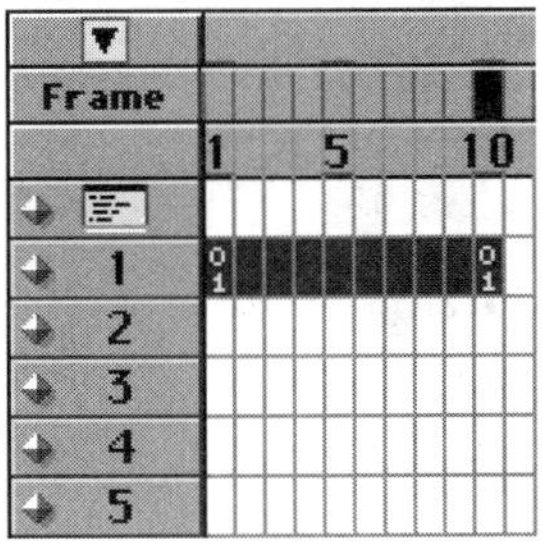

Figure 39. In the score, select the key frames and all the frames between them.

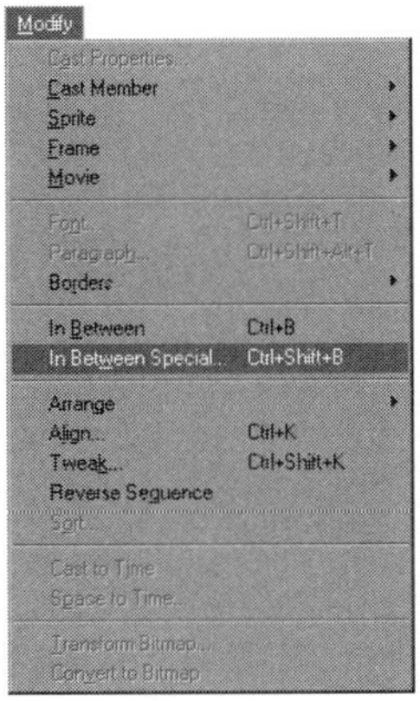

Figure 40. Choose **In Between Special** from the **Modify** menu.

2. Drag the cast member you wish to stretch or squeeze **(Figure 36)** from a cast window onto Director's stage to create the first key frame in your animation.
3. Click the score window to make it active, and click the cell that you just created so that it's selected (if not already).
4. In the score, select a later frame in the same channel that the first first key frame occupies to set up your second key frame **(Figure 37)**. The more empty frames that are between the first and second key frames, the more gradual will be your stretching or squeezing.
5. Choose Paste Cells from the Edit menu to place your sprite into this second key frame, and onto the stage. Now drag the handles on the selection rectangle that surrounds this sprite to stretch or squeeze it **(Figure 38)**.
6. In the score, select all the cells from the starting point to the ending point of your animation by dragging across them **(Figure 39)**. Be sure to include the key frames in this selection.
7. Choose In Between Special from the Modify menu **(Figure 40)**.
8. Make sure that Size is the only check box selected in the In Between Special dialog box.
9. Click Tween to place the animation into the score.

✔ Tip

- You can animate a sprite stretching or squeezing while moving across the stage by combining two In-betweening features at the same time. In step 5 above, move the second key frame sprite to a new location on the stage in addition to stretching or squeezing it. Also in step 8, select both the Size and Position check boxes.

To In-between the foreground or background color of sprites:

You can use the In Between Special command to change the foreground or background color of a sprite over a range of frames. This only works on shape or 1-bit bitmap cast members.

1. In the score, click the desired frame in the desired channel to indicate where your color In-between will begin.
2. Drag the desired cast member from the cast window onto the stage. Remember that this cast member must be either a shape or 1-bit bitmap for the color In-between to work properly.
3. Choose Tool Palette from the Window menu **(Figure 41)**.
4. Select the cell in the score that contains the sprite placed in step 2 above.
5. Choose the desired foreground and background colors for your sprite by clicking the color chips in the Tool Palette **(Figure 42)**. These are the starting colors for your color In-between.
6. Choose Copy Cells from the Edit menu **(Figure 43)**.
7. In the score, select a later frame in the same channel that the first key frame occupies to set up the the second key frame of your color In-between.
8. Choose Paste Cells from the Edit menu.
9. Choose the desired foreground and background colors for your second key frame sprite by clicking the color chips in the Tool Palette **(Figure 42)**. These are the ending colors for your color In-between.
10. In the score, select all the cells between your two colored sprites, including both of them **(Figure 44)**.

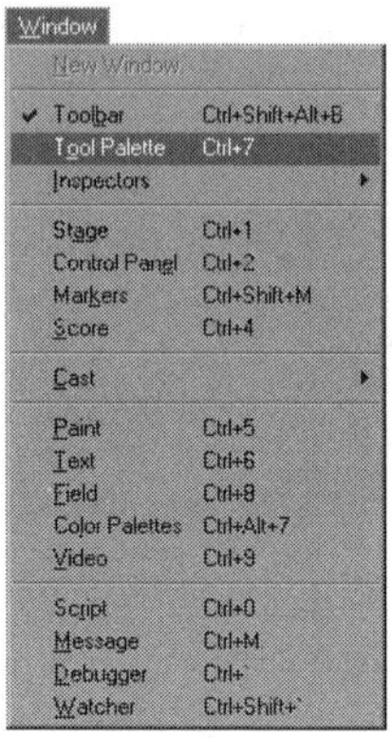

Figure 41. Choose **Tool Palette** from the **Window** menu.

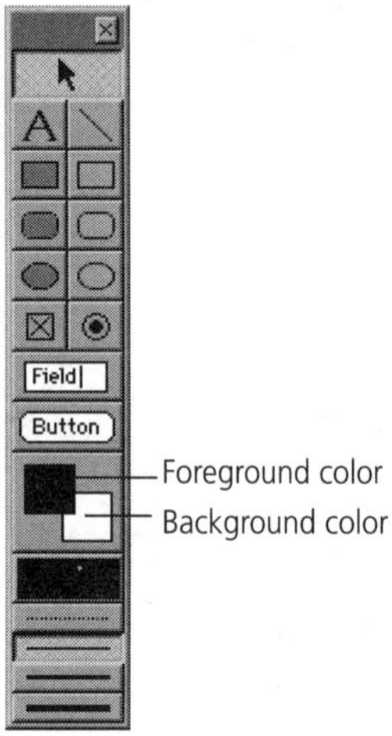

Figure 42. In the **Tool Palette**, select the colors for your sprite.

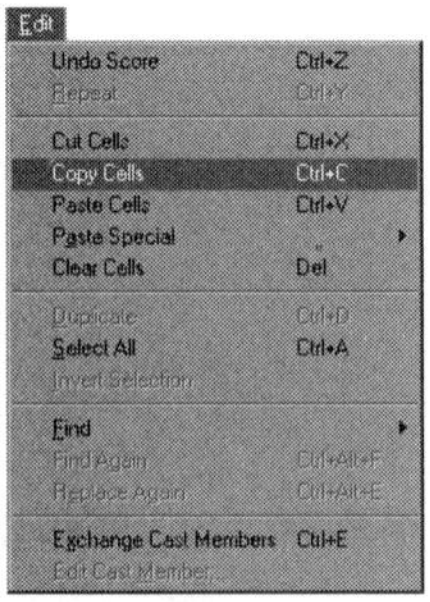

Figure 43. Choose **Copy Cells** from the **Edit** menu.

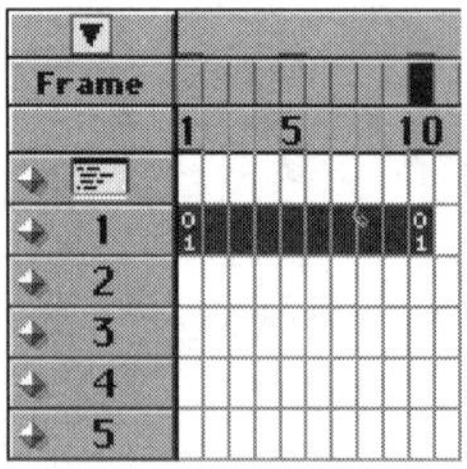

Figure 44. In the score, select all the cells between your two colored sprites, including both of them.

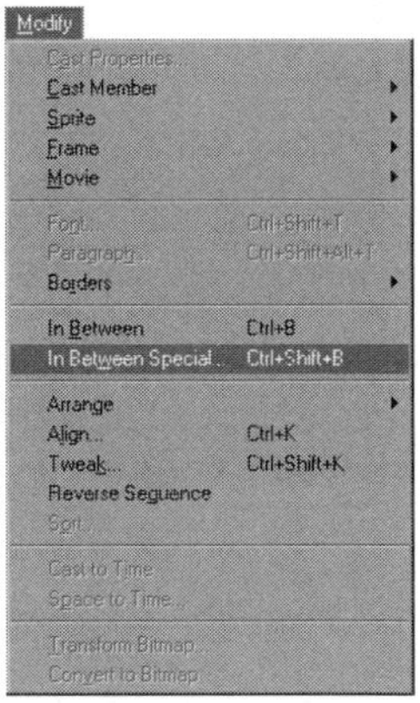

Figure 45. Choose **In Between Special** from the **Modify** menu.

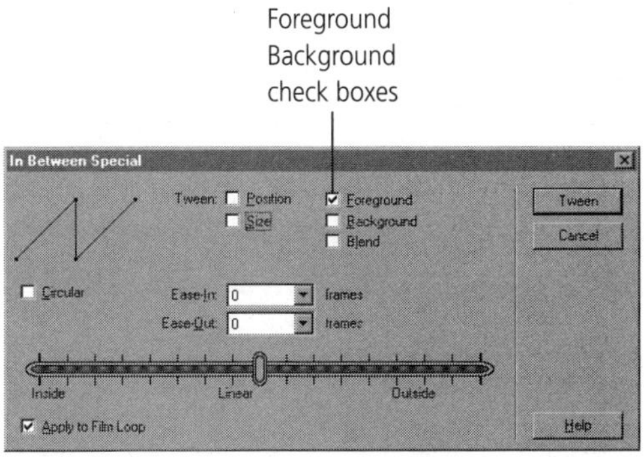

Figure 46. Check the Foreground or Background check box in the **In Between Special** dialog box to indicate which color you are In-betweening.

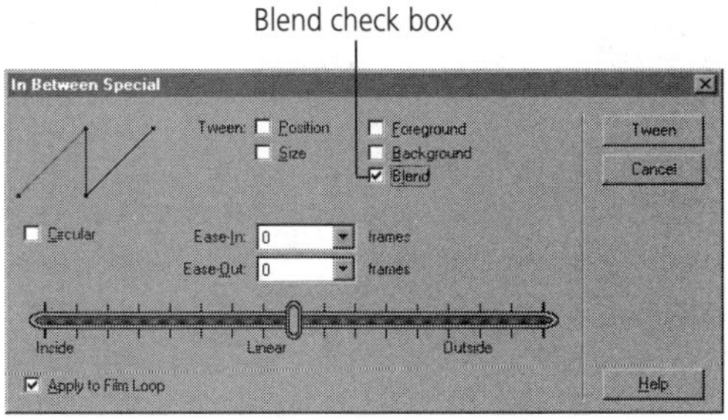

Figure 47. Check the **Blend** check box in the **In Between Special** dialog box.

11. Choose In Between Special from the Modify menu **(Figure 45)**.
12. Check the Foreground or Background check box in the In Between Special dialog box to indicate which color you are In-Betweening **(Figure 46)**. You can actually check both to In-between both colors at the same time.
13. Click Tween to place the color In-between into the score.

Note: Director generates colors for a color In-between by referencing the active color palette. The In-between colors correspond to colors in the palette which lie between the starting and ending colors you specify in the key frames. If the palette colors between your starting and ending colors don't form a gradient, you will find that the color In-between isn't very effective since the transition between colors is not gradual. So for best results, choose starting and ending colors where the colors between them in the active palette are gradually changing from the first to the second. *(See page 139 in the Color in Director Chapter on creating a blend of colors in a color palette)*

To In-between the blend setting of a sprite:

You can make a sprite appear to fade in or fade out by In-betweening its blend setting.

1. Place a sprite with the starting blend setting in a cell of the score
2. Place a sprite with the ending blend setting in a later cell of the score. *(See page 65 on changing the blend setting)*
3. Select the cells between the cells in step 2, including both of those cells.
4. Choose In Between Special from the Modify menu. Check the Blend check box and click Tween **(Figure 47)**.

To create a circular animation path with In-Between:

Setting up an In-between animation for a circular path is very similar to setting up a curved In-between animation *(see page 154)*. The main difference is that the last key frame sprite of your circular animation shares the same position on the stage as the first key frame sprite. This is necessary for defining a circular path. To define the roundest possible circular path, use five key frames arranged on the stage as shown in **(Figure 48)**. The fifth key frame sprite overlaps the first, so four are only visible.

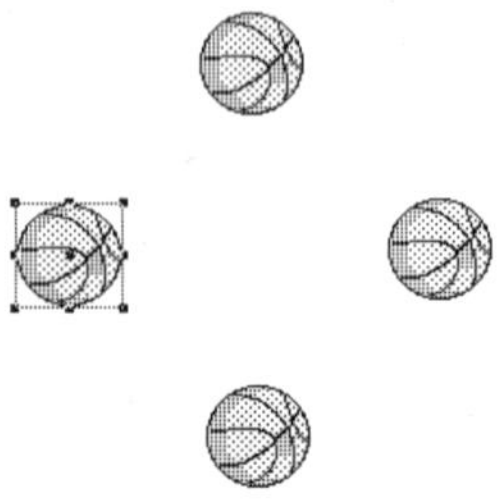

Figure 48. To define the most accurate circular path, use five key frame sprites. The first and fifth key sprites overlap here.

Be sure to check the Circular checkbox in the In Between Special dialog box **(Figure 49)**. The Inside/Outside slider determines if the circular path stays inside or outside the boundary defined by the positions of your key frame sprites, and how curved the path is.

Circular checkbox

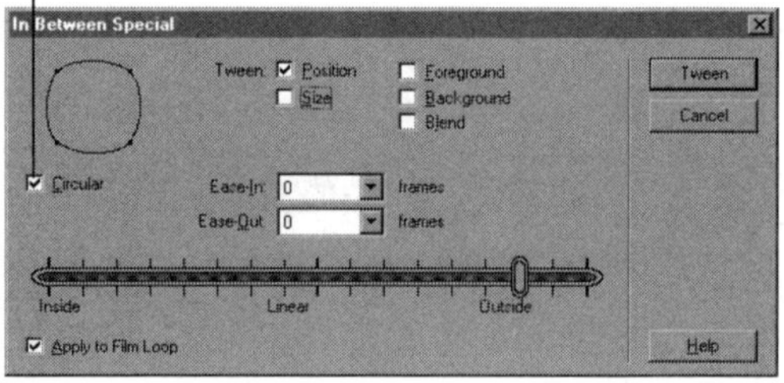

Figure 49. Check the **Circular** checkbox in the **In Between Special** dialog box.

REAL-TIME RECORDING

One of the most direct ways to animate objects in Director is to use its Real-time recording feature. With Real-time recording, you move a single cast member or a film loop cast member around the stage using the mouse, and Director records its movement and its movement rate to the score automatically. This is especially useful if you want to animate an object along a natural, free-flowing path, featuring many changes in direction.

The major drawback to this approach is that the motion generated by your hand is often considerably less smooth than you might like. However, after you record a cast member's motion in real-time, you can go back and adjust individual frames in your score.

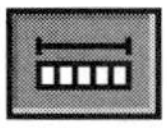

Figure 50. Click the **Selected Frames Only** button in the control panel to record in a specific range of frames.

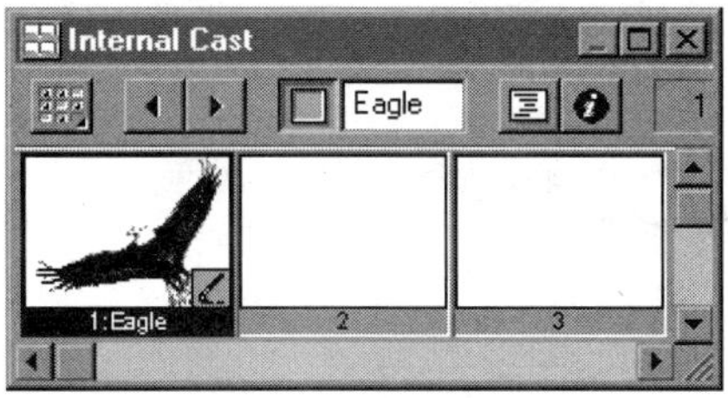

Figure 51. In a cast window, click the cast member you wish to animate with Real-time recording.

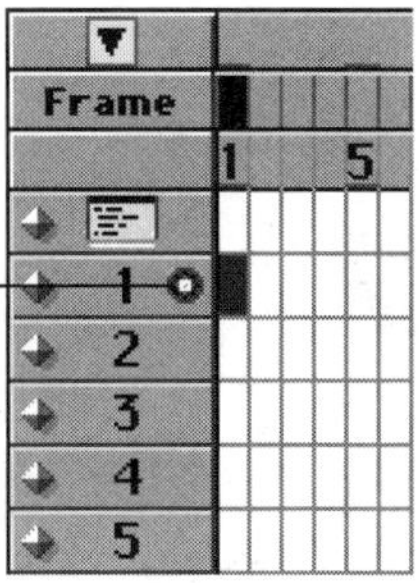

Figure 52. Hold down the Control key and the Spacebar to select Real-time recording

Figure 53. Click the mouse pointer on the stage and the selected cast member appears.

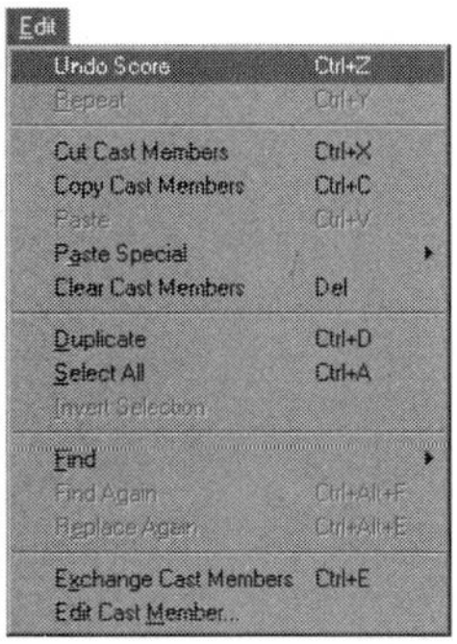

Figure 54. Choose **Undo** from the **Edit** menu.

To Real-Time Record:

1. In the score, click the desired frame in the desired channel to indicate where your Real-time recording should begin. To record in a specific range of frames, select those frames and click the Selected Frames Only button **(Figure 50)** in the control panel.
2. In a cast window, click the cast member you wish to animate so that it's selected **(Figure 51)**.
3. Move the mouse pointer to the location on the stage where you will begin your animation (don't drag the cast member to the stage).
4. Hold down the Control key and the Spacebar. A Real-time record indicator appears next to the number of the channel that you are recording in **(Figure 52)**.
5. Drag to begin recording your animation path. Notice that as soon as you click the mouse, the cast member you selected appears automatically on the stage **(Figure 53)**.
6. Release the mouse button to end your Real-time recording session. Director places this animation into the score.
7. If you don't like the animation, choose Undo from the Edit menu **(Figure 54)** and start again.

✔ **Tips**

- Remember that Real-time recording requires you to select a cast member from a cast window, but **not** to drag it on the stage, as you normally would. If you do drag the cast member on stage first, you will probably record the cast member twice.
- If you begin to record your animation from a frame that contains other cast members, those cast members will be recorded in the frames through which you are Real-time recording. To avoid this, you might want to real-time record from a totally empty frame, and then copy and paste your recorded frames into their proper place in the score.
- If Real-time recording seems too sensitive to your mouse movements, you can make it less so by slowing down the tempo at which Director records. To do this, set a new tempo in the control panel window by entering a new value (in frames-per-second) in the Tempo display **(Figure 55)**. Once recorded, you can reset the tempo value to its higher rate to play back your animation.
- You can create a handwriting-type effect by selecting the cells of your Real-time recorded animation, then clicking the Trails checkbox in the score **(Figure 56)**. As your sprite moves across the stage, it leaves behind a trail.

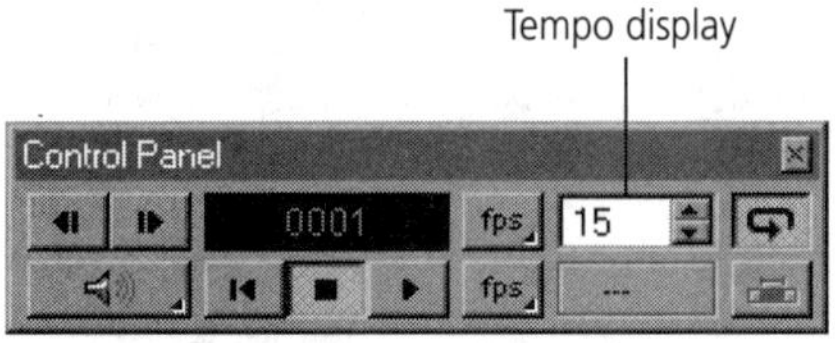

Figure 55. In the control panel, enter a lower value in the Tempo display if the mouse movements are too sensitive while you are Real-time recording.

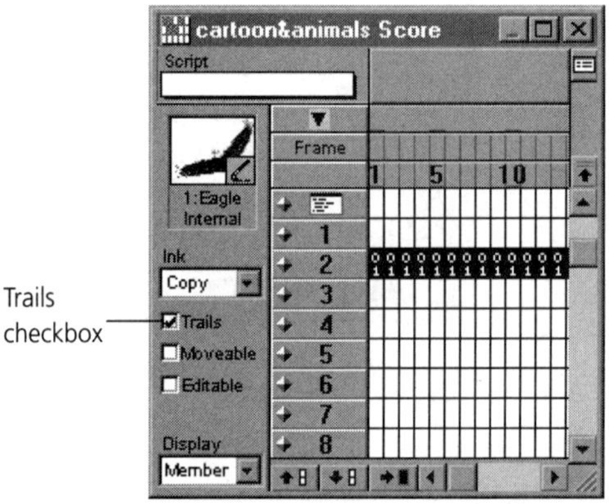

Figure 56. Select the cells of your Real-time recorded animation and click the **Trails** checkbox in the score so that your sprite leaves a trail on the stage.

Real-Time Recording

CREATING FILM LOOPS

Figure 57. A film loop cast member consists of a sequence of frames.

Think of a film loop as an animated cast member. Instead of consisting of just one image, it's actually composed of a plurality of frames that form an animated sequence—perhaps a dog running **(Figure 57)**, a globe spinning, a helicopter hovering, and so on. The beauty of a film loop is that you treat it as a single cast member, which can greatly simplify your work in the score.

Film loops can be used with Director's In Between command and Real-Time Recording feature to create complex animations. For instance, the film loop of a bird flapping its wings can be "in-betweened" to move from one side of the screen to another. As the bird moves across the stage, its frames are simultaneously alternating.

Like conventional cast members, a film loop is kept in a cast window. It is identified by the film loop icon **(Figure 58)**.

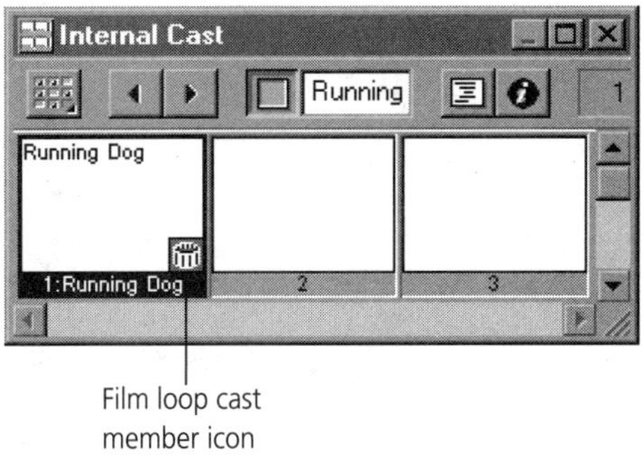

Figure 58. A cast window.

Note: A film loop cast member is inserted into your movie like any other graphical cast member—by dragging it to the stage or into cells in the score. A film loop cast member must occupy enough continuous cells in the score in order for all of its frames to have a chance to play. For example, if a film loop consists of four frames, the film loop cast member should be placed through at least four continuous frames in the score, so that during playback, all of its frames are displayed.

Note: Even though you've placed a film loop into your movie, it will not appear to animate if you step through its frames using the control panel, or if you drag Director's playback head across the frames in the score. Film loops animate only when you play your movie.

Note: You cannot apply score ink effects to film loops. These effects must first be applied to the individual sprites that make up a film loop.

To create a film loop:

1. Choose Import from the File menu to import your film loop's individual cast members into a cast window. Be sure to import them in the order in which they should appear in the loop.
2. In the cast window, select all of the individual cast members that will make up the film loop animation **(Figure 59)**. Hold down the Control key while clicking each cast member to select them together.
3. Drag the selected cast members from the cast window into a desired position in the score, where they are automatically placed into a single frame **(Figure 60)**.
4. With the score still active, choose Space to Time from the Modify menu to transfer your cast members into multiple frames **(Figure 61)**.
5. In the Space to Time dialog box, enter a value of 1 for the Separation.
6. Make sure the cells of your animated sequence are selected in the score
7. In a cast window, select an empty cast member position, and choose Film Loop from the Insert menu.
8. Type a name for the film loop and click OK **(Figure 62)**.

✔ **Tips**

- As a shortcut, you can create a film loop by dragging a selection of frames from the score window directly into a cast window.
- A film loop itself can be composed of other film loops. For example, suppose you have two film loops placed in the score, one of a walking man, and the other of a running dog. You can create a single film loop which includes of both of these loops.

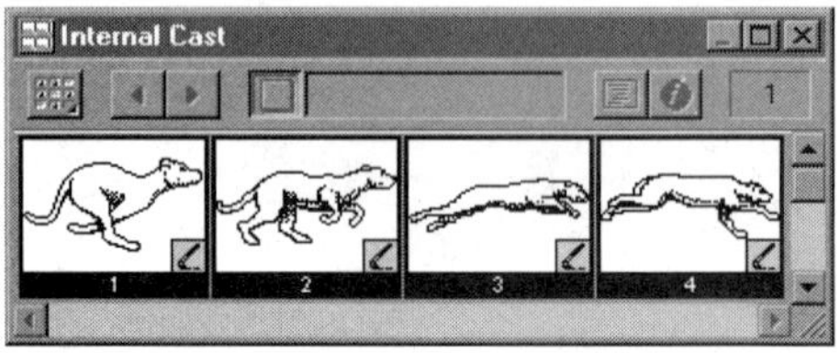

Figure 59. In the cast window, select all the cast members that will make up your film loop animation, as shown here for a running dog film loop.

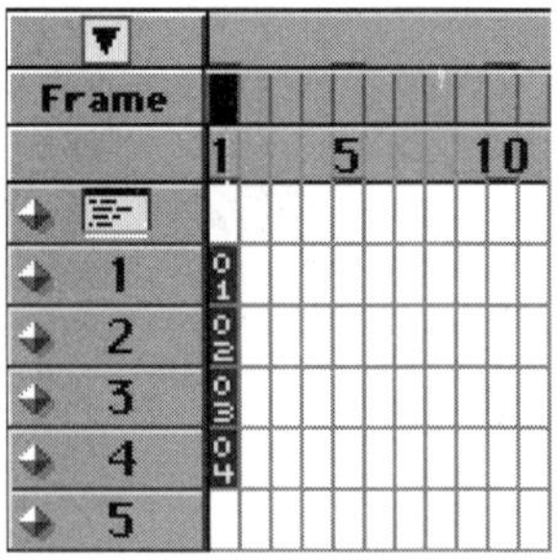

Figure 60. Drag the selected cast members from the cast window into the score.

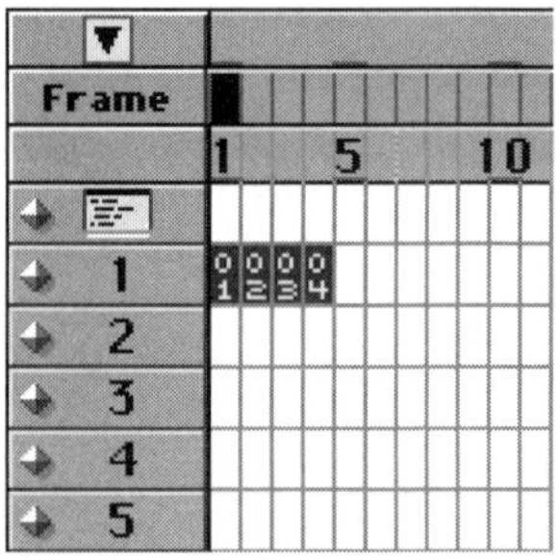

Figure 61. Transfer your film loop cast members into multiple frames using **Space to Time** from the **Modify** menu.

Figure 62. Type a name for your film loop In the **Create Film Loop** dialog box.

Create a Film Loop

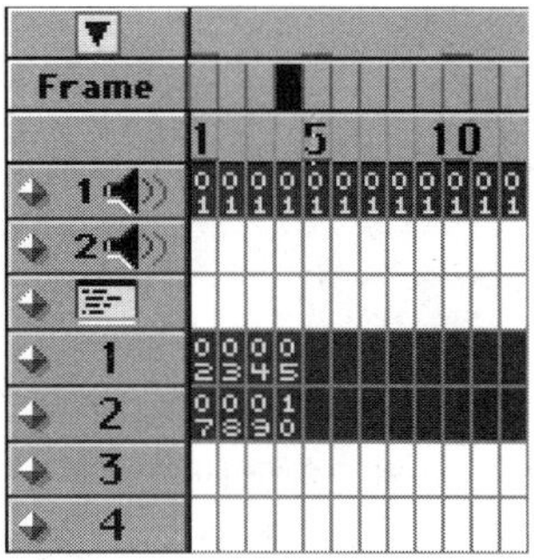

Figure 63. Select the cells that contain all the sequences that will be part of your film loop.

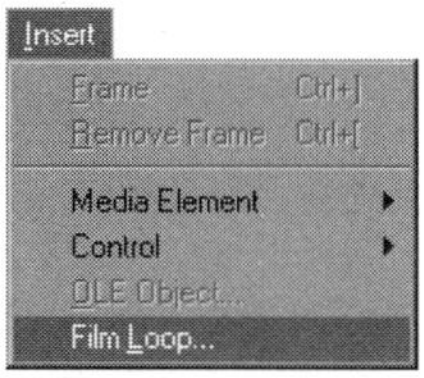

Figure 64. Choose **Film Loop** from the **Insert** menu.

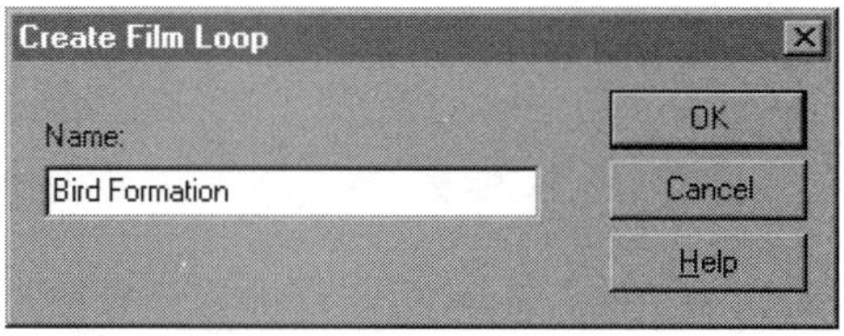

Figure 65. Type a name for your film loop In the **Create Film Loop** dialog box.

To create a multichannel film loop:

A film loop can consist of more than one channel of animation, where each channel features its own animated element. For instance, a film loop might consist of three birds flying in formation (each bird would have been originally animated in its own channel). Also, film loops can include sound effects from the sound channels.

1. In the score, create an animation for the first channel that will be featured in your multichannel film loop, just as you would normally create an animated sequence.
2. Create the animations for all the other channels that will be featured in your multichannel film loop, also placing any sound effects into the sound channels that you wish to include.
3. In the score, drag to select all the frames in all the channels you've just created, so they are highlighted **(Figure 63)**. Use Control-click to select non-adjacent cells.
4. Open a cast window, and select an empty cast member position.
5. Choose Film Loop from the Insert menu **(Figure 64)**.
6. Type a name for the film loop and click OK **(Figure 65)**.

To Real-time record with a film loop:

You can use Real-time recording to record a path for a film loop cast member to follow across the stage (very similar to Real-time recording with a non-film loop cast member described earlier in this chapter). As your film loop cast member cycles through its frames during playback, it will also move across the stage. This is a great technique to use to set up animations such as birds flapping their wings across the stage.

1. In the score window, click the desired frame in the desired channel to indicate where your Real-time film loop recording will begin. To record in a specific range of frames, select those frames and click the Selected Frames Only button in the control panel.
2. Select the film loop cast member in a cast window **(Figure 66)**.
3. Move the mouse pointer to the location on the stage where you wish to begin your animation.
4. Hold down the Control key and the Spacebar, and drag to begin recording your animation path.
5. Release the mouse button to end your Real-time recording session. Director places this animation into the score.

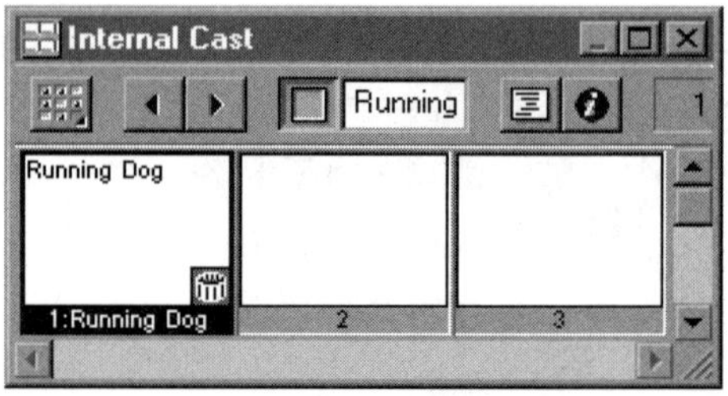

Figure 66. Select the film loop cast member in a cast window with which you will be Real-time recording.

In-between with a film loop:

Making use of the In-between feature with a film loop cast member creates a powerful animation effect. For example, you can animate a film loop cast member of a racing dog, having it travel across the stage in any variety of predetermined paths while its frames alternate. This can be accomplished by simply setting up several key frames and using the In Between command with a film loop cast member. You can specify a straight, curved, or circular path for your film loop cast member to follow, just as you can with a regular bitmap cast member. Use the In Between or In Between Special commands described on pages 152–160. Follow the same steps given there, but simply select a film loop cast member from a cast window.

DIGITAL VIDEO 10

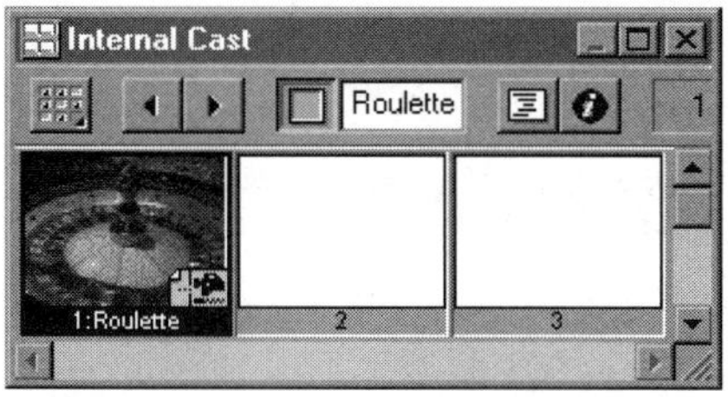

Figure 1. QuickTime movies and Video for Windows become digital video cast members when imported.

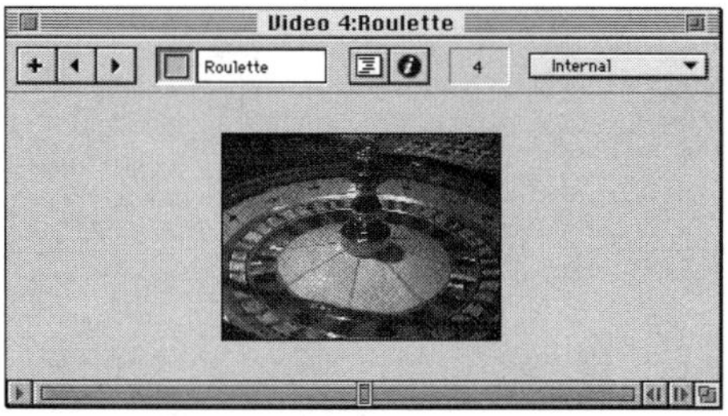

Figure 2. The video window.

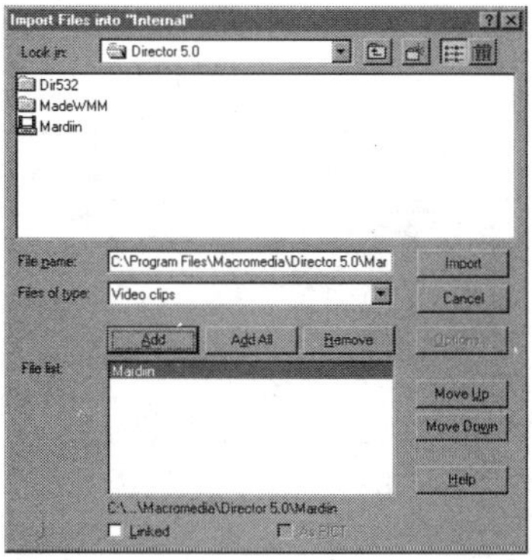

Figure 3. Choose **Video clips** from the **Files of type** pop-up menu in the **Import** dialog box.

Director for Windows allows you to import either QuickTime movies, or Video for Windows (.AVI files), which are both referred to as digital video throughout the Director application. Once imported, a QuickTime movie or a Video for Windows becomes a digital video cast member in a cast window **(Figure 1)**. You incorporate a digital video cast member into your Director movie as you would any other graphical cast member, by placing it on the stage through an appropriate range of frames.

Director provides very basic editing capability for digital video inside the video window **(Figure 2)**. You are limited to rearranging frames by cutting, copying, and pasting. For more extensive editing features, you will need to use a video editing application.

To import a digital video:

1. Choose Import from the File menu.
2. Choose Video clips from the Files of type pop-up menu **(Figure 3)**, and add the desired files to be imported.
3. Click Import.

Note: Digital videos are always imported linked to their original files. This means that if you edit a digital video in Director, you will permanently change the original file. Also, any changes you make to a digital video file outside Director are automatically reflected in Director. When you transfer your Director movie or projector to another system, all digital video files must be included.

To place a digital video into a Director movie:

A digital video cast member is placed into your movie the same way in which you incorporate any other graphical cast member, by dragging it from a cast window onto the stage, or directly into the cells of the score.

1. Open the cast window which contains your digital video cast member **(Figure 4)**.
2. Choose Score from the Window menu **(Figure 5)**.
3. Drag your digital video cast member from its cast window into an animation channel in the score and into the appropriate frame where the video should begin playing.
4. Position the digital video cast member on the stage as it should appear in your movie by dragging it to the desired location.

Note: Director starts to play your video when the playback head reaches the frame in which it is contained. But in order for the video to play to completion, it must be extended over enough frames in the score to match its playing length, otherwise it will end without finishing, much like a sound. For example, if you know the duration of your video to be 5 seconds, and your movie frame rate is 30 FPS (frames-per-second), then your digital video should occupy approximately 150 frames. The best way to determine the appropriate number of frames is to first extend the video over more frames than necessary using the In Between command *(see page 57)*. Second, play your movie back with the score window open, and note in which frame your video finishes playing.

Note: You can set your video to loop by checking the Loop option in its Cast Member Properties box **(Figure 6)**.

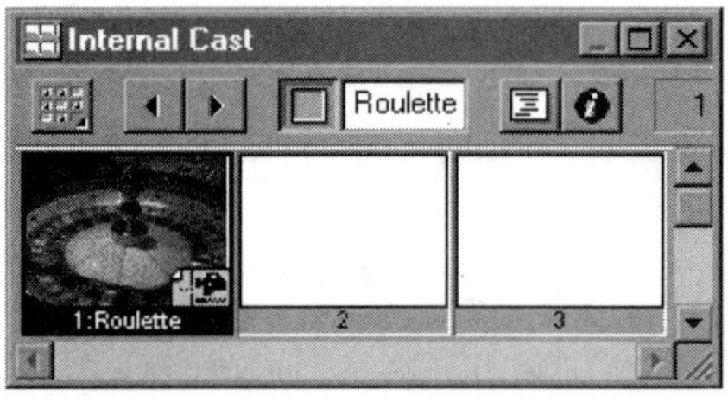

Figure 4. Open the cast window which contains your digital video.

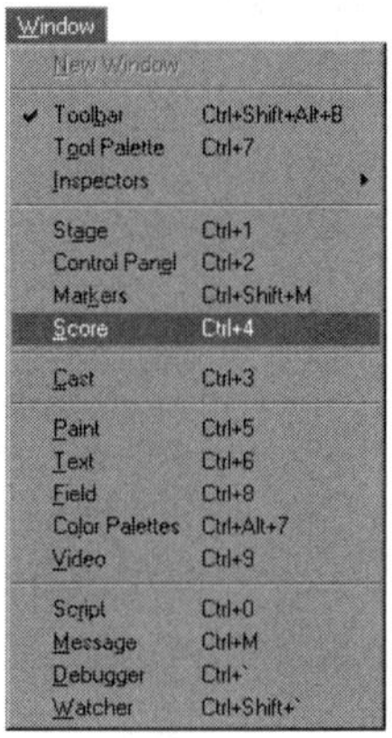

Figure 5. Choose **Score** from the **Window** menu.

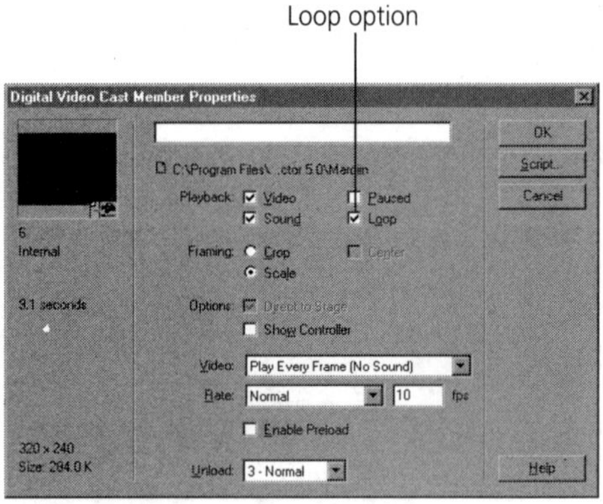

Figure 6. Check the **Loop** option in the **Digital Video Cast Member Properties** dialog box.

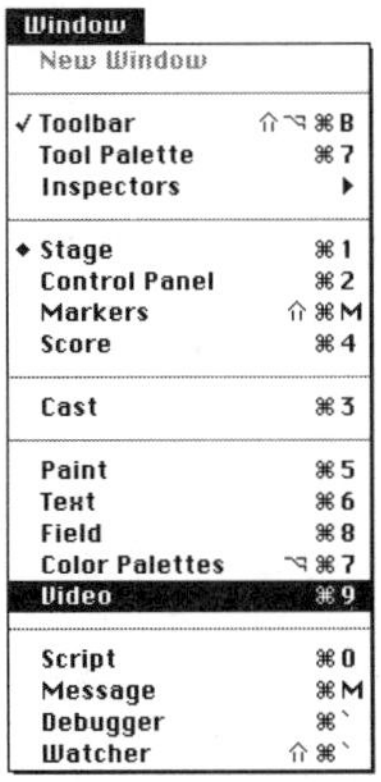

Figure 7. Choose **Video** from the **Window** menu.

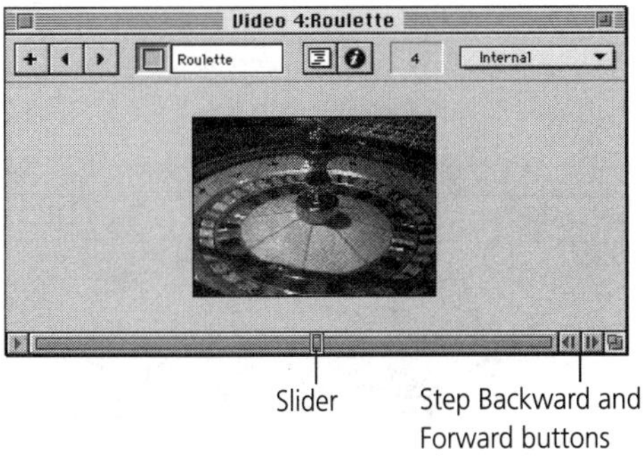

Figure 8. In the video window, use the slider or the **Step Backward** and **Forward** buttons to display the first frame in the range of frames you wish to copy or cut.

Figure 9. Hold the Shift key and drag the slider to select a range of frames in the video window.

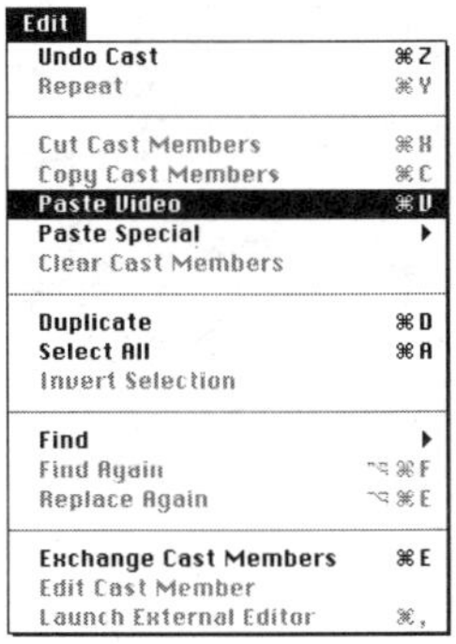

Figure 10. Choose **Paste Video** from the **Edit** menu.

If the Loop option is checked, your video will repeat from the beginning when it reaches its end, assuming that the video occupies enough frames in the score.

✔ Tip

- You can ensure that a video finishes playing by setting a tempo in the tempo channel using the Wait for End of Digital Video option. *(See page 193 in the Movie Tempo Chapter)*

To cut, copy, or clear video frames:

1. Choose Video from the Window menu **(Figure 7)**.
2. Go to the first frame in the range of frames you wish to copy or cut by using the Step backward and forward buttons, or by dragging the slider bar in the video window **(Figure 8)**.
3. If you want to select a range of frames, hold down the Shift key and drag the slider until the last frame in your range is displayed. The portion of the slider which corresponds to your range turns black **(Figure 9)**.
4. Choose either Cut Video, Copy Video, or Clear Video from the Edit menu.

To paste a frame or frames into a digital video:

1. Use the Previous and Next cast member buttons in the video window to display the digital video cast member into which you wish to paste video frames. If you are pasting into a new digital video, Director prompts you to enter a filename for this new cast member when you paste.
2. Using the slider, display the frame in the video window before which you want your frame or range of frames to be pasted. Your frame(s) will be inserted at this point.
3. Choose Paste Video from the Edit menu **(Figure 10)**.

To crop a digital video:

You can crop a video so that only a portion of its rectangular area is visible during play. Doing so hides a section of your video, but does not permanently delete it.

1. In the cast window, select the digital video cast member that you wish to crop **(Figure 11)**.
2. Click the Cast Member Properties button in the cast window **(Figure 11)**.
3. Check the Crop option in the Digital Video Cast Member Properties dialog box **(Figure 12)**. Check the Center option if you want your cropped video centered in its new rectangular area.
4. Click OK.
5. Open the score window and select the cells which contain the video.
6. On the stage, drag the handles that surround your video to crop it.

To scale a digital video:

You can scale a video so that it takes on the dimensions of any rectangular area.

1. Select the video in the cast.
2. Click the Cast Member Properties button in the cast window.
3. Check the Scale option in the Digital Video Cast Member Properties dialog box **(Figure 13)**
4. Click OK.
5. Open the score window and select the cells which contain the video.
6. On the stage, drag the handles that surround your video to scale it.

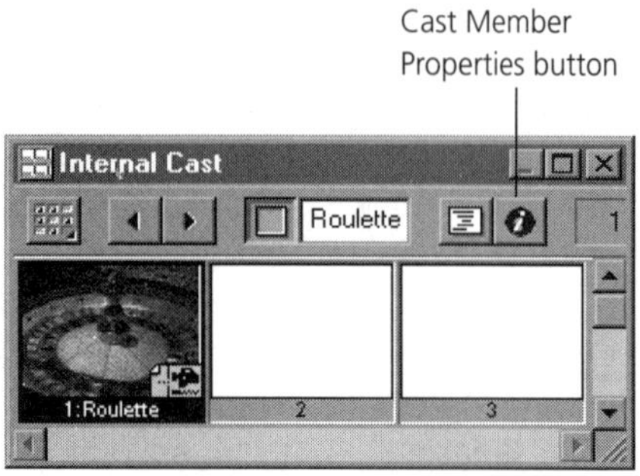

Figure 11. Select the digital video cast member you wish to crop in the cast window and click the **Cast Member Properties** button.

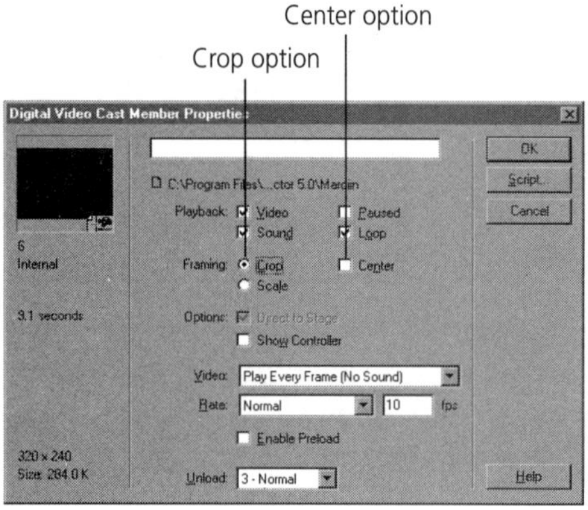

Figure 12. Check the **Crop** option in the **Digital Video Cast Member Properties** dialog box.

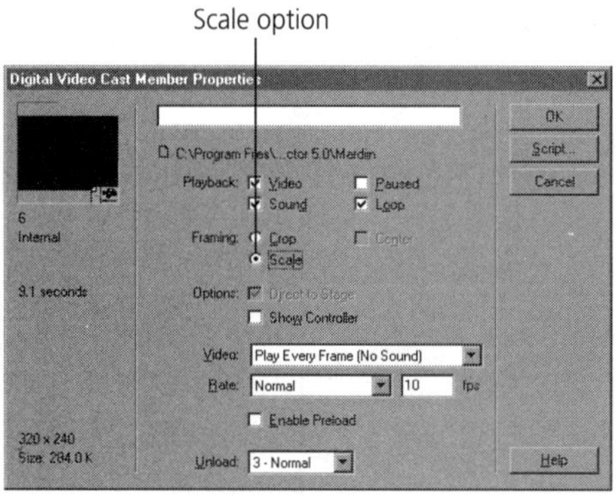

Figure 13. Check the **Scale** option in the **Digital Video Cast Member Properties** dialog box.

CREATING TEXT IN DIRECTOR 11

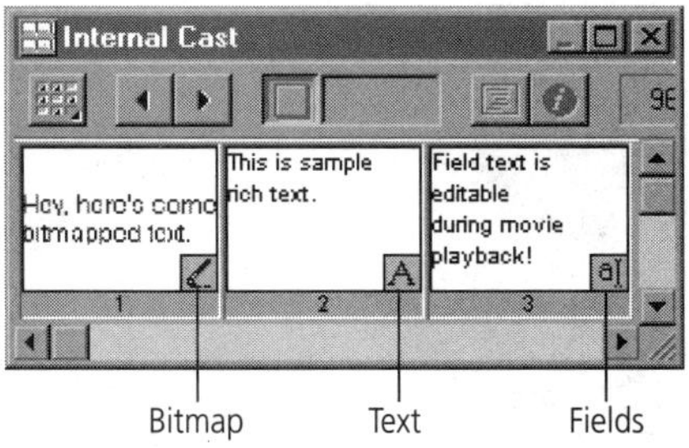

Figure 1. Director supports three different types of text: bitmapped, rich text (or simply text cast members), and fields.

Director supports three different types of text that you can incorporate in your movies. These are bitmapped text, rich text, and fields **(Figure 1)**. Each type has its advantages. A summary of each is given below.

Bitmapped text is created in Director's paint window. You can apply all the effects and tools in the paint window to bitmapped text, like to any other painted image. Bitmapped text animates the fastest. The down side is that bitmapped text cannot be edited once it is created and placed into a cast window (words cannot be rearranged, new fonts can't be applied, and so on).

Rich text (simply referred to as "text" throughout Director) is created using Director's text window, or with the Text tool found in the Tool Palette. Of the three text types, rich text has the most extensive formatting controls. Unlike bitmapped text, rich text can be edited after it has been created. The text window provides the features of an elementary word processor, offering definable tabs, margins, paragraph formatting, line spacing, and other controls. Rich text can also be edited directly on the stage.

A **Field** cast member is created with the Field tool in the Tool Palette, or in the field window. The distinguishing feature of a field cast member is that its text can be edited while a movie is playing. This is useful in an interactive movie, where users type in data. Field cast members should only be used when absolutely necessary since they animate the slowest, and require that the same fonts be installed on any system that will be running your movie.

BITMAPPED TEXT

Bitmapped text is created in Director's paint window. The most notable feature of bitmapped text is that it cannot be edited once it's created. If you decide you want to change a word, a typeface, the text's spacing, and so on, you must erase the original text and start over again. On the other hand, like any other bitmap image, bitmapped text can be selected and then modified with a variety of Director's paint window effects—for instance, it can be rotated, warped, flipped, and so on *(see page 105 in the Paint window chapter)*. It can also be easily incorporated into other painted artwork you might have. The print quality of bitmapped text is poor. Fields offer the best print quality *(see page 179)*. Bitmapped text requires more storage space than rich text or fields.

When you create text in the paint window, that text automatically becomes a bitmap cast member, where it can be dragged to the stage and assigned to the score like any other cast member.

With bitmapped text, it is not required to have the same fonts installed on those systems where you play the movie.

To create bitmapped text:

1. Choose Paint from the Window menu to open Director's paint window **(Figure 2)**.
2. Click the Text tool icon in the paint tool palette to select it **(Figure 3)**.
3. Click the mouse anywhere in the paint window to select the location where your text will be placed. A text box containing a blinking insertion point appears at this spot.
4. Choose Font from the Modify menu to open the Font dialog box, where you can select the desired font, size, and style **(Figures 4–5)**.

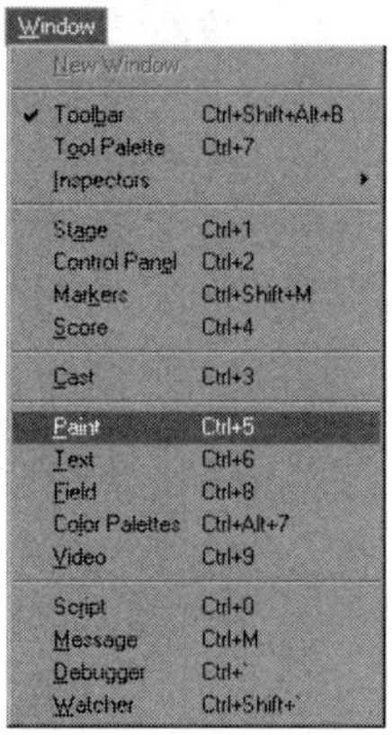

Figure 2. Choose **Paint** from the **Window** menu.

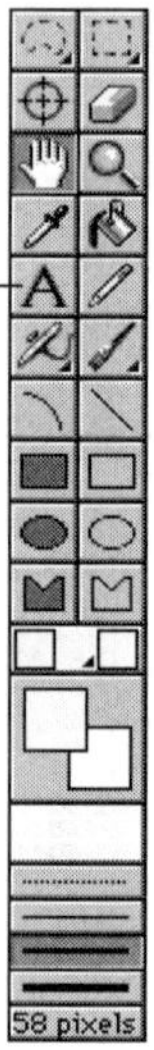

Figure 3. Select the Text tool in the paint window tool palette.

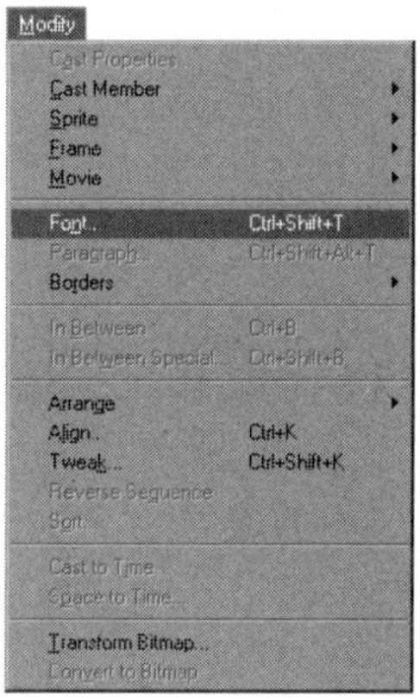

Figure 4. Choose **Font** from the **Modify** menu.

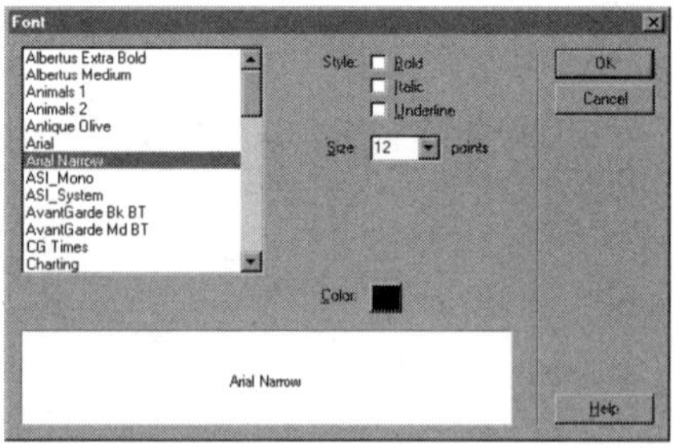

Figure 5. Set the desired font, size, and style in the **Font** dialog box.

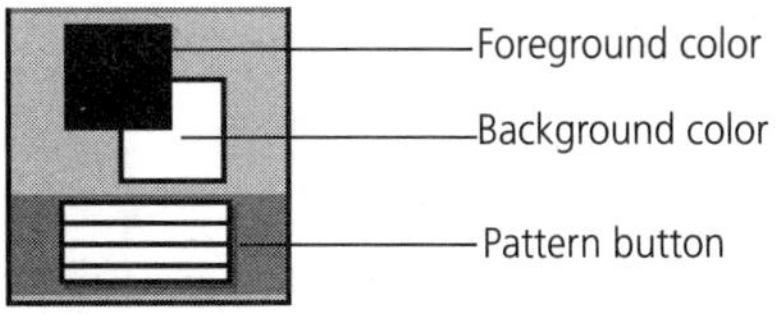

Figure 6. Select the text colors by clicking the **Foreground** and **Background** color chips. Apply a pattern to the text by clicking the **Pattern** button.

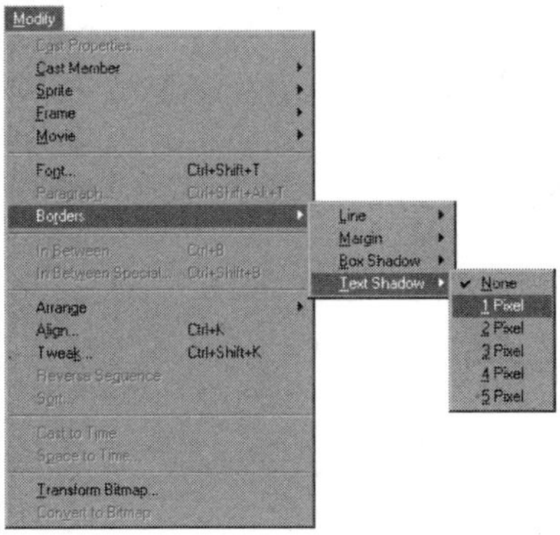

Figure 7. Add a drop shadow to the text by selecting **Borders** from the **Modify** menu, and selecting **Text Shadow** from the pop-up menu.

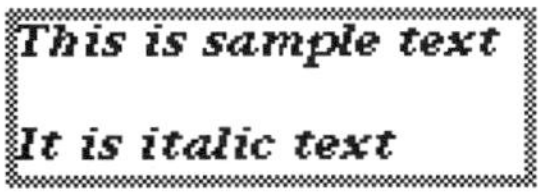

Figure 8. A text box with sample text.

Figure 9. The **Warp** effect from the **Effects** toolbar was used to alter this bitmapped text.

5. Click the Foreground and Background color chips in the paint tool palette to color the text. The Foreground chip sets the color of the text itself, while the Background chip sets the color of the box that surrounds the text. You can also apply a pattern to the text by clicking the Pattern button in the tool palette **(Figure 6)**.
6. To add a drop shadow to the text, choose Borders from the Modify menu, and select Text Shadow from the pop-up menu. In the Text Shadow submenu, choose the number of pixels that the shadow should offset the text by **(Figure 7)**.
7. Type in your text **(Figure 8)**. Press Enter to start a new line.
8. To move the text to a new location on screen, drag the text box by its border.

✔ Tips

- Remember that bitmapped text can be altered with the variety of effects in the paint window's Effects toolbar. Director's Warp effect was used to make the text sample in **(Figure 9)** appear to have dimension.
- From the cast window, you can double-click a bitmapped text cast member and Director automatically opens the image in its paint window.

RICH TEXT

All the limitations of bitmapped text—the fact that once you place the text, you can no longer edit it, and that such text prints poorly to laser printers—are overcome by rich text (simply referred to as "text" throughout Director). Rather than being bitmapped (built pixel-by-pixel), this text type is created by mathematical graphics routines. The benefit of rich text is that it can easily be edited, resized, and otherwise altered once it becomes a cast member in your movie, making it more flexible than the bitmapped text created in the paint window. On the downside, this variety of text can't be rotated or otherwise distorted for special effect, as bitmapped text can. Also, Director animates rich text more slowly than bitmapped text.

There are two ways to create rich text cast members in Director. The first is to create and position the text directly on the stage, using the Text tool **(Figure 10)** in the Tool Palette. The second approach is to type your text into Director's text window **(Figure 11)**, which in turn places the text in a cast window (as a cast member), where it can be dragged to the stage at a later time. The first approach is the quickest, most straightforward method of incorporating rich text into a movie. The second is best if you need more extensive formatting controls, or would like to create a number of text cast members at one time, and place them throughout your movie later on.

If you create a projector, rich text is converted into bitmaps, so you don't need to have the same fonts installed on those systems where you play the movie.

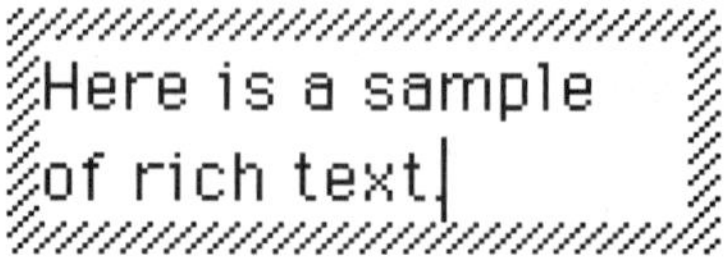

Figure 10. The Text tool in the Tool Palette is used to create and position a rich text cast member directly on the stage.

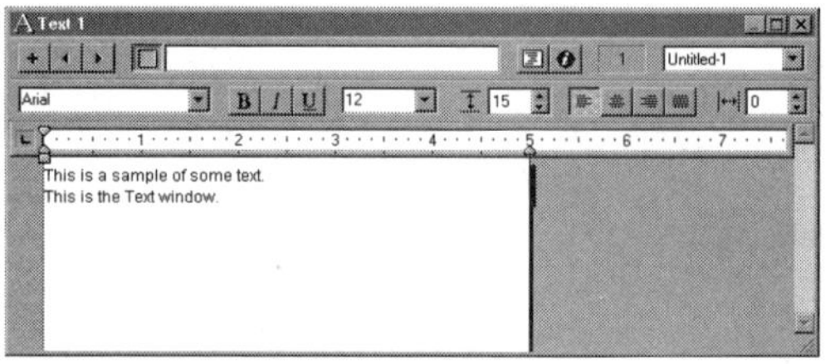

Figure 11. The text window.

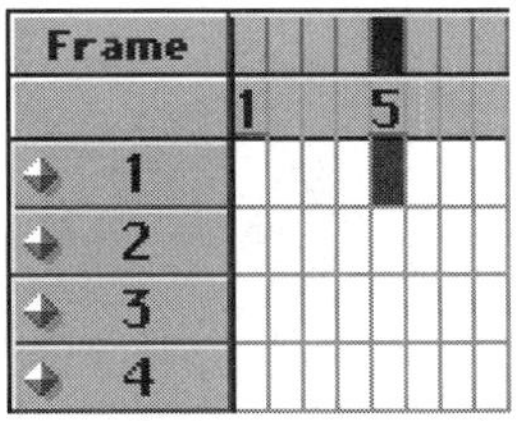

Figure 12. Select a cell in the desired animation channel where you wish to place a rich text cast member.

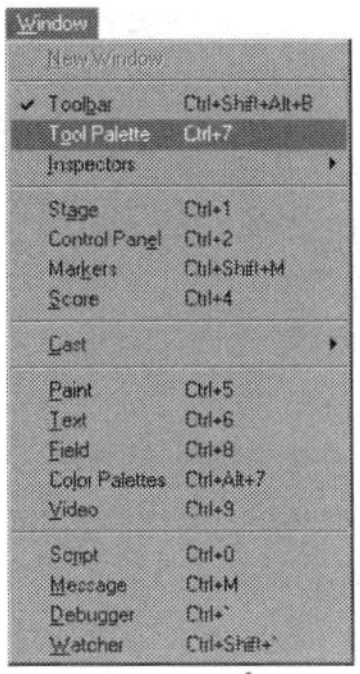

Figure 13. Choose **Tool Palette** from the **Window** menu.

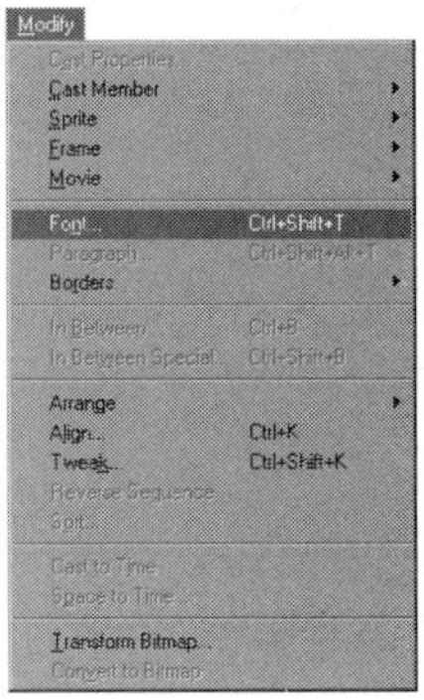

Figure 14. Choose **Font** from the **Modify** menu.

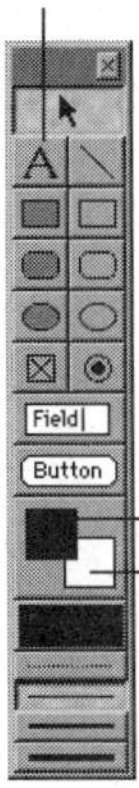

Figure 15. Click the Text tool in the Tool Palette.

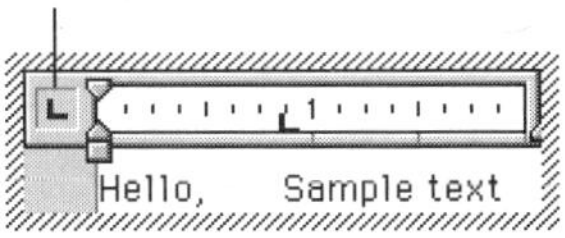

Figure 16. Use the Ruler to set tabs in the text box.

To create rich text directly on the stage:

1. In Director's score window, select the cell in the desired animation channel where you wish to place a rich text cast member **(Figure 12)**.
2. Choose Tool Palette from the Window **(Figure 13)**.
3. In the Tool Palette, click the Text tool **(Figure 15)**.
4. Position the crosshair pointer on the stage, and click the mouse to place a text box there.
5. You can set the text's font, size, and style by choosing Font from the Modify menu **(Figure 14)**, and making the appropriate selections in the Font dialog box.
6. In the Tool Palette, click the Foreground and Background color chips to assign color to your text. The Foreground color applies to the text itself, while the Background color applies to the text box **(Figure 15)**.
7. Type your text into the text box. Text wraps around to a new line automatically as you type.
8. When you've finished typing, click outside the text box to make it final. The text is placed on the stage and in the active cast window.

✔ Tips

- After step 4 above, choose Ruler from the View menu to display a ruler over the text box, which allows you to set tabs **(Figure 16)**. Click the tab well repeatedly to select the type of tab you wish to set. Click on the ruler to set a tab. To remove a tab, drag it off the ruler.
- You can convert rich text and field cast members into bitmap cast members (but not the other way around). Select the text or field cast member in a cast window and choose Convert to Bitmap from the Modify menu.

To create rich text with the text window:

1. Choose Text from Director's Window menu **(Figure 17)**.
2. Use the controls in the text window to set the font, style, size, alignment, spacing, and kerning settings for your text **(Figure 18)**,
3. To set a tab, first click the tab well repeatedly to select the type of tab you wish to set **(Figure 19)**. Click on the ruler to set a new tab. To remove a tab, drag it off the ruler.
4. To set margins, drag the indent markers (left, first-line, or right indents) on the ruler **(Figure 19)**
5. Type your text in the text window. The text will be formatted automatically in the style that you specified. Text wraps around to a new line as you type. You can also press Enter to begin a new line.

   The text that you type will automatically be entered as a cast member in Director's cast window, where you can drag it to the stage and assign it to the score.
6. When you've finished typing, you can either close the text window, or, if you would like to create more text cast members, click the New cast member button at the top of the text window **(Figure 18)**. Director will clear the window, and create another cast member position in the cast window to accommodate the new text.

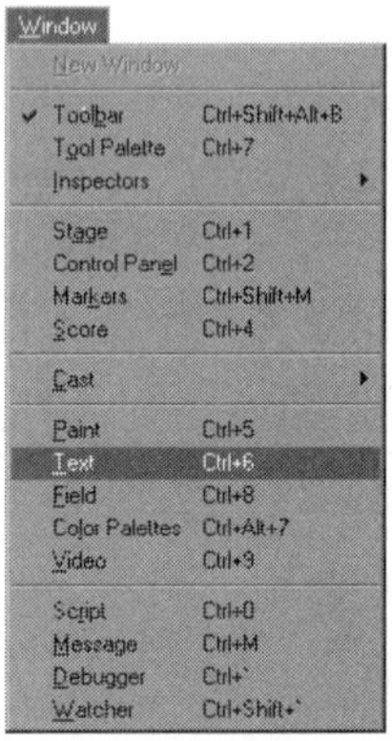

Figure 17. Choose **Text** from the **Window** menu.

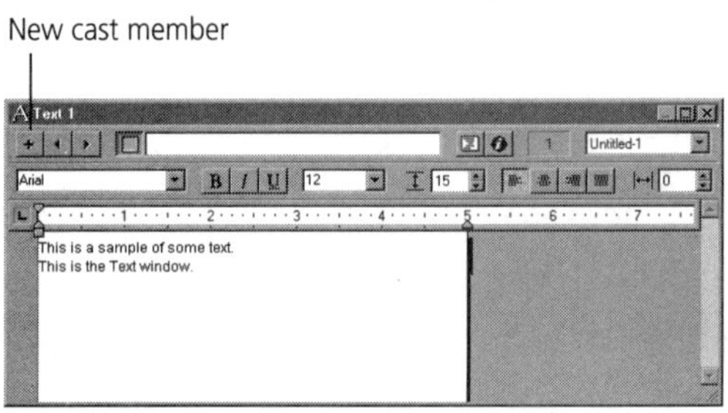

Figure 18. Use the controls in the text window to set the font, style, size, alignment, spacing, and kerning settings for your text.

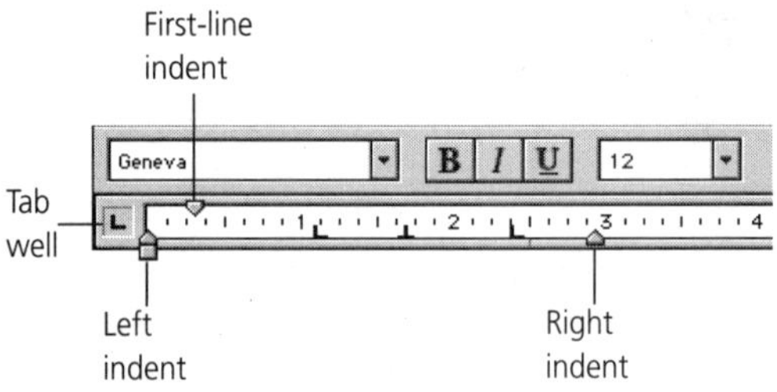

Figure 19. Tabs and margins are set in the text window's ruler.

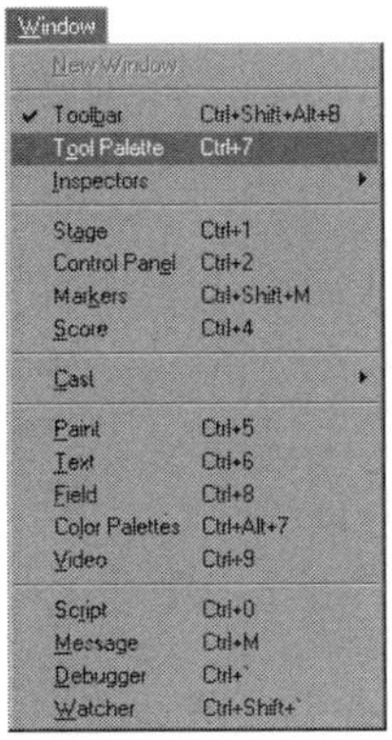

Figure 20. Choose **Tool Palette** from the **Window** menu.

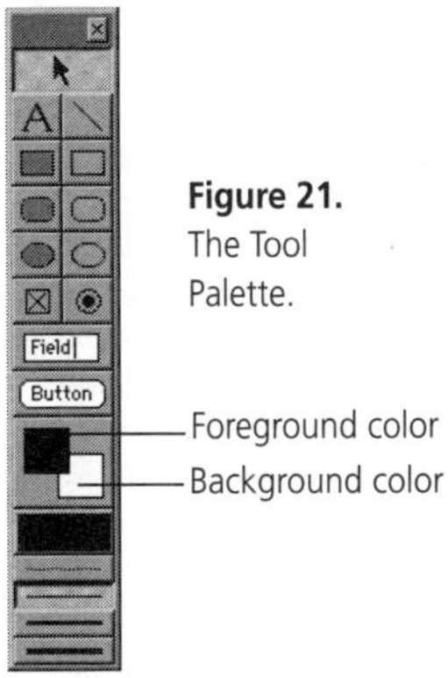

Figure 21. The Tool Palette.

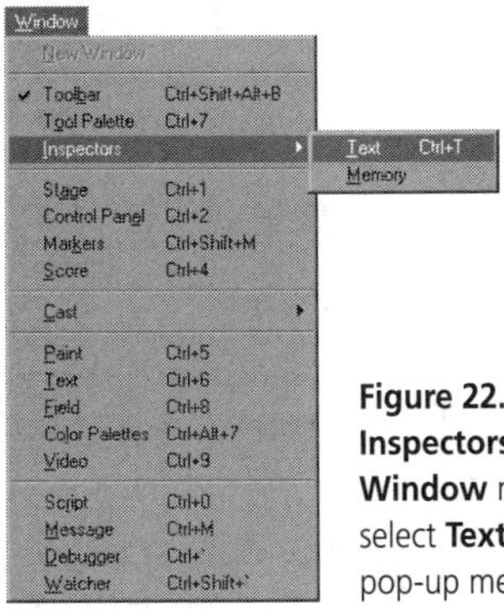

Figure 22. Choose **Inspectors** from the **Window** menu and select **Text** from the pop-up menu.

Figure 23. Use the Text Inspector to make formatting changes to your text cast members.

optional

7. If you would like to add color to your text or the box surrounding it, choose Tool Palette from the Window menu **(Figure 20)**.
8. To change the color of text, first select the section of text you wish to color by dragging across it. Then click the Foreground color chip in the Tool Palette **(Figure 21)** and select a color from the pop-up menu.
9. To change the color of the text box, click the Background color chip in the Tool Palette and select a color from the pop-up menu.

To edit text in the text window:

Once a text cast member has been placed in your score, it's often easiest to edit the text right from the stage. To edit text using the text window, however, simply open the cast window and select the text cast member you wish to edit. Then choose Text from the Window menu to open the text window for the selected cast member (you can double-click the cast member to open the text window).

Using the Text Inspector

The Text Inspector is simply another tool for changing the formatting of your text. It has most of the controls found in the text window. The convenience of the Text Inspector is that you can change the formatting of text directly on the stage without having to open the text cast member in the text window.

1. Choose Inspectors from the Window menu, and select Text from the pop-up menu **(Figure 22)**.
2. Select the cell in the score that contains the text cast member you wish to change on the stage.
3. Make the desired formatting adjustments in the Text Inspector window **(Figure 23)**.

Anti-alias text feature

Anti-aliasing reduces the jagged edges and curves of text. It is most useful for larger point sizes where rough edges can be noticeable. The anti-alias feature is available only for rich text, and is on by default.

To change the anti-alias setting for text:

1. In the cast window, select the text cast member whose anti-aliasing setting you wish to change.
2. Choose Cast Member from the Modify menu and select Properties from the pop-up menu **(Figure 24)**.
3. In the Text Cast Member Properties dialog box, click on the appropriate anti-alias option **(Figure 25)**.

To import text:

Director allows you to import text files saved in the rich text format (RTF).

1. Choose Import from the File menu **(Figure 26)**.
2. In the Import dialog box, choose text as the file type to import.
3. Add the text file and click Import. The text file is imported as a single cast member unless the file contains page or column breaks. Each time Director encounters a page or column break, it creates a new cast member for the text.

✓ Tip

- You can apply three of Director's score ink effects to rich text, namely Copy, Background Transparent, and Blend. In the score window, select the cell or range of cells that contains the desired text sprites, and then click the Ink pop-up menu to make an ink selection **(Figure 27)**.

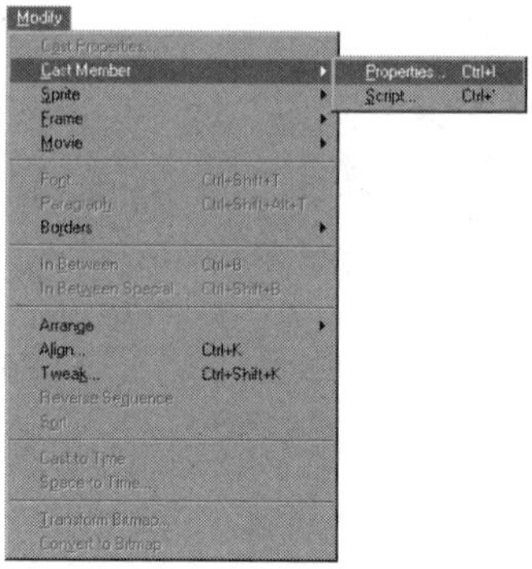

Figure 24. Choose **Cast Member** from the **Modify** menu and select **Properties** from the pop-up menu.

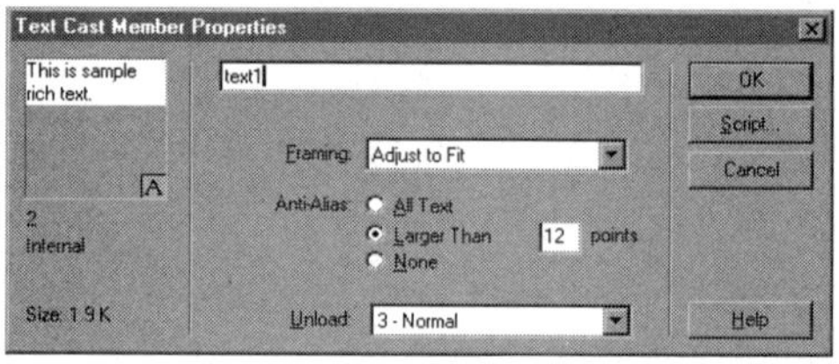

Figure 25. Click on the appropriate anti-alias option in the **Text Cast Member Properties** dialog box.

Figure 26. Choose **Import** from the **File** menu.

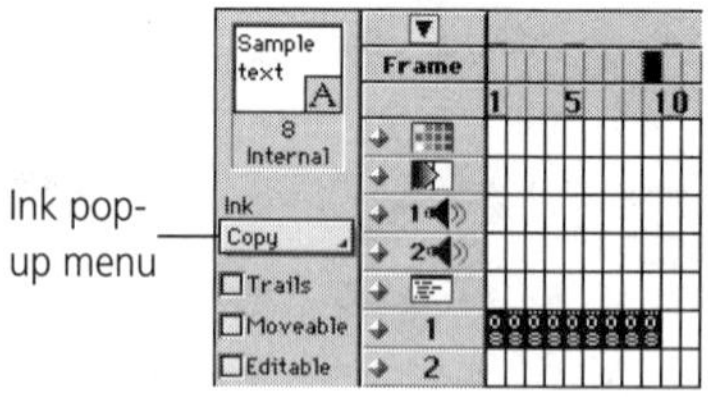

Figure 27. Use the **Ink** pop-up menu in the score to apply one of three ink effects to your text sprites.

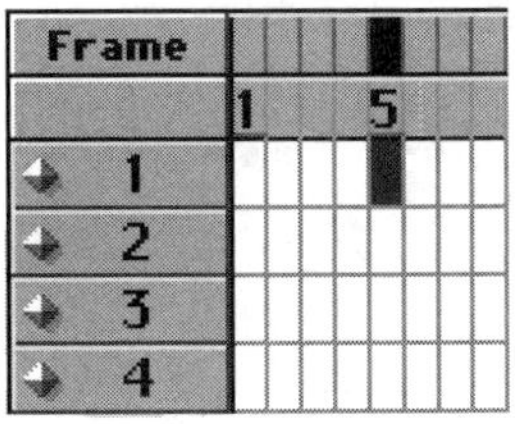

Figure 28. Select a cell in the desired animation channel where you wish to place your field cast member.

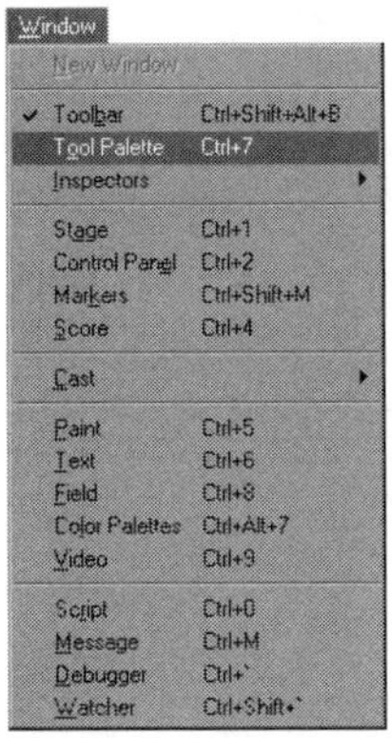

Figure 29. Choose **Tool Palette** from the **Window** menu.

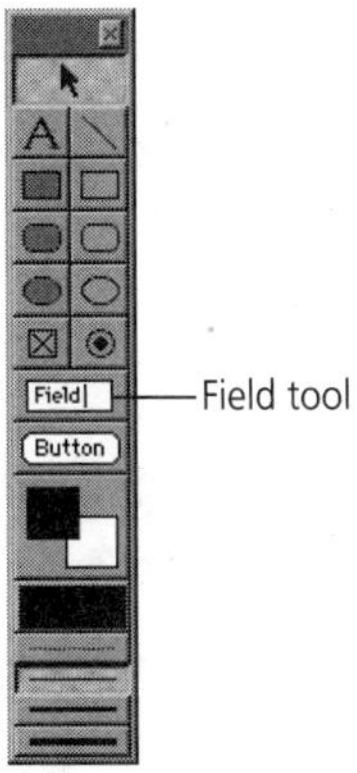

Figure 30. Click the Field tool in the Tool Palette.

FIELDS

Working with fields in Director is very similar to working with text cast members. The main difference with field cast members is that their text is editable during movie playback, adding an interactive dimension. This allows you to create movies where your users change and enter text data on the stage. For example, you might want to incorporate your user's name into the actual movie, by asking him or her to enter it during the course.

Another feature of fields is that their print quality is higher than either bitmapped or rich text.

You should only use fields if you need either editable text during playback, or high print quality, since there are several important disadvantages: Of the three text types, fields animate the slowest; fields require that any system which plays your movie have the same fonts installed, even if your movie is played as a Projector; formatting controls are more limited with fields than with text cast members.

To create a field directly on the stage:

Creating a field on the stage is very similar to creating a text cast member on the stage. *(See page 175)*

1. In the score, select the cell in the desired animation channel where you wish to place your field cast member **(Figure 28)**.
2. Choose Tool Palette from the Window menu **(Figure 29)**.
3. Click the Field tool in the Tool Palette **(Figure 30)**.
4. Position the crosshair pointer on the stage, and click the mouse to place a field text box there.
5. Choose Font from the Modify menu to set the field's font, style, and size.

To make a field editable during movie playback:

1. Select the field cast member in the cast window.
2. Click the Cast Member Properties button in the cast window.
3. In the Field Cast Member Properties dialog box, check the Editable option **(Figure 31)**.

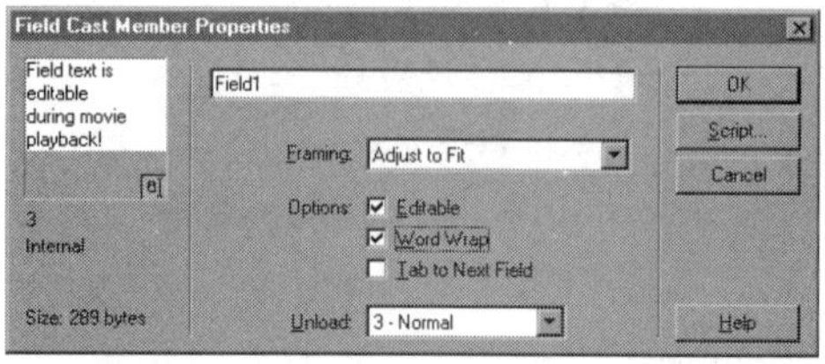

Figure 31. Check the **Editable** check box in the **Field Cast Member Properties** dialog box.

✔ Tip

- If you want a field cast member to be editable only during certain frames in your movie, select the appropriate cells in the score and check the editable check box in the score **(Figure 32)**. If the Editable option in the Field Cast Member Properties dialog box is set, the score's editable option is ignored, and the field will be editable in every frame where it is present.

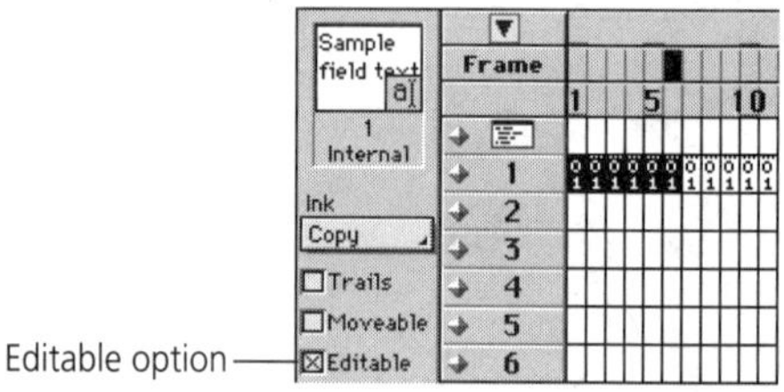

Figure 32. Check the **Editable** check box in the score.

To edit a field during playback:

Whenever your movie is playing and an editable field sprite is present on the stage, you can click on it and then type to edit its contents. Its parent cast member in the cast window *is* changed as you type.

To create a field cast member using the field window:

The field window is similar to the text window, except that the ruler (tabs and indents) as well as spacing and kerning controls are not available.

1. Choose Field from the Window menu **(Figure 33)**.
2. Type your text in the field window **(Figure 34)**. When you close the field window, a field cast member is created in the current cast window, from where it can be dragged and placed onto the stage.

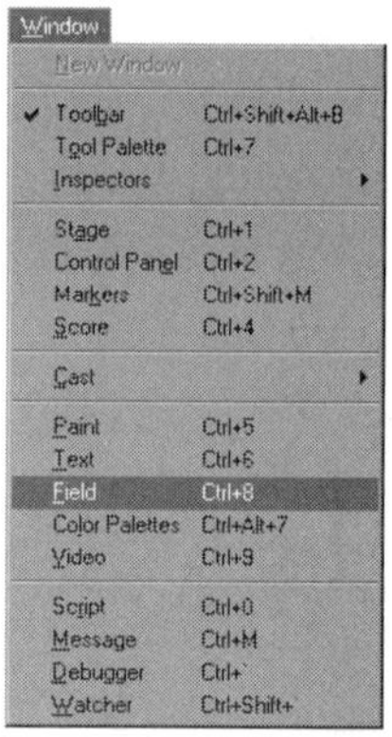

Figure 33. Choose **Field** from the **Window** menu.

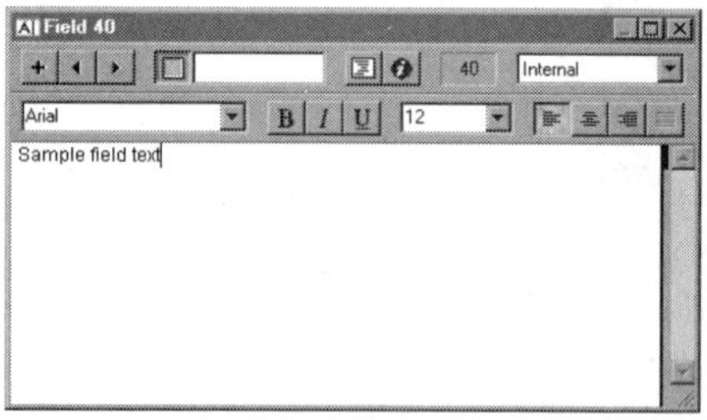

Figure 34. The field window.

SOUND IN DIRECTOR 12

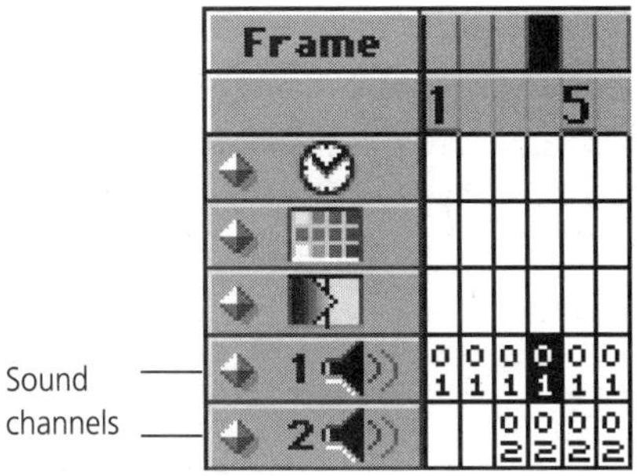

Figure 1. Sounds are placed in one of two sound channels in the score.

Adding musical scores, sound effects, and voice-overs to Director movies is easy. Simply import a sound file, and place its cast member in a range of frames in one of Director's sound channels **(Figure 1)**. If there's any trick to this, it's deciding which frames the sound should play in. For example, if you want Director to play the sound of footsteps as a character walks across the screen, you'd first animate the character and then note in which frames his feet touch the ground. You'd then place your footstep sound in these frames, assigning it to one of the score's two sound channels. Another movie might call for playing a musical score throughout an entire animation rather than timing it to specific events. In this case you would place the music into a sound channel through a range of frames.

Windows actually supports only one sound channel. Director can play more than one sound at a time since it mixes them together. It does so through using Macromedia's MACROMIX.DLL technology. This file must be installed on your PC to be able to play more than one sound at a time. The MinMaxChannels value in the DIRECTOR.INI file determines how many sounds Director can mix. Its default value is 4. The maximum is 8 mixed sounds.

You can mix two sounds by using the score's sound channels. In order to mix additional sounds, you will need to use special Lingo commands. This chapter focuses on using the score's two sound channels.

IMPORTING AND CREATING SOUND

To import a sound into a cast window:

1. In a cast window, select the cast member position into which you'll import your sound. If you do not select a particular cast position, Director will place your sound in the first available slot **(Figure 2)**.
2. Choose Import from the File menu **(Figure 3)**.
3. In the Import dialog box, choose Sounds from the Files of type pop-up menu **(Figure 4)**. This tells Director to display only Sounds in the file selector box.
4. Add the desired sound, and click Import. Director places your sound in the cast window. Now it's ready to be assigned to the score.

✔ Tips

- Ordinarily when you import a sound, Director copies the contents of the sound file into your movie. This can significantly increase the disk size and memory requirements of the movie. To avoid this, check the Linked option in the Import dialog box before importing a sound file. This tells Director to refer to the original sound file when necessary, rather than copying its entire contents into your movie.
- When you import a sound into Director, the sound can only be played *as is*. Other than volume, Director has no controls for editing the sound's various attributes, such as pitch. You can't even use Director's tempo channel to alter the sound's playback speed. Changes made to Director's tempo will affect the animation rate, but not the sound.

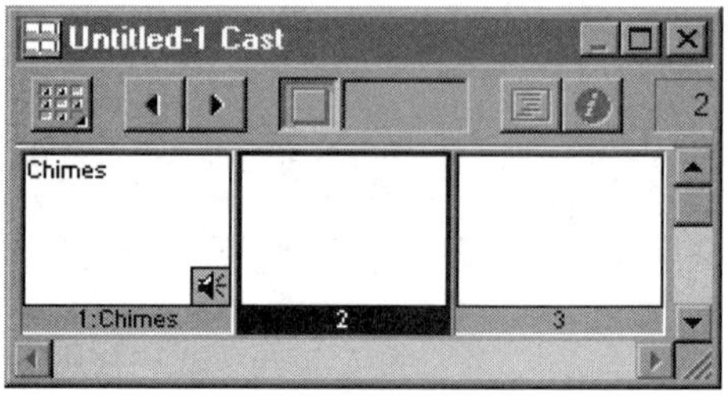

Figure 2. Select a cast member position in a cast window into which you'll import a sound.

Figure 3. Choose **Import** from the **File** menu.

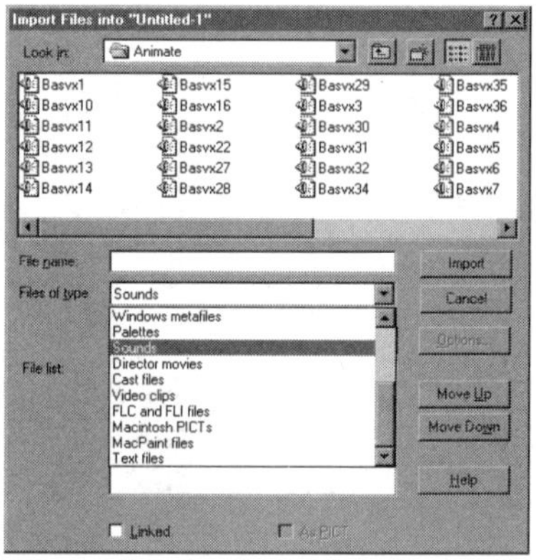

Figure 4. Choose **Sounds** from the **Files of type** pop-up menu in the **Import** dialog box.

About MIDI

Besides playing digitized sound files, Director can also play sound effects and music by controlling a MIDI instrument such as a keyboard synthesizer, drum machine, or sequencer that has been attached to your PC. Using these types of instruments allows your movie to play a very rich and intricate musical score; it is, however, a complex process. First, your PC needs a special MIDI interface that allows it to work with MIDI equipment. Second, Director requires that you use a series of somewhat cryptic commands to control the instruments properly. This topic falls beyond the scope of this book. For more information consult your Director reference manual.

✔ Tips

- Director for Windows accepts sounds saved either as AIFF, AIFC, or WAVE files. These formats are standards supported by most, if not all, sound digitizers and editors for Windows. Most libraries of prerecorded "clip-sounds" support these formats as well.
- An intricate soundtrack—especially one with long-lasting sounds such as voice overs and musical scores—can slow your entire movie down. This is a particularly important issue if you intend to play your movie on a wide variety of PC's; while a top-of-the-line Pentium PC may keep pace, a run-of-the-mill 486 model might be overtaxed and slow your movie significantly. So try to think ahead about the types of PC's likely to play your movie, and design your soundtrack accordingly.
- Sounds in digital videos (QuickTime for Windows or AVI movies) cannot be mixed with sounds played through the sound channels. Whichever sound starts playing first prevents the other type from playing.

To set the volume of your movie:

1. Choose Control Panel from the Window menu **(Figure 7)**.
2. Click the Volume button in the control panel **(Figure 8)**, and select the desired volume level from the pop-up menu. This setting controls the volume of your entire movie.

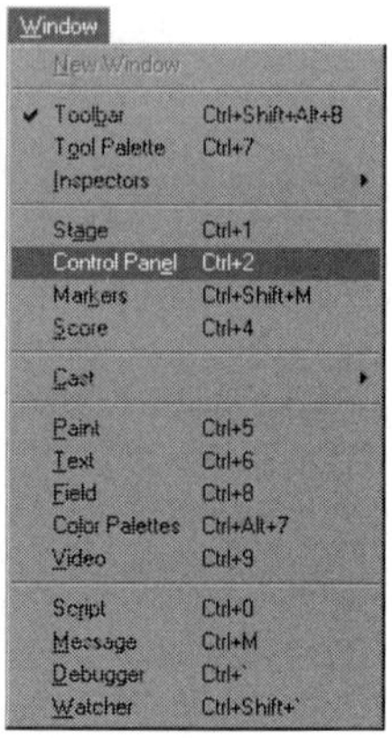

Figure 7. Choose **Control Panel** from the **Window** menu.

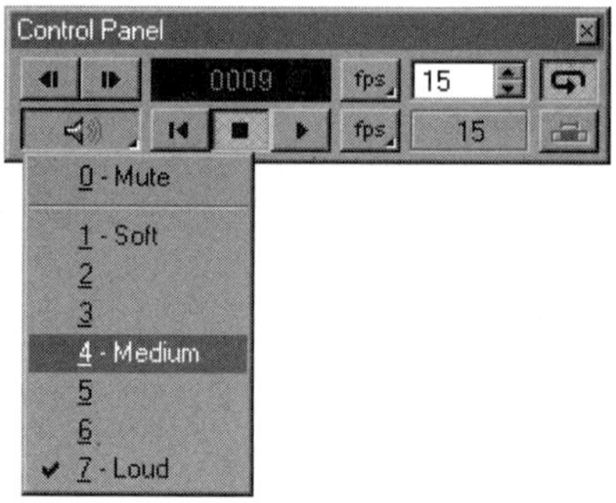

Figure 8. Click the **Volume** button in the control panel, and select the desired level from the pop-up menu.

Set Volume

Sound production outside Director

The process of making ambitious movies in Director will inevitably require custom sounds that you'll have to create from scratch.

For serious sound production you'll want to use a third-party sound editing application that can record sounds at high resolutions from a variety of sources, such as microphones, tapedecks, and musical synthesizers. Such applications also allow you to edit sounds, cutting out unwanted noise and adjusting pitch, volume, and other characteristics. Some popular programs available for Windows are Sound Forge from Sonic Foundary, and Wave Lab from Steinberg. If you see yourself heading into sound production, you'll probably want to upgrade your sound card to one that has higher quality analog to digital conversion for clearer sound recording. One such card is Audio media 3.

Note: However you create your custom sounds, make sure that they are saved as AIFF, AIFC, or WAVE files, since these are the only sound formats that Director for Windows accepts.

PLACING SOUND

To place sounds in the score:

1. In the score window, click the frame (or drag across a range of frames) in the desired sound channel to indicate where your sound should be placed **(Figure 9)**.
2. Choose Frame from the Modify menu and select Sound from the pop-up menu **(Figure 10)**.
3. In the Frame Properties: Sound dialog box, select the sound you'd like to place in the score (a sound must have already been imported into Director's cast window to appear in this list). With a sound selected, click the Play button to hear a preview, or click OK to place it in the score **(Figure 11)**.

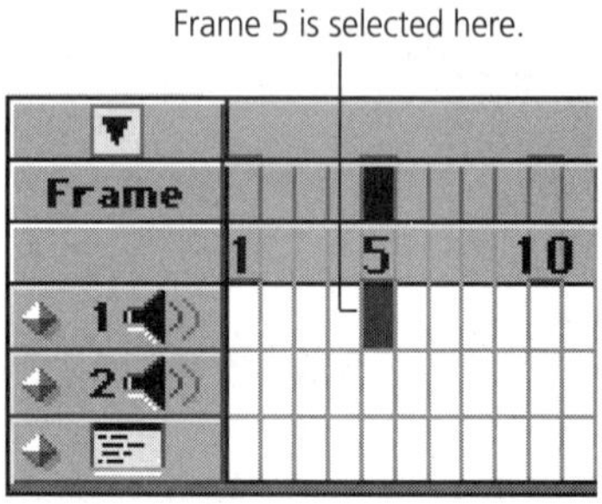

Figure 9. Select a frame or range of frames in a sound channel in which your sound will be placed.

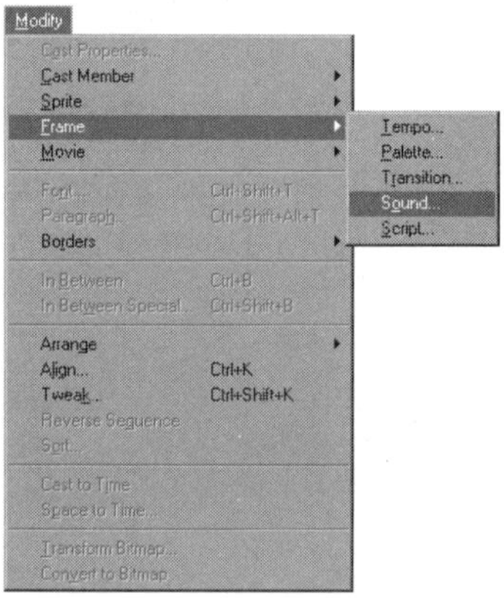

Figure 10. Choose **Frame** from the **Modify** menu and select **Sound** from the pop-up menu.

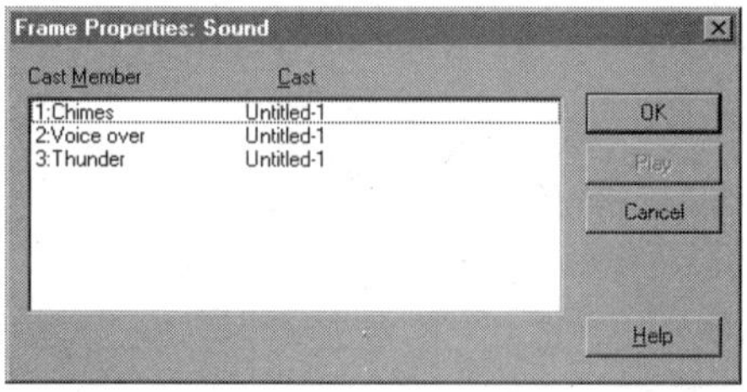

Figure 11. Select a sound to be placed in a sound channel.

To extend sounds to play completely:

Most sounds need to be assigned to a range of frames in order to play completely—a laser blast, for instance, might require 20 frames, while a musical score could fill hundreds. If a sound is assigned to fewer frames than its duration demands, it will cut off prematurely. For instance, if a sound is designed to last two seconds, and the movie tempo is set at 30 fps, then the sound needs to be assigned to at least 60 frames. If it's assigned to only 45 frames, it will end in its last frame without finishing. If you find that your sound is ending prematurely,

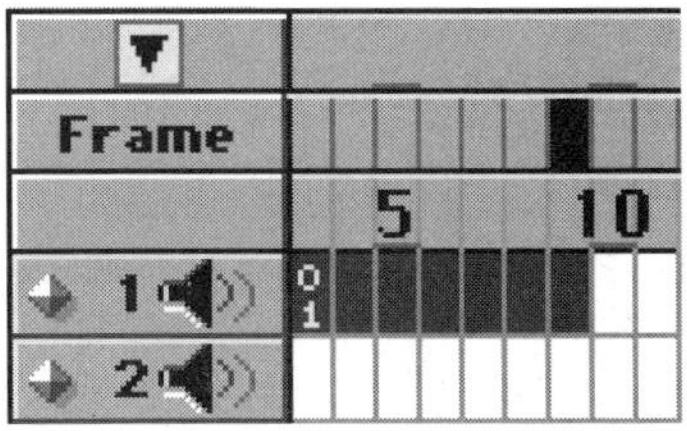

Figure 12. Select a range of frames through which you'll extend a sound.

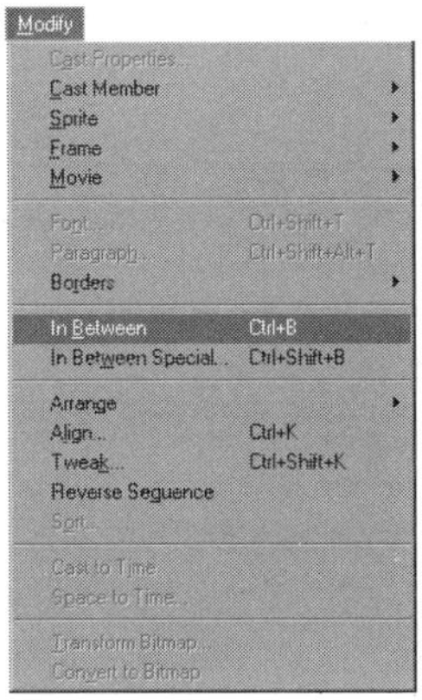

Figure 13. Choose **In Between** from the **Modify** menu.

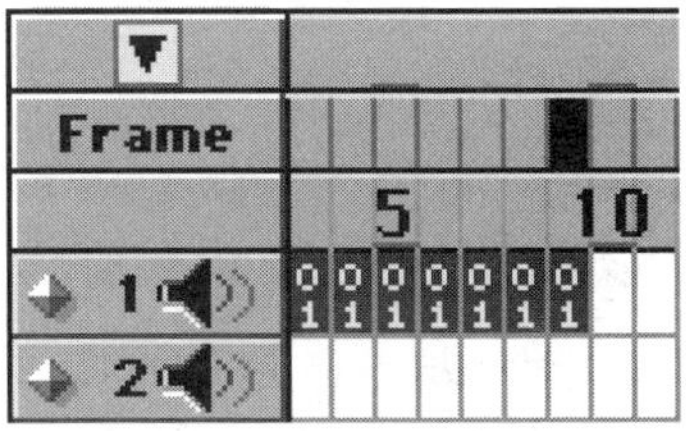

Figure 14. The sound is extended through all the highlighted frames.

you simply have to extend the sound to occupy additional frames in the score.

1. In the score window, click the last frame that your sound occupies, and drag to highlight the additional frames to which you will extend the sound **(Figure 12)**.
2. Choose In Between from the Modify menu **(Figure 13)** to extend the sound through all of the highlighted frames **(Figure 14)**.
3. Rewind and play the movie to confirm that your sound now plays completely. If it still cuts off, simply extend the sound into even more frames by repeating the steps above.

✔ Tips

- If you assign a sound to more frames than it requires, the sound will not repeat, unless it has been set to loop. *(See the section "To loop a sound" on page 188 for more info)*
- To quickly determine the number of frames a sound requires, use the steps above to extend it into more frames than it can possibly require (for example, if you know that a laser blast sound effect will require roughly 20 frames, then extend it to 40 or 50). Then play back your movie with the score window open and visible. As the movie plays, Director will highlight each frame it moves through. Simply listen for your sound, and note at which frame in the score it finishes. Now you know how many frames the sound really requires, and can cut out any extra frames it occupies.
- You can also ensure that a sound finishes playing by setting a pause in the tempo channel that waits until the end of a sound. *(See the section "To set a pause in the movie's tempo" on page 193 in the Movie Tempo chapter)*

To loop a sound:

Often you'll want a particular sound to play repeatedly throughout your movie. For example, you might want the sound of a chirping bird to play over and over, or you might want the sound of background music to loop continuously. Setting up such repetitions is easy.

1. Place your sound cast member into the score and extend it through as many frames as you wish it to play **(Figure 15)**. When you extend the sound, you should account for the number of repetitions desired. For instance, if a sound normally requires 10 frames to play completely, and you want it to repeat five times, then you should extend it through 50 frames.
2. In the cast window, select the sound cast member that you placed into the score.
3. Choose Cast Member from the Modify menu and select Properties from the pop-up menu **(Figure 16)**.
4. In the Sound Cast Member Properties dialog box, click the Loop check box **(Figure 17)**.

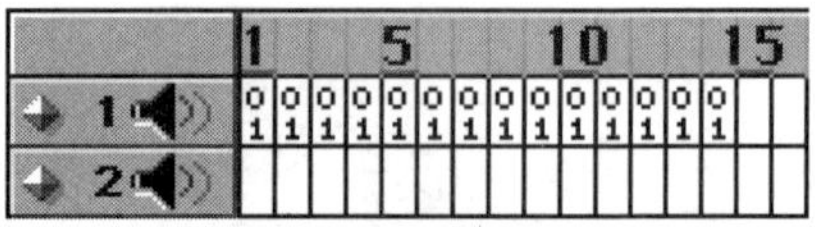

Figure 15. Place the sound through a continuous range of frames you wish it to play in.

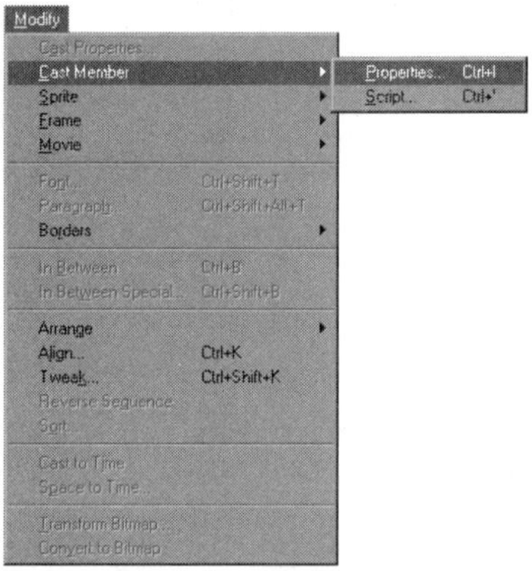

Figure 16. Choose **Cast Member** from the **Modify** menu and select **Properties** from the pop-up menu.

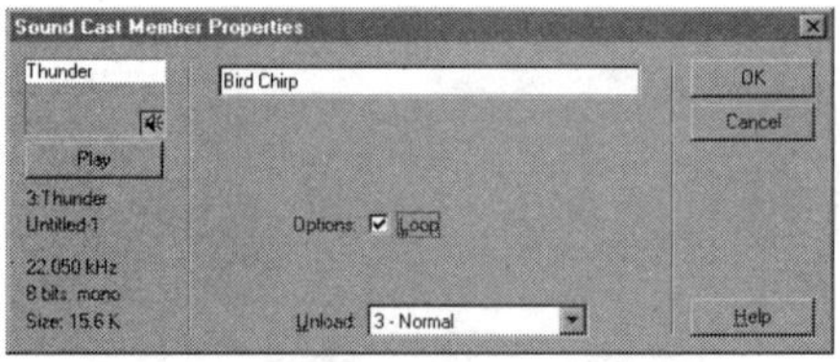

Figure 17. Click the **Loop** option in the **Sound Cast Member Properties** dialog box.

SETTING SCENE TRANSITIONS 13

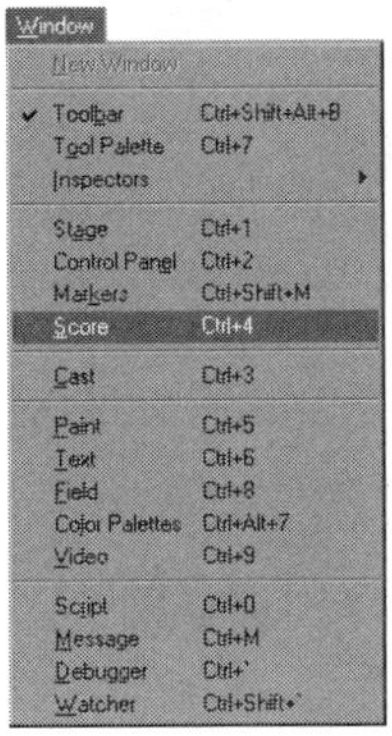

Figure 1. Choose **Score** from the **Window** menu.

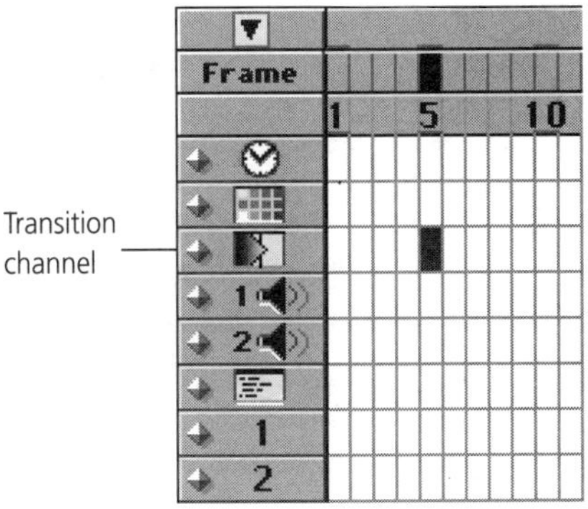

Figure 2. Select a cell in the transition channel where you want a transition to occur.

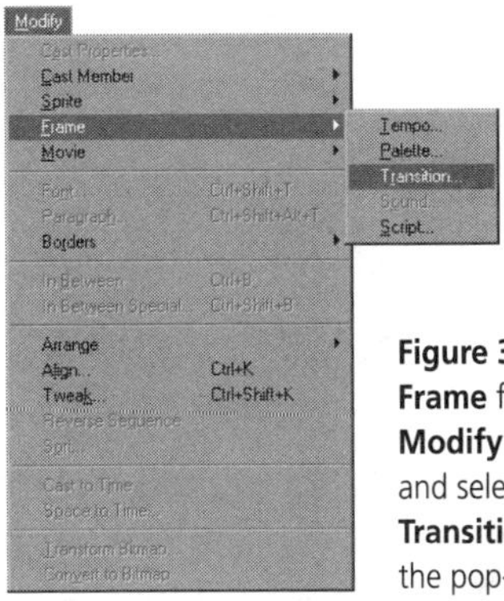

Figure 3. Choose **Frame** from the **Modify** menu and select **Transition** from the pop-up menu.

Director offers more than 50 special effects **transitions** such as dissolves, wipes, and fades that you can use to smoothly move from one scene in a movie to another (a scene is a sequence of related action that takes place on Director's stage). Without transitions, scenes simply cut abruptly from one to another, often creating a jarring effect for the viewer.

Transition's are placed into the transition channel of Director's score, at the particular frame where you wish the transition to occur.

To set a transition:

1. Choose Score from the Window menu to open Director's score **(Figure 1)**.
2. In the transition channel, select the cell at the particular frame in which the transition should occur **(Figure 2)**. The transition begins between the frame that you select, and the frame that precedes it. To transition between two scenes, you'd set the transition at the first frame of the second scene and not at the last frame of the first scene.
3. Choose Frame from the Modify menu, and select Transition from the pop-up menu **(Figure 3)**, or double-click the cell you've selected in the transition channel.

4. In the Frame Properties:Transition dialog box, click the transition that you wish to apply **(Figure 4)**. Use the dialog box's scroll bars to move throughout all of the transition types. ***Note:*** Director features too many transition types to cover here. Fortunately, each type is identified with a descriptive name. Experiment with the different transition types before selecting one for your scene.
5. Click the Entire Stage radio button if the transition should apply to Director's entire stage. Click the Changing Area Only button if the transition should apply only to areas of the stage that are changing from one scene to the next (in other words, where sprites are present, but then are not, or vice versa).
6. Use the Duration and Smoothness slider bars to give the transition a custom duration time and smoothness (smoothness refers to the size of pixel "chunks" used to dissolve one scene or introduce another).
7. Click OK to apply the selected transition to your score. The transition is placed into the active cast window as a transition cast member **(Figure 5)**.

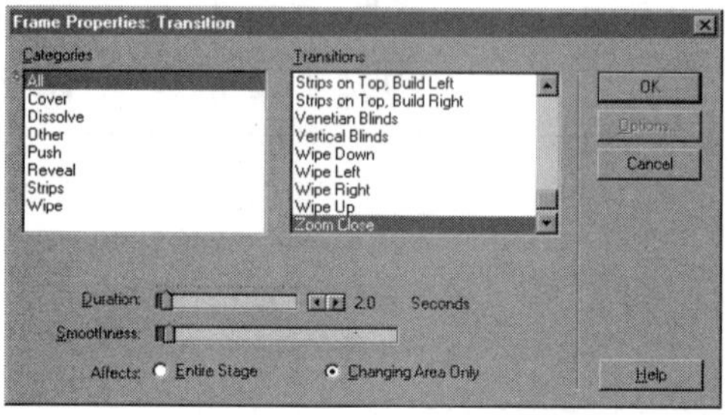

Figure 4. Select the desired transition in the **Frame Properties:Transition** dialog box.

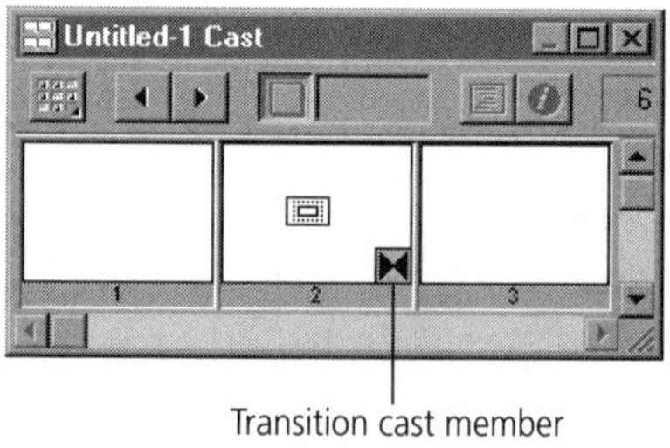

Figure 5. The transition becomes a cast member.

To add Xtra transitions to Director:

Director 5 allows you to add new transitions by installing them as Xtras. *(Also see the Xtras chapter on page 225)*

1. Copy your Xtra transition file into the Xtras folder in the Director application folder. This installs the new transition. You need to restart Director for this transition to be available.
2. Double-click the cell in the transition channel in the score where you wish a transition to occur.
3. In the Frame Properties:Transition dialog box, your Xtra transition is now available to be selected.

MOVIE TEMPO 14

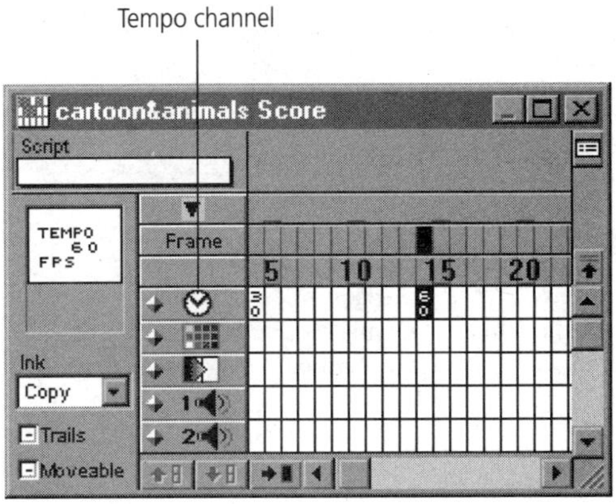

Figure 1. The tempo of your movie is set in the tempo channel of the score.

Director plays your movie at a particular **tempo**, or speed, which you can easily adjust. The movie's tempo is measured in **frames-per-second** (fps), which means the higher the tempo rate (15 fps, 24 fps, 30 fps, etc.), the faster Director plays back animation. With a high tempo (say, 60 fps), you can make sprites zoom across the stage, while you can use a low tempo (perhaps 7 fps) to create a slow-motion effect.

Your movie's tempo is set in the tempo channel of Director's score **(Figure 1)**. Although one tempo can apply to an entire movie, you can also vary your tempo on a frame-by-frame basis.

There are two important things to know about the effects that tempo settings have on your movie: First of all, while the tempo you set affects the speed at which cast member sprites are animated on stage, it does not affect the playback rate of sounds or digital videos.

Secondly, while you may set a high tempo in a movie, the PC that Director is running on must be advanced enough to keep up with that pace. If a particular scene calls for the animation of a large number of sprites, or if it features special ink effects, or if cast members are painted at high color depths (such as 32-bit color), or if there are complex transitions or color palette manipulation at work, your PC may simply not be able to manage all this without slowing the scene's tempo. If this is the case, you must either settle for this slow playback speed, buy a faster PC, or redesign the movie's scene so that it is less demanding.

To set a new tempo in the score:

When you set a new tempo in the tempo channel, that tempo applies to all the following frames of your movie (until you set another tempo change).

1. Choose Score from the Window menu to open Director's score **(Figure 2)**.
2. In the tempo channel, select the cell where you would like a new tempo to occur **(Figure 4)**.
3. Choose Frame from the Modify menu, and select Tempo from the pop-up menu **(Figure 3)**.
4. In the Frame Properties:Tempo dialog box, slide the Tempo scroll bar to set the movie's tempo in frames per second **(Figure 5)**.
5. Click OK to apply the tempo change to the score. Director now uses this tempo setting to play the frame you selected in step 2, and all the frames to the right of it (until, that is, you set a new tempo).

✓ Tips

- You can also open the Frame Properties:Tempo dialog box by double-clicking a cell in the tempo channel.
- If your movie will be played on a wide variety of PC models, try to set a tempo that even low-end PC's will be able to keep up with. Otherwise, owners of low-end PC's such as 386/33's may be disappointed with your movie's playback performance. The best way to determine how well a particular PC will play your movie is to play it on that machine and compare the movie's set tempo to its actual playback tempo. *(See page 194)*

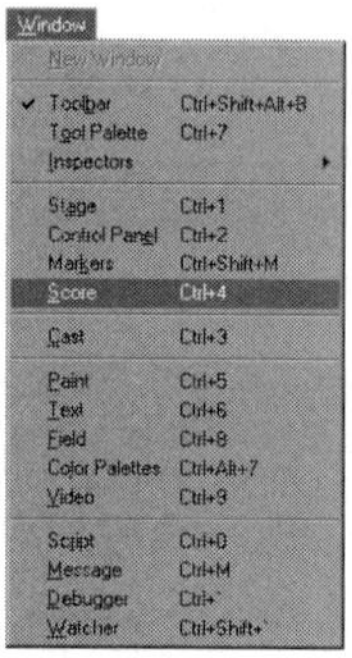

Figure 2. Choose **Score** from the **Window** menu.

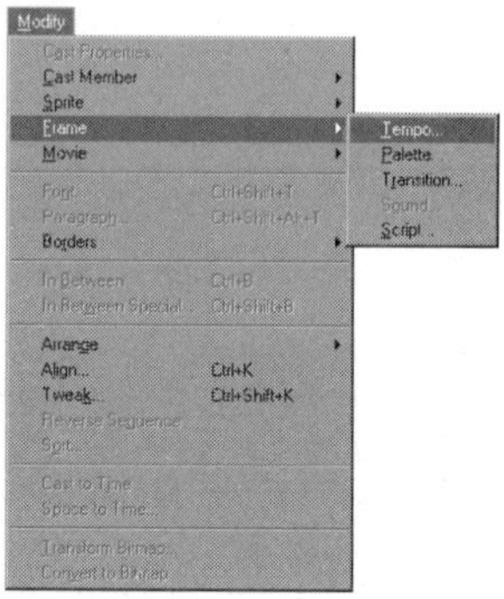

Figure 3. Choose **Frame** from the **Modify** menu, and select **Tempo** from the pop-up menu.

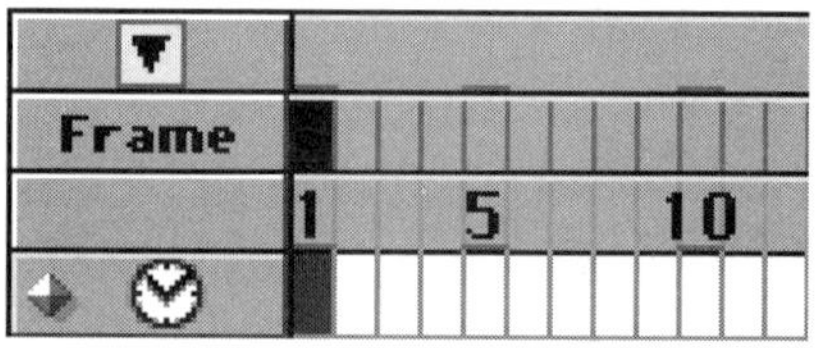

Figure 4. Select a cell in the tempo channel where you would like a new tempo to occur.

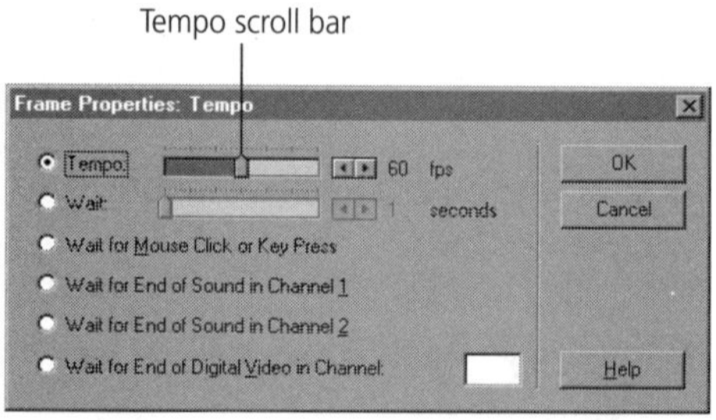

Figure 5. Use the **Frame Properties:Tempo** dialog box to set the movie's tempo in frames-per-second.

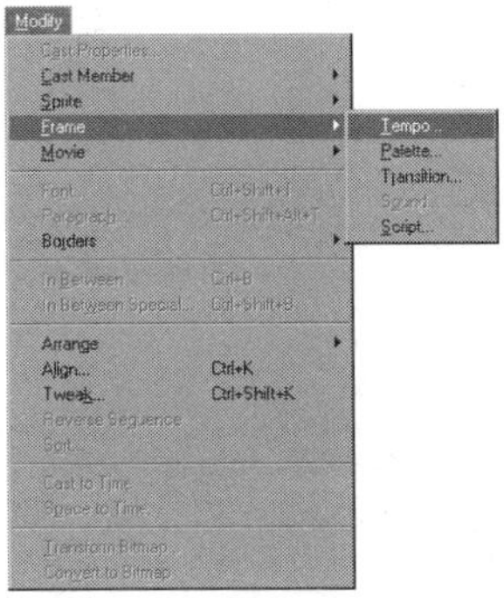

Figure 6. Choose **Frame** from the **Modify** menu, and select **Tempo** from the pop-up menu.

Figure 7. Select one of five **Wait** options in the **Frame Properties:Tempo** dialog box.

To set a pause in the movie's tempo:

Director's Frame Tempo command allows you to create a pause in the playback of your movie. You can pause the action for a specified number of seconds, or create a pause that waits for a certain event to occur such as a mouse click or key stroke.

1. In the tempo channel of the score window, select the frame where you would like to set a pause.
2. Choose Frame from the Modify menu, and select Tempo from the pop-up menu **(Figure 6)**.
3. In the Frame Properties:Tempo dialog box, select the Wait option you wish to use by clicking the appropriate radio button **(Figure 7)**. If you are creating a timed pause, use the Wait scroll bar to specify the duration in seconds. If you want Director to wait for a digital video clip to finish playing, be sure to specify which of the score's animation channels contains the clip.
4. Click OK to apply the pause to the score.

Note: If you create a pause that waits for a sound or digital video to finish, make sure that the sound or video clip begins playing before the frame where the pause takes place. In other words, a sound or digital video clip must already be in progress for this type of pause to work as expected.

To compare actual playback tempo versus the set tempo:

Director tries to play a movie at the particular tempo you've set in the tempo channel. Unfortunately, the actual playback speed may fall short when complex animations are featured. This is very likely on a low-end PC. Fortunately, Director makes it easy to compare this actual tempo to the tempo you've set on a frame-by-frame basis.

1. Set the desired tempo for your movie as outlined on page 192.
2. Choose Control Panel from the Window menu to open the control panel **(Figure 8)**.
3. Click Rewind in the control panel.
4. Click the control panel's Step forward button to step through your movie one frame at a time.
5. In the control panel, compare the Actual Tempo to the Tempo display setting for each frame in your movie **(Figure 9)**. The Actual Tempo value is how fast the computer has managed to play back the given frame. The Tempo display setting shows the target frame rate you've set in the tempo channel for the given frame.

✔ **Tip**

- You can adjust the target tempo for each frame by clicking the arrows in the Tempo display in the control panel **(Figure 9)**. The effect is the same as setting a tempo in the tempo channel for the given frame. A tempo you set in the tempo channel overrides any value you set in the control panel's Tempo display.

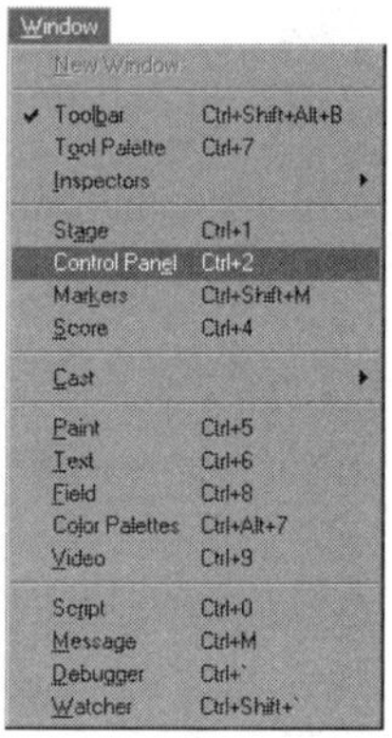

Figure 8. Choose **Control Panel** from the **Window** menu.

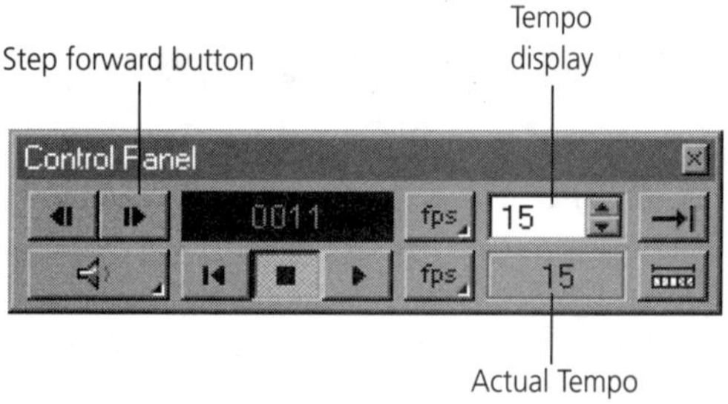

Figure 9. The control panel shows the Actual Tempo of a single frame, and the Tempo display setting for that frame.

Actual Playback Tempo vs. Set Tempo

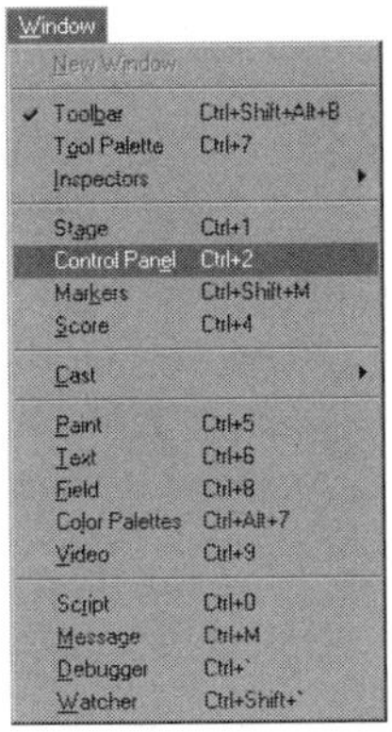

Figure 10. Choose **Control Panel** from the **Window** menu.

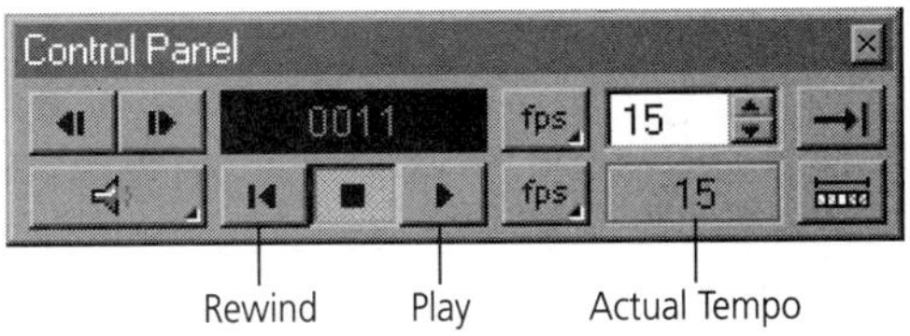

Figure 11. The control panel.

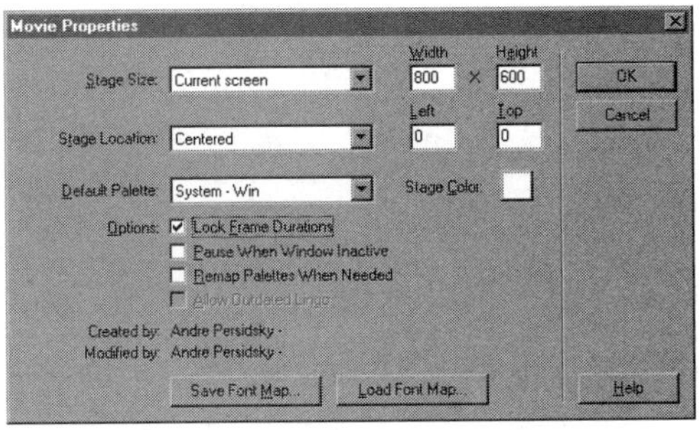

Figure 12. Check the **Lock Frame Durations** option in the **Movie Properties** dialog box.

Locking playback speed

When you've determined the proper tempo for your movie, you can then "lock" that speed so that it's used by whatever PC your movie happens to play on. Doing so guards against your movie being played too fast on more advanced PC's but does not prevent the movie from playing back *slower* when run on a less sophisticated PC. If you're trying to set the movie's tempo to play workably on even low-end PC's, you should establish a tempo that even those PC's can keep up with, and then lock it in.

To lock your movie's playback speed:

1. Set the desired tempo for your movie as outlined on page 192.
2. Choose Control Panel from the Window menu **(Figure 10).**
3. Use the control panel to rewind and then play back your movie from beginning to end **(Figure 11)**. In doing so, Director records the actual speed at which it plays each frame, and stores these values in the Actual Tempo display in the control panel. If the movie branches off into multiple segments (for instance, in an interactive presentation), make sure you play through all of these segments.
4. Choose Movie from the Modify menu and select Properties from the pop-up menu. In the Movie Properties dialog box, check the Lock Frame Durations option **(Figure 12)**. Each frame is now locked to play at the actual speed that was recorded in step 3. To unlock the movie's playback speed, uncheck the Lock Frames Duration option.

CREATE A PROJECTOR 15

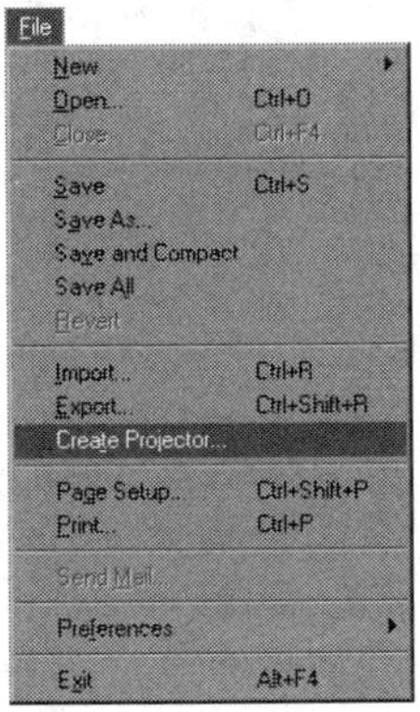

Figure 1. Choose **Create Projector** from the **File** menu.

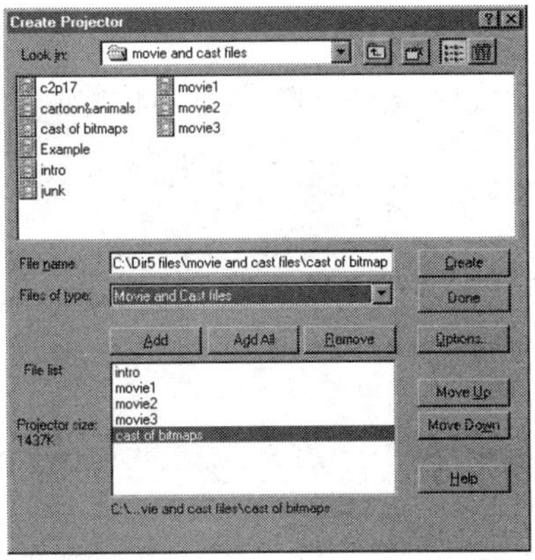

Figure 2. Select and add movie and cast files to your projector file list in the **Create Projector** dialog box.

When you wish to distribute your Director movie to the public, you need to create a projector—a play-only version of your movie (or sequence of movies) that runs like any application. Your users don't need to own a copy of Director to run your projector. Anyone can watch your projector movie as long as their computer meets the minimum hardware requirements.

A projector file cannot be opened or edited in Director, preventing users from modifying your movie. Only the original source movie files can be opened in Director.

To create a Projector:

1. Choose Create Projector from the File menu **(Figure 1)**.
2. In the Create Projector dialog box, select the movie or external cast file that you wish to include in your projector **(Figure 2)**.
3. Click the Add button. You can add as many movies and external casts as you wish to a single projector file by repeating steps 2–3. When you play the projector, its movies will play one after the other, in the order in which they appear in the file list (also called play list), assuming that you have selected the Play Every Movie option in the Projector Options dialog box. *(See page 200)*
4. Click the Options button to set projector options in the Options dialog box. *(See page 200)*
5. Click Create. The Save dialog box appears.
6. Type the name of your projector and click Save.

7. To play a projector, double-click its icon **(Figure 3)**.

Figure 3. Double-click a projector icon to start the projector.

Note: If any of the movies included in your projector have links to external files, such as to digital videos or sounds, those files must be included along with the projector file in order for your users to be able to properly run the projector. Be sure to include all linked files in the same folder along with the projector.

How to organize files for distribution

Creating a projector that consists of many movie files in its play list has its drawback. If you wish to change a single movie in the play list, you must recreate the entire projector each time. A more efficient way to organize your production is to create a projector that consists of a single short movie, which in turn, launches all the other movie files that form your multimedia production. This is accomplished by incorporating a Lingo script in the short projector movie, such as in **(Figure 4)**, that branches to each of your movies *(see page 220 in the Lingo through Interactivity chapter for details on scripts that branch)*. These other movie files are not projectors, but are Director movies. You can protect them from being opened and edited by using the Update Movies command. *(See page 199)*

The other movie files that your projector launches should be included in the same folder as the projector file **(Figure 5)**, as well as any external casts and linked files. With this type of organization, you are free to edit any of the movies that your projector launches, without having to recreate the projector file.

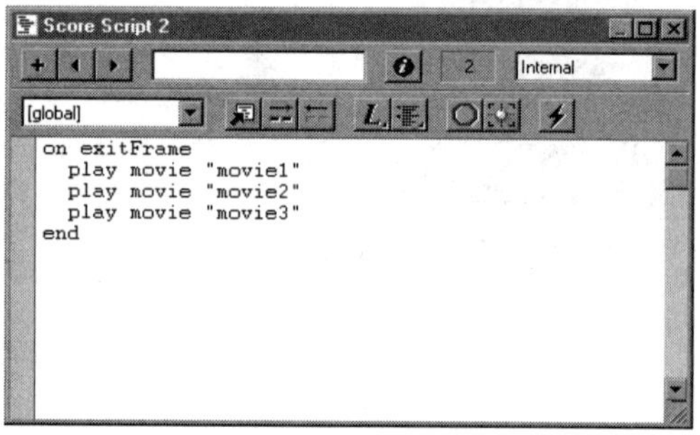

Figure 4. This is a frame script that launches three other Director movies. You can keep your projector file small, and your production more manageable, by using a projector to launch your movies, rather than incorporating all of your movies in a single large projector file.

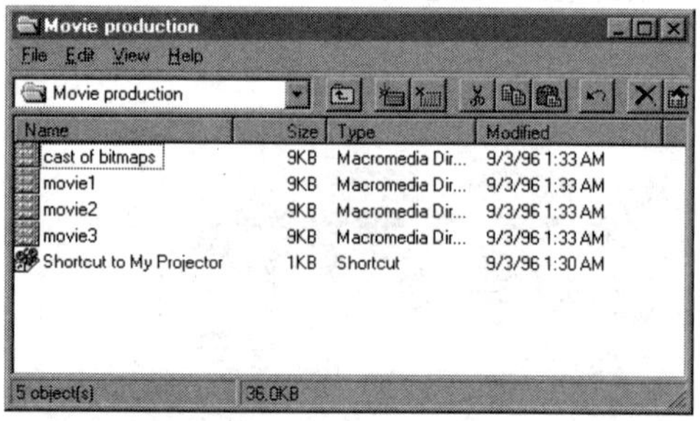

Figure 5. This is a good way to organize your files for distribution. The movie and cast files here have been protected using the **Update Movies** command.

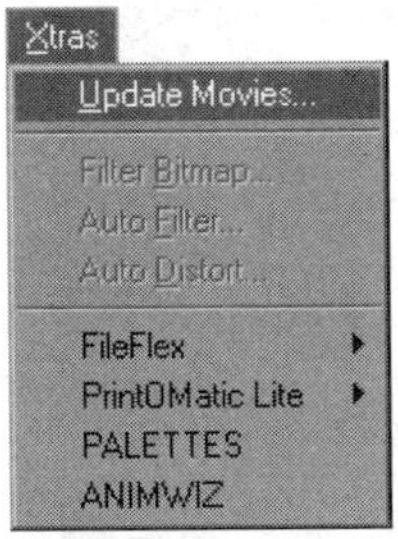

Figure 6. Choose **Update Movies** from the **Xtras** menu.

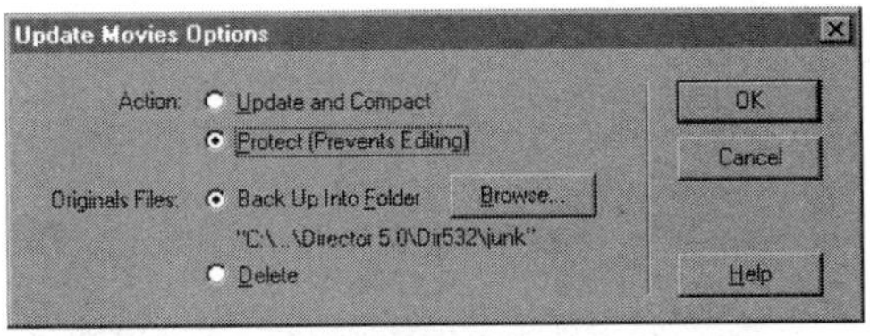

Figure 7. Click the **Protect** radio button in the **Update Movies** dialog box.

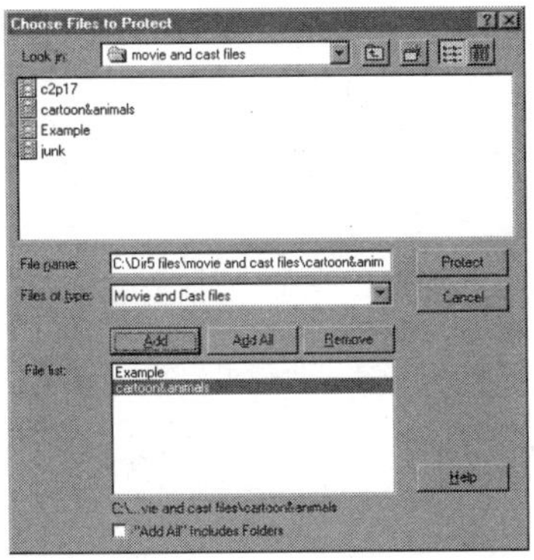

Figure 8. Select the movie and cast files you wish to protect by selecting them individually in the file box, and then clicking **Add**.

To protect movie and cast files using Update Movies:

You can use the Update Movies command under the Xtras menu to protect movie and cast files from being opened and edited in Director. When you create a projector file that launches other movies, you may want to protect those other movie files, which are not themselves projectors. You will very likely want to do this if you will be distributing your multimedia production.

The Update Movies command is also used to update older versions of Director movies, and to compact current Director movie files. *(See page 12 in the Basics chapter)*

1. Choose Update Movies from the Xtras menu **(Figure 6)**.
2. Click the Protect radio button in the Update Movie dialog box **(Figure 7)**.
3. Click the Back Up into Folder radio button if you wish to place the original movie and cast files into a specified folder. Click the Browse button to select the folder in which to place these original files.

Or

3. Click the Delete button if you wish the new protected files to overwrite the originals. Make sure that you have backed up the original files since you cannot unprotect them.
4. Click OK
5. In the Choose Files to Protect dialog box **(Figure 8)**, select a movie or cast file you wish to protect and click Add. Repeat this step to add all the files you wish to protect to the list at the bottom of the dialog box. Click Add All to add all the files in the current folder to the list of files to protect.
6. Click Protect.

Note: There is no way to unprotect a movie or cast file once it has been protected. Make sure to backup the original files before you protect them.

Projector Options

The Projector Options dialog box allows you to set general settings that affect all the movies in your projector. These settings take precedence over any settings you set in the Movie Properties dialog box. Click Options in the Create Projector dialog box to open it **(Figure 9)**.

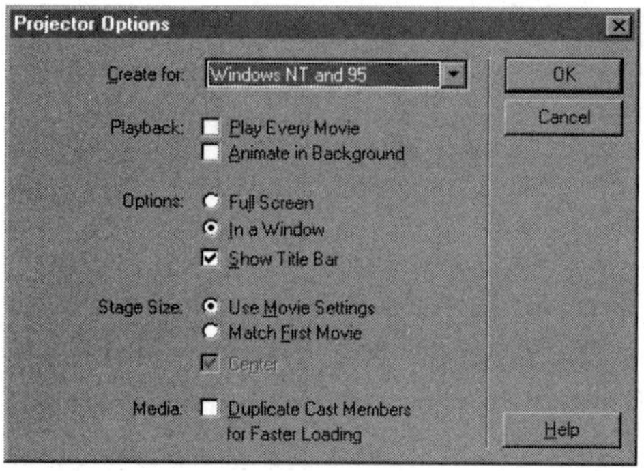

Figure 9. Click the **Options** button in the **Create Projector** dialog box to open the **Projector Options** dialog box.

Create for:

Click the Create for pop-up menu to select the type of computer system your projector will play on. On the Windows platform, your options are: Windows 3.1, Windows NT, and Windows 95 **(Figure 10)**. You can run a Windows 3.1 projector on Windows 95 and NT.

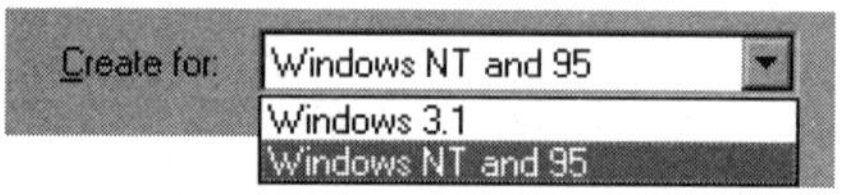

Figure 10. Click the **Create for** pop-up menu to select the type of computer system your projector will play on.

Playback:

If you check the Play Every Movie option, all the movies you add to the projector play list will be played in the order they are listed. If not checked, only the first movie on the list is played. This first movie can activate other movies, regardless of whether this option is set, by branching to them using Lingo.

Check the Animate in Background option if you wish your projector to continue playing even if you click outside of it on the desktop. If not checked, the projector stops playing if you click outside of it.

Options:

Check the Full Screen option if you wish your movie to occupy the full screen when playing. The desktop is hidden, and any menu bar used in your movie is displayed at the top of the stage. Click the In a Window button to display the movie in a normal sized window. Show Title Bar is available when the In a Window option is selected. If checked, the window which displays your movie has a title bar. This window is moveable only when it has a title bar.

Stage Size:

If the Use Movie Settings button is clicked, the stage size takes on the dimensions of each new movie in the projector play list that is opened. If the Match First Movie button is clicked, the stage size retains the dimensions of the first movie in the play list.

If the Center option is checked, the stage is automatically centered on the screen (this comes in handy when the stage is smaller than the full screen dimensions). Projectors that run on Windows are always centered.

Media:

Check the Duplicate Cast Members for Faster Loading option if you wish to improve the speed at which your movies are loaded. The tradeoff is that the projector file will be larger.

INTERACTIVITY THROUGH LINGO 16

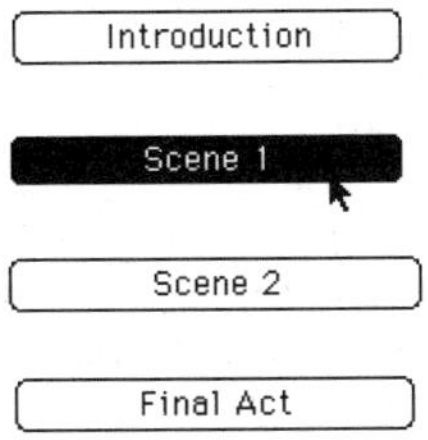

Figure 1. A menu of scene choices is shown here, composed of four interactive buttons.

Lingo is Director's scripting language that adds the intelligent, interactive dimension to your multimedia productions. Through Lingo, you enable users to communicate with your movie; they can type in text, click on sprites, and your movie can respond to these inputs in limitless ways.

Lingo allows your movie to go beyond what is normally possible when authoring only through the score. For instance, you can use Lingo to offer your users navigational control over the order in which scenes of your movie are played. A common example of this involves a multimedia presentation that offers a menu of scene choices **(Figure 1)**.

This chapter introduces you to the basics of writing Lingo scripts. It is organized into the following four sections:

Introduction to scripts and script windows defines scripts, script types, and explains how to create scripts in script windows.

Making sprites and cast members interactive teaches you how to make your sprites and cast members respond to mouse input.

Navigation explains how to write scripts that allow users to navigate through the scenes of your movie in a non-sequential order.

Handlers, messages, and events explains how Director knows which scripts to run and when.

INTRODUCTION TO SCRIPTS AND SCRIPT WINDOWS

What is a Lingo script?

A Lingo script is a set of instructions written in Lingo code that tells Director how your movie should respond when specific events occur during play. Examples of events include user input through the mouse and keyboard. Other events are non-input oriented such as the playback head entering a new frame (events are described in detail on page 221).

Suppose a user clicks the mouse on a particular sprite in your movie. Should something happen? If you want your movie to respond to an event such as a mouse click, you need to write a script. Your movie can respond in many ways. For example, you can write a script that causes a sprite's color to change when a user clicks on it. In fact, scripts can be written that allow user inputs to affect virtually every aspect of your movie, such as sound, positions of sprites, the path the playback head follows through a movie, text output, and many other attributes for limitless interactive possibilities.

The instructions in a Lingo script are organized into handlers. A **handler** is a set of Lingo instructions that is activated by an event in your movie (technically, a handler is activated by a message which is sent when an event occurs). Handlers, messages, and events are described in detail on pages 221–224. One script can contain multiple handlers.

All handlers start with the work **on**, and end with the word **end** as in **(Figure 2)**. The word after **on** is the message the handler should respond to. The instructions inside a handler (between **on** and **end**) are executed when the handler receives a matching message.

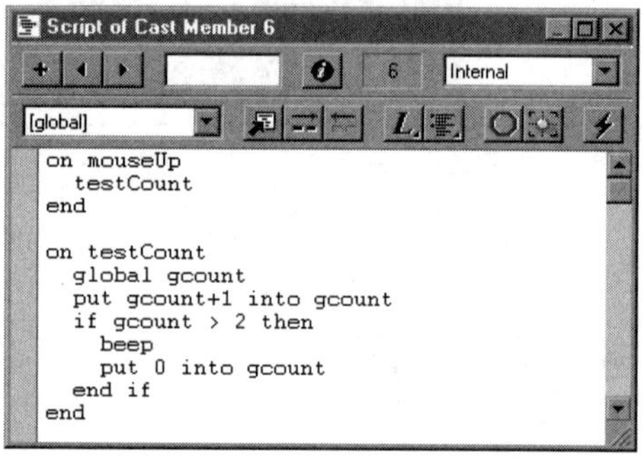

Figure 2. This script is composed of two handlers: the mouseUp handler and the testCount handler.

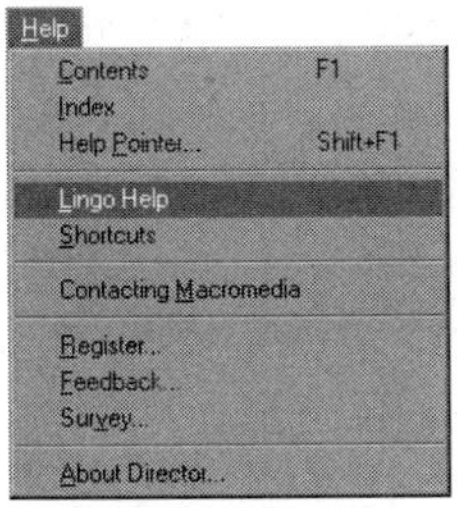

Figure 3. Choose **Lingo Help** from the **Help** menu.

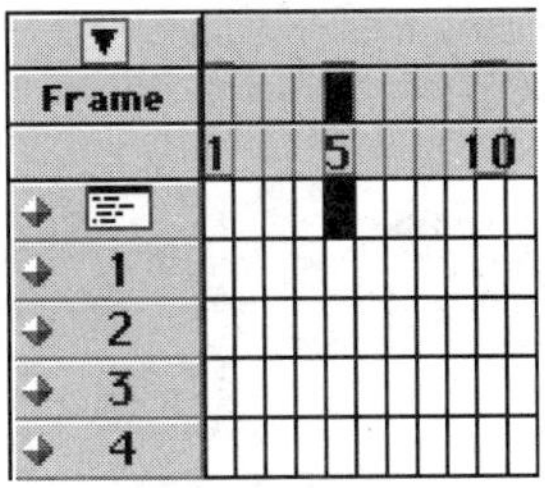

Figure 4. Select the fifth frame in the script channel.

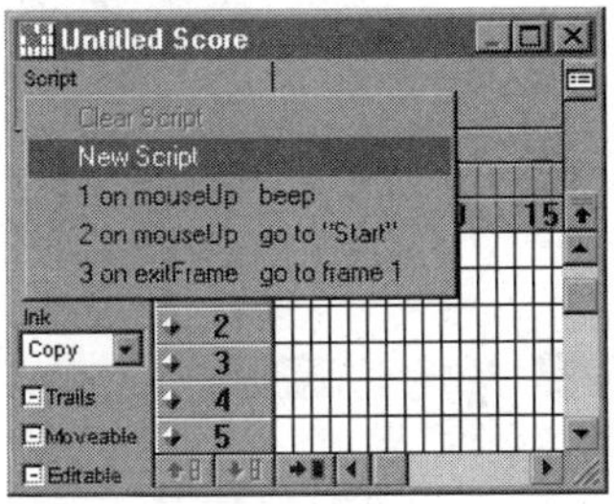

Figure 5. Choose **New Script** from the **Script** pop-up menu in the score window.

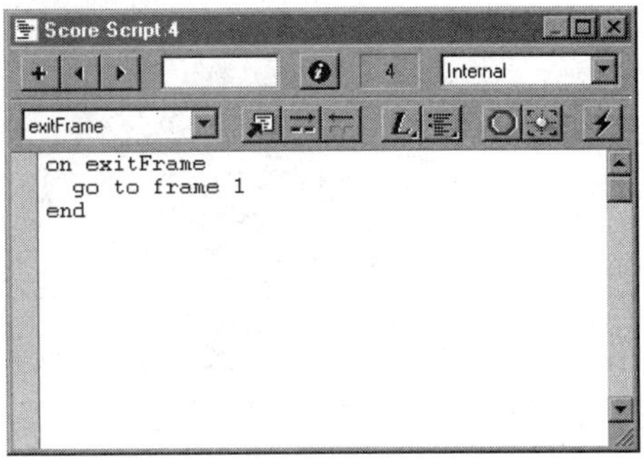

Figure 6. This is example script 1.

Writing a script

Lingo scripts are written in script windows, which can be opened in several ways in Director. How you open a script window is important since it determines the type of script it will contain. A script window's type is indicated in its title bar. *(See pages 207–209 for a description of the five script types, and how to open the corresponding script windows)*

The Lingo instructions written in scripts need to conform to the language rules of Lingo. Lingo instructions are valid combinations of Lingo elements, which are introduced throughout this chapter in sample scripts. All Lingo elements are defined in Director's Lingo dictionary. Open it by choosing Lingo Help from the Help menu **(Figure 3)**.

Example script 1

The following steps create a handler that causes the playback head to jump to frame 1 each time it reaches frame 5 as your movie is playing. The script that contains this handler is called a frame script since it is assigned to a frame in the script channel.

1. Choose Score from the Window menu.
2. Select the fifth frame in the script channel **(Figure 4)**.
3. Choose New Script from the Script pop-up menu in the score window to open a script window **(Figure 5)**.
4. In the script window that opens, type **go to frame 1** on the middle line **(Figure 6)**. The first and last lines are are automatically provided.
5. Close the script window.
6. Choose Control Panel from the Window menu.
7. Rewind the movie to frame 1.
8. Click Play in the control panel. You can see the playback head looping between frames 1 and 5 in the score.

Analysis of Example script 1

You wrote a handler in a frame script that causes your movie to loop between frames 1 and 5. The first line of the handler **on exitFrame** tells Director to run the instructions in the body of the handler when the playback head exits the frame which contains the script, in this case the fifth frame. The body of the handler holds the statement **go to frame 1**, which tells Director to move the playback head to frame 1, thus creating a loop in your movie. The **end** keyword is required at the last line of each handler.

To automatically insert Lingo elements into a script window:

The Alphabetical Lingo and Categorized Lingo buttons **(Figure 7)** in the script window allow you to select and insert Lingo elements into your script.

1. Click the Alphabetical Lingo button and select the Lingo element from the pop-up menu **(Figure 8)** that you wish to insert into your script at the cursor

Or

2. Click the Categorized Lingo button and select the Lingo element by category from the pop-up menu **(Figure 9)** that you wish to insert into your script.

✔ **Tip**

- Lingo is not case-sensitive. However, it is wise for the sake of readability to be consistent with case in your scripts. Follow the conventions used in the Lingo Dictionary, as well as those provided in the example scripts throughout this chapter.

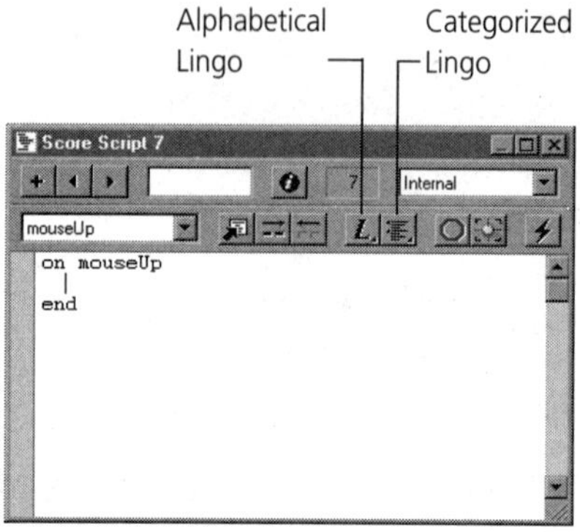

Figure 7. The **Alphabetical** and **Categorized** Lingo buttons allow you to insert Lingo elements automatically into your scripts.

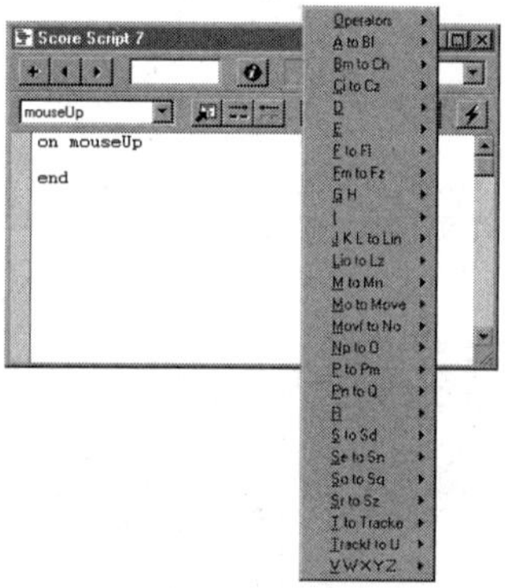

Figure 8. Click the **Alphabetical** Lingo button to select a Lingo element for insertion into your script.

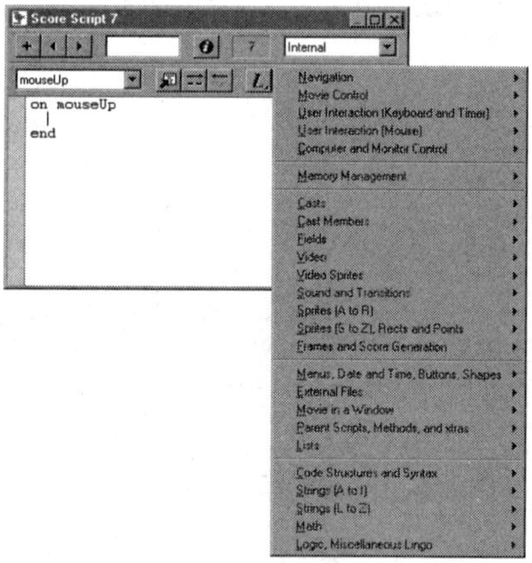

Figure 9. Click the **Categorized** Lingo button to select a Lingo element by category for insertion into your script.

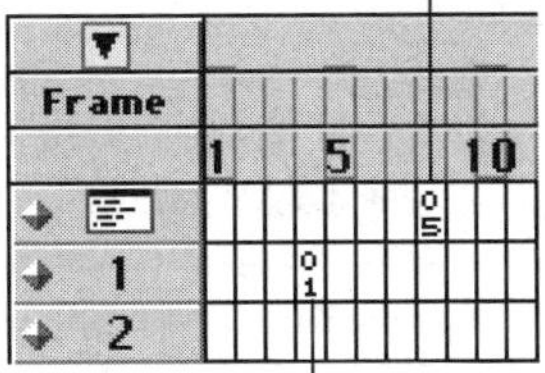

Figure 10. Frame and sprite scripts are assigned in the score. They are also referred to as score scripts.

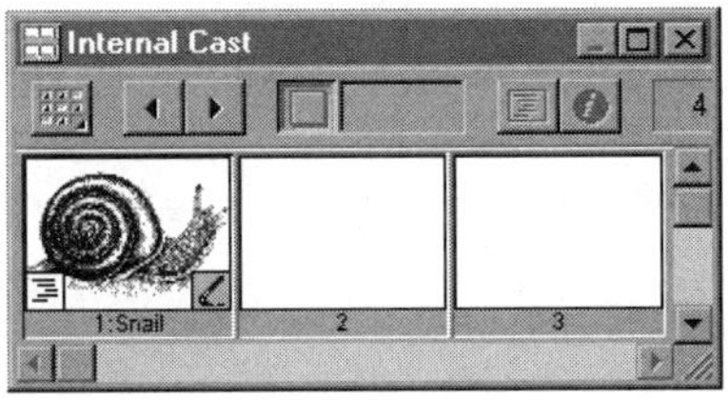

Figure 11. A cast member script is assigned to a cast member. A script symbol appears in the bottom-left corner of a cast member thumbnail when it has an assigned script.

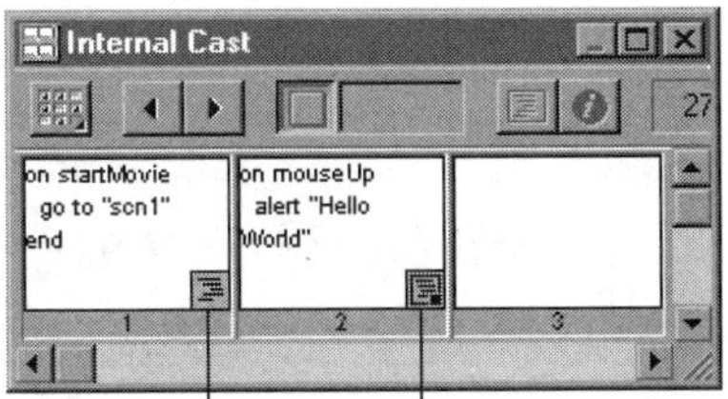

Figure 12. Movie, score, and parent scripts are themselves cast members and are stored in cast windows.

Script types

There are five script types in Director. These are sprite scripts, frame scripts, cast member scripts, movie scripts, and parent scripts (parent scripts are an advanced Lingo topic beyond the scope of this book). Sprite, cast member, and frame script types are described in detail on pages 211, 212, and 216 respectively.

A script type is determined by the object the script is assigned to in Director **(Figures 10–11)**. Sprite scripts are assigned to sprites, frame scripts are assigned to frames in the score's script channel, cast member scripts are assigned to cast members, and movie scripts are assigned to the entire movie— not to an individual object. Sprite and frame scripts are referred to as score scripts since they are both assigned in the score window.

Which script type you choose to write handlers in determines how accessible those handlers are to your movie. Handlers in a cast member script are available to be executed only when the corresponding cast member is clicked or receives input through the keyboard during playback. Likewise, handlers in a sprite script are available to be executed only when you click on the corresponding sprite, or the sprite receives input through the keyboard.

Handlers in a frame script are available to be executed only when Director is entering or exiting the frame where the script is assigned.

Handlers in movie scripts are the most accessible since they are available at anytime during playback.

All script types except cast member scripts are themselves cast members, and are stored in cast windows **(Figure 12)**.

To change a script's type to another script type:

You can change any movie, score, or parent script's type. You cannot change a cast member script's type.

1. Select the script in the cast window whose type you wish to change **(Figure 13)**.
2. Click the Cast Member Properties button in the cast window.
3. Click the Type pop-up menu in the Cast Member Properties dialog box **(Figure 14)**, and select a new type.

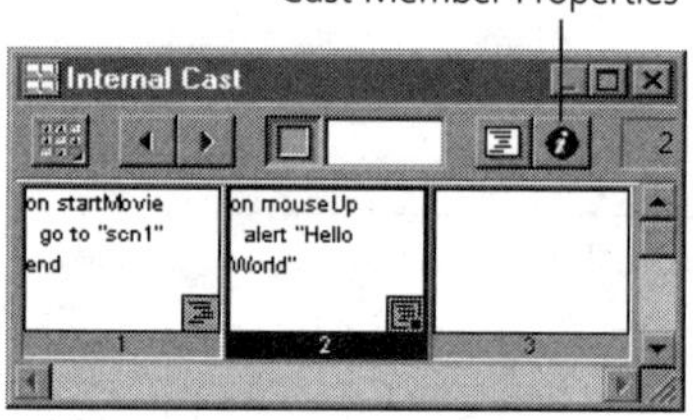

Figure 13. Select the script whose type you wish to change and click the **Cast Member Properties** button.

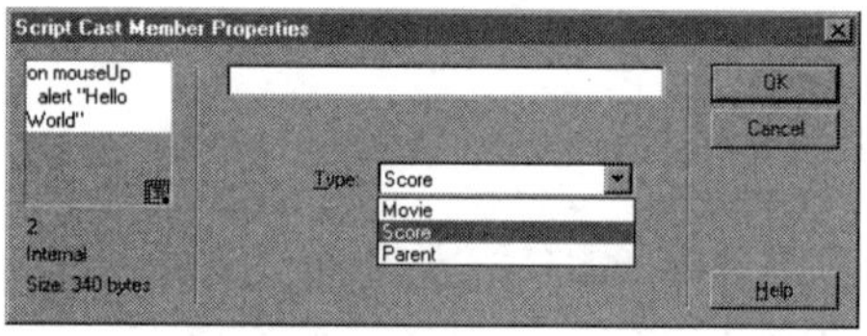

Figure 14. Click the **Type** pop-up menu in the **Cast Member Properties** dialog box and select a new type.

Script windows

Lingo scripts are edited in script windows. The title bar in a script window indicates the type of script being edited. A cast member script is edited in a script of a cast member window. Sprite and frame scripts are edited in score script windows (remember that they are classified as score scripts). And a movie script is edited in a movie script window. The only difference between script window types is how they are opened in Director. *(See below)*

To open a new score script window:

Sprite and frame scripts are created in score script windows.

1. Open the score window.
2. Choose New from the Script pop-up menu in the upper left side of the score window **(Figure 15)**. A score script window appears.

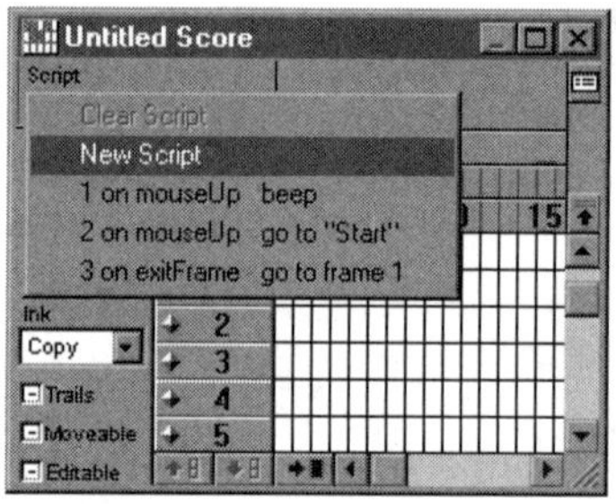

Figure 15. Choose **New Script** from the **Script** pop-up menu in the score window.

To open a cast member script window:

1. Open the Cast window.
2. Select a cast member that you wish to attach a script to, or edit its existing script **(Figure 16)**. These are limited to bitmap, PICT, shape, text, field, or button cast member types.

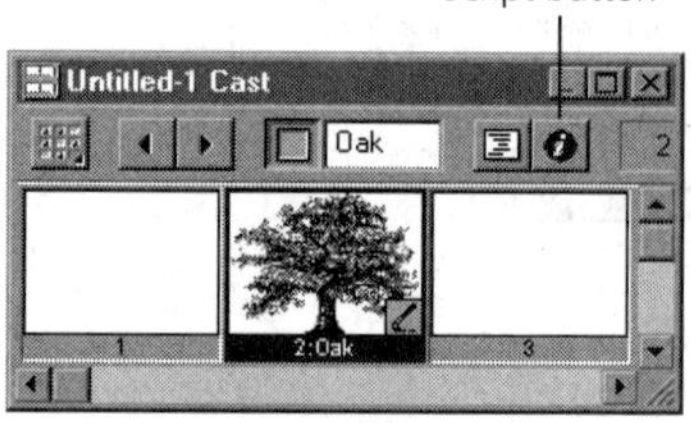

Figure 16. Open a cast member script window by selecting a cast member, then clicking the **Script** button.

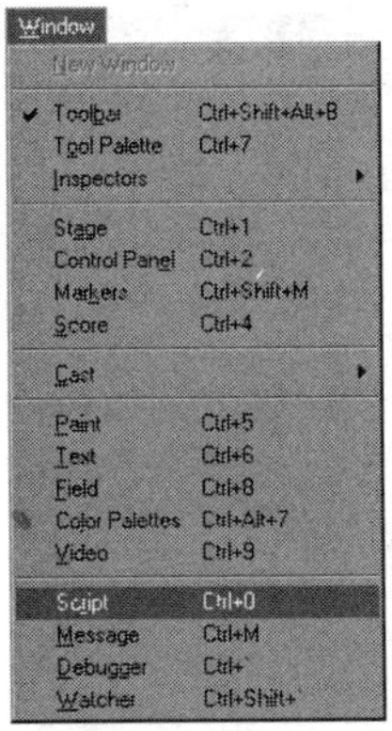

Figure 17. Choose **Script** from the **Window** menu.

New Script

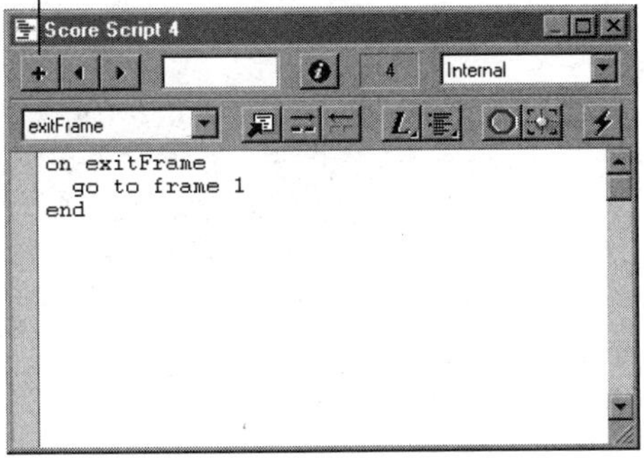

Figure 18. Click the **New Script** button in any opened score, cast member, or movie script window to open a new movie script window.

3. Click the script button in the cast window to open the cast member script window. A cast member that has a script already attached to it displays a script symbol in the lower left corner of its thumbnail.

✔ **Tip**

- You can also open a cast member script window by clicking the Script button in the cast member properties dialog box for a selected cast member.

To open a new movie script window:

1. Choose Script from the Window menu **(Figure 17)**.

Or

2. Click the New script button in any opened score, cast member, or movie script window **(Figure 18)**. *(See page 208 on opening score and cast member script windows)*

MAKING SPRITES AND CAST MEMBERS INTERACTIVE

A very direct way in which a user can interact with your movie is by clicking on sprites. What your movie does in response to such input is entirely up to you, the author. For instance, you may want to set up a sprite so that its size, color, or position changes when it is clicked. You can even change the cast member a sprite is based on when clicked, as you might want to do for a customized button that changes appearance when clicked.

This section explains how to write scripts that make sprites and cast members respond to mouse clicks. In the process, sprite and cast member script types are described in detail.

Example script 2

The following script sets up a sprite so that when it is clicked, your movie produces a beep sound. This is an example of a sprite script (defined on next page).

1. Choose New from the File menu and select Movie from the pop-up to create a new movie.
2. Create a cast member using one of the shape tools in the paint window.
3. Place the cast member in frame 1, channel 1 of the score.
4. With the sprite cell selected in frame 1 of channel 1, choose New Script from the Script pop-up in the score.
5. In the script window that opens, type **beep** in the middle line of the script **(Figure 19)**. The other two lines are automatically provided.
6. Close the script window.
7. Choose Loop Playback under the Control menu **(Figure 20)** to set it.
8. Playback your movie. Notice that when you click within the sprite on the stage, you hear a beep.

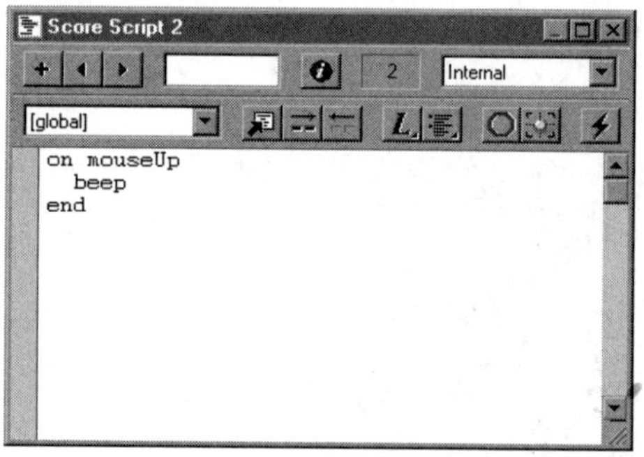

Figure 19. This is example script 2.

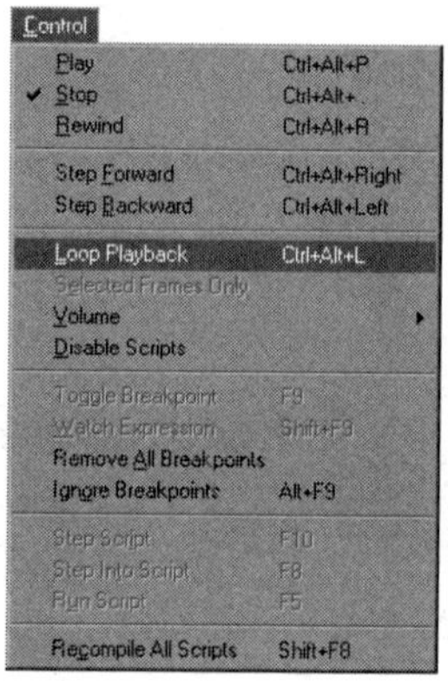

Figure 20. Choose **Loop Playback** from the **Control** menu.

Analysis of Example script 2

The first line **on mouseUp** tells Director that when the mouse is clicked and released over the sprite, the instructions in the body of the script should be executed, in this case, the **beep** command. You can change the first line to **on mouseDown** and the beep will be heard as soon as the mouse is clicked on the sprite.

This script is assigned to a single sprite. The script becomes activated only when the particular sprite in the particular frame that the script is assigned to is clicked. The script does not apply to other sprites based on the same cast member unless it has been assigned to them as well.

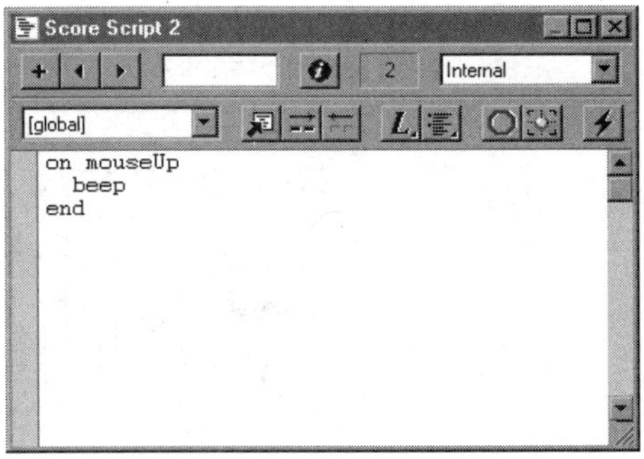

Figure 21. This is a sample score script.

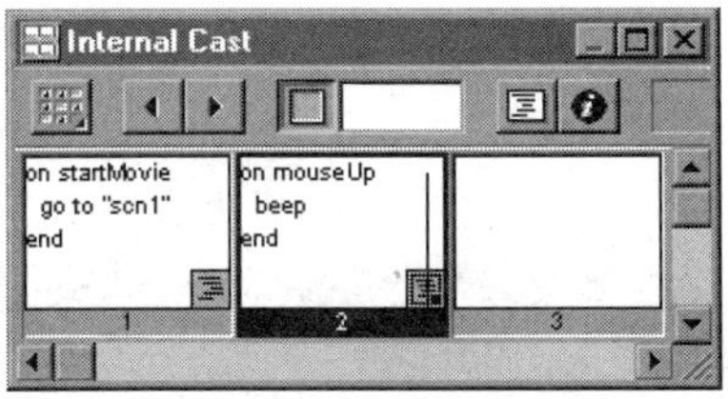

Score script

Figure 22. Select the desired score script cast member you wish to edit and click the script button in the cast window.

Script Preview button

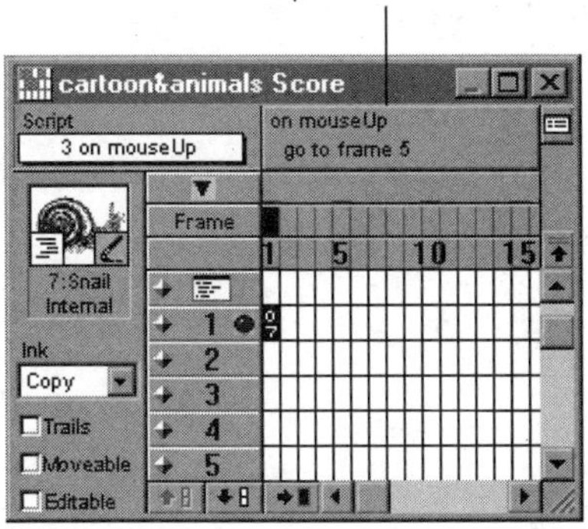

Figure 23. Click the **Script Preview** button in the score window to open the score script that has been assigned to the selected cell.

Sprite Scripts

Sprite scripts are scripts that are assigned to sprites in the cells of the score *(see page 46 for a definition of sprites)*. Sprite scripts are also referred to as **score** scripts **(Figure 21)**. Sprite scripts are created and edited in score script windows. Sprite scripts are themselves cast members, and are stored in cast windows.

Sprite scripts require user input through the keyboard or mouse in order for their instructions to be executed. Generally, a user must click on a sprite during playback in order for its script to run.

A sprite script applies only to the sprite in the frame where it is assigned. If you wish a sprite to be interactive across multiple frames, you must assign the sprite script to each sprite in the range of frames, or use a cast member script instead. *(See page 212)*

By assigning different sprite scripts to sprites based on the same cast member throughout your movie, a single cast member, such as a button, can perform multiple functions depending on which frame during your movie it is clicked.

To edit an existing sprite script:

1. Open the cast window.
2. Select the desired score script cast member you wish to edit **(Figure 22)**. Click the script button in the cast window and the score script window appears.

✓ Tips

- You can open and edit a score script that is already assigned to a particular cell by selecting that cell in the score, and clicking the Script Preview button in the upper-right side of the score **(Figure 23)**. This button displays the first two lines of the score script associated with the selected cell.
- You can also open an existing score script by double-clicking it in the cast window.

To assign scripts to sprites:

1. Open the score window
2. Select the cell or cells that contain the sprites you wish to assign a script to.
3. In the Script pop-up menu, choose an existing score script to assign to your selected sprite(s) **(Figure 24)**. Score scripts are listed in the pop-up menu by numbers, which correspond to their positions in the cast window, and by their first line of Lingo code.

Figure 24. Choose an existing score script from the **Script** pop-up menu to assign to your selected sprites.

Cast member scripts

A cast member script is a script that is attached to a cast member **(Figure 25)**. The instructions in a cast member script are executed when its corresponding cast member is clicked on the stage, or when the cast member is a field, and a key is pressed during movie playback.

The usefulness of a cast member script is that its Lingo instructions will run in any frame where the cast member is activated, unlike a sprite script. For example, you may want a button cast member to always produce the same response when clicked, regardless of which frame it is clicked in.

If a sprite has both a cast member script and a sprite script associated with it, the sprite script takes precedence. This is important to keep in mind when you are determining which type of script to use. If a cast member should always perform the same function throughout your movie, such as causing a jump to a certain movie segment, then use a cast member script. On the other hand, if your cast member responds differently depending on where it is activated in your movie, assign sprite scripts to the sprites based on the cast member.

Unlike movie, score, and parent scripts, cast member scripts are not cast members; instead, they are attached to cast members.

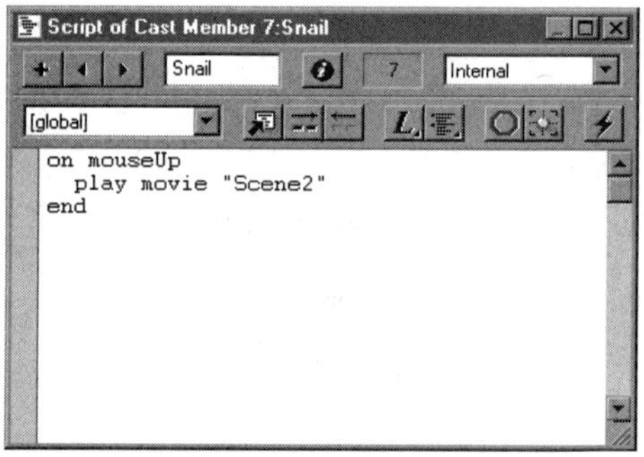

Figure 25. This is a sample cast member script.

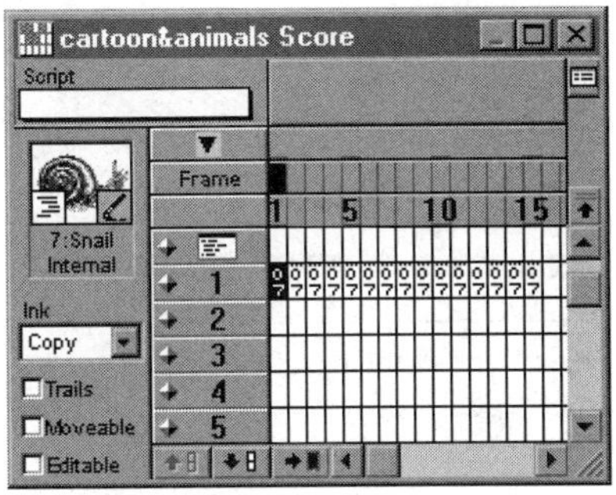

Figure 26. Place a cast member into frames 1–15 in channel 1 of the score.

Figure 27. Example script 3.

Example script 3

The following script is very similar to the script in example 2, except that it is a cast member script. You can click any sprite based on the cast member in any frame, and this script will run and produce a beep sound and a short message.

1. Place a cast member through frames 1–15 in channel 1 of the score **(Figure 26)**.
2. Open the cast window and select the cast member in step 1.
3. Click the Script button at the top of the cast window.
4. In the script window that opens, type **beep** in the middle line of the script. Type **alert "Hello World"** on the line beneath it so that your script is identical to the one in **(Figure 27)**. The first and last lines are provided automatically.
5. Close the script window.
6. Choose Loop Playback under the Control menu to set it.
7. Playback your movie. Notice that when you click the cast member in any frame on the stage, you hear a beep and see the message "Hello World".

Analysis of Example script 3

You created a cast member script and attached it to a cast member. The first line **on mouseUp** tells Director that when the mouse is clicked and released over the cast member, the instructions in the cast member script's mouseUp handler should be executed, in this case, the **beep** command, and **alert** command. The **alert** command prints the message Hello World to the screen.

NAVIGATION

You can offer your movie viewers the choice of being able to jump to various segments of your movie while it is being played—they are not limited to watching from start to finish. This is accomplished by writing scripts that move the playback head to different frames in a movie. These scripts are typically setup to respond to user input, such as clicking the mouse on a particular sprite (such as a button), or pressing a certain key. This section describes steps for writing scripts for very common situations involving navigation, including scripts for pausing a movie. In the process, frame scripts are described in detail, as well as some additional language elements of Lingo.

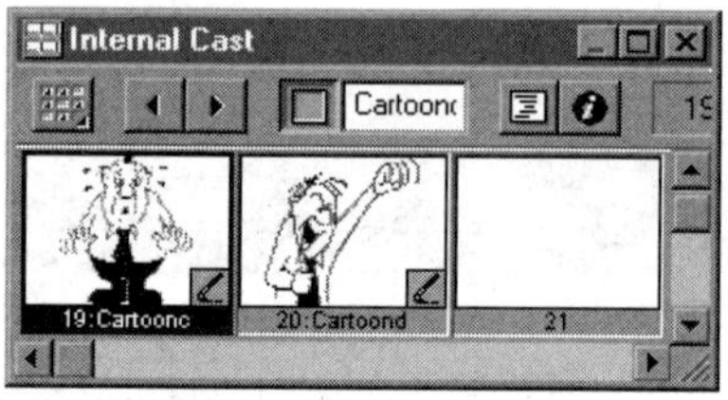

Figure 28. Select the cast member to which you will attach a script.

Example script 4

The following steps create an interactive cast member, which causes your movie to jump to a new frame when it is clicked.

1. Open the cast window and select a cast member that appears in your movie **(Figures 28)**.
2. Click the Script button at the top of the cast window. A script window appears.
3. On the middle line of this script, type **go to frame number (Figure 29)**. In the **number** field, enter the actual frame number that you wish the playback head to jump to (e.g. **go to frame 57**).
4. Close the script window to enter the script. When you playback your movie, clicking this cast member whenever it appears on the stage causes Director to jump to the frame you specified in the script.

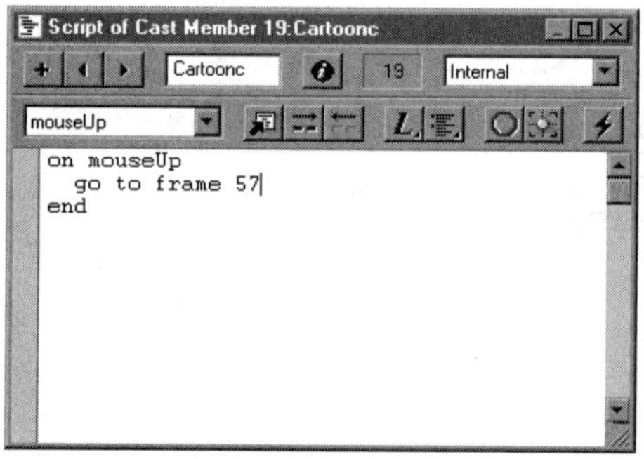

Figure 29. Example script 4.

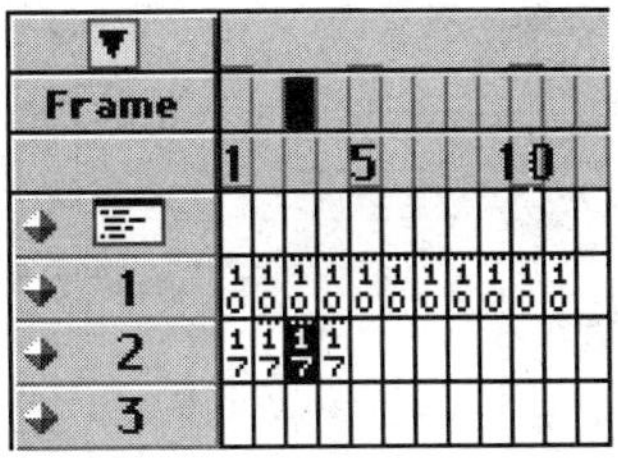

Figure 30. Select a sprite to which you will assign a score script.

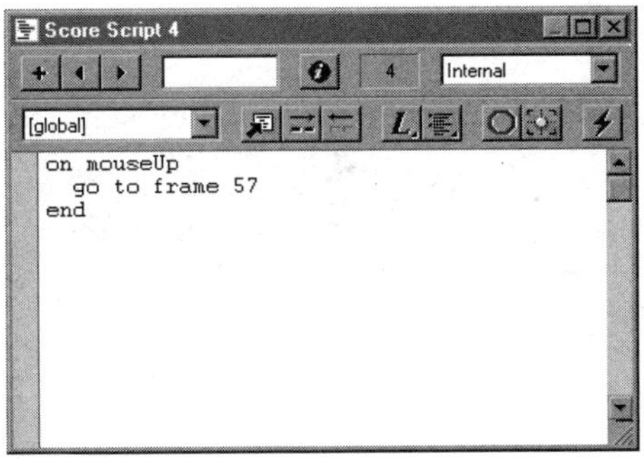

Figure 31. Example script 5.

Analysis of Example script 4

You created a cast member script. The first line of the script **on mouseup** instructs Director that whenever the mouse is pressed and released on this cast member, this mouseUp handler should be executed. In this case, the result is that the **go to** command is executed, which causes the playback head to jump to the specified frame number.

Example script 5

The following steps create an interactive sprite that causes your movie to jump to a new frame when it is clicked. This is similar to example script 4, except that it applies to a single sprite.

1. Open the score window.
2. Select the sprite in the cell that you wish to assign this score script to (remember a sprite script is a type of score script) **(Figure 30)**.
3. Choose New from the Script pop-up menu in the score. The lines **on mouseup** and **end** automatically appear in the script **(Figure 31)**.
4. On the middle line of this script, type **go to frame number**. In the **number** field, enter the actual frame number that you wish the playback head to jump to (e.g. **go to frame 57**). Don't change the rest of the script.
5. Close the script window to enter the script. To activate this script, click this specific sprite during your movie.

✔ Tip

- Since your sprite in this example is interactive in a single frame, you will probably want to add a pause in that frame to ensure that the user has a chance to click it. *(See Example script 6 on page 216 to pause your movie using a frame script)*

Frame scripts

Frame scripts are scripts which are assigned to cells in the script channel of Director's score. Unlike sprite and cast member scripts, frame scripts don't require user input to be activated. Frame scripts are generally used when you want Lingo instructions to be available for activation in a certain frame or range of frames. A frame script handler is executed when the playback head is in the frame where the script is assigned, and the appropriate message is sent to trigger the handler. *(See page 221 for an explanation of messages)*

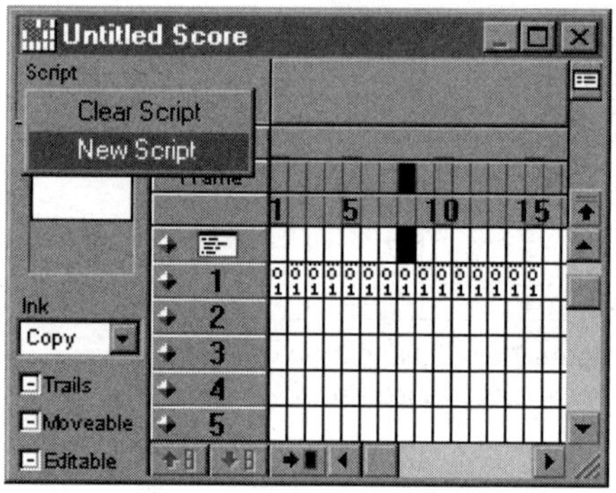

Figure 32. Select the frame in the script channel where you wish to set a pause for your movie.

Example script 6

The following steps create a frame script which causes your movie to pause in a specific frame during playback.

1. Open the score window and select the frame in the script channel where you wish your movie to pause **(Figure 32)**.
2. Choose New from the Script pop-up menu at the top left side of the score. A script window appears with the text **on exitFrame** and **end** already in place.
3. Type **pause (Figure 33)**.
4. Close the script window.

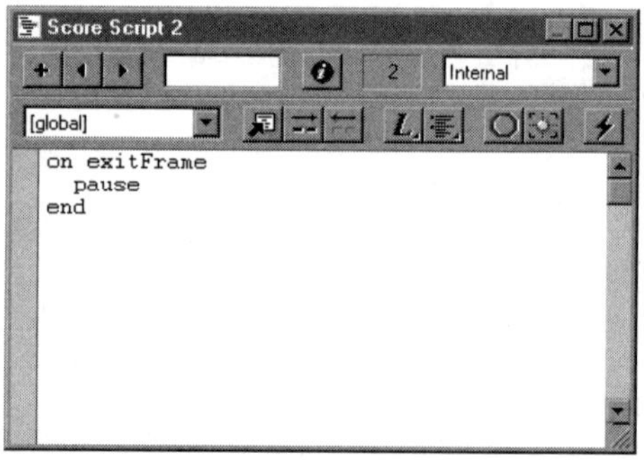

Figure 33. Example script 6

✔ Tip

- You can create a loop in your movie by typing **go to frame number** in step 3 above, where **number** refers to a frame number that precedes the current frame. During playback, when Director reaches the frame with this frame script, your movie jumps back to the specified frame and will start looping within this movie segment.

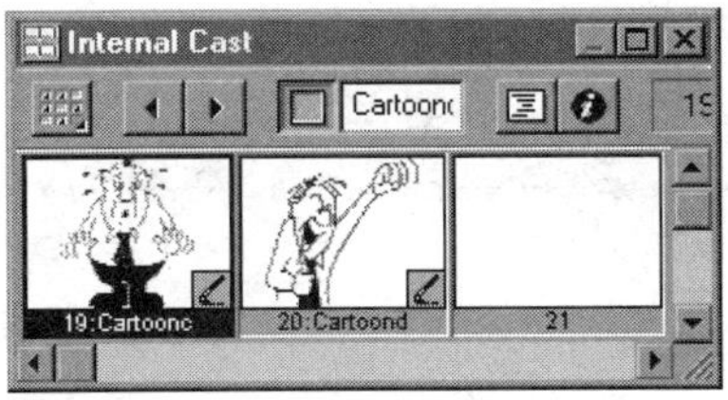

Figure 34. Select the cast member to which you will attach a script.

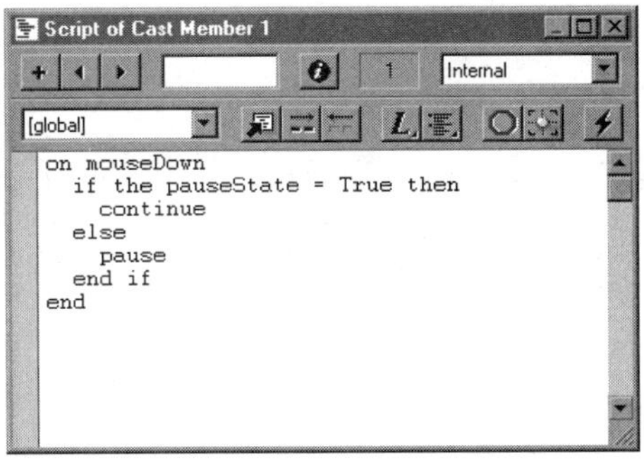

Figure 35. Example script 7

Analysis of example script 6

You created a frame script which causes your movie to pause in the frame where you assigned the script. During playback, when Director reaches this frame, the Lingo handler **on exitFrame** tells Director to run the body of the script when the playback head exits the frame (the Lingo handler **on enterFrame** would cause the script to run at the start of the frame). In this case the **pause** command is executed which tells Director to stay in the current frame. Your movie will remain paused until you stop the movie, or another script becomes activated that moves the playback head to a new frame. Such a script could be attached to a sprite in this frame, which causes the movie to jump to a new frame when the sprite is clicked.

Example script 7

The following steps create an interactive cast member, which functions as a pause button. When the cast member is clicked, the movie pauses. When the cast member is clicked again, the movie resumes play.

1. Open the cast window and select a cast member that appears in your movie **(Figure 34)**.
2. Click the Script button at the top of the cast window.
3. Type in this script **(Figure 35)**.

```
on mouseDown
  if the pauseState = TRUE then
    continue
  else
    pause
  end if
end
```

4. Close the script window to enter the script.

Analysis of example script 7

You wrote a cast member script. The first line **on mouseDown** causes Director to execute the body of this handler whenever the cast member is clicked. The next line **If the pauseState = TRUE then continue** checks to see if the movie is currently paused. If it is paused, the **continue** command is executed and the movie resumes play. If the movie is not paused, then the command after the **else** statement is executed, which is **pause**.

PauseState is a Lingo function that returns the **TRUE** value when the movie is paused, and **FALSE** when it is not.

The If-then structure evaluates a statement. If the statement is true, the command after **then** is executed. If the statement is false, the command after the **else** is executed (lookup the **If** keyword entry in the Lingo dictionary for more details on the if-then structure).

To use the go to command to jump to a frame relative to the current frame:

You can use the Lingo **go to** command to jump to a frame that is a certain number of frames before or after the current frame. To jump to a frame that lies before the current frame, include the statement **go to frame -x** in your handler **(Figure 36)**, where **x** is the number of frames before the current frame that you wish to jump to. Similarly, to jump to a frame somewhere after the current frame, include the statement **go to frame x**.

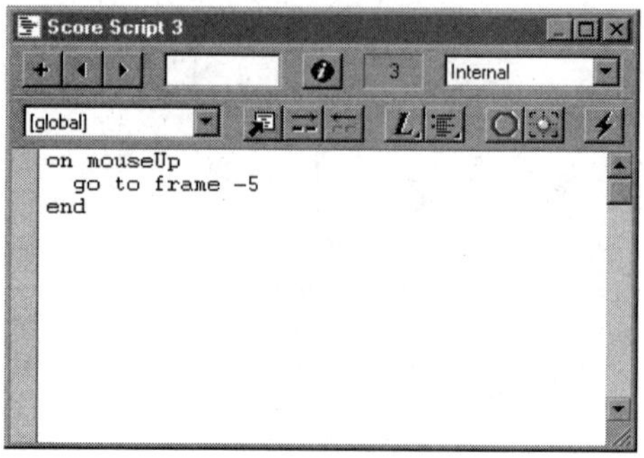

Figure 36. When this script handler is activated, it causes your movie to jump to the frame which is five frames before the current frame.

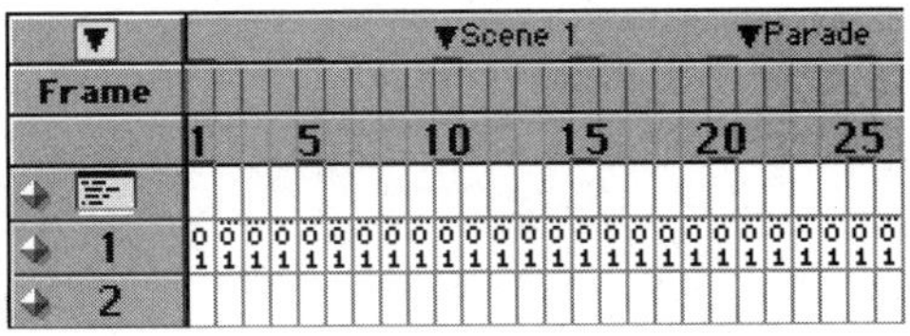

Figure 37. Markers are used to label different segments of your movie.

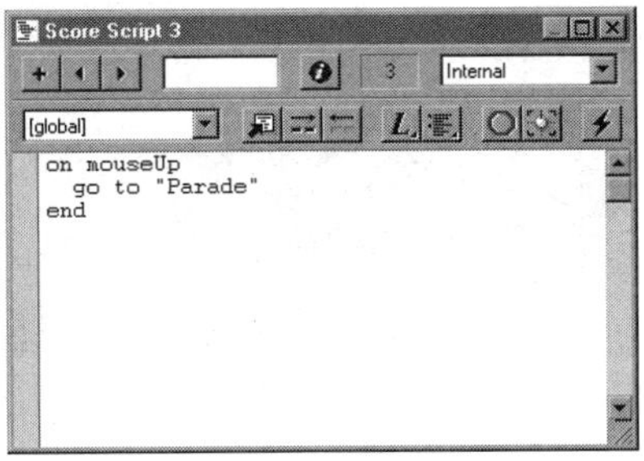

Figure 38. This Lingo statement go to "Parade" jumps to the segment of the movie labeled Parade.

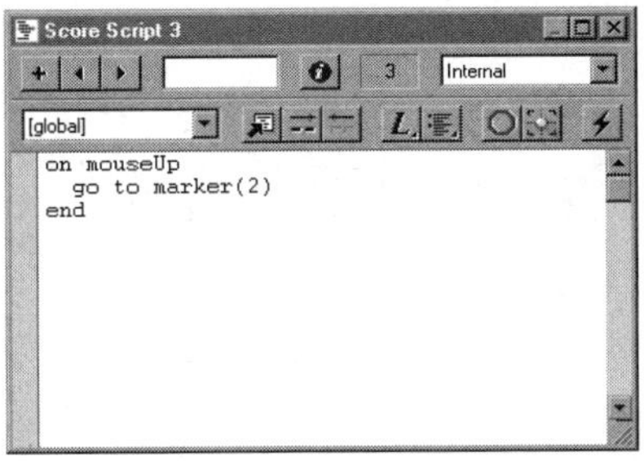

Figure 39. The Lingo statement go to marker(n) jumps to the nth marker ahead of the current frame.

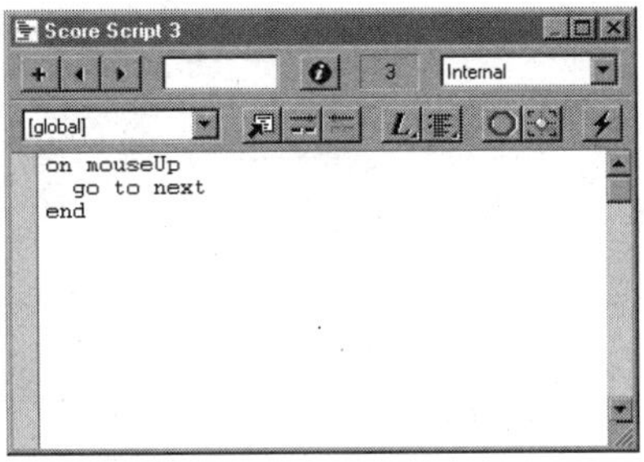

Figure 40. The Lingo statement go to next jumps to the next marker after the current frame.

To use the go to command to jump to a marker label:

You can use the **go to** command to move the playback head to a specific marker instead of to a frame number. Markers are used to label different segments of your movie **(Figure 37)**. *(See page 58 in the Score, Stage, and Sprites chapter for more information on creating markers)*

The advantage of using markers rather than frame numbers with the **go to** command is that frame numbers often change while you're editing in the score, whereas a marker name marks a specific movie segment independently of any frame number.

Use the **go to** command to jump to a marker by typing **go to "marker"** in your handler, where **marker** is the name of the marker you wish to jump to **(Figure 38)**.

To jump to a marker relative to the current frame:

Lingo allows you to refer to a marker in relation to how many markers it is ahead of or behind the current frame. To jump to the nth marker ahead of the current frame, include the statement **go to marker(n)** in your script, such as **go to marker(2) (Figure 39)**. This tells Director to jump to the second marker after the current frame. Similarly, to jump to the nth marker before the current frame, include the same statement, but make **n** a negative number. You can also jump to the next marker after the current frame by using the statement **go to next (Figure 40)**. To jump to the marker immediately before the current frame, use **go to previous**. These commands are equivalent to **go to marker(1)**, and **go to marker(-1)**.

Branching

In Director, **branching** is the process where the playback head jumps to a certain movie segment, plays that segment, and then returns back to the original frame that caused the jump. Suppose your movie offers a tour of different restaurants. Let's say that this movie starts with a main menu of button sprites, each corresponding to a specific restaurant you can view. When you click a button, Director jumps to a particular restaurant segment, plays that segment, and returns back to the main menu. This branching is best accomplished by using the Lingo branch command **play** in your scripts.

To write a script that branches to a marker or frame:

1. Open a script window for the script where a branch should take place.
2. Type **play "marker"**, and include the marker name you wish to branch to **(Figure 41)**. You can also type **play frame number** where **number** is the frame to branch to.
3. At the end of the movie segment that is branched to in step 2, place the command **play done** in the appropriate script. This command returns the playback head back to the original frame from where the branch occurred **(Figure 42)**.

✔ **Tip**

- You can branch to a different movie by using the Lingo statement **play movie "moviename"**, where **moviename** is the name of the movie file **(Figure 43)**. To branch to a specific frame in a different movie, use the statement **play frame "frame" of movie "moviename"**, like in **(Figure 44)**.

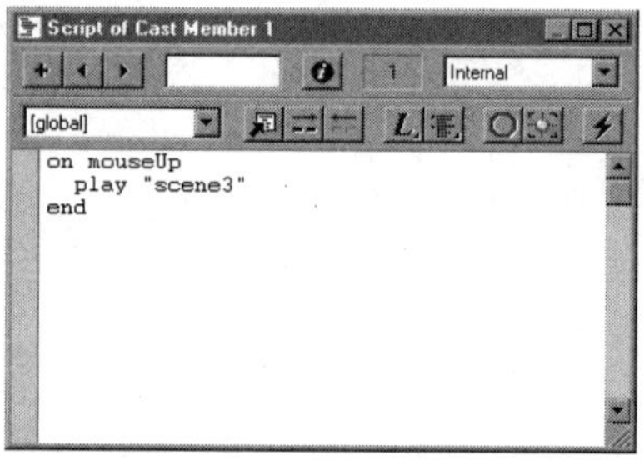

Figure 41. Type play "marker", and include the marker name you wish to branch to.

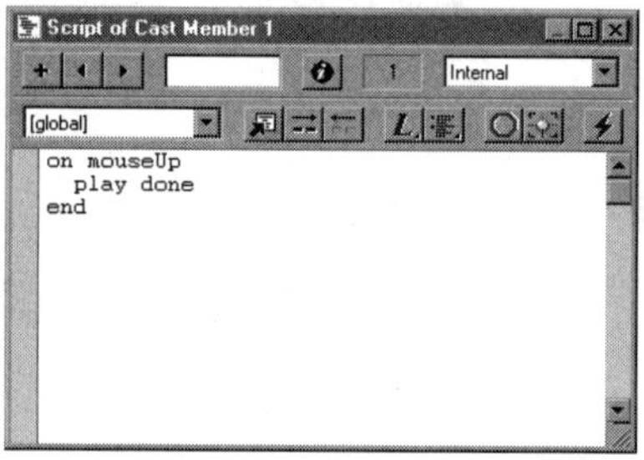

Figure 42. The play done command returns the playback head to the frame where the branch occurred.

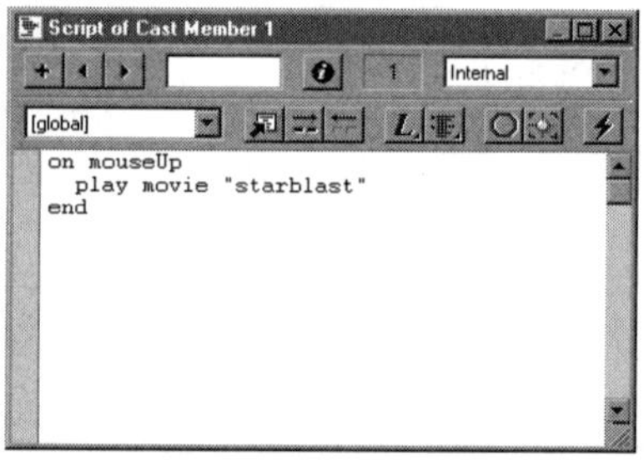

Figure 43. The play movie command branches to a different movie.

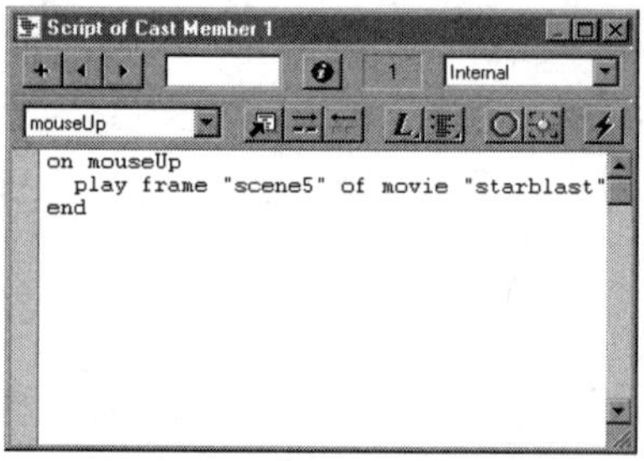

Figure 44. This script branches to a specific frame in a different movie.

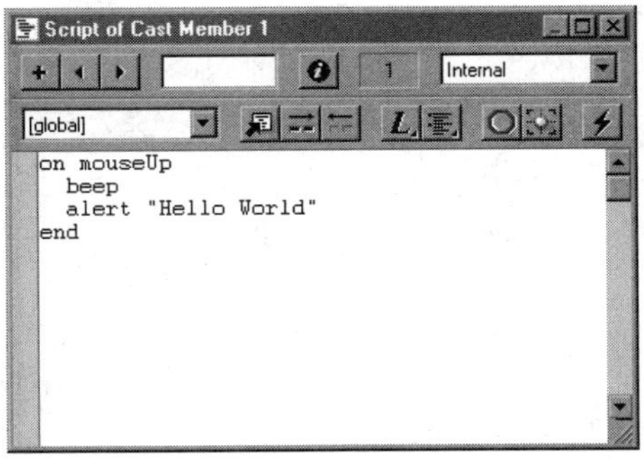

Figure 45. This script contains a mouseUp handler.

Event	Message
A window is activated	activateWindow
A window is closed	closeWindow
A window is deactivated	deactivateWindow
Playback head enters current frame	enterFrame
Playback head exits the current frame	exitFrame
No event occurred	idle
A key is pressed	keyDown
A key is released	KeyUp
Mouse button pressed	mouseDown
Mouse button released	mouseUp
Movie starts playing	startMovie
Movie stops playing	stopMovie
A specified amount of time passes without a specified event occurring	timeOut
A window is maximized or minimized	zoomWindow

Figure 46. These are the 14 built-in events that can occur while a movie is playing, and the corresponding messages they send. You can write handlers which respond to any of these messages. You can also create handlers which respond to messages that you define (these types of handlers operate very much like functions. This topic is beyond the scope of this book.)

HANDLERS, MESSAGES, AND EVENTS

Handlers

A Lingo script is composed of one or more handlers. A handler is a set of Lingo instructions that is activated by a specific event during the playback of your movie (technically by a message which is sent in response to an event, *see section below*).

A handler always starts with the word **on** followed by the name of the message the handler should respond to. For example:

```
on mouseUp
  beep
  alert "Hello World"
end
```

This handler **(Figure 45)** responds to the mouseUp message, which is sent when the mouse button is released. The body of the handler script, which is the indented part, contains the commands which are executed when the handler is triggered by the matching message. These commands are run in the order they are listed.

Handlers can be stored in any of the five script types discussed on page 207. Which script type you place a handler or handlers in is important since it directly affects when those handlers are available to receive messages for activation. *(See How handlers receive messages, page 222)*

What are events and messages?

Events are the actions that occur in your movie that cause messages to be sent. Handlers in turn respond to these messages. There are 14 built-in events that can occur while a Director movie is playing **(Figure 46)**. About half of these events are caused by inputs from the user, such as clicking the mouse button, pressing a key, activating a window, or closing a window. The other half of the built-in events are actions that occur in your movie which don't directly relate to user input, but are nonetheless events that you may want a handler to respond to. Such events include a frame being entered or exited, and the movie being started or stopped. For example, when the following handler **(Figure 47)** receives the exitFrame message, it causes the movie to jump to frame 1.

```
On exitFrame
  go to frame 1
end
```

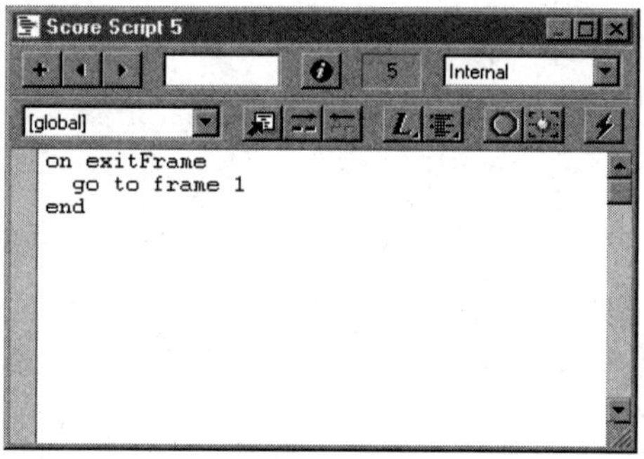

Figure 47. This script contains a handler which responds to the exitFrame message.

How do handlers receive messages?

When an event occurs, its corresponding message is sent in a specific order to a group of objects in Director. Lingo checks to see if any one of these objects has a script attached to it which contains a matching handler. If so, that handler is executed.

The objects that messages are sent to in general are a primary event handler (defined on page 224), an activated sprite, an activated sprite's cast member, the current frame, and the movie. Which of these objects a message is sent to and in what order depends on the type of message.

Generally, when an object receives a message and its script contains a matching handler for that message, this handler is executed, and the message does not continue on to other objects (the exception to this is the primary event handler, which passes a message along).

The order in which Director sends messages to objects

MouseUp, **mouseDown**, **keyUp**, and **keyDown** messages are sent to objects in one of two possible orders. If the mouse pointer is positioned over a sprite (including field sprites) when any one of these

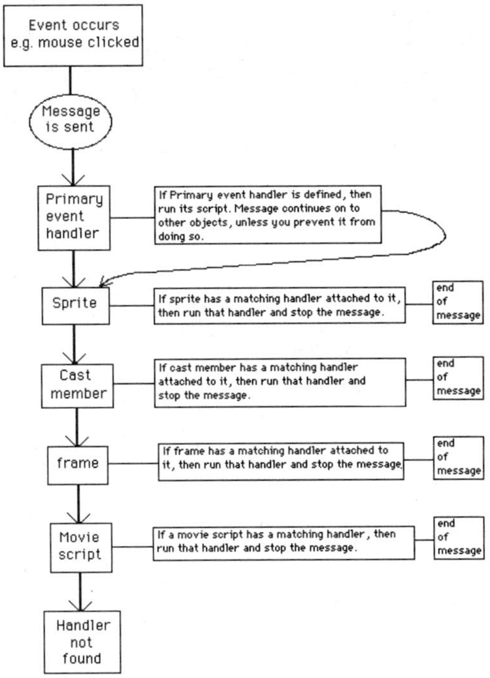

Figure 48. This chart shows where mouseUp, mouseDown, keyUp, and keyDown messages get sent when the mouse pointer is positioned over a sprite.

messages is generated, then the message is sent to objects in the following order: **(Figure 48)** primary event handler, activated sprite, the activated sprite's cast member, the current frame, and the movie (which can have many movie scripts, all of which are checked for a matching handler). If the mouse pointer is not positioned over a sprite when the message is generated, then the order is as follows: primary event handler, the current frame, and movie scripts.

Both the **enterFrame** and **exitFrame** messages are sent to the current frame (technically to the script channel in the current frame), and then to movie scripts. If the current frame has a script assigned to it that contains a handler for one of these messages, that handler is executed.

The **timeOut** message is sent to a primary event handler, and then to movie scripts. A timeOut message gets sent when a user doesn't touch the mouse or keyboard for a specified amount of time.

The **idle**, **activateWindow**, **closeWindow**, **deactivateWindow**, **startMovie**, **stopMovie**, and **zoomWindow** messages are sent directly to movie scripts.

Where to place handlers

Understanding the order in which messages are sent to objects is important, since it will affect where you place your handlers. For example, if a mouseUp message is generated when the mouse pointer is positioned over a sprite, the message first goes to the sprite script before it goes to the cast member script. Therefore, if the sprite and cast member both have handlers attached to them, the sprite handler takes precedence. You can use this to your advantage. For example, you can have many sprites in your movie all based on the same cast member, yet each can perform a different function when clicked.

Primary event handlers

There are four events for which you can define a primary event handler. The messages that correspond to these events are mouseUp, mouseDown, keyDown, and timeOut. Primary event handlers provide the first opportunity for your movie to respond to these messages.

You need to define a primary event handler in order for it to respond to one of these messages. Following are the Lingo terms you use in defining a primary event handler, and the messages they correspond to:

Term	Message
keydownScript	keyDown
mousedownScript	mouseDown
mouseupScript	mouseUp
timeoutScript	timeOut

The following handler sets up a primary event handler for a mouseDown message:

```
on startMovie
set the mousedownScript to "go to frame 5"
end
```

This handler would be placed in a movie script **(Figure 49)**, since the startMovie message is sent exclusively to these types of scripts. Movie scripts are a good place to initialize variables and properties.

After this script is executed, anytime a mouseDown message occurs, the playback head will jump to frame 5, regardless of what frame the mouse click occurs in, or where the mouse pointer is positioned.

To turn off the primary event handler for the mouseDown message, you would use the following Lingo statement:

```
set the mousedownScript to EMPTY
```

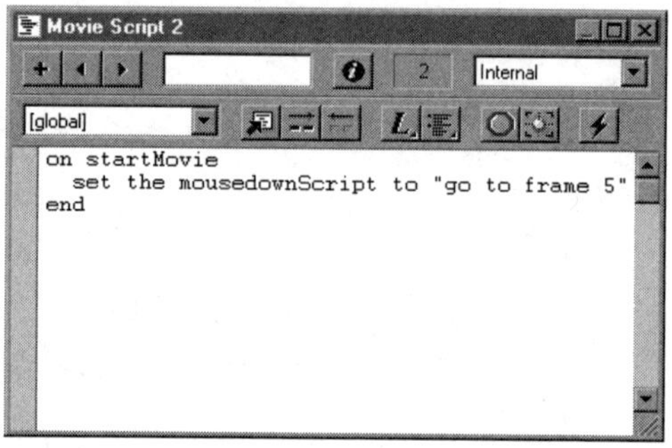

Figure 49. This script defines a primary event handler for a mouseDown message.

Figure 1. Install Xtras by placing them into the Xtras folder in the Director application folder, or in a second location (see main text).

Figure 2. The **Filter Bitmap** and **Auto Filter** commands under the **Xtras** menu are used to apply image filters to bitmapped images.

Director's open architecture allows you to incorporate third party software modules called Xtras, which extend its functionality in many ways. For example, you can add new cast member types, expand Director's built-in set of transition effects, and even add new authoring tools—all by installing Xtras in Director.

There are five types of Xtras in Director: image filters, transition Xtras, cast member Xtras, Lingo Xtras, and tool Xtras. Each is described in this chapter.

To install an Xtra:

Your Director 5 CD-ROM contains a handful of Xtras in the Xtraprtn folder.

An Xtra (any type) is installed into Director for Windows by placing its file into the Xtras folder in the Director application folder **(Figure 1)**. Director can also find Xtras placed in a second location. For Windows 95 and NT, this location is in the Xtras folder in Program Files\Common Files\Macromedia. For Windows 3.1, this location is in Windows\Macromed\Xtras.

You can place the Xtra file up to five layers deep in these locations. Relaunch Director in order for it to recognize the newly installed Xtra. An Xtra file can contain more than one Xtra.

Xtras are not saved into projector movies. If your projector uses Xtras, you should place the Xtras into an Xtras folder in the same folder where your projector resides.

Image filters

You can use image filters from Adobe Photoshop or Premiere to modify your bitmapped cast members in Director. Image filter Xtras are accessed using the Filter Bitmap and Auto Filter commands **(Figure 2)** under the Xtras menu.

Transition Xtras

Transition Xtras are transitions that you can add to the standard transition choices provided by Director in its Frame Properties:Transition dialog box. When you apply an Xtra transition in the transition channel, the Xtra transition becomes a transition Xtra cast member in a cast window **(Figure 3)**. *(See page 190 in the Setting Scene Transitions chapter on how to set an Xtra transition)*

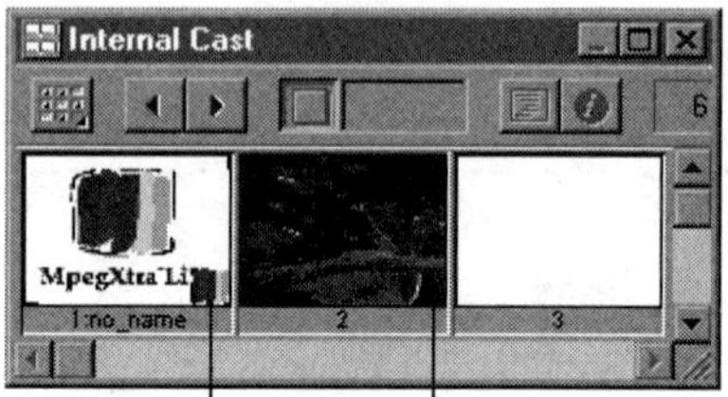

Figure 3. Xtra and transition Xtra cast member types are shown.

Xtra cast members

Xtra cast members can be many different objects. They are not limited to be a specific media type like a bitmap or text. Their type cast be quite abstract. For example, an Xtra cast member can be an interactive digital video, a database, or even a utility program that aids you in generating cast members, like the Auto Distort command.

When Xtra cast members are installed, they appear under the Insert menu **(Figure 4)**. When you choose an Xtra cast member from the Insert menu, it is placed into a cast window from where it can be assigned to the score.

An Xtra cast member can have its own custom Options dialog box and About box. If these are defined, they are accessed from the Xtra Cast Member Properties dialog box **(Figure 5)**. Open it by selecting the Xtra cast member in the cast window and clicking the Cast Member Properties button.

An Xtra cast member can also have its own media editor, which you can open by double-clicking the Xtra in the cast window.

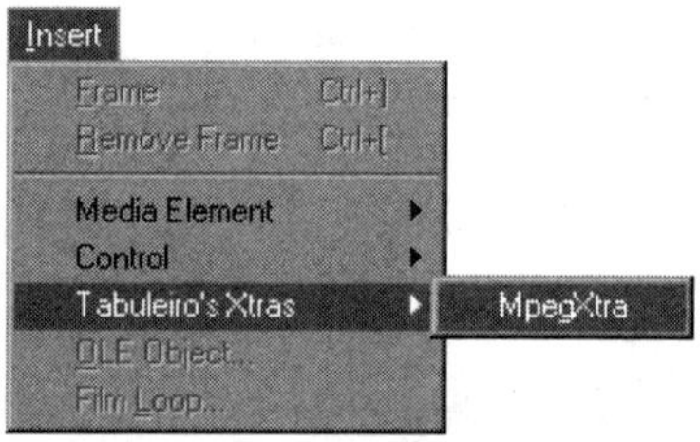

Figure 4. Insert an Xtra cast member into a cast window by choosing it from the Insert menu.

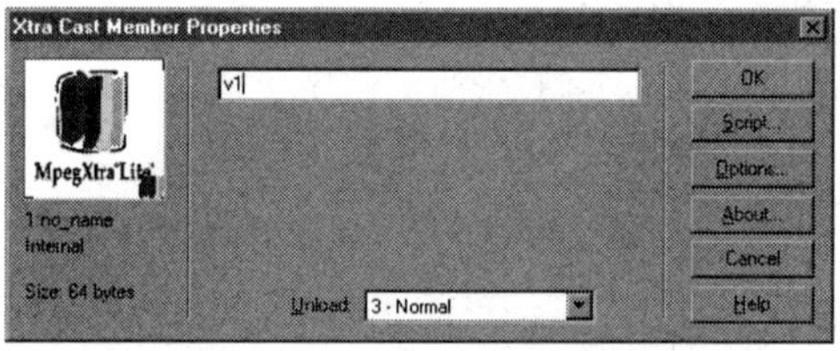

Figure 5. An Xtra cast member may have a custom **Options** dialog box and an **About** box, both of which are opened from the **Xtra Cast Member Properties** dialog box.

Figure 6. Tool Xtras are located under the **Xtras** menu.

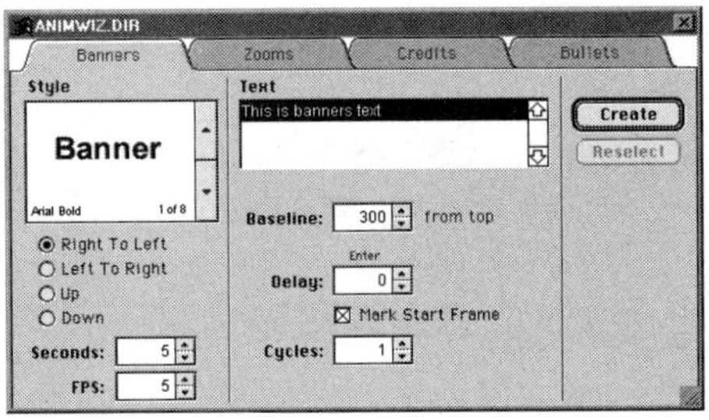

Figure 7. Animation Wizard is an example of a tool Xtra.

Lingo Xtras

Lingo Xtras add new language elements to Lingo—Director's scripting language. By adding Lingo Xtras, you expand the power of Lingo without having to wait for the next release of Director. You can open Lingo Xtras by using the Lingo openXlib command. *(See the Lingo dictionary for this entry)*

Tool Xtras

Tool Xtras are software modules that aid in the authoring of a Director movie. When you install a tool Xtra, it is accessible from the Xtras menu **(Figure 6)**. Director 5 comes with several preinstalled Tool Xtras. One is called Animation Wizard.

Animation Wizard **(Figure 7)** allows you to quickly create moving banners, zoom effects, scrolling credits, and bullets. Animation Wizard inserts these effects directly into your score, saving you a lot of time. Open Animation Wizard by choosing it from the Xtras menu (Animation Wizard was implemented as Auto Animate in Director 4).

Developing Xtras

Xtras are written in C language. If you are a C programmer and are interested in creating Xtras, see the Xtras Developer Kit on your Director 5 CD ROM located in folder Macromed\Xdk_dir5.

Xobjects

Xobjects are software modules that were used in previous versions of Director to extend its functionality. Xtras are meant to replace Xobjects. Xobjects don't have the custom user interface capability of Xtras, and require complex Lingo commands to be controlled. You can still use Xobjects in Director 5. This may be an issue if you are updating a Director 4 movie that uses them *(See Xobjects in the Lingo Dictionary)*.

Appendix A: Glossary

Anti-aliasing
Removes or reduces the rough and jagged edges around an image.

Bit depth
The number of bits used to display each pixel. In Director, bit depth can be set to 1, 2, 4, 8, 16, 24, and 32-bit color.

Cast window
A Cast window is the storage area in Director that contains your multimedia elements, such as graphics, sounds, color palettes, film loops, buttons, QuickTime movies, and scripts.

Control Panel
Provides VCR-type control over the playback of your movie, including Rewind, Play, and Step Forward buttons.

Cast member
An individual multimedia element that can be incorporated into your movie, such as a graphic, sound, film loop, color palette, or QuickTIme movie.

Cell
The individual storage units that make up the Score. Each cell contains information about one cast member.

Channel
A row of cells in the Score window. Each channel holds a specific cast member type. There are 48 animations channels, 5 effects channels (Tempo, Palette, Transition, Sound 1 & 2) and a script channel.

Color cycling
A color effect, where colors are rotated through a specified range in a color palette. Cast members that appear in these colors appear to pulsate and change color.

Color depth
The bit depth of a cast member, indicating how many colors it can display.

Common palette
A specially constructed palette that incorporates many of the colors shared by your entire cast. Its purpose is to replace the many cast member palettes your movie may be using with a single palette that can display your entire cast in approximately accurate colors.

Current frame
The frame that is currently displayed on the Stage. You can change the current frame by using the frame counter in the Control Panel, or the Playback head in the Score window.

Current palette The color palette used to display the colors of the cast members in the current frame on the Stage. You can change the current palette in the Palette channel of the Score.

Foreground Sprites that appear to be in front of other sprites on the Stage are in the foreground. A sprite's foreground priority is determined by its placement in the animation channels. A sprite closer to the bottom animation channel (channel 48) is closer to the foreground.

Foreground color The main color used to paint artwork in the Paint window, and to paint QuickDraw shapes and text in the Tool Palette. It is selected using the Foreground color chip.

Frame A column of cells in the Score window, that represents a segment of time in your movie. Each frame contains information about what your cast members are doing in that time segment.

Film loop A cast member that is composed of a sequence of graphical cast members to form a looping animation.

In-Between A command in Director that helps create an animation sequence, by filling in the frames between two key frames that you specify.

Ink Effects Ink effects determine how your sprites appear when they overlap each other and background artwork on the Stage. Ink effects are applied to sprites using the Score window's ink pop-up menu. Ink effects can also be applied to cast members to permanently affect their colors, by using the paint window's Ink pop-up menu.

Mask An image that allows you to control which parts of an artwork selection are transparent (you can see background artwork through these parts) and which parts are opaque. A mask could be used to make the windows in a house transparent, and the rest of the house opaque.

Movie The term used to describe any multimedia animation created in Director.

Palette A subset of colors used to display your cast members. Only one color palette can be active at a time.

Playback head The position of the Playback head in the Score window indicates which frame is currently displayed on the Stage. You can drag the Playback head to display different frames on the Stage.

Projector A play-only version of a Director movie. Projectors cannot be opened or edited in Director and are the best way to distribute your movies to the public. It is not necessary to own a copy of Director to run a projector movie.

Real-time recording A feature in Director that allows you to record the path of mouse movements, and then substitute any graphical cast member to follow this path to form an animation.

Registration point A reference point used to align the positions of cast members in an animation sequence.

Score A frame-by-frame record of your movie, used to direct all your cast members. The Score is organized into 48 animation channels, 5 effects channels (Tempo, Palette, Transitions, Sound 1 & 2), and one script channel.

Stage The background upon which your movie animations are played and viewed.

Step Recording The most basic animation technique in Director, where you arrange and record each frame on an individual basis to create an animation sequence.

Tempo The rate at which the frames of your movie are played. Tempo is measured in frames-per-second.

Appendix B: List of Keyboard Shortcuts by Menu

File Menu

New Movie	Control-N
New Cast	Control-Alt-N
Open	Control-O
Close	Control-F4
Save	Control-S
Import	Control-R
Export	Control-Shift-R
Page Setup	Control-Shift-P
Print	Control-P
General Preferences	Control-U
Exit	Alt-F4

Edit Menu

Undo	Control-Z
Repeat	Control-Y
Cut	Control-X
Copy	Control-C
Paste	Control-V
Clear	Delete
Duplicate	Control-D
Select All	Control-A
Find Text	Control-F
Find Handler	Control-Shift-;
Find Cast Member	Control-;
Find Selection	Control-H
Find Again	Control-Alt-F
Replace Again	Control-Alt-E
Exchange Cast Members	Control-E

View Menu

Next Marker	Control-right arrow
Previous Marker	Control-left arrow
Zoom in	Control-+
Zoom out	Control--(minus)
Show Grid	Control-Shift-Alt-G
Snap to Grid	Control-Alt-G

Insert Menu

Insert Frame	Control-]
Remove Frame	Control-[

Modify Menu

Cast Member Properties	Control-I
Cast Member Script	Control-' (apostrophe)
Sprite Properties	Control-Shift-I
Sprite Script	Control-Shift-' (apostrophe)
Movie Properties	Control-Shift-D
Movie Casts	Control-Shift-C
Font	Control-Shift-T
Paragraph	Control-Shift-Alt-T
In Between	Control-B
In Between Special	Control-Shift-B
Bring to Front	Control-Shift-up arrow
Move Forward	Control-up arrow
Move Backward	Control-down arrow
Send to Back	Control-Shift-down arrow
Align	Control-K
Tweak	Control-Shift-K

Control Menu

Play	Control-Alt-P
Stop	Control-. (period)
Rewind	Control-Alt-R
Step Backward	Control-Alt-left arrow
Step Forward	Control-Alt-right arrow
Loop Playback	Control-Alt-L
Volume:Mute	Control-Alt-M

Toggle Breakpoint	F9
Watch Expression	Shift-F9
Ignore Breakponts	Alt-F9
Step Script	F10
Step into Script	F8
Run Script	F5
Recompile All Scripts	Control-Shift-Alt-C

Window Menu

Toolbar	Control-Shift-Alt-B
Tool Palette	Control-7
Text Inspector	Control-T
Stage	Control-1
Control Panel	Control-2
Markers	Control-Shift-M
Score	Control-4
Cast	Control-3
Paint	Control-5
Text	Control-6
Field	Control-8
Color Palettes	Control-Alt-7
Video	Control-9
Script	Control-0
Message	Control-M
Debugger	Control-` (back single quote)
Watcher	Control-Shift-` (back single quote)

A

B

C

D

E

F

G

H

Index

T

U

V

W

X

Z